Conducting Educational Research

Conducting Educational Research

A COMPARATIVE VIEW

R. Murray Thomas

BERGIN & GARVEY
Westport, Connecticut • London

Library of Congress Cataloging-in-Publication Data

Thomas, R. Murray (Robert Murray), 1921–
    Conducting educational research : a comparative view / R. Murray
Thomas.
        p.   cm.
    Includes bibliographical references (p.   ) and index.
    ISBN 0–89789–609–2 (alk. paper).—ISBN 0–89789–610–6 (pbk. :
alk. paper)
    1. Education—Research—Comparative method.   I. Title.
LB1028.T446   1998
370′.72—dc21   98–18506

British Library Cataloguing in Publication Data is available.

Library of Congress Catalog Card Number: 98–18506
ISBN: 0–89789–609–2
        0–89789–610–6 (pbk.)

First published in 1998

Bergin & Garvey, 88 Post Road West, Westport, CT 06881
An imprint of Greenwood Publishing Group, Inc.

Printed in the United States of America

The paper used in this book complies with the
Permanent Paper Standard issued by the National
Information Standards Organization (Z39.48–1984).

10 9 8 7 6 5 4 3 2 1

Copyright Acknowledgments

The author and publisher gratefully acknowledge permission for the use of the following material:

Excerpts from A. Diver-Stamnes and R. M. Thomas (1995), *Prevent, Repent, Reform, Revenge*. Westport, CT: Greenwood. By permission of the publisher.

Figure 10-2: "Projected World Population Increase." Reprinted, by permission, from *International Comparative Education*, R. M. Thomas, ed., 1990. Butterworth-Heinemann.

Figure 10-3: "Path Analysis of School Principals' Influence." From W. K. Hoy, C. J. Tarter, and L. Witkoskie (1992), "Faculty Trust in Colleagues: Linking the School Principal with School Effectiveness," *Journal of Research and Development in Education*, 26(1), pp. 38–45. By permission of the publisher.

Figure 2-1: "A Framework for Comparative Educational Analysis" was adapted from M. Bray and R. M. Thomas (1995), "Levels of Comparison of Educational Studies: Different Insights from Different Literatures and the Value of Multilevel Analyses," *Harvard Educational Review*, 65(3), pp. 472–490. By permission of the publisher.

To
Minnabeth T. Garrison
and
Elinor T. Guinn

Contents

Tables and Figures

Tables

Figures

Preface

Most research in the field of education is of a comparative nature. Comparisons are drawn between nations, regions of the world, schools, classrooms, teachers, individual students, ethnic groups, religious denominations, males and females, methods of instruction, teaching materials, learning goals, evaluation techniques, testing programs, and much more. Comparisons are also drawn across time— early events compared with later ones, yesteryear compared with today and tomorrow.

Although there are many books about educational research and many about comparative education, I have not found any that focus precisely on the process of conducting comparative education research. The purpose of the present volume is to help fill that gap in the professional literature.

The book is comparative in an additional sense as well, in that the chapters compare diverse sources of research topics, aims of research projects, methods of gathering and classifying data, ways of interpreting the outcomes, and options for reporting and publishing the results.

The contents have been designed chiefly for two kinds of readers—for students who are planning research projects and for staff members of such organizations as ministries of education, school systems, bureaus of educational research, and educational-aid agencies. To achieve its purpose, the book describes the principal steps in designing and implementing research, illustrating each step with a host of examples of comparative studies.

Finally, I wish to express my appreciation to T. Neville Postlethwaite, who, over the years, has generously shared with me his rich fund of knowledge of educational research, and to Mark Bray who inspired me to write this book. I am also grateful to Paul Pedersen for his support and to the members of the Greenwood Publishing Group's editorial staff for the care and precision they invested in producing this volume.

1

Components of Educational Research

This book is designed to explore in detail a range of topics that people can profitably consider as they plan research projects. This opening chapter introduces readers to five general stages that make up the process of conducting educational studies. The stages focus on choosing what to compare, specifying the research problem, collecting information, organizing and summarizing information, interpreting the results, and reporting the outcomes.

Chapters 2 through 15 explain the five stages in considerable detail. A final chapter speculates about future developments in comparative research. But before identifying the topics and describing where they are discussed in later chapters, I need to explain what the term *comparative education* is intended to mean throughout the book.

In its most inclusive sense, *comparative education* refers to inspecting two or more educational entities or events in order to discover how and why they are alike and different. An *educational entity* in this context means any person, group, or organization associated with learning and teaching. An *event* is any activity concerned with promoting learning.

This broad definition of comparative education is in contrast to the more typical way the term has been used. In much educational discourse, *comparative education* has referred solely to the study of educational likenesses and differences between regions of the world or between two or more nations, as reflected in the assertion by Walberg, Zhang, and Daniel (1994, p. 79) that "By definition, the field of comparative education concerns national comparisons." Or sometimes studies of provinces or states within a country have also appeared in the comparative-education literature. However, limiting the notion of educational comparisons to regions, nations, and provinces leads to a pair of unfortunate kinds of neglect. First, it dismisses from consideration a very large body of research, including studies focusing on comparisons between local education systems, schools, classrooms, language groups, religious denominations, social classes, age levels, genders, individual students, and more. Second, it diverts attention from the advantages of multiple-level comparisons, such as those involving (a) individual teachers within different schools of different nations or (b) subtypes of ethnic groups within nations of two or more world regions. Therefore, by adopting an inclusive, wide-ranging definition of comparative education, I hope to avoid the shortcomings of the more traditional restricted meaning of the term.

As already mentioned, the role of this introductory chapter is to offer a brief preview of what the rest of the book is about. The preview focuses first on the nature of typical comparisons, then continues with examples of the book's main sections: (1) choosing what to study, (2) collecting information, (3) organ-izing and summarizing information, (4) interpreting results, and (5) reporting outcomes.

THE NATURE OF TYPICAL COMPARISONS

The word *compare is* often used with two slightly different meanings. In its first sense, *compare* implies identifying similarities between two or more things, that is, recognizing features they share in common. Then the word *contrast* is used to indicate the differences between those things—identifying ways they are not alike. However, sometimes people use *compare* to mean both the similarities and differences. It is this second sense of *compare* that is intended throughout the following chapters.

To illustrate the nature of typical comparisons, we can inspect three ways of categorizing them: (a) by space or time, (b) by general aims, and (c) by the qualitative and the quantitative.

Space or Time

Research can be conducted along either—or both—of two dimensions: space and time. Space studies involve the simultaneous inspection of two or more *categories of people* (demographic entities), *geographic areas, institutions* and/or *technologies* (ways of doing things) in terms of the same aspect of education. The aspect of education that is the central focus of a study can be referred to as the *target feature* or *target variable*, such as pupils' reading skills, ways of funding education, or colleges' student-admission policies. Illustrative titles of space studies are:

—Reading Scores in Two Schools: Privileged versus Under-Privileged Pupils
—Public Funding of Schools in Zambia, Mozambique, and South Africa in 1997
—Current Student Admission Procedures: Harvard, Stanford, and Yale

Time studies involve inspecting educational phenomena at different chronological periods within the same organizational or demographic entity, as reflected in such titles as:

—Administrative Control of Rivertown's Schools in the 1950s and 1990s
—The Evolution of the French Ministry of Education: 1800 to 1940
—Tests of a Retarded Child's IQ: Age 8 to 18.

Some investigations combine space and time:

—Student Exchanges Within the European Community, 1978 and 1998
—Trends in Financing Cairo's Private and Public Schools
—Ethnic Groups' Access to Medical Education: India in 1920 and 1960.

In short, authors of necessity make decisions about which spaces and/or times they intend to compare.

General Aim

Most comparative studies have one—or some combination—of four types of aims: the descriptive, explanatory, predictive, or evaluative.

The purpose of *descriptive* research is to tell the status of an aspect of education as found among the people, institutions, or technologies that are being compared. Thus, descriptive studies involve the choice of a target aspect (or several aspects) of education and of two or more places or times at which that aspect is described. Again, the term *target* here refers to a particular facet of the educational enterprise, such as science curriculum, achievement testing, foreign language instruction, teacher education, budgeting practices, and the like. Examples of descriptive studies are:

—Teachers' Salaries: Canada's Provinces Compared
—Ways of Teaching Foreign Languages
—One School's Disciplinary Practices: 1950-1990.

The aim of *explanatory* studies is not only to describe two or more sets of people or technologies, but also to explain the *why* behind the observed likenesses and differences between the things being compared. In other words, explanatory research is designed to reveal causes of similarities and contrasts. Thus, authors are obliged not only to select one or more target aspects, as in descriptive studies, but also to choose other aspects of the education system or the society that likely account for the similarities and differences in the target variables. Explanatory studies can bear such titles as:

—Causes of School Drop-Outs in Developed versus Developing Nations
—Political Influences on Multicultural Curricula in Plural Societies
—Effects of Climate on Teaching Practices: Tropical and Temperate Zones.

Predictive studies involve description *plus* explanation *plus* an envisioned future that will find the target aspect either in a different condition than it is at the present time or perhaps in much the same condition. Frequently the description focuses on both the past and the present so that trends in past development can be observed and explained. The explanation identifies causes of the observed trends. Then a proposal is offered about how and why those causal factors will likely operate in the future. On the basis of this proposal, an imagined description of the target variable is provided for a future date. Authors of predictive studies must therefore choose (a) the target aspect whose status is to be described for the past and present, (b) the past and present times that the target's status is depicted, (c) the aspects of the education system and the society that are likely causes of the status of the target variable, and (d) the time in the future for which the prediction will be made. Typical titles of predictive studies include:

—Expected University Enrollments in Beijing by 2010
—Computers in Rural Classrooms: Present and Future
—Prospects for Religious Education in Russian Schools.

Evaluative studies involve the same components as the descriptive variety *plus* judgments of how adequately the target aspect measures up to standards of desirability. Therefore, investigators must select the target aspect that is to be described and also choose criteria by which the status of the target aspect is to be assessed. The titles of such investigations typically reflect their evaluative nature:

—Mathematics Achievement in 32 Nations
—Ratings of School-Building Quality in Stockholm
—Winning Exhibits in the City's Science Fair.

Comparative investigations usually combine two or more of the above types. For example, a predictive study involves not only description and explanation but may also include evaluation.

Qualitative Versus Quantitative Investigations

Recent decades have witnessed a continuing debate that pits advocates of qualitative research against proponents of quantitative methods (Eisner & Peshkin, 1990; LeCompte & Preissle, 1993). Although there is some lack of agreement about exactly what *qualitative* and *quantitative* should mean in comparative studies, I believe the following definitions reflect the essence of the two approaches.

Qualitative research compares the characteristics of one educational entity with those of another entity, with no concern for amounts or frequencies of the characteristics being studied. Examples of projects using qualitative methods are:

—The Philosophical Foundations of Two Types of German Secondary Schools: The Gymnasium and the Gesampschule
—Individual Learning Styles of Five Dyslexic Adolescents
—Cultural Backgrounds of Immigrant Children.

Quantitative research, on the other hand, compares the amounts or frequencies of the characteristics that are being investigated.

—Trends in Four Schools' Tuition Fees: 1977-1997
—The Correlation Between Educational Level and Recidivism Among Prison Inmates
—Teachers' Ratings of 20 Moral-Education Topics: Taiwan and the United States

In my opinion, the typical qualitative-versus-quantitative argument is ill conceived. The proper issue is not whether one of these approaches is generally superior to the other. Instead, the issue is: What circumstances determine which of the approaches will be the more appropriate? In effect, the choice of an investigative method depends on the nature of the particular question the investigator hopes to answer. Some questions call for qualitative techniques. Others require the inclusion of amounts and frequencies.

Oftentimes both qualitative and quantitative information are desired. Consider these three instances.

—In an article about discipline methods in U.S. schools, Donohue (1996) described the child-raising practices of theologian John Wesley's [1703-1791] mother, then quoted present-day court decisions about corporal punishment and cited the 1992 incidence of paddling in Texas (140,928 cases) and Alabama (53,443 cases) schools.
—A report on British vocational education described program improvements (more student control over their learning experiences, closer links between schools and businesses) that helped attract nearly "136,000 students into business studies in 1995, over two times the number in 1990" (McCafferty, 1996, p. 2).
—A study of the influence on American children of sex and violence on television combined qualitative descriptions of program content with quantitative information: "[there were] about 50 crimes—including a dozen murders—in every hour of prime time [viewing]. Since 1955, TV characters have been murdered at a rate one thousand times higher than real-world victims" (Impoco, 1966, p. 60).

Summary

Comparative studies can be viewed from several perspectives, including those of space/time, types of general aims (descriptive, explanatory, predictive, evaluative), and the patterning of qualitative and quantitative methods. Additional perspectives inspected in Chapter 2 focus on ways of understanding fundamental conditions affecting educational endeavors and ways of solving problems faced in the conduct of education.

With this brief introduction to comparative viewpoints as a foundation, we next consider the five earlier-mentioned stages in comparative research: (1) choosing what to compare, (2) collecting information, (3) summarizing information, (4) interpreting results, and (5) reporting the outcomes.

STAGE 1: CHOOSING WHAT TO STUDY

Researchers use a variety of approaches in deciding what they intend to study. For instance, graduate students looking for potential thesis topics may extract research issues from their recent reading fare—reading fare that suggests a hypothesis or theory to test, the kernel of an idea that deserves expansion, a controversy to be settled, a different type of education system to investigate, and the like. In other cases, a topic may derive from a person's present job—a department of education may compare two budgeting systems, inspect three methods of teaching reading to bilingual pupils, contrast counseling procedures, and more. Once researchers have selected the aspects of education they wish to compare, their next task is to state the research problem in a clear, convincing fashion.

Stating the Research Question and Rationale

A statement of the key issue being investigated usually appears in the opening section of the research report, along with a rationale explaining why such an issue is worth studying. The presentation often begins with the rationale which then leads into the questions that are the focus of the study. Here are three examples. The first compares instructional media used for teaching geometry. The second compares the learning environments of Australian and Japanese secondary-school students. The third compares the development of Islamic education from one era to another. In the first example, the research questions are stated outright. In the second and third, although the issues to be studied are not cast in question form, the questions are implied in the stated purposes of the studies.

1. *Title:* Is More Always Better? The Separate and Combined Effects of a Computer and Video Program on Mathematics Learning.

    The introductory rationale: Only a short time ago, teachers employed mainly a "chalk-and-talk" strategy, while students learned with paper-and-pencil tools. However, current educational systems expose learners to a large variety of technologies utilizing video programs and computer software. Access to these devices raises three important questions: (a) To what extent does a two-media educational environment (such as, for example, a combination of both video and computer programs) facilitate achievement more than either of its components alone? (b) Are there combined and/or separate effects of video and computer programs on students' intrinsic motivation? (c) To what extent do the levels of mindfulness differ under the different media environments? The present investigation addresses these questions by examining a study unit in geometry taught with the aid of a computer and/or video program. (Adapted from Mevarech, Shir, & Movshovitz-Hadar, 1992)

2. *Title:* Students' Conceptions of Learning and Their Use of Self-Regulated Learning Strategies. A Cross-Cultural Comparison.

   The introductory rationale: There are many clear descriptions of the characteristics of students who are good at regulating their own learning progress. Typically, self-regulators are characterized as purposeful, strategic, and persistent in their learning. They possess the ability to evaluate their own progress in relation to their goals and to adjust subsequent behavior in light of those self-evaluations. They are self-initiators who exercise personal control of the methods needed to attain the learning goals they have set for themselves. Although the published descriptions of good learners provide important information about students in classrooms, they do not tell why or how students become self-regulators. To date, self-regulated learning theory and research in the social cognitive tradition have focused on classroom environmental variables found in Western academic settings. This study extends the notion of environment to include that of cultural contexts. It investigates whether Japanese and Australian students, operating in different educational contexts, have the same conceptions of learning and use the same set of strategies to regulate their learning. (Adapted from Purdie, Hattie, & Douglas, 1996)

3. *Title:* Pedagogy, Power, and Discourse: Transformation of Islamic Education.

   The introductory rationale: Strong revivalist Islamization movements have recently emerged in a number of Muslim countries as a traditionalist response to modernity. They aspire to imbue all forms of knowledge with traditional Islamic values and arrest the secularization and modernization of knowledge. The movement is rooted in the history of Muslim societies, where religious discourses mediated power and social control. This study will examine the historical evolution of knowledge and power linkages in Islamic societies and the use of Islamic education to reproduce and establish specific discourses of power. (Adapted from Talbani, 1996)

Summary

In the foregoing discussion, the initial phase of conducting comparative education research has been portrayed as consisting of two principal steps— (a) deciding on what to compare and (b) casting the results of this decision in the form of one or more research questions that are accompanied by a rationale explaining why such questions are worth investigating. The researcher's next task is that of identifying the kinds of information needed for answering the questions.

STAGE 2: COLLECTING INFORMATION— METHODS AND INSTRUMENTS

Every research project entails gathering information.   Ways that one project differs from another are in the kind of information sought, in the collection methods, and in the instruments used in the collection process.

The Kind of Information Sought

The type of information to be collected is often implied in the statement of the research question.   For instance, comparing the effectiveness of computer programs and videos in teaching geometry implies that the investigators would need to test students' achievement in geometry and to assess students' levels of intrinsic motivation both before and after the learners studied a geometry unit. In order to judge the effect of cultural contexts on Australian and Japanese pupils' ability to regulate their own learning, a researcher would need to identify significant features of Australian and Japanese classroom conditions and to evaluate pupils' learning goals, persistence, and ability to assess their own study techniques and progress.   Tracing the connection between Islamic education and political power over the centuries requires that the investigator compile historical accounts of the development of Islam, of the evolution of Western secular science and education, and of the current clash between Islamic tradition and the secularization of the curriculum.

Thus, the research questions serve as an initial guide to the types of information to gather.   To refine this initial impression, the investigator devises a research design in the form of a detailed plan specifying the most suitable approaches to collecting data and describing techniques for accomplishing this task.   A detailed plan is apt to be most efficient if the researcher is acquainted with the advantages and disadvantages of a wide variety of data-gathering methods.   The most popular of these methods are introduced in the following paragraphs.

A variety of terms have been used to identify ways of gathering data.   Some terms identify general approaches to collecting information—*case study, historical analysis, ethnography, survey, correlational comparison, experiment.* Other terms refer to direct data-gathering techniques used within the approaches— *content analysis, interviews, observations, tests,* and *questionnaires.*   At this point, I merely define the types and offer examples of titles that might appear in studies of each type.   In Stage II (Chapters 4 through 7) the types are described in detail, along with their advantages, limitations, and conditions of application.

General Approaches to Gathering Data

The term *general approach* refers to the kind of data to be collected without specifying the instruments and specific steps employed in gathering information.

Case Studies

A case study is an intensive description of a single person, group, institution, social movement, or event. The usual purpose is to furnish a multifaceted, individualized understanding of the people or objects being studied. Case studies assume a comparative form when two or more people, institutions, or events are the focus or when the same entity is viewed on successive occasions.

—Discipline Problems in Two Classrooms: Inner City versus Suburb
—Home Support for School Achievement: An In-depth View of Four Families
—One School Principal's Administrative Style at Ages 40 and 55

Historical Analyses

The purpose of historical research is to describe what happened in the past in some aspect of education. The description often includes the analysis of the social-psychological context within which that aspect emerged. Frequently, historical studies not only chronicle what happened but also attempt to account for the causes behind the events.

Historical research depends heavily—often exclusively—on content analysis. The investigator's time is spent searching through books, journals, letters, memoirs, newspapers, laws, contracts, and the like to discover what occurred and why. Additional methods of gathering data for historical accounts include interviews and direct observations as sources of information about recent events.

In order to qualify as comparative education, a historical study must have at least one of two potential foci. The focus may be on two or more time periods in the life of the same person, group, institution, technology, community, nation, or such.

—The Development of Mozart's Creative Skills in Childhood and Midlife
—Social-Class Levels and Schooling: The Case of Scotland, 1850-1950
—Attitudes of Episcopalians toward Sex Education, the 1930s and 1990s

Or the focus may be on a parallel set of educational events in the lives of two or more entities.

—Educational Liberalism in Brazil: Echoes of 19th Century Russia
—Children's Life Conditions and Academic Achievement in Canada and the United
   States: A Historical Perspective
—Educational Revolution from Above: Thatcher's Britain and Gorbachev's Soviet
   Union

Ethnography

The term *ethnography* originated in the discipline of cultural anthropology, a word encompassing data-gathering techniques intended to "provide diverse perspectives toward education and contribute to the authentic portrayal of a complex, multifaceted human society" (LeCompte & Preissle, 1993, p. 28). Ethnographic investigations typically assume the form of case studies in which the researcher witnesses an ongoing educational event in order to record what occurs. The investigator may view the event from the perspective of either an outside observer or an active participant.

—Informal Learning Activities in Two African Villages
—Rituals in Representative Christian Schools: Catholic, Quaker, Evangelical
—Hidden Goals: Teachers' Unstated Aims Reflected in Their Interactions with Students

Surveys

A survey provides an overview of the status of some feature of the educational enterprise or of some aspect of the society that relates to education. Surveys assume a comparative form when the results are reported for more than one group, institution, or event.

—Chinese and Japanese Parents' Attitudes Toward Vocational Schools
—Entrance Tests Used in Ten Provincial Colleges
—Student Behavior at Interscholastic Sporting Events: Football, Tennis, and Volleyball

Correlational Comparisons

Frequently researchers are interested in discovering what happens to variable *B* when there is a change in variable *A*. Thus, conducting correlational studies involves collecting data about two or more entities, each of which varies in amount, frequency, or quality. Then the two sets are compared to determine how much change—if any at all—in one set has been accompanied by change in the other set.

—Does improving children's diets result in their succeeding better with their school work?
—Do vocational schools prepare students more adequately for the labor market than general-education schools?
—Does increasing school expenditures increase pupils' achievement? If so, by how much?
—Are students happier under strict discipline than under lax discipline?

Experiments

In comparative education, an experiment involves treating two or more similar individuals or groups in different ways in order to discover how the different ways influence some outcome of interest.

There are several popular experimental designs. One of the most common is the *pretest-treatment-posttest* variety. Imagine that, in teaching young children to read, we wish to learn how a phonics approach compares with a sight-word approach. In the pretest phase, we collect a group of children and test their prereading skills—their ability to recognize likenesses and differences in visual symbols, distinguish among similar sounds, and trace figures from left to right on a page. We then divide the children into two groups, Group A and Group B, so that the range of prereading skills in Group A is the same as in Group B. In effect, we place as many children with high-, with medium-, and with low-level prereading abilities in Group A as we place in Group B, so we now have two matched groups.

The treatment phase will last six weeks. During this time, Group A is taught reading by a phonics method and Group B by a sight-word method.

The posttest phase comes at the close of the six weeks, when we test all of the children's reading skills—their comprehension, their ability to figure out the meanings of new words, and their fluency in reading aloud. On the basis of the posttest results we draw conclusions about (a) how the phonics and sight-word methods compare in regard to the groups in general and (b) how different individual children fared under the method they experienced.

In summary, experiments involve manipulating the treatment of people in educational contexts. The pretest-treatment-posttest design is only one of many designs available. Additional types are identified in Chapter 5, with each type described in terms of its forms, strengths, weaknesses, and applications. Studies employing experiments can bear such titles as:

—Results of Psychoanalytic, Nondirective, and Confrontational Counseling
—Centralized Versus Decentralized Hiring of Teachers
—The Influence of Six Over-the-Counter Drugs on Students' Ability to Memorize

Specific Techniques of Data Collection

Within a general approach, an investigator employs specific instruments and steps for compiling the needed information. Popular techniques include content analysis, interviews, observations, tests, and questionnaires.

Content Analyses

The process of content analysis entails searching through one or more communications to answer questions that an investigator brings to the search. In the past, the most common kinds of communications have been written or printed documents—letters, memoirs, reports, books, articles, field notes, laws, regulations, and more. However, 20th century technology expanded the realm of communications to include audio recordings, still photographs, motion-picture films, video recordings, and the like. In comparative-education research, techniques of content analysis have been increasingly applied to these more recent sources of information. Although the term *content analysis* as a label for a research method did not appear until the 1950s, the practice of analyzing documents is of very ancient origin, pursued in past centuries in such fields as history, religion, philosophy, science, and literary criticism. Content analysis in comparative education represents a specialized application that involves (a) focusing on educational institutions and their relationships to individuals' lives or to society in general and (b) inspecting not just a single communication but, rather, studying two or more so as to identify likenesses and differences among them. Comparisons can involve documents from different times, different places, and different authors.

> —*Different Times:* Changes in the Contents of New York's Secondary-School Industrial Arts Instructional Manuals, 1944-1994.
> —*Different Places:* General-Education Requirements in Four Private Universities.
> —*Different Authors:* Science-Education Objectives à la Darwin, Einstein, and Fermi.

Interviews

Talking with informants enables researchers to gather diverse types of information—the informants' patterns of thought, abilities, moral values, interests, ambitions, plans, judgments of other people, and recall of events. Interviews may be conducted directly—face to face—or via telephone, two-way radio, or electronic computer. For the purpose of data collection, interviews have several advantages over printed questionnaires. Unlike questionnaires, interviews permit the researcher to rephrase questions that respondents do not understand, and interviews allow respondents to elaborate their ideas at length. Interviews may be used in any of the general research approaches noted above— case studies, historical analyses, ethnographies, correlational studies, surveys, and experiments.

Observations

The term *observation* refers to a researcher's directly witnessing an event and then remembering the event or else recording it as a written account, a taped report, or a mark on a checklist or rating scale. Observations are typically important in conducting case studies, ethnographic investigations, and experiments. They are less frequently used in historical analyses and surveys.

Tests

Tests consist of physical, psychomotor, or mental tasks people are asked to perform. The words *physical, psychomotor,* and *mental* are not labels for entirely separate functions but, rather, are terms used to identify the most apparent characteristics of a performance. Such acts as swimming a kilometer, lifting sacks of rice, and scattering flower seeds appear to require much physical skill and minimal thought. Driving a tractor or typing phrases from a book on a computer keyboard involve a combination of physical coordination and mental work and thereby qualify as psychomotor activity. Solving an algebra equation or creating a short story is a mental act involving little or no physical effort.

Tests are often labeled in terms of the purposes they are intended to serve. Achievement tests are designed to reveal how well someone has mastered particular learning objectives. Intelligence tests are supposed to measure people's general mental competence and thereby help in predicting how well they should succeed with cognitive tasks in general. Aptitude and ability tests are also used for making predictions. However, unlike general intelligence measures, aptitude tests are typically designed to assess how well a person is prepared to master a specific kind of skill (manual dexterity, spatial reasoning, clerical efficiency) or kind of knowledge (mathematics, logic, aesthetics). Personality tests are expected to reflect how people view themselves and the world they inhabit.

Tests are commonly used in experiments and surveys and sometimes are included in case studies, ethnographic investigations, and historical accounts.

Questionnaires

Questionnaires are printed forms containing queries for respondents to answer. The questions can be of a factual nature (the marital status of a pupil's parents, the mother's occupation, the kinds of chores the child does around the house, and such) or can focus on the respondent's opinions, attitudes, interests, likes, and dislikes. Two advantages of questionnaires are that they permit a researcher to collect data from a large number of respondents in a short period of time, and the responses are in a more convenient form for summarizing the results than is usually true of information gathered by means of interviews.

STAGE 3: ORGANIZING AND SUMMARIZING INFORMATION

Once the information has been collected, the researcher's next job is that of organizing and summarizing the results so readers can readily understand the pattern formed by the data. This assignment typically begins with classifying the data in a pattern from which conclusions can be drawn. Statistical summaries, tables, and graphs often serve for casting the results in an easily comprehended form. Therefore, researchers face the task of choosing an appropriate classification system and selecting statistical and graphic displays that may help readers grasp the outcomes of the research.

Suitable Classification Schemes

Perhaps the most important way people render a mass of information understandable is by dividing it into classes or categories. This process of classification pervades everyone's daily life and functions as an essential element of virtually every research effort. The act of classifying enables an investigator to extract from a conglomeration of data those features most pertinent to the research question at hand and to organize the features into a pattern that lends itself to comprehensible interpretation. The following examples from journal articles furnish an impression of the variety of categories that can be employed in different comparative studies.

1. *Article title:* Effects of four physical education teaching methods on development of motor skill, self-concept, and social attitudes of fifth-grade children (Emmanoel, Zervas, & Vagenas, 1992).
   Classification categories: (a) pupils by gender, (b) four teaching methods, (c) types of motor skill, (d) self-concept levels, (e) social attitudes.

2. *Article title:* A content assessment and comparative analysis of prison-based AIDS education programs for inmates (Martin, et al., 1995).
   Classification categories: (a) U.S. states, (b) individual prisons within states, (c) incidence of AIDS (acquired immune deficiency syndrome)—by prisons, and by prison population versus general population, (d) prisons with AIDS educational programs versus those without, (e) educational program features—aims, contents, methods of instruction, program assessment.

3. *Article title:* Comparing educational output (Bottani, 1995).
   Classification categories: (a) nations, (b) subject-matter categories, (c) 49 types of indicators (various family characteristics, nations' cultural features, social and economic conditions) that might explain the differences in students' performance in the countries studied.

4. *Article topic:* Varying methods of teaching mathematics in different countries, and the results of the methods in terms of student achievement (Bracey, 1993).
   Classification categories: (a) nations, (b) five strategies for teaching mathematics, (c) three levels of complexity of symbol manipulation required by the strategies, (d) students' socioeconomic levels, (e) students' success on mathematics tests that include (f) diverse types of problems.

In each of these studies, after the researchers have tabulated their raw data into the proper categories and manipulated the categories in relation to each other, they are prepared to summarize the results in the form of narratives, statistical results, or tabular and graphic displays.

Levels of Precision

Summaries of information can be offered at various levels of specificity. As authors prepare their conclusions, they are faced with decisions about how detailed their summaries should be. Such decisions are influenced by several considerations, including the precision of the available data, the complexity of the information to be conveyed, and the space available. Three examples of levels of precision are displayed in Table 1-1, with the descriptions in the right column cast in more detail than those in the left column.

Table 1-1

Levels of Precision

Less Detailed Summaries	More Detailed Summaries
—In reading ability, students in Finland performed better than students in Italy, Hungary, and Venezuela.	—The average scores on reading tests taken by nine-year-olds in four countries were 569 for Finland, 529 for Italy, 499 for Hungary, and 383 for Venezuela.
—Tanzania's first president, Nyerere, was a product of the British colonial education system.	—Julius K. Nyerere, Tanzania's first elected president, during his boyhood had attended a school organized by the British colonial government for the sons of chiefs. Later he traveled to the British Isles to complete a degree at Edinburgh University.
—By the early 1990s, school violence in the United States had risen to an alarming level. Students often stayed home from school for fear of suffering harm at the at the hands of juvenile offenders.	—Studies of violence in U.S. schools in the early 1990s indicated that on a typical day an estimated 100,000 students carried guns to school, 160,000 stayed out of school to avoid possible harm, 40 were injured or killed by firearms, 6,250 teachers were threatened with bodily injury, and 260 teachers were assaulted.

Statistical and Graphic Summaries

Statistics enable researchers to furnish succinct, precise summaries of large amounts of data, summaries in the form of percentages, averages, the bunching together or spreading out of data, the extent of correlation among variables, and more. Hence, an investigator can convey comparisons of teachers' academic preparation by reporting that 67% of the teachers in Province A and 93% in Province B held bachelor degrees. Or the average annual per-student expenditure in School District X can be reported as $470.18 and in School District Y as $983.64. The interquartile range of students' scores on a mathematics test can be described as extending across 26 points in School D but across only 13 points in School E (with the interquartile range representing the spread of scores for the middle 50% of the students who took the test). The correlation between hours of study and history-test scores in a sample of college women was +.76 and in a sample of college men was +.63. Such statistics, and a variety of other popular types, along with their appropriate uses, are inspected in Chapter 9.

The reader's task of comparing quantities of such data can often be much simplified if the statistics are displayed in tabular form. Consider, for example, the average scores earned by students on science tests administered to 15-year-olds in four counties at five-year intervals between 1977 and 1997 (Table 1-2).

Table 1-2

Average Science Test Scores in Four Counties

County	1977	1982	1987	1992	1997
Domingo	62.1	67.0	65.8	74.7	79.9
Marston	68.7	66.4	77.0	78.2	83.1
St. Ives	78.4	72.3	69.7	66.6	67.8
Taft	60.1	61.2	63.4	60.1	55.7

Although tables are effective for concisely communicating an array of quantities, tables often require careful study to reveal information that is more readily communicated in graphic form. A glance at Figure 1-1 enables a reader to readily grasp the 20-year trends in students' scores in the four counties included in the science testing. If Table 1-2 were the only summary available, readers could extract the science-testing trends only by concentrated effort.

Another type of chart useful for summarizing the science-test results is shown in Figure 1-2. The chart summarizes the Domingo County students' performance in terms of the group's average score (the black horizontal line), spread of scores for the middle 80% of the group (the shaded vertical line), and the total range—from the lowest score to the highest (the black vertical line). A variety of other graphic styles are offered in Chapter 10.

Figure 1-1

Trends in Average Science Test Scores in Four Counties

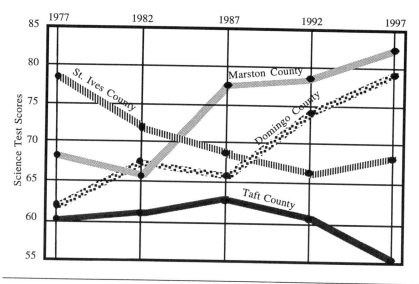

Figure 1-2

Science Score Distributions—Domingo County 1977-1997

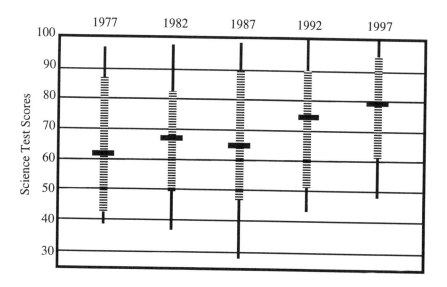

STAGE 4: INTERPRETING THE RESULTS

The purpose of the interpretation portion of a research report is to inform readers of what the investigator believes the results mean. In strictly descriptive studies, there need be no mention of what meaning the author may attach to the results. The results are simply cast before the reading audience. Such is the case with census data telling how many children of different age levels attend school. The enrollment figures are reported, and it is up to the readers to decide what significance those data may imply. However, most comparative studies go beyond description to include explanation (estimates of causes and effects), prediction, and/or evaluation. In those instances, the researcher provides interpretation.

Sources of Interpretation

There appear to be three main sources of the meaning an investigator assigns to data. The first is preplanned. The second is generated during the progress of the study. The third comes as a surprise.

Answering the Research Questions

In the preplanned variety, the meaning derived from the results is determined by the initial set of questions, problems, theories, or hypotheses the researcher was seeking to investigate by conducting the study. This source typically appears in the statement of the research problem at the beginning of the study. Thus, the interpretation at the end of the research report consists of answering the questions posed at the beginning. Here are two examples of this linkage between an initial question and the interpretation derived from the research results. The first example is from a survey of the reading achievement of sixth-grade pupils in the African nation of Zimbabwe, a study comparing the reading skills of pupils in different school environments. The second example is from a comparison of the attitudes toward academic achievement between secondary-school students of Chinese and European heritage living in New Zealand.

The Zimbabwe Case. *Two research questions.* What proportion of sixth-grade pupils have sufficient reading skill to succeed in seventh grade? Do identifiable environmental factors appear to help account for differences in the reading ability of pupils in different schools?

Survey results. A team of Zimbabwe educators cited 33 reading-test items that they deemed essential for pupils to master if the pupils were to succeed in seventh grade. At the very minimum, pupils should master at least 50% of the items, but it would be more desirable if they mastered 70% or more. The results of testing 2,509 children in 143 schools (representing all regions of the nation) showed that only 38.1% of the pupils reached the minimum level and only

13.3% reached the desirable level in reading skill. There were significant differences between schools in average reading ability.

Interpretations. Clearly, the great majority of sixth-graders were inadequately prepared for the reading tasks of seventh grade. Comparisons of students' reading-test scores and school conditions showed that pupils performed better in reading when their schools had more complete classrooms (enough desks, writing materials, bookshelves), piped water, electricity, full-time female teachers, older teachers (over age 30), academically qualified teachers, and lower pupil-teacher ratios (Ross & Postlethwaite, 1992, pp. 43-44).

The New Zealand Case. *Two research questions.* Statistics on educational achievement in New Zealand showed that students of Chinese heritage surpassed students of all other ethnic groups. Whereas 6.3% of college-age youths in the general population attended higher-education institutions, among youths of Chinese parentage the percents were 15.7% for females and 19.3% for males (Chung & Walkey, 1989, p. 139). Questions may then be asked about whether attitudes toward academic success help account for such differences: Specifically, (a) what attitudes toward academic achievement are expressed by secondary-school students of Chinese and European parentage and (b) what attitudes about academic achievement do such students attribute to their parents?

Research results. A sample of 159 Chinese-heritage and 159 European-heritage students completed questionnaires designed to assess (a) their fear of academic failure, their achievement orientation, and their academic aspirations and (b) their fear of parents' responses to the students' failure, their parents' aspirations, their parents' achievement orientation, and the students' obligation to parents. Significant differences were found in the responses of the two groups of students.

Interpretations. "It is clear that the Chinese students have a higher educational orientation than do the Europeans. In addition to higher levels of academic aspiration and overall achievement orientation, they show a higher fear of academic failure. These characteristics also appear to be related to attributed parental attitudes, with the Chinese students indicating higher expectations on the part of their parents, together with a greater sense of obligation to their parents and a greater fear of their parents' response if they should fail. . . . It is perhaps not surprising that such significant differences should . . . be reflected in the great over-representation of Chinese students, particularly Chinese male students, in New Zealand's [higher education] institutions" (Chung & Walkey, 1989, pp. 150-151).

Discovering Interpretations in the Data

A second source of interpretation does not derive from preconceived questions. Instead, what the data can mean is extracted from inspecting the information that has been collected. The investigator approaches the compiled information with the question, "I wonder what meaning this material may hold?" Such an approach is sometimes referred to as "following the data." The investigator is like an explorer opening a new trail through uncharted territory. A typical way this can happen is illustrated by the following example.

A researcher who, in the past, had written extensively about the Indonesian education system was given a copy of the new Indonesian national education law that went into effect in 1989. The law superseded an original 1950 version with which the researcher was already acquainted. As he read the new law, he found himself periodically deciding that the new version was an improvement over the old one. These decisions were initially quite casual and intuitive rather than the result of his systematically applying specific evaluation criteria to the document. But soon he wondered exactly what it was about the new law that caused him to consider it superior to the old one. To solve this dilemma, he carefully reread the document, pausing each time that he intuitively "felt" it was superior, and he asked himself what characteristic of the law at that juncture had led him to such an opinion. By this a process of analysis, he was able to identify six features that distinguished the new law from the old. He labeled these characteristics *comprehensiveness, equity, clarity, relevant differentiation, balance of control,* and *flexibility.* The six then served as criteria which he applied in a systematic comparison of the 1950 and 1989 versions. The resulting comparison was subsequently published as a journal article entitled "Education Law as a Mirror of Maturity: The Indonesian Case" (Thomas, 1990a).

Profiting from Unexpected Outcomes

A third source of interpretation is the surprise variety. It usually comes as an unexpected revelation in the midst of a project. At first appearance, the revelation may seem to be an error, as if something went wrong with the study. It is viewed as an error because the result is not what the investigator expected— it conflicts with the researcher's predictions. But when such an outcome is seen from a more open-minded perspective, the apparent mistake can be transformed into a valued serendipitous finding. Significant scientific advances occasionally occur this way. In 1772, Joseph Priestly, the English chemist who is credited with discovering oxygen, happened to create carbonated water while studying the qualities of gases in the atmosphere. Radioactivity was accidentally discovered in 1896 by Henri Beckquerel, who wrapped some photographic plates in a black cloth, covered them with a sheet of aluminum, then happened to put some uranium-compound crystals on top. When he took the plates out of a drawer a few days later, he was amazed to find that the crystals had fogged the photographic plates, similar to the way light would affect them. A British bacteriologist, Alexander Fleming, in 1928 noticed that a culture of bacteria in a petri dish in his laboratory was gradually being dissolved by mold that had developed from air-borne spores settling on the dish. He was at first disturbed at the destruction of his precious bacteria; but then he analyzed this curious phenomenon and in the process discovered penicillin.

In the field of comparative education, unintentional insights also occur, even though less dramatic than the discovery of soda water, radioactivity, or penicillin. For instance, in Ambert's introduction to her paper entitled "Toward a Theory of Peer Abuse" she explains that:

> The topic of peer abuse emerged rather unexpectedly as I was analyzing two sets of open-ended questions in students' autobiographies. Students' written recollections of what had made them the most unhappy and then the most happy at four stages in their early lives were being coded for sources of unhappiness and happiness. The goal of this analysis was to test for the relative salience of parents in students' lives. Not only were we able to count the frequencies of parents, peers, and other sources of happiness/unhappiness mentioned, but peer abuse as a specific aspect of unhappy events became one of the salient results of the analysis [and launched the present separate study of peer abuse]. (Ambert, 1995, p. 177)

Interpretations and Their Support

The term *interpretations* is used here to mean generalizations that researchers offer about the outcome of their investigation. Critical readers are seldom willing to accept an author's conclusions without understanding why those interpretations are warranted. Thus, authors typically defend their conclusions by citing data or a line of logic to buttress their judgments. In way of illustration, consider these two examples of linking an interpretation to supporting evidence.

The interpretation: The educational atmosphere of students' homes is a critical influence on how well students succeed in science education.
The evidence: A study of 260,000 students in 23 nations showed that "in nearly all countries 10-year-old and 14-year-old children from homes with more reading resources and parents with more years of education performed better on the science tests than children from poorer homes with respect to these. Even when compared with school organizational and teaching factors, the home influences were still very strong in both developed and developing countries" (Postlethwaite & Wiley, 1992, p. 157).

The interpretation: As analysts ponder the effects of student exchanges within the European Union, they should recognize that the notion of a European community-of-the-intellect is not entirely new.
The evidence: " 'Today there are no longer Frenchmen, Germans, Spaniards, even Englishmen: whatever people say, there are only Europeans. All have the same tastes, the same feelings, the same customs, because none has experienced any particular national formation.' This is not the statement of some Bureaucrat at Brussels, but was written by Voltaire in 1740. However, while this perception might have applied to the small intellectual élite among [Voltaire's] contemporaries educated in the same scientific and humanistic traditions, the situation had changed radically by the time of the French

Revolution half a century later" when strong nationalistic divisions emerged (Rüegg, 1993, p. 42).

Description and Inference

As investigators summarize the information they have collected, they need to decide whether their conclusions are to be descriptive or inferential. The term *descriptive* in the present context refers to statements that relate only to people, institutions, or events that have been directly measured or assessed. In contrast, *inferential* refers not only to conclusions about things directly observed but also to other people, institutions, or events to which those conclusions are assumed to apply.

Descriptive Interpretations

Sometimes people intend their summaries to concern only the things they have directly studied. Such is the case when a psychologist examines two autistic children, then describes the two in terms of their similarities and differences without offering any opinions about autistic children in general. It is also the case when a history teacher tests her students' knowledge of the American Revolution and summarizes how well her group performed compared to the students in a different class. Such summaries can assume various forms— verbal portrayals, graphs, or statistics. For example, as a verbal portrayal, the psychologist may write:

Autistic Child A is far more self destructive and divorced from reality than Child B. Child A often strikes his head against the wall and frequently responds with a blank stare when asked questions. Child B occasionally tugs at his hair but does not hit his head; he is prone to answer questions with at least a grunt or nod or shake of the head.

As a statistical summary, the history teacher may report that the average (mean) score for her class on the American-Revolution test was 80.7, whereas the average for the other class was 73.2. She may also report that the scores in her class ranged from 63 to 100, while scores in the second class extended from 37 to 98.

Inferential Interpretations

However useful it may be to describe an individual's or group's performance, researchers frequently wish to extend the results of their studies to encompass more people, institutions, or events than they have examined. In other words, the people or institutions that the investigator has directly inspected are seen as merely a sample of a broader population to which the conclusions might be applied. From studying six autistic children, an investigator may choose to draw inferences about autistic children in general. From testing the history knowledge of two classrooms of students, a researcher may hope to say something useful about how well other students in other schools will likely profit from a similar style of history instruction.

The importance of distinguishing between description and inference lies in the fact that investigators who choose to extend their conclusions beyond the group they have directly appraised are obliged to offer evidence of why such an extension is warranted. They are obligated to suggest how much faith readers can place in the belief that the people they studied represent an accurate sample of the broader population to which the conclusions are being applied. The key question is: To what extent are judgments drawn about the sample likely to be in error when those judgments are extended to a greater range of people or events? Techniques for answering this question are offered in Chapter 9.

Later in this book, descriptions of many styles of interpretation are offered in the three chapters that comprise Stage IV.

STAGE 5: REPORTING THE OUTCOMES

The final phase of a research project consists of reporting the results to an appropriate audience. Reports can assume many forms, including master's-degree theses, doctoral dissertations, books, chapters within books, articles in academic journals, articles in popular periodicals (magazines, newspapers), in-house publications, microfiche or microfilm reproductions, and documents on the computer Internet. Each of these outlets has its own advantages and limitations, as illustrated in a comparison between theses and journal articles in terms of the length of a report, its chance of acceptance, its cost to the author, the publishing time lag, and breadth of dissemination (Table 1-3).

In the closing sections of this book, the two chapters that comprise Stage V identify the advantages and limitations of a variety of other forms of disseminating research, and they offer guidelines for designing and submitting reports for publication. When researchers are preparing reports, they should have in mind the type of publishing outlet they hope to use, since the way research is written up is influenced by the requirements of the publication medium for which it is intended.

CONCLUSION

The purpose of this opening chapter has been to introduce a typical sequence of tasks that investigators perform when conducting comparative education research. Then Chapters 2 through 15 describe the research tasks in detail. The final portion of each of those chapters offers a "Research Project Checklist" that consists of a list of questions identifying key elements of the chapter that researchers can profitably consider when designing their own projects.

Table 1-3

Two Forms of Research Reports:
Theses and Journal Articles

<u>Graduate Student Thesis</u>   <u>Academic Journal Article</u>

Length and Detail

Unlimited length and detail.   Length and detail restricted by
                                      journal policy.

Likelihood of Acceptance

Acceptance is determined solely by the   Acceptance for publication is
judgment of the student's advisory   determined by (a) editors' and
committee.   selected referees' judgments of
                                                research quality, (b) length of the
                                                report, (c) the journal's theme and
                                                editors' current interests, (d) the
                                                quantity and quality of other
                                                submitted articles. (The leading
                                                journals often accept no more than
                                                20% of articles they receive.)

Cost to the Author

Unless the student has a research grant,   Some journals pay the entire cost
the cost of issuing the thesis is borne   of publication, some charge the
entirely by its author.   author a fee, and others require that
                                                  the author subscribe to the journal
                                                  in order to have an article accepted.

Publishing Time Lag

The student and the advisory committee   The journal's editors determine how
determine when the thesis will be issued.   much time will elapse between the
                                                day the article is first received at the
                                                editorial office and (a) when the
                                                author will be notified of acceptance
                                                and (b) when the article appears in
                                                print. The time lag for acceptance
                                                can vary from two months to a year
                                                or so. The lag between acceptance
                                                and publication can vary from six
                                                months to three or four years.

Table 1-3 continued

**Two Forms of Research Reports:
Theses and Journal Articles**

<u>Graduate Student Thesis</u>   <u>Academic Journal Article</u>

Breadth of Dissemination

Graduate Student Thesis	Academic Journal Article
The reading audience is usually confined to a few interested individuals at the institution in which the author produced the thesis.	The audience includes individual subscribers, users of libraries that have the journal, and people who learn of the article via a computer network.

Stage I:

Choosing What to Study

The pair of chapters in Stage I identify sources of questions to investigate, describe alternative aims of research studies, inspect ways to state research questions, and consider the importance of presenting a rationale in support of the issues being investigated.

2

Sources and Aims of Research Topics

This chapter is designed to answer three sets of questions:
1. What are typical sources of ideas for research projects?
2. What are the aims investigators hope to reach with the topics they choose? In other words, what kinds of outcomes do they hope to produce?
3. What are the basic premises underlying typical theories used for explaining why educational events occur as they do?

SOURCES OF QUESTIONS TO INVESTIGATE

Researchers derive ideas for topics from various sources. The following discussion identifies kinds of sources and illustrates linkages between typical origins and the topics they can stimulate.

Two principal reservoirs of research ideas are communications and problems met in the conduct of educational enterprises.

Communications consist of what people say (oral) and write (printed). Useful oral communications include lectures, speeches, conversations, discussions, debates, criticisms, advice, proposals, and more. Useful printed communications include journal and magazine articles, newspaper stories and editorials, books, encyclopedias, letters, diaries, legal documents, government reports, school board minutes, conference proceedings, and the like.

Problems faced in the daily conduct of education are likewise a fertile origin of research ideas, since dedicated teachers and administrators are continually trying to improve the efficiency of their work. To help with this effort, they either conduct studies themselves or enlist the aid of researchers interested in such issues.

But whatever the immediate stimulus may be, it is usually helpful to have in mind a broad array of possible topics from which to choose. Then, from that array, researchers can select what they wish to compare. The following examples

illustrate what I mean by *an array of possible comparisons.* Later in Stage I
these matters are discussed in greater detail.

The Array of Possible Comparisons

Because there are thousands of potential comparisons, it is useful to know
methods of organizing them so they can be surveyed systematically.   The
following paragraphs describe three such methods—a cube display, a set of
encyclopedia topics, and a taxonomy of educational objectives.

A Cube Display

Figure 2-1 offers a three-dimensional way of exhibiting comparative
possibilities (Bray & Thomas, 1995, p. 475). The first dimension is geographi-
cal/locational. It contains seven levels: world regions/continents, countries,
states/provinces, districts, schools, classrooms, and individuals. This dimension
could be expanded by the addition of further intermediate levels. For example,
schools within districts could be grouped into clusters, and individual students
within a classroom could be placed together in work groups for the study of
mathematics, reading, or science.

The second dimension represents nonlocational demographic groupings, with
the illustrated groups based on ethnicity, religion, age, gender, socioeconomic
status, and an entire population. Further groups could be added, including ones
founded on citizenship, language spoken, political affiliation, health condition,
tested intelligence, source of family income, educational attainment, and more.

Aspects of the educational enterprise and of society are combined along the
third dimension, although it is also possible to cast the education system and
society as separate dimensions, thereby producing a four-dimensional model.
Only four of a multitude of educational aspects are pictured in the figure—
learning objectives, curriculum, teaching methods, and administrative structure.
Only four of a host of potential societal variables are portrayed—parents' asso-
ciations, political change, labor market conditions, and population growth.

Every comparative study involves all three dimensions so that a given study
can be located in one or more cells in the diagram. For instance, the shaded cell
represents a research project comparing learning objectives for ethnic groups in
two or more nations.

In summary, the cube suggests a way of looking at possible comparisons, but
it does not offer a definitive list of options along each dimension. To expand the
options that comprise each dimension, researchers can turn to more specific
classification systems. The following example demonstrates one way to extend
the aspects of education that are located on the third dimension of Figure 2-1.

Figure 2-1

A Framework for Comparative Education Analyses

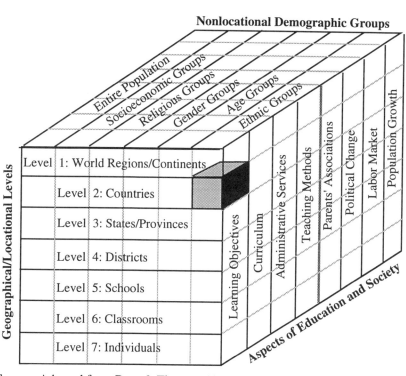

(Source: Adapted from Bray & Thomas, 1995, p. 475.)

A Set of Encyclopedia Topics

A systematic classification of potential comparisons can be developed by deriving topics from an educational encyclopedia and reassembling them into major categories and subcategories. How this is accomplished can be demonstrated with items drawn from Husén & Postlethwaite's *International Encyclopedia of Education* (1985, 1994).

The process of organizing such a schema consists of examining the contents of an encyclopedia's index in order to identify suitable topics, then reorganizing the topics into an outline that subsumes more specific items under more general ones. The complete outcome of the process is too lengthy to present here. However, the pattern that the final product may assume can be illustrated with the following segment of a more extensive schema. First, general headings are selected and labeled: (1) social/philosophical foundations, (2) curriculum, (3) teaching/learning activities, (4) characteristics of learners, (5) organization and management (administration), (6) educational personnel, and (7) research techniques. Then, more detailed topics, representing descending tiers of greater specificity, are listed under each heading. Here are the early items in the third general category:

3. Teaching/learning activities
  3.1 Learning objectives
    3.1.1 Types of objectives
      3.1.1.1 Cognitive
      3.1.1.2 Psychomotor
      3.1.1.3 Affective/emotional
      3.1.1.4 Behavioral
    3.1.2 Educational standards
  3.2 Methods of teaching
    3.2.1 Classroom teaching
      3.2.1.1 Lecture
      3.2.1.2 Demonstration
      3.2.1.3 Discussion
      3.2.1.4 Group work
      3.2.1.5 Experimentation
      3.2.1.6 Sociodrama
      3.2.1.7 Individual projects
      3.2.1.8 Mastery-learning
      3.2.1.9 Ausebel's verbal model
      3.2.1.10 Bruner's discovery model

3.2.1.11 Carroll's model
3.2.1.12 Freinet method
3.2.1.13 Herbartian approach
3.2.1.14 Montessori's system
3.2.1.15 Rogers' experiential plan
3.2.1.16 Socratic dialogue
3.2.1.17 Wittrock's generative learning
  3.2.2 Distance teaching
    3.2.2.1 Correspondence
    3.2.2.2 Radio
    3.2.2.3 Television
    3.2.2.4 Computer-assisted
  3.2.3 Individualized instruction
    3.2.3.1 Tutoring
    3.2.3.2 Apprenticeship
    3.2.3.3 Self instruction
    3.2.3.4 Dalton plan
    3.2.3.5 Decroly method
    3.2.3.6 Keller plan

Further second-level headings in the teaching/learning-activities outline can be (3.3) learning materials and equipment and (3.4) evaluating learners' progress. To continue the outline, we would next list subtopics under each of those headings.

In addition to using an encyclopedia to generate topics, we can turn to sources of even more specific issues that fit within the sorts of categories displayed in the above outline. For example, an investigator intending to conduct a study in the realm of learning objectives may profit from inspecting the *Taxonomy of Educational Objectives* that Benjamin Bloom and others devised.

A Taxonomy of Educational Objectives

Bloom and his associates first defined three major domains into which instructional objectives could be placed—the cognitive, the affective (emotional), and the psychomotor (Bloom, 1956; Krathwohl, Bloom, & Masia, 1964; Anderson & Sosniak, 1994). Then within each domain, they created categories they believed would accommodate all the types of specific objectives that educational programs are typically designed to pursue. The structure of their taxonomy can be illustrated with an excerpt from the cognitive domain.

The six major classes of objectives are those focusing on knowledge, comprehension, application, analysis, synthesis, and evaluation. The items within each class are ones that could be adapted to any subject-matter field in the curriculum—language arts, mathematics, science, social science, fine arts, vocational subjects, and others. The nature of the subcategories within a major class can be demonstrated by those under the heading *knowledge* (Bloom, 1956, pp. 52-88). Each item begins with the phrase *Knowledge of*:

1.1 Specifics
    1.1.1 Terminology
    1.1.2 Specific facts
1.2 Ways and means of dealing with specifics
    1.2.1 Conventions
    1.2.2 Trends and sequences
    1.2.3 Classification and categories
    1.2.4 Criteria
    1.2.5 Methodology
1.3 Universals and abstractions in a field
    1.3.1 Principles and generalizations
    1.3.2 Theories and structures.

These generic entries are converted into a form applicable to a specific subject-matter area by appending to each entry a phrase identifying the subject-matter field. For instance, for the subject of algebra the resulting statements become:

1.1.1 Knowledge of terminology in algebra, 1.1.2 knowledge of specific algebra facts, 1.3.1 knowledge of algebra principles and generalizations, and so on.

In like manner, each of the other five major classes also subsumes a series of more precise types of objectives. Thus, a person intending to compare instructional objectives may well find Bloom's taxonomy useful in suggesting aspects of objectives to include.

A question can now be asked about why researchers should concern themselves with inspecting a broad array of possible comparisons if they already have in mind a specific issue that interests them? The answer is that considering an extensive range of potential topics can often guide investigators toward improving their project by incorporating aspects that otherwise would have been overlooked. For example, someone planning to compare instructional methods in six classrooms might profit from using the encyclopedia outline for devising the categories into which teachers' methods will be placed. Or, the cube in Figure 2-1 could alert a researcher who is studying student achievement to analyze data at more than one geographical level (state, district, school), so as to reveal differences among states, among districts within states, and among schools within districts.

Finally, almost every research project includes a phase that is typically referred to as "a review of the literature." The review consists of the investigator learning what has been done in the past in relation to (a) defining his or her research topic, (b) selecting methods of data collection, and (c) interpreting the results. Surveying the array of potential comparisons can be one important feature of such a review.

Sources of Topics and Research-Project Aims

The following sketches of eight research projects illustrate connections among (a) the source of a topic, (b) the event leading to the choice of the topic, and (c) both the general and specific aims of the project.

1. *The topic source*: A professor's research agenda

A university professor interested in the decentralization of educational administration was conducting a series of studies about transferring administrative decision-making responsibilities from the provincial level to the school-district level. In connection with this project, he suggested that one of his doctoral advisees carry out her dissertation research as a segment of the decentralization program. The topic he recommended to her was: "A comparison of three methods of devolving responsibility for hiring teachers for rural schools."

General aim: Contribute to a broader research project.

Specific aim: Discover the consequences of three methods of assigning local authorities the task of hiring teachers.

2. *The topic source*: A speech at an educational conference

While attending a conference, a graduate student doubted the accuracy and wisdom of a conference speaker's declaring that:

"In the primary grades, reading instruction for boys should begin later and advance at a slower pace than for girls because (a) girls mature at a faster rate than boys, (b) girls score higher than boys on reading tests, and (c) more boys than girls require remedial reading instruction."

The student's doubt became the basis of the topic he chose for his master's thesis. He planned to analyze reading-test scores of primary-grade boys and girls, focusing attention on how well individual children succeeded rather than focusing solely on the average score for each sex. On the basis of the results, he recommended that the pacing of reading instruction be founded on each child's reading skills rather than on the conference speaker's generalization about the two sexes.

General aim: Assess a conference speaker's assertion.

Specific aim: Compare the effectiveness of different paces of reading instruction, focusing on individual pupils rather than on girls as a group and boys as a group.

3. *The topic source*: Reports of students' interest in studying science

The impetus behind a science educator's decision to conduct a research project came from two published reports that traced a decline over the secondary-school years in students' interest in studying science. In an effort to discover ways to heighten student interest, he studied the effects that a "results-prediction" technique had on learners' attitudes. The technique, used in teaching genetics concepts to high school biology students, consisted of the instructor requiring class members to predict the outcome of genetics experiments before the experiments were actually conducted. The purpose of requiring prediction was to enhance learning "by focusing students' attention on the concepts under consideration and by motivating students to seek verification of their predictions" (Sinclair, 1994, p. 153). A comparison of the performance of students under the results-predication approach with the performance of ones not obliged to offer predictions showed that both groups scored equally well on tests, but the "prediction activities augmented classroom participation, promoted critical analysis, and enhanced student interest in the lesson" (Sinclair, 1994, p. 153).

General aim: Evaluate a remedy for an educational problem

Specific aim: Test the instructional effectiveness of having students try to predict the outcome of experiments in the field of genetics.

4. *The topic source*: Books about Vygotsky's theory of learning

One definition of *theory* is: "A set of beliefs that explain why events occur as they do." The label *activity theory* has been attached to a set of beliefs advanced by a Russian psychologist, Lev Semenovich Vygotsky (1896-1934). Activity theory proposes that learning consists of a sequence of phases in which actions alternate with thought. First, learners take action in a problem situation; then they think about how successful that action has been and they subsequently apply the resultant knowledge the next time they face a similar problem. In effect, action leads to contemplation, which leads to revised action, which then leads to further contemplation, which leads to further revised action, and so on (van der Veer & Valsiner, 1994). A team of researchers who had read books about Vygotsky's work applied his activity theory toward discovering when, during the process of learning a new card game, adults' question-asking contributed most to their mastering the game—(a) in the introductory-acquisition phase (acquiring the game rules and strategies) or (b) in the implementation phase (playing the game). From conducting experiments with teaching the game to adults in tutoring sessions, the researchers concluded that "The results confirm the view that questions answered during knowledge implementation more effectively aid comprehension than those answered during acquisition" (Fishbein, et al., 1990, p. 163).

General aim: Apply a theory

Specific aim: Determine when, during the process of learning a card game, the players profit most from asking questions.

5. *The topic source*: Articles in professional journals

In American schools, the academic achievement of students from cultural origins other than mainstream American culture is often below average. Some research published in professional journals has identified students' lack of familiarity with the English language as the chief cause of low achievement, whereas other studies have cited a disadvantaged socioeconomic background as a more significant cause. In an effort to cast light on this controversy, Kennedy and Park (1994) compared the home language, socioeconomic background, and academic records of 1,952 Mexican-American and 1,131 Asian-American eighth-graders. The results of their study suggested that the chief influences on academic success differed between the two ethnic groups.

"Much of the association of home language with academic performance for Mexican-American students could be explained by socioeconomic background and social psychological variables [self-concept, cultural variations in oral and written logic, student aspirations]. In contrast, for Asian-American students, speaking a language other than English in school [was more often associated with getting higher course grades but with getting] lower standardized test scores in reading" (Kennedy & Park, 1994, p. 188).

General aim: Explore alternative causes.

Specific aim: Discover the extent of association among (a) Mexican-American and Asian-American students' home language, (b) a variety of sociocultural factors in their lives, and (c) the students' grades and reading-test scores.

6. *The topic source*: Articles in professional journals

For researchers Anne Cunningham and Keith Stanovich, the impetus to compare ways of teaching young children to spell came from journal articles describing the success of the Simultaneous Oral Spelling method. The method requires that children spell a word by (a) pronouncing the word as presented to them in printed and spoken form, (b) pronouncing the name of each letter while writing the word, and (c) repeating the whole word again. Cunningham and Stanovich sought to learn how important the writing portion of the method was to promoting spelling skill. To do so, they had first-grade children study spelling under three conditions —writing words, typing words on a computer, and spelling words by manipulating letter tiles. They discovered that having children write words was the best method, "even under conditions where the post-training spelling assessment was done on the computer and with tiles" (Cunningham & Stanovich, 1990).

General aim: Compare educational procedures.

Specific aim: Evaluate the effectivness of three methods of practicing spelling.

7. *The topic source*: A computer search of the subject matter of books and articles

The advent of computerized lists of books and articles on educational topics has greatly enhanced the efficiency of searching the professional literature to discover which topics have been studied thoroughly and which have been neglected. When two staff members at the University of Iowa's center for gifted education conducted such a search, they concluded that a category of youths which rarely drew scholars' attention was that of students with extremely high academic talent in particular fields of knowledge (English, mathematics, natural sciences, social studies). To help fill in this knowledge gap, Colangelo and Kerr analyzed the test results of 5,615 students who had achieved a perfect score in one or more academic fields during a nationwide college testing program that included 729,606 participants. The results of the study showed that:

"Boys had a higher incidence of perfect scores [than girls] in each subtest except English. Asians and Whites were overrepresented among perfect scorers, and all other ethnic groups were underrepresented. 'Perfection' in one academic area did not assure comparable high performance in other academic areas. Few perfect scorers planned college majors or careers in the disciplines in which they attained perfect scores" (Colangelo & Kerr, 1990, p. 404).

General aim: Contribute to a neglected area of knowledge.

Specific aim: Among students of very high academic talent, discover the degree of relationship among their test scores across different subject areas by student gender and ethnic background.

8. *The topic source*: A college counselor from Indonesia attended a three-month workshop on counseling techniques in the United States. Upon his return to Indonesia, he integrated elements of several techniques to form an approach to diagnosing and treating learning difficulties that seemed compatible with Indonesian culture. To assess the effectiveness of the approach, he devised a continuing research program that involved collecting information from counselors who adopted his system. He then used the information to change the approach in ways that suited different regions' school facilities, personnel, and pupils (Sukmadinata, 1978).

General aim: Transfer an educational practice from one context to another.

Specific aim: Appraise counseling techniques imported from the United States for their suitability in a variety of Indonesian contexts.

The foregoing eight examples illustrate a few of the wide variety of sources of research ideas and suggest aims of the resulting projects. Additional general aims include those of replicating earlier research, refining an educational practice, evaluating instructional materials, assessing traditional procedures or "conventional wisdom," generating a new or revised theory of cause and effect, and more.

CLASSIFYING AIMS OF RESEARCH STUDIES

Developing a convenient framework for surveying aims of research topics can entail (a) dividing investigators' motives into two principal categories (*understanding* and *acting constructively*) and then (b) under each motive, identifying illustrative research topics within the four types of research aims introduced in Chapter 1—description, explanation, prediction, and evaluation. The contents of the following section are assembled on such a framework.

The terms *understanding* and *acting constructively* identify two varieties of research often labeled (a) *basic* or *pure* and (b) *applied* or *practical*.

The concept *understanding* reflects people's need to comprehend how their world operates. In seeking to promote understanding, the researcher's motive is simply to understand life, without intending to apply that knowledge to solving practical problems. This is often the case with studies in atomic physics, astronomy, molecular biology, chemistry, social history, anthropology, sociology, psychology, and the like. In comparative education, basic-research investigators hope to learn the status of educational enterprises and how they function, whether or not such information might be useful for improving the efficiency or quality of those enterprises. They pursue such topics as:

—Educational Effects of Short-Term Military Occupation: Burma and Japan
—The Status of Religious Education in Five Industrialized Societies
—The Relation Between Mothers' Occupational Status and Children's School
   Success

The concept *acting constructively* reflects people's need to solve problems they face in their lives. Applied-research investigators are driven by a desire to improve the conduct of education through problem solving. The applied nature of their work is often implied in the titles of their studies.

—The Effectiveness of Three Methods of Teaching Logic: Lectures, Debates, and
   Computers
—When and Where Nationally Adopted Textbooks Work Best

The concepts *understanding* and *acting constructively* are partially linked, in that individuals' attempts to act constructively are based on their beliefs about how the world operates. Thus, a research project may be designed to provide the understanding needed for solving a problem. Such could be the intent of studies entitled:

—Physiological Versus Environmental Causes of Stuttering
—The Effects on School Attendance of Market-Driven Economies and Centrally
   Planned Economies

DEVISING BASIC AND APPLIED RESEARCH TOPICS

The following section introduces sources of both basic and applied research topics, beginning with the basic-research goal of extending people's knowledge of the world and—in the particular case of comparative education—extending people's knowledge of education systems and of the sociopolitical contexts within which those systems operate.

The Motive Behind Basic Research:
To Understand Educational Phenomena

As suggested earlier, research projects that focus on understanding usually have one or more aims—those of describing, explaining, predicting, or evaluating target variables. The principal goals of such studies are often reflected in the projects' titles.

Describing means depicting the status of target variables at two more times or places.

—The Increase in Adult-Controlled Afterschool Activities for Children: 1970-1995
—The Popularity of the 'Reading Recovery' Plan for Teaching Children Who Have
   Difficulty Learning to Read: New Zealand, the United Kingdom, and the United
   States

Explaining means accounting for how and why the target variables arrived at their particular condition.

—The Influence of Language, Culture, and Attitude on Learning Mathematics and Science: A Review of the Literature
—Causes of Delinquency: Interactions among Family, School, and Juvenile Offenders

The line of reasoning adduced for explaining educational events is often cast in the form of a theory or model linking causes to effects. Because such theories so often play a critical role in comparative education research, they deserve the detailed attention that is provided in the final section of this chapter.

Predicting means foretelling the future condition of the target variable.

—Expected Results of Sex Education in Public Schools
—The Impact of Population Growth on Schooling in Subsahara Africa: 2010 and 2050

Evaluating means judging the desirability of the target variables' condition.

—Summer Setback: The Drop in Children's Math Skills Over a Long Vacation
—Assessing the Effectiveness of Two Speech-Disorder Treatments

The Motive Behind Applied Research:
To Solve Problems Met in the Conduct of Education

When a researcher's goal is to act constructively for the improvement of some aspect of education, the four general aims assume a slightly different form.

Describing means establishing the status of the target variable as a foundation for adopting a course of action.

—Students' Health Insurance Costs: 1977-1997
—High School Dropout Rates by State and School District

Explaining means identifying what, if anything, needs to be changed in order to improve the condition of the target variable.

—Effects of Television Violence on Pupils' Moral Values
—Sleep, Drugs, and Learning Efficiency

Predicting means estimating the future condition that the target variable will assume if particular actions are taken.

—Likely Consequences of Failed School-Bond Elections
—Alcohol on the College Campus: Estimating Academic Achievement among Heavy, Moderate, and Light Drinkers

Evaluating means judging how desirable the results of some action have been.

—Good News, Bad News: An Appraisal of Single-Subject Research Techniques in Counseling Psychology
—Diverse Effects of High-School Tracking

In summary, as researchers formulate their projects, they can profit from deciding the extent to which their aim is to foster understanding of educational events compared to furnishing guidance toward solving educational problems. It is useful as well for investigtors to determine the extent to which their project will include description, explanation, prediction, and evaluation.

USING THEORY TO EXPLAIN EDUCATIONAL EVENTS

As mentioned earlier, an important motive behind certain investigators' choice of research topics is their desire to apply, test, or criticize a theory.

The term *theory* can be defined in various ways. One dictionary version is: "A coherent group of general propositions used as principles of explanation for a class of phenomena" (Flexner, 1987, p. 1967). Another is: "A more or less verified or established explanation accounting for known facts or phenomena" (Webster's, 1989, p. 1471). The word *theory* is also sometimes used as a synonym for such terms as *explanatory scheme, model, paradigm,* or *hypothesis.* However, for present purposes, I have adopted a slightly more detailed rendition. First, I offer a meaning for the word *facts*: "Facts or data are either discrete observations and measurements of people, institutions, or events, or else they are summaries of such observations and measurements." Then *theory* is defined as: "A proposal about (a) which facts are most important for understanding an educational phenomenon and (b) which relationships among facts are most significant for clarifying the causes of the phenomenon."

Dozens of theories in the field of education and in related social sciences are available to researchers to account for educational events. The diversity of those theories can be illustrated with the following 16 examples that represent a limited number drawn from the entire assortment of such schemes. Each example includes a title, the theory's foundational precepts, and typical applications in education.

Structural-Functional Theory

In the social sciences, structural-functional theory proposes that a society has a given structure that is sustained by functions appropriate to that structure—such structural features as a particular style of producing and consuming goods, established roles people play (including their place in a social-class system), and established values and institutions.   The task of the education system is to perpetuate the structure. Thus, according to proponents of a structural-functional perspective, the kind of comparative research that is most enlightening consists of studies that clarify the way education supports the form of a society. From cross-cultural research, scholars hope to extract general principles that account for how and why different education systems operate as they do. Typical applications of structural-functional theory are illustrated in McGinn's (1987) tracing the evolution of the French national education system from the time of Napoleon I to the present day and Kelly's (1987) analyzing the transfer of that system to France's Southeast Asian colonies in the early 20th century.

Two criticisms directed at structural-functional theory are that (1) it accounts more adequately for social conservatism and stability than for social change and (2) it has not explained adequately why daily teaching in the classroom takes place as it does (Lundgren, 1985, pp. 1957-1962).

Human-Capital Theory

A human-capital or human-resource perception of education centers on issues of how education contributes to, or detracts from, individuals' economic productivity. "The basic assumption of the notion that education is a form of investment in human capital is that education raises the productivity of workers and that the higher earnings of the educated reflect the value of their product" (Woodhall, 1985, p. 1503). Economists and political scientists are often interested in analyzing educational events from a human-capital, human-resource, or manpower-development point of view. Studies employing human-resource theory bear such titles as *Human Capital: A Theoretical and Empirical Analysis, with Special Reference to Education* (Becker, 1993), *Education Finance Reform and Investment in Human Capital: Lessons from California* (Fernandez, 1995), and "Gender Differences in the Returns to Schooling and in School Enrollment Rates in Indonesia" (Deolikar, 1993).

Conflict Theory

A conflict view of human affairs focuses on divisions within the society—divisions between individuals, groups, and institutions. From a conflict-theorist's vantage point, dissent and friction are not deviations to be deplored but, instead, are normal conditions that contribute to personal and social change and development. "Conflict turns the wheels of history, because the endpoint of one conflict is a new lineup of resources, which in turn becomes the basis for the formation of new interests and new conflicts" (Collins, 1993, p. 292).

Conflict theorists seek to discover who belong to groups that are in conflict, what the motives of the dissidents are, what strategies are employed by the antagonists, and how effective the strategies have been. Four convictions that underlie one version of conflict theory are that:

1. Each social resource produces a potential conflict between those who have the resource and those who do not. "The basic dimensions of resources and, hence, social conflicts are: (a) economic resources [in the form of]. . . material conditions; (b) power resources, best conceived as positions within control networks; and (c) status or cultural resources [that will provide]. . . control over social rituals [such as education], producing group solidarity and group symbolism" (Collins, 1993, p. 290).
2. Potential conflicting interests become effective to the extent that they are mobilized relative to the mobilization of opposing interests.
3. Conflict engenders subsequent conflict.
4. Conflicts diminish as resources for mobilization are used up.

Applications of conflict theory for explaining educational change are found in such works as *Schooling in East Asia* (Thomas & Postlethwaite, 1983) and Kravetz's (1983) analysis of conflicts over bilingual education policies in the United States.

Marxist Theory

A widely influential form of conflict theory is the dialectical-materialism explanation of social systems proposed by a pair of 19th-century German social philosophers, Karl Marx (1818-1882) and Frederich Engels (1820-1895). A basic tenet of Marxist theory is that people's modes of thought and social relations are determined chiefly by the system of producing and distributing goods within their society.

> The mode of production in material life determines the general character of the social, political, and spiritual processes of life. It is not the consciousness of men which determines their existence; but, on the contrary, their social existence determines their consciousness. (Marx, 1859, p. 43)

Marx asserted that societies naturally evolve through three successive stages—feudalism (aristocratic land owners exploit the peasants), capitalism (bourgeois entrepreneurs exploit the workers), and state socialism or communism (all resources of the production and distribution of goods and services in a classless society are controlled by the working masses so that no one is exploited). Marxist doctrine holds that education in each social system is designed to support the production and distribution patterns (political, economic, and cultural practices) of that particular system (Marx, 1859, 1898; Marx & Engels, 1848).

Books in the field of international education that offer Marxist explanations of events include Paulo Freire's *Pedagogy of the Oppressed* (1970/1993), Martin Carnoy's *Education and Cultural Imperialism* (1974), and Robert Arnove's *Education and Revolution in Nicaragua* (1986).

Correspondence Theory

In keeping with a structural-functional viewpoint, correspondence theory proposes that education and work (meaning occupations and the economic system) correspond to each other in structure and content, and that the role of the education system is to maintain the existing social structure. Studies conducted from a correspondence-theory perspective reflect researchers' belief that it is useful to compare educational operations with the world of work.

In a Marxist version of correspondence theory,

> The bureaucratic organization of schools parallels that found in business; the hierarchical relations among administrators, teachers, and students are similar to the social relations between managers and workers; the lack of control students have over their education and the alienation they often feel as a result reflect a similar lack of control and alienation that workers find in their adult economic lives; and the extrinsic rewards—grades, test scores—in schools, parallel the use of extrinsic rewards—wages—found in the workplace. (Rumberger, 1985, p. 1030)

World-Systems Theory

A world-systems interpretation of educational events proposes that the entire socioeconomic-political-cultural world should be included in any effort to account for the overall condition of modern-day societies, including the effort to explain the operation of a society's educational enterprises. In today's world, socioeconomic conditions of one nation affect the welfare of others. Trans-national corporations that locate facilities in multiple regions influence the types of workers employed and the training they receive. Governments that maintain colonial control over dependent societies affect the sorts of education available in those societies.

Chase-Dunn and Grimes credit sociologists with creating the phrases *world economy, world market,* and *world system* in the 1970s when

> a rapidly growing group of social scientists recognized that national "develop-ment" could only be understood contextually, as the complex outcome of local interactions with an aggressively expanding European-centered "world" economy. Not only did these scientists perceive the global nature of economic networks . . . but they also saw that many of these networks extend back at least 500 years. Over this time, the people of the globe became linked into one integrated unit: the modern "world system." (Chase-Dunn & Grimes, 1995, p. 387)

Educational studies founded on a world-systems viewpoint include Coombs' *The World Crisis in Education* (1985) and Axinn and Sudhaker's *Modernizing World Agriculture* (1972). Ways of conducting such analyses are described in

Hopkins and Wallerstein's *World-Systems Analysis: Theory and Methodology* (1982).

Dependency Theory

The dependency version of world-systems analysis was developed and disseminated during the 1960s to explain how one society relates to others, so that some are at higher levels of socioeconomic development than others, and some must rely on others for their subsistence. One of the progenitors of dependency theory, particularly among Marxist writers, was the concept of imperialism, represented chiefly in the colonial control of most of Africa, Asia, and the Pacific Islands by European and North American powers and by Japan prior to World War II. In Central and South America the imperialism was internal, with a small elite of European heritage controlling the economy and suppressing the culture of native peoples. Since World War II, as so many colonized peoples have attained political independence, their societies have been viewed by dependency theorists as still subservient to the former colonialists.

Among publications that inspect education systems from a dependency perspective are *Education and the Colonial Experience* (Altbach & Kelley, 1991), *Predicting Development, Dependency, and Conflict in Latin America* (Alschuler, 1978), and *Schooling in the Pacific Islands—Colonies in Transition* (Thomas & Postlethwaite, 1984).

Liberation Theory

As a variant of dependency theory, liberation theory adopts a "humanistic approach to questions of development. The underlying assumption is that members of the underdeveloped societies are oppressed by the powerholders of their own societies, who control the relevant economic resources such as land, industry, and wealth . . . [so] the main remedy for overcoming this oppression lies in the education of the oppressed to be aware of their condition. This practice is called 'consientizacao' by the Brazilian educationist Paulo Freire" (Fagerlind & Saha, 1989, pp. 25-26).

Books reflecting a liberation-theory focus are Freire's *The Politics of Education: Culture, Power, and Liberation* (1985), Ivan Illich's *Deschooling Society* (1971), and David West's *Authenticity and Empowerment: A Theory of Liberation* (1990).

Societal-Development Theory

The word *development* identifies one kind of change, the kind that pictures societies progressing, becoming better rather than retrogressing and becoming worse. Development theory is intended to answer such questions as: What are the indicators of societal development? Which conditions promote development and which retard it? How can constructive conditions be fostered and destructive ones be avoided? What part can education play in development?

Among studies featuring development theory are *Social Change and History: Aspects of the Western Theory of Development* (Nisbet, 1969), *Education's Role in National Development Plans* (Thomas, 1992), and *Social Transformation: A General Theory of Historical Development* (Sanderson, 1995).

Modernization Theory

As one way of looking at societal development, *modernization theory* is employed in studies that focus on the role of education in nations' efforts to adopt increasingly complex forms of technology aimed at enhancing the production and distribution of goods and services. In other words, how does education contribute to, or detract from, the modernization process?

Research that considers how education is related to modernization is found in such sources as *Perspectives on Modernization: Toward a General Theory of Third World Development* (Abraham, 1980) and *Gender and Development: Rethinking Modernization and Dependency Theory* (Scott, 1995).

Information-Integration Theory

The interpretation of human behavior proposed by Norman H. Anderson and his colleagues focuses on how people integrate information in their attempts to derive meaning from their experiences. Integration theory is founded on the conviction that "thought and action typically arise from multiple causes acting together" (Anderson, 1991a, p. 1). To explain educational events from an information-integration perspective, a researcher's task includes (a) identifying the kinds of information that contribute toward making a decision in an educational context, (b) determining the sources of the different kinds of information, and (c) estimating the strength of each kind and the role it plays in effecting a decision.

The multiple factors that people weigh in generating their judgments and actions include values, attitudes, moral knowledge, their own and others' motivations, and features of the particular persons and conditions in the present episode. The process of integrating the multiple factors consists of assigning positive and negative weights to each factor (in terms of the goal or goals being pursued), then applying a kind of intuitive algebra to the collection of factors so as to produce a decision about the event at hand. Although people perform the computation automatically, as their intellectual maturity advances they can become at least partially aware of their decision-making process and thereby bring it under greater intentional control.

Representative studies employing information-integration theory are "Cognitive Algebra of Interpersonal Unfairness" (Farkas, 1991) and "Moral Algebra of Harm and Recompense" (Hommers & Anderson, 1991).

Darwinian Theory

When Charles Darwin in 1859 published *The Origin of Species,* he set the foundation for the dominant present-day conceptions of how biological inheritance affects people's aptitudes and performance in educational settings. From Darwin's fundamental tenets have grown subtheories often grouped under such titles as *ethology* (the study of the behavior of animals—including humans—in natural environments), *psychobiology* (the study of how body structures relate to behavior), and *sociobiology* (the study of the biological bases of how members of a species act toward one another and toward members of other species).

Examples of educational research that draws heavily on some form of Darwinian theory include Arthur Jensen's *Genetics and Education* (1972) and *Educability and Group Differences* (1973); G. Stanley Hall's classic *Health, Growth, and Heredity* (1965); and S. D. Smith's *Genetics and Learning Disabilities* (1986).

Ecological Theory

Whereas Darwinian theory focuses primary attention on people's inherited biological nature, *ecological* or *contextual theory* emphasizes the ways environmental conditions interact with inherited nature to determine the patterns of people's thought and action.

In devising one version of ecological theory, Roger W. Barker at the University of Kansas noted that traditional psychology showed ways in which people differed from one another but failed to trace the great variations in thought, feeling, and action that an individual person experiences during a typical day. He asserted that a large portion of the variation in a single child's life could be accounted for by the environments or *behavior settings* through which that child commonly moves. In effect, ecological theorists contend that a great deal of a child's behavior can be accounted for by the characteristics of the contexts the child encounters. This viewpoint has been illustrated in such studies as *One Boy's Day* (Barker & Wright, 1951), *Big School, Small School* (Barker & Gump, 1964), and *Habitats, Environments, and Human Behavior* (Barker, 1978).

A more recent variant of ecological theory offered by Urie Bronfenbrenner of Cornell University analyzes environments in terms of how immediately they impinge on an individual's daily life (Bronfenbrenner, 1979, 1993). The most immediate level is the *microsystem,* such as a child's home, school, and peer group that dictate the child's activities, the child's roles, and the quality of the child's interpersonal relations. The next level of analysis is labeled the *mesosystem*, consisting of interactions among home, school, and peers. More distant are *exosystems*, events outside the child's immediate experience but ones that still affect the child (the parents' workplaces, school board decisions, friends of the child's siblings). Each of these systems is set within the general society's cultural milieu that displays a particular pattern of governance, custom, language, and more. Research conducted within this variety of ecological theory is found in *Two Worlds of Childhood: U.S. and U.S.S.R.* (Bronfenbrenner, 1972), "Home School Research" (Wright, 1988), and *Development in Context: Acting and Thinking in Specific Environments* (Wozniak & Fischer, 1993).

Behaviorist Theory

The late Harvard University psychologist B. F. Skinner is perhaps the best known of all the advocates of a behaviorist interpretation of individual and group action. As a theory of learning, behaviorism is founded on the conviction that the consequences which follow a person's actions determine whether that person will act in the same way on similar occasions in the future. If the consequences have been pleasant (rewarding, reinforcing), the tendency to behave in the same way again is strengthened. If the consequences have been unpleasant (punitive, nonreinforcing), then the tendency to behave that way again is weakened. Thus, in Skinnerian behaviorism, the term *learning* refers to the process of people habitually acting the same way when under similar stimulus circumstances because past consequences have been satisfying (Skinner, 1969, 1974). Traditional behaviorists, because of their emphasis on the effect of consequences, avoid talking about such unseen entities as *mind* and *thought*. They focus, instead, on people's observable actions and the observable consequences that follow such actions, since behaviorists believe that *teaching* or *guiding people's learning* requires only the manipulation of the consequences that people experience in their lives.

Illustrative studies employing behaviorism as an analytical tool are "The Shame of American Education" (Skinner, 1984), *Human Operant Conditioning and Behavior Modification,* (Davey & Cullen, 1988), "Separate and Combined Effects of Methylphenidate and Behavior Modification on Boys with Attention-Deficit Hyperactivity Disorder in the Classroom" (Pelham, et al., 1993), and "Combining Noncontingent Reinforcement and Differential Reinforcement Schedules as Treatment for Aberrant Behavior" (Marcus & Vollmer, 1996).

Social-Learning Theory

Social-learning theorists, such as Stanford University psychologist Albert Bandura, agree with behaviorism's emphasis on the importance of consequences in forming people's beliefs and habits. However, unlike behaviorists, social-learning proponents are quite willing to talk about such things as *mind* and *thoughts*. They also differ with behaviorists' account of how a person first achieves a new behavior. They contend that most of what people know and do is acquired by imitation (modeling)—copying what they see and hear other people do. In other words, most learning is the result of social interaction, either directly (seeing what others do) or vicariously (reading or hearing about what others do) (Bandura, 1986).

Research projects that interpret educational events from a social-learning viewpoint include *Juvenile Delinquents, the Martial Arts, and Behavior Modification: An Experimental Study of Social Intervention* (Demoulin, 1987) and "Behavior Modeling Training and Generalization: Interaction of Learning Type and Number of Modeling Scenarios" (Bryant & Fox, 1995).

Curriculum and Instructional Theory

Theories of curriculum design and instruction are proposals about how best to organize and purvey educational content. Curriculum designs typically include consideration of the learning objectives to be achieved, the subject-matter content to be used in pursuing the objectives, suitable learning materials, effective instructional methods, and ways of evaluating the learners' progress. Decisions about such matters are founded on curriculum planners' ideas about the abilities of the learners and about the skills and knowledge learners need in order to thrive in their particular society. Studies that employ theories of curriculum design and instruction can be of many kinds, involving comparisons between two or more sets of objectives, types of content, learning materials, methods of instruction, assessment techniques, types of students, types of teachers, or social contexts.

Representative research projects include *Television and the Preschool Child: A Psychological Theory of Instruction and Curriculum Development* (Lesser, 1977), *The Management of Ignorance: A Political Theory of the Curriculum* (Inglis, 1985), *Education as a Human Right: A Theory of Curriculum and Pedagogy* (Vandenburg, 1990), and *Radical Curriculum Theory Reconsidered: A Historical Approach* (Hlebowitsh, 1993).

Additional Theories

The 16 sorts of theories reviewed in the above paragraphs represent only a portion of the viewpoints that can be used in the design and interpretation of comparative studies. Additional models that can serve those purposes bear such labels as *gender theory* (Eccles, 1994; Gilligan, 1982), *group socialization theory* (Harris, 1995), *information theory* (Henry, 1996), *interactionist deliquency theory* (Bartusch & Matsueda, 1996), *meaning theory* (Colomb, 1989), *resistance theory* (Foley, 1991; Giroux, 1983), *responsive curriculum theory* (Anwkah, 1983), *reproduction theory* (Apple, 1982; Foley, 1991), *self-*

efficacy theory (Telljohann, Everett, Durgin, & Price, 1996), *social-class theory* (Goldthorpe, 1996), *strain theory* (Farnworth & Leiber, 1989), *value theory* (Foster, 1991), and far more.

CONCLUSION

Students and practitioners in the field of education and in allied disciplines (psychology, sociology, anthropology, economics, history) often appear to feel at a loss when they are expected to come up with ideas for research projects. The purpose of this chapter has been to assist them with that task by suggesting a diversity of sources and aims of research topics and by offering examples of topics. Research efforts often include the aim of interpreting events in terms of theories that help dictate the type of data to collect and the kinds of conclusions to draw from data analyses. In this chapter I have illustrated several types of theories that can be adopted to guide the conduct of comparative studies.

RESEARCH PROJECT CHECKLIST

1. From which (if any) of the following sources do I derive my research topic?

___A teacher's (professor's) suggestion   ___A colleague's or friend's suggestion

___The content of a speech or lecture   ___A debate or discussion

___A television or radio program   ___A newspaper or popular magazine

___An academic journal   ___A book (textbook, scholarly

___A diary, biography, letters   publication)

                                   ___A research report

___Other (specify)_____

2. Which (if any) of the following categories identify the general aim of my research?

___To *understand* the nature of an aspect of education

     ___To describe the aspect's status

     ___To explain causes of the aspect's condition

     ___To predict the aspect's future condition

     ___To evaluate the desirability of the aspect

___To propose *constructive action* for improving an aspect of education

     ___To describe the status of the aspect as a foundation for adopting a course of action

     ___To explain what needs to be changed to improve the aspect

     ___To predict the outcome of the aspect if certain action is taken

     ___To evaluate the results of an action that has been taken

3. Does the aim of my project include explaining the condition of the target variable in terms of one or more recognized theories? If the answer is yes, then what is the title or nature of the theory or theories?

3

Specifying the Research Problem

Once a researcher has selected a topic to study and has identified the aim to be achieved, the next task is to cast the topic in an efficient form and to buttress the choice of the topic with a convincing line of reasoning. This task requires decisions about (a) how best to state the research issue, (b) how to identify and define key terms, and (c) how to formulate a supporting rationale.

STATING THE ISSUE TO BE INVESTIGATED

Three ways to state a research problem are as a topic, as a question, or as a hypothesis.

A topic statement is like the title of a book or article.

—Social Class, Intelligence, and School Success
—Ethnic Groups' Political Strategies in Curriculum Change
—Regional Contrasts in Literacy Education: Southeast Asia and the Middle East

Stating an issue as a question identifies the sort of answer the research is expected to provide in resolving the issue.

—What is the relationship between students' social-class status, their levels of intelligence, and how well they succeed in school?
—To what extent do ethnic groups adopt political strategies to effect changes in schools' curricula, what is the nature of such strategies, and which ethnic groups most actively employ the different strategies?
—What similarities and differences exist between Southeast Asia and the Middle East in the forms, extent, and success of literacy education?

A hypothesis represents a probable answer to the research question, but the probability of the answer is yet to be tested by means of the research activities.

—Students' success in school is positively correlated with their social-class status and their level of intelligence.

—Political strategies that ethnic groups attempt for effecting curriculum change include lobbying legislators, electing members of their group to school boards, writing letters to newspapers, and conducting public demonstrations. Some groups use particular strategies more often and more successfully than do other groups.

—Literacy education in the Middle East region, as contrasted with literacy education in Southeast Asia, is conducted in larger-group settings, is provided more often for males than for females, and progresses at a slower pace due to the complexity of the written language.

A question now can be asked about which of these three methods is the best. Or, more precisely, under what circumstances is one of the methods superior to the others?

Although a research problem stated as a topic may suffice as a title for a book or article describing the outcome of the research, a topic form rarely furnishes an investigator the clear guidance needed for choosing research methods, gathering data, and interpreting the results. This means that the preferred way of stating the problem is either as a question or as a hypothesis.

There are at least two circumstances in which an investigator may favor the hypothesis over the question. One is when there is good reason to believe that a proposed solution to the research issue is correct, but that belief still needs to be corroborated by evidence. The other is when the investigator is applying a statistical test to the data that will be collected, and casting the problem as a hypothesis renders statistical testing more convenient. (A detailed explanation of such testing is offered in Chapter 9.)

But the vast majority of research problems can be expressed as questions involving such queries as who, how, which, why, what, when, where, how much, and how frequently.

—Who were the principal figures in educational development in mid-19th-century Scandinavia, and how did they exert their influence?

—Which indicators of academic aptitude are the best predictors of university entrants' subsequent academic success: (a) entrance-test scores, (b) secondary-school grades, or (c) letters of recommendation?

—What is the effect of class size on primary-school pupils' achievement in reading, mathematics, and the arts?

—When during a child's development is it most appropriate to provide sex education, in what sequence should particular topics be offered, and why in that sequence?

—Where do school officials plan to build new schools, and what criteria do they use for reaching that decision?

—How much of the variation among nations' literacy levels is related to the size of the nations' expenditures on education?

—How often do male teachers take sick leave compared to female teachers, and what illnesses do they cite as the cause of their infirmity?

It is also the case that questions can appear in more than one form.

—In Argentina, Brazil, and Venezuela, how do secondary-school history books portray different ethnic groups' roles in the development of those countries?

—The purpose of the present study is to discover the ways secondary-school history books in Argentina, Brazil, and Venezuela portray the roles of different ethnic groups in those nations' development.

—The central concern of this investigation is how the roles of different ethnic groups in national development are depicted in the history texts used in the secondary schools of Argentina, Brazil, and Venezuela.

Frequently a research project is designed to answer questions at more than one level of specificity. Major questions subsume minor ones whose answers contribute to resolving the major questions.

—How did immigration over the period 1967-1997 affect the conduct of schooling in Canada, Germany, and the United States?
  1. In each country, who immigrated, from where, when, and in what amounts?
  2. What characteristics of immigrants influenced schooling in Canada, Germany, and the U.S., and what was the nature of the influence of immigrants':
     2.1 Language skills?
     2.2 Family customs?
     2.3 Aspirations and goals?
     2.4 Attitudes toward education?
     2.5 Economic status?
  3. What problems did the education systems in the three countries incur as the result of such immigration?
  4. How did education officials in the three countries cope with those problems?

DEFINING KEY TERMS

After the research problem has been stated, an important step is that of defining exactly what is intended by the key words and phrases being used. The terms *key words* and *key phrases* refer to concepts at the core of the research project, concepts that must be adequately understood if the project is to be conducted with proper care and if the procedures and outcomes are to be precisely explained to readers. Some of the most basic terms are typically found in a research study's title or topic question. In the following examples, each key term is underlined.

—<u>Ethnic Groups' Political Strategies</u> in <u>Curriculum Change</u>
—<u>Students' success in school</u> is <u>positively correlated</u> with their <u>social-class status</u> and their <u>level of intelligence.</u>
—<u>Literacy education</u> in the <u>Middle East region,</u> as contrasted with literacy education in <u>Southeast Asia,</u> is conducted in <u>large-group settings,</u> is <u>provided more often</u> for males than for females, and advances at a <u>slower pace</u> due to the <u>complexity of the written language.</u>

Researchers usually deal with the matter of defining terms in one or more of five ways: (1) offer no definition, on the assumption that readers already know exactly what a term is supposed to mean, (2) offer one or more synonyms, (3) provide a concise, abstract dictionary description of the author's intended use of the term, (4) furnish examples of situations that both the author and the readers have experienced or examples of knowledge they hold in common, or (5) define the term by the operations performed in assessing the degree of the concept's presence.   Consider, now, advantages and disadvantages of each of these approaches.

No Definition

One obvious difficulty with an author's using key terms without defining them is that so many words and phrases mean different things to different people. Some words in the above examples carry widely agreed-upon meanings and thus call for no explanation. Such seems to be the case with *male* and *female.* (However, even *male* and *female* may require clarification in research that involves issues of homosexuality, feminine-versus-masculine personality traits, or the like.) Other words whose meanings at first glance appear unambiguous can later be recognized as subject to diverse interpretations. This point can be demonstrated with *ethnic group, intelligence, literacy,* and *Middle East region.*

Meanings for *Ethnic Group*

People often disagree about the meaning of such words as *ethnic, race,* and *minorities.* To illustrate, in a study of teachers' behavior in Israeli elementary schools, Saad and Hendrix (1993, p. 21) wrote that:

Israeli society is heterogeneous, composed of a great variety of ethnic Jewish groups that immigrated from over 100 countries. In addition, Israeli society includes an Arab minority that constitutes about 17% of the population and adds another element of diversity.

The authors then divided the Jewish population into two "geocultural groups"—the Askenazim (of European-American descent) and Sephardim (of Asian-African descent). But they failed to explain (a) whether they intended this bipartite division to be one of ethnicity, (b) whether the separation of Jews from

Arabs was an ethnic distinction, and (c) which characteristics distinguish the "great variety of ethnic Jewish groups" from each other.

In other instances, the context in which *ethnic* appears may lead some readers to infer meanings reflecting their own political interpretations of social systems, perceptions not necessarily shared by other readers. For example, Rippberger's (1993, p. 51) examination of bilingual education in Mexico and the United States led her to conclude that "A term such as 'ethnic group' . . . implies that the politically dominant group has no ethnicity but is the 'standard' for other (presumably non- or substandard) groups."

Furthermore, *ethnic* is sometimes coupled with a companion word that may cause readers some confusion. In Taylor's (1981) investigation of cultural assimilation in the United States, she adopted the term *religioethnic*, with the meaning she assigned to *religio* probably more obvious to readers than her meaning for *ethnic*. Groups that Taylor compared were identified by such labels as U.S. White Protestant, U.S. Black Protestant, Dutch Protestant, Irish Catholic, Italian Catholic, English Protestant, and the like. Therefore, *ethnic* could mean either a person's place of residence and racial designation (U.S. Black) or the homeland of the individual's ancestors (Holland). The sense of *ethnic* was rendered even more complex when individuals who identified their religion as Protestant and their nationality as English, Scottish, Welsh, or British were all grouped under the English Protestant category.

Finally, the word *Chinese* is sometimes used as an ethnic designator. But the category *Chinese* is itself composed of a second level containing an estimated 56 groups, including the Han, Manchu, Chuang, Hui, Miao, Yi, Mongols, and more. These second-level groups can themselves consist of subgroups. The Han classification is composed of nine major ethnolinguistic groups, including the Cantonese, Fujian, Keijia, and Wu. And the process may not stop at this level but can descend to additional strata of groups whose members exhibit cultural traits in common.

In short, when the word *ethnic* or *ethnicity* is a key term in a research project, it would be unwise for the investigator to assume that readers will bring identical meanings to the word. Failing to define precisely what the word is intended to mean in the context of the researcher's study could be a critical mistake.

Meanings for *Intelligence*

Judgments of people's intelligence are usually made either by someone informally observing how accurately and promptly people answer questions or by someone interpreting the scores earned on formal oral or written tests. The fact that not everyone concurs on what constitutes *intelligence* is revealed in continuing disagreements about:

(a) whether intelligence is a single overall mental trait, so that a person with more of the trait is better able to succeed in every aspect of mental activity than a person with less of the trait; or, instead, there are multiple areas of intelligence, and a person can be more adept in one area than in another.

(b) the sorts of questions-to-answer or acts-to-perform that are accurate indicators of intelligence.

Perhaps the most obvious evidence of this disagreement is found in the fact that when individuals take several different intelligence tests, they often fail to succeed equally well on all tests (Martin, Blair, & Bledsoe, 1990; Prewett, 1992; Raggio, 1993; Razel, 1989). In effect, people's patterns of performance can be uneven across different sorts of test items. A person who scores high in defining words may be no more than moderately adept at solving mathematical-reasoning problems and may do rather poorly on memory for musical tones. A second person may do well in all three of these tasks. A third person may earn high marks in reading maps and diagrams, but prove only average in creating novel ways to complete a rhyme. In other words, the correlation is less than perfect— and sometimes rather low—between people's success on one intelligence test and on another test that contains different kinds of items. Such results suggest that intelligence is not a single, unified human trait but, rather, is composed of a variety of different kinds of ability that are related to each other in different degrees (Gardner, 1983; Guilford, 1967; Harris & Harris, 1971). This means that researchers who employ *intelligence* as a key concept in a study cannot assume that members of their reading audience will understand exactly what the concept means without a precise explanation of how the term is being used in the project at hand.

Meanings for *Literacy*

Exactly what constitutes literacy is an incessant issue of debate in the field of education. The debate centers chiefly on two questions: What types of skill does literacy include, and what level of competence qualifies a person to be classified as literate?

In regard to skill, does *literacy* refer solely to reading ability, or does it also encompass writing and perhaps the comprehension of quantities (sometimes called *numeracy*) and a grasp of cultural customs (*social literacy*) and technologies (*computer literacy*)? Is an individual considered literate if he or she can read and write in one language, but that language is not the dominant medium of communication of the society in which the person currently lives?

Even more controversial than types of skill is the matter of levels. Sometimes people who can do no more than read and write their own names have been deemed literate. In other instances, the ability to render a sophisticated interpretation of a complex legal document has been the skill demanded. Such a high standard has occasionally been applied by a dominant political group to prevent outsiders of modest educational attainment from voting in elections in which demonstrated literacy is required for participation. Furthermore, the desired level can become elastic when defined as *functional literacy*. A UNESCO definition of functional literacy proposes that:

> A person is functionally literate who can engage in all those activities in which literacy is required for effective functioning of his group and community and also for enabling him to continue to use reading, writing, and calculation for his own and the community's development. (Limage, 1990, p. 232)

Such a definition is imprecise because the literacy demands in the life of a farm laborer or a fishing-boat's deckhand are notably different from the demands in the lives of atomic physicists and newspaper editors.

In sum, it is insufficient to use the words *literacy* and *literate* as key concepts in research without specifying the sorts of skills and levels of competence intended in the particular study at hand.

Meanings for *Middle East Region*

People generally bring the same meaning to such geographical terms as *Egypt, the Pacific Ocean, Hong Kong, the Pyrenees,* and the *Suez Canal,* so those place names can be used in a research report without further explanation. However, other terms can puzzle readers. This is true of *Middle East Region, Southeast Asia, Central Europe, Mediterranean Region, Pacific rim countries, Western U.S.,* and *Baltic States.* Does *Middle East* include Ethiopia, Turkey, and Afghanistan? Does the *Pacific rim* include islands of the Pacific, such as Papua New Guinea, Tahiti, and the Aleutians?

Thus, when geographic designators are key words in a research project, they often cannot properly be left without clarifying the meaning they bear in the project.

Clarifying with Synonyms

Occasionally a synonym is sufficient to convey a researcher's meaning. "*Chancellor* means *head of state*." "In Indonesia, a *dosen* is a *college instructor*." "A *post-secondary institution* is a *college, institute,* or *university*." However, in other instances, a synonym is insufficient. It is not enough to say that *Middle East* is the same as *Mideast* or *Near East*.   Nor is *racial origin* an adequate substitute for *ethnic*. Key terms usually call for more complete definitions than synonyms provide.

Dictionary Definitions

Sometimes dictionary definitions are adequate.   Other times they fail to represent precisely what an investigator intends. Consider these four (Flexner, 1987).

Ethnic—pertaining to or characteristic of a people, especially a group sharing a common and distinctive culture, religion, language, or the like.

Intelligence—capacity for learning, reasoning, understanding, and similar forms of mental activity; aptitude in grasping truths, relationships, facts, meanings, et cetera.

Literacy—the quality or state of being literate, especially the ability to read and write.

Middle East—(loosely) the area from Libya east to Afghanistan, usually including Egypt, Sudan, Israel, Jordan, Lebanon, Syria, Turkey, Iraq, Iran, Saudi Arabia, and other countries of the Arabian peninsula.

The specific nature of the three research projects described earlier can serve as a guide to how useful these dictionary definitions may be. For instance, the definition of *ethnic* seems unduly general for an investigator's purposes, because it fails to identify which features the members of a social faction would have in common to make them an ethnic group for purposes of political action. Would they need to be alike in one or more such features as home language, birth place, religion, length of time in their present society, skin color, or occupational status?

In a similar way, *intelligence* is defined in too broad a fashion to indicate, among many kinds of thought and action, which ones are being compared with people's social-class status and school achievement. Phrases like "similar forms of mental activity" and "et cetera" fail to delimit the meaning of *intelligence,* leaving readers free to fill in whatever additional characteristics they wish.

The definition of *literacy* has the virtue of specifying literacy skills as being those of reading and writing, but it fails to indicate the level of performance needed to qualify a person as literate.

Defining *Middle East* by naming the countries encompassed by the term is a great help. However, perhaps not all of the dictionary's countries are being studied in the present research project. Or perhaps other nations, such as Ethiopia and Afghanistan, are included in the study. Thus, the investigator may choose to offer his or her own list by stating: "For purposes of the present research, the term *Middle East Region* refers to . . ." and then name the nations.

Defining by Shared Experience or Knowledge

Citing countries in the Middle East is an instance of defining by shared knowledge. Readers of research reports either already know the location of the intended countries or can easily discover the location by inspecting a map. Hence, readers accurately share the author's meaning for the term.

A different procedure can be adopted for clarifying a researcher's use of *ethnic* The desired shared knowledge results from a two-step process. The investigator:

1. Identifies each ethnic group by a generally understood label, then

2. Describes significant ways that those groups differ from each other. The phrase *significant ways* refers to characteristics of a group (a) that apparently influence the group's behavior in relation to the target variable and (b) that differentiate one group from another.

The following example illustrates this process as applied in an imagined study conducted in Israel where the ethnic groups of interest are labeled *Jews* and *Palestinians*. A question can be asked about how Jews and Palestinians differ from each other in relation to the target variable, *political strategies*. In other words, what characteristics of Jews and Palestinians distinguish between the two groups in the political strategies they adopt for effecting curriculum change? From our knowledge of the groups, we propose that they differ significantly in:

   a. Which group wields the greater political power: Jews versus Palestinians.
   b. Their view of the proper portrayal of religion in the curriculum: a Judaic versus Islamic perspective.
   c. Their favored language of instruction: Hebrew versus Arabic.
   d. The ways their group's rights, privileges, and obligations are depicted.
   e. The line of logic adduced in defense of their positions expressed in items b, c, and d.

As these five features are described for each group, it becomes apparent that not everyone within one of the ethnic groups agrees entirely about such matters. Thus, we may wish to divide each of the two general ethnic categories into two or more subtypes. For example, we might end up with four ethnic groups— extreme Jews, moderate Jews, moderate Palestinians, and extreme Palestinians— who have somewhat different opinions about curriculum change, with moderate Jews and Palestinians closer to agreeing with each other than are extreme Jews and Palestinians. It seems likely that the moderates may employ somewhat different strategies than the extreme groups; those differences can be made more evident with our four-fold division of groups than if we compiled data only under the more general designations of *Jews* and *Palestinians*.

By means of the above process, we arrive at a definition of *ethnic* that precisely fits the nature of our research project. Our definition of *ethnic groups* is introduced to readers in some such manner as the following:

> For the purposes of the present study, four ethnic groups are defined in terms of the positions they hold regarding five variables—political power, religion in the curriculum, language of instruction, rights and obligations, and supporting rationales. The following description specifies each group's position on each variable.

The resulting detailed description provides the desired shared knowledge (researcher's and reader's) of what *ethnic* means in this particular investigation.

The same two-step procedure can be used to provide shared knowledge about the exact meaning intended for a variety of imprecise key terms in other research projects, such as terms involving religious, political, social, occupational, economic, or recreational groups. In addition, the process can usefully be applied in comparisons of rural versus urban schools, large versus small schools, centralized versus decentralized administrative systems, formal versus nonformal programs, complex versus simple languages, developed versus underdeveloped societies, strong versus weak economies, democratic versus socialistic forms of governance, and more.

A particular form of shared-knowledge is often known as a *behavioral definition*, one in which the meaning of a term is identified by listing observable acts that comprise the term. For instance, *child abuse* may be defined as "Anyone physically or verbally treating a child in ways that appear to cause immediate or long-term damage to the child's physical, intellectual, social, or emotional well-being." The definition can then be rendered more specific by adding observable symptoms of damage, such as:

(a) Physical damage—The child displays bruises, cuts, swellings, weeping, cowering.
(b) Intellectual—The child expresses unusually distorted views of the physical and social world and/or displays diminished learning ability.
(c) Social—The child increasingly avoids social contacts (isolates self) or is unusually aggressive and abusive in dealing with other people.
(d) Emotional—The child habitually avoids trying new tasks and/or says he or she is "no good." Or, with little or no apparent provocation, the child frequently weeps, flies into rages, and/or destroys objects.

In a research effort focusing on child abuse, the investigator can then observe which of the ways that adults treat children increase the incidence of these symptoms of damage.

Other phrases that can profitably be defined in the form of behaviors include *teaching techniques, supervisory methods, play therapy, peer counseling, curriculum planning, classroom discipline, drug education, school success,* and *political strategies.*

At first glance, the foregoing procedures may not seem worth the trouble they require to identify the specifics that comprise a shared-knowledge definition. However, such processes prove their value in the precision of communication they foster and in the guidance they offer researchers for selecting appropriate data collection methods. This point will be demonstrated later in Stage III.

Operational Definitions

As already mentioned, defining a key term operationally consists of specifying the techniques used for measuring or assessing the degree of the characteristic that the term signifies. This technique can be illustrated with the words *literacy* and *intelligence*.

Two Definitions of Literacy

In one study, investigators sought to discover the extent to which 2,659 patients using emergency departments of two large city hospitals were functionally literate in relation to their own health care. For this purpose, literacy was defined as a patient's achieving a satisfactory score on the *Test of Functional Health Literacy in Adults* (Williams, et al., 1995):

> One section of the test measured patients' ability to read and understand passages from preparation instructions for an upper GI [gastro-intestinal] tract radiograph series, a Medicaid application, and a standard hospital informed-consent document. The other portion evaluated patients' ability to understand labeled prescription vials, blood glucose test results, clinic appointment slips, and financial information forms. (Do you know. . . , p. 13.)

A different operational definition used extensively in international studies since the 1940s has been one which states that a person is judged literate if he or she can accurately read, and then answer questions about, the content of a textbook designed for the fourth grade of the primary school. Such a definition then becomes more precise if (a) the particular book or passage of reading material is identified (because books that ostensibly are suitable for fourth-graders often differ in their levels of difficulty) and (b) the minimum proportion of questions that must be answered correctly is specified (such as "at least 75% of the questions"). Smith (1995) has noted that in recent years this standard for literacy has been raised in many studies from the fourth-grade level to that of the typical eighth-grade textbook.

Defining Intelligence

In research programs, judgments of people's intelligence are usually founded on the scores individuals earn on one or more intelligence tests. If researchers are to know the exact skills measured by a given test, they are obliged to inspect the types of items that comprise the test and to learn the extent of correlation between one variety of item and another. Therefore, an operational definition of intelligence consists of naming the particular test used, describing its types of test items, and identifying the abilities that each type apparently assesses. Illustrative types of ability are: vocabulary knowledge, verbal reasoning, mathematical reasoning, computational accuracy, perceptual speed, eye-hand coordination, classification accuracy, divergent thinking, and fertility of solutions. However, these few examples represent no more than a limited number of the many abilities represented in the domain of intelligence tests.

Summary

It is apparent that researchers have available a variety of ways to define key terms employed in their projects. Defining terms precisely carries an investigator a long way toward recognizing the most appropriate methods and materials for collecting the evidence needed to answer the research questions.

DEVISING A RATIONALE

A rationale typically consists of a line of reasoning that performs one or both of two functions: provides a context within which to place the present research project and suggests why such research is worthwhile. It is useful for an investigator to devise a rationale at an early stage of planning a study, since it compels one to think clearly about where and how such a study will make a contribution to knowledge. However, preparing a satisfactory rationale requires a sufficient understanding of the field of knowledge in which the intended study is located. If the investigator lacks such an understanding, then the initial version of the rationale will likely be incomplete and perhaps somewhat off target, requiring subsequent revision based on a survey of existing research in the field. Efficient methods for conducting a survey of the professional literature are described in Chapter 5.

In journal and magazine articles, an author's final version of the rationale typically appears early in the report, often as a brief set of introductory statements. In master's degree theses and doctoral dissertations, the rationale is often quite detailed, sometimes divided between two chapters—(a) the opening chapter, which explains the problem to be investigated and the reasons it is considered important, and (b) the second chapter, which reviews the literature in the realm of the research problem in order to show what other investigators have found and to suggest how the present study contributes to that body of knowledge.

The following four examples from journal articles illustrate ways rationales can set the stage for a research project.

In the first example, the opening paragraphs inform readers of the two types of comparison that the article provides: (a) a comparison between the only two European colonies left in East Asia and (b) a comparison across time—past, present, and expected future.

Hong Kong and Macau have much in common. Both are colonies of European powers, populated mainly by Chinese, heavily dependent on commerce, and scheduled for reintegration with the People's Republic of China (PRC) at the end of this century. However, their patterns of education display major differences. Perhaps surprisingly, little comparative work has explored the reasons for these differences. The most obvious cause of divergence lies in the contrasting colonial histories of the two territories, for Hong Kong was colonized by the

British while Macau was colonized by the Portuguese. A second cause lies in the different sizes of the territories' populations and economics.

Using a historical perspective, this article considers both contemporary patterns and anticipated future developments. Since both Hong Kong and Macau will soon again become part of China, a major question concerns the extent to which a common political framework will bring convergence of patterns in education. (Bray, 1992, p. 322)

The second example opens with a concise description of the problem area treated in the article, then tells how the present study is intended to clarify a puzzling aspect of that area. Sources of the author's evidence, cited in brackets, are keyed to a list of references at the end of the article. The body of the article is then designed to compare pupils of different age levels.

One of the most pressing concerns among educators is the large number of school children who achieve below grade level. One important and seemingly obvious strategy for preventing academic failure is seeking help from a knowledgeable classmate, parent, or teacher. Seeking help can be more beneficial than giving up prematurely, more adaptive than waiting passively, and more efficient than persisting unsuccessfully on one's own [for discussion of the instrumental role of help-seeking in learning, see Nelson-LeGall, 1985]. Yet, despite their awareness of potential academic failure and despite the availability of assistance that might prevent failure, many children do not actively seek help with their school work when it is needed [Good, Slavings, Hare, & Emerson, 1987; Karabenick & Knapp, 1988]. The goal of the present research is to begin to understand why this is the case. (Newman & Goldin, 1990, p. 92)

The third example is structured in much the same pattern as the second but offers statistics and more references to support the work's basic assertion that alcohol use among college students is widespread and poses serious consequences both for individuals and for society. The rationale then identifies a gap in the body of information about college drinking, a gap the present study is intended to help fill. The comparisons drawn in the article are between moderate and heavy drinkers and among the contexts in which drinking occurs.

One group of drinkers whose alcohol consumption raises public health and safety concerns is college students. A recent survey revealed that 81.5% of college students drink alcohol, and significant percentages of college students are moderate (37%) or heavy (19%) drinkers [O'Hare, 1990]. Furthermore, the more a college student drinks, the more he or she is likely to experience alcohol-related problems such as injury, memory loss, fights/arguments, or academic difficulties [O'Hare, 1990]. Alcohol abuse remains a source of concern to most college administrators, and 97% of campuses engage in alcohol education and abuse-prevention efforts [Mager, 1988].

Programs designed to prevent alcohol abuse often target the contexts that are associated with excessive drinking [e.g., Mills, Neal, & Peed-Neal, 1983].

However, more information is needed about the contextual determinants of excessive drinking. Identification of the interpersonal and intrapersonal situations associated with excessive drinking would facilitate prevention efforts and would guide educators and counselors in the development of focused interventions to reduce abusive drinking. This study focuses on college students who drink alcohol regularly but have not been identified as problem drinkers; the situational contexts that differentiate heavy drinkers from light and moderate drinkers are evaluated. (Carey, 1993, p. 217)

In the fourth example, the author begins by explaining that he has generated a theory out of other researchers' work (which he cites in brackets) and that the study reported in his article was designed to test hypotheses derived from that theory.

Many writers have suggested that the effects of high school tracking [separating students into college-preparatory and vocational streams] on student achievement vary among schools, but none has offered a compelling theory for why this may occur [Heyns, 1974; Hauser, Sewell, and Alwin, 1976; Rosenbaum, 1984]. I use existing knowledge about tracking to develop hypotheses for between-school differences in tracking's effects. Building on the work of Sorensen [1970], I argue that the impact of tracking varies according to the structural characteristics of school tracking systems. I also consider claims that tracking has different effects in public and Catholic schools [Gamoran and Berends, 1987; Page and Valli, 1990]. I test these hypotheses by applying methods of multi-level contextual analysis to data on tracking and achievement in a national sample of high schools. (Gamoran, 1992, p. 812)

CONCLUSION

The three aims of this chapter have been to (a) describe ways people can choose to state their research problem, (b) illustrate methods of defining key terms, and (c) show how a rationale offered at the outset of a project enables researchers to locate their problem in an appropriate domain of knowledge and to indicate what their intended study can contribute to that domain. Performing these three activities before selecting ways to collect data will greatly simplify the task of choosing the data collection methods and will enhance the likelihood that the methods will be well suited to the needs of the study.

RESEARCH PROJECT CHECKLIST

In planning their investigations, researchers can profit from answering the following queries:

1. In which form do I intend to state my research problem?
 ___As a topic or title
 ___As a question
 ___As a hypothesis

2. Will the statement be in the form of a single problem or more than one problem?
 ___A single problem
 ___Two or more problems at the same level of specificity
 ___Two or more problems, with constituent subproblems subsumed under more general ones

State the problem or problems: _____

_____

3. In the above statement of my problem, I underline each *key word* or *key phrase* that needs to be defined with the meaning intended in my research. Then, on the following lines, I list each key word or phrase beside the form of definition I intend to use for that term.

 ___No definition (meaning of the term is obvious)_____

 ___Synonym_____

 ___Dictionary type of definition_____

 ___Shared knowledge definition_____

 ___Operational definition_____

4. What functions do I intend to include in the rationale I prepare for my study?

 ___Locate the study in the context of similar research in the field
 ___Indicate the contribution that the intended study can make to the field
 ___Identify sources of other studies or controversies related to the intended study
 ___Identify one or more theories or hypotheses to be tested by the study
 ___Identify which things will be compared in the study
 ___Other (describe)_____

Stage II:

Collecting Information—
Methods and Instruments

The process of collecting information can be viewed as consisting of six phases:

(a) identifying the kinds of information needed to answer the research questions
(b) locating sources of that information
(c) establishing criteria to guide the choice of which sources will be most appropriate
(d) applying the criteria to select the most suitable sources of data collection
(e) devising efficient methods and instruments for gathering the information
(f) compiling the desired data by means of those methods and instruments

In Stage II, Chapter 4—entitled "Surveying the Professional Literature"—focuses on phases (a) and (b) in the data-collection process. Chapter 5 ("Approaches to Gathering Data") and Chapters 6 and 7 ("Data Collection Techniques") are concerned with phases (e) and (f). The approaches described in Chapter 5 include case studies, historical analyses, ethnography, surveys, correlational studies, and experiments. The specific methods and instruments that can be employed in those approaches include content analyses, interviews, and observations as reviewed in Chapter 6 and by tests and questionnaires as described in Chapter 7.

In preparation for Chapters 4 through 7, the following discussion addresses phases (c) and (d)—the creation and application of criteria for choosing among data-collection methods.

Apparently everyone applies standards in choosing which data-collection methods to use. However, researchers can differ in the degree to which their standards are (1) intuitive, subconscious, and unstated or (2) intentional, reasoned, and clearly described. Intentional, reasoned criteria are the more desirable, since they function under the conscious control of the researcher and thus can be applied systematically in the selection of data-collection techniques.

In way of illustration, consider ways that the following four kinds of standards or conditions can guide the choice of research methods. In this overview, each standard is identified by a label, a question that defines the nature of that standard, and an example of how the standard could be applied in a particular research project.

AIM APPROPRIATENESS

The most obvious criterion is that of aim appropriateness as reflected in the question: Which data-collection method best suits the objectives of the study? Or, how likely will a given data-collection method furnish information that convincingly answers the research question?

The investigative techniques that will best achieve the objectives of a study are usually rather obvious. Consider, for instance, the proper techniques for discovering likenesses and differences between the educational backgrounds of the inventor Thomas Alva Edison and the automaker Henry Ford. Clearly, such a project does not lend itself to conducting an experiment, an opinion survey, or direct observations of—and interviews with—the two men. Instead, the project calls for parallel case studies carried out by content analyses of historical materials and perhaps by interviews with people who either knew Edison and Ford or else who have made an intensive study the their lives.

As a second example, consider a study with the aim of showing how four schools rank in terms of the effectiveness of their programs for teaching primary-grade children to read. Potential ways of gathering information would be: (a) to observe the teaching of reading in each school's primary classes, (b) to survey pupils' reading skills by means of individual or group tests (test children on one occasion), or (c) to conduct an experiment (pretest at the beginning of the school year, then posttest at the end). Of these options, the experiment seems the most appropriate, for it reflects how much children apparently learned in the programs over the period of a school year. The first method—observing classroom teaching—reveals teachers' instructional procedures, but fails to show how well children progress under those procedures. The second method—one-time testing—shows how well pupils read on a single occasion but does not account for how well they could already read at the beginning of the school year. The experiment, although likely the best alternative, is still not perfect, since it cannot show how children's reading activities outside of the school program may have contributed to their skills. Thus, the pretest-posttest plan might profitably be supplemented with a questionnaire survey in which parents describe the type and amount of reading their children do at home.

It is the case, however, that the data-collection process that would be most appropriate for the aim of a study may be altered or abandoned because of conditions relating to one or more of the following factors—subject suitability, context appropriateness, and cost.

SUBJECT SUITABILITY, EVENT SUITABILITY

The term *subject* refers to the people or events that will be the source of the desired information. The question to ask is: What methods of data collection are most appropriate for acquiring information from different kinds of subjects?

The characteristics of people that may affect the suitability of data-collection techniques are people's abilities and attitudes. For instance, interviews are more appropriate than questionnaires for collecting the opinions of people whose reading and writing skills are limited. Furthermore, when the subjects are reluctant to offer their opinions for fear of revealing themselves, information about their attitudes can more appropriately be drawn from observations of their behavior than from interviews or questionnaires.

The issue of event-suitability involves a researcher deciding what form an event should assume in order to serve as an accurate source of information. It seems apparent that the aim of much of education is to prepare people to act constructively in the events they encounter—in such events as voting in an election, shopping in a store, judging the honesty of an acquaintance, choosing a vocation, speaking before a group, filling out an income tax form, and hundreds more. The most direct, realistic way to assess how well students have learned to act in an event is to test them under real-life conditions—a kind of on-the-job evaluation. But there can be marked disadvantages to depending on spontaneous, real-life events for evaluating how well instruction has succeeded. The most obvious problems involve the timing and control of events, as can be illustrated in the case of a class in medical first-aid procedures. The timing problem derives from the fact that real-life medical emergencies appear on rare, unpredictable occasions. A researcher cannot wait for such occasions in order to appraise students' skills. Furthermore, when a medical emergency does occur, letting a novice control the treatment runs the risk of injury to the patient. Thus, if the evaluation of students is to be feasible, it needs to depend on simulated situations rather than real-life events. The dual aim of such simulations is to mirror life as accurately as possible and to enable the investigator to determine the time the simulated event will occur and to control how it progresses. For assessing the effectiveness of first-aid instruction, this aim could be achieved by having live actors (perhaps class members) feign various symptoms. Or the simulated event could take the form of a videotaped real-life or dramatized accident or illness. The researcher could then assess students' first-aid skills by testing their ability to diagnosis the portrayed disorders and to describe or demonstrate treatment.

CONTEXT APPROPRIATENESS

The context-appropriate standard concerns the possible influence exerted on the data-collection process by conditions of the environment in which research information is gathered. A question identifying this standard is: What environmental setting will promote the most efficient means of collecting data? Or, stated differently, what factors may significantly affect the ease of data collection and the accuracy of the obtained information? The following examples illustrate two sorts of context variables that would influence the obtained information.

In a study of junior high school students' experiences with illicit drugs, a researcher hoped to interview students individually but was prevented by the school's rule that students' anonymity must be maintained when sensitive social issues were discussed—issues of religious belief, moral values, political convictions, drugs, alcohol, tobacco, and the like. Thus, it was necessary for the researcher to replace the interviews with an anonymous questionnaire survey.

A woman studying high school students' opinions of popular public figures was assigned a room adjacent to the school's gymnasium for conducting interviews. She had intended to tape record each session. However, the noise from physical education classes in the gymnasium interfered so seriously with the recorded material that she was obliged to abandon the tape recorder and depend solely on handwritten notes.

COST

Sometimes a data-collection approach that is well suited to the research aim is rejected because the cost would be excessive. Costs can be of several kinds, including financial outlay and time. This standard can be stated as: What are the financial and time arrangements that support data-gathering methods well suited to the aim of the research project?

When the available money is inadequate to cover the expense of a preferred data-collecting technique, then some change will obviously be required in that technique. In a study of high school students' skills in handling materials in chemistry laboratories, a shortage of funds for transporting members of the research staff can result in limiting the scope of the research to a single city's schools rather than extending it to a sampling of schools throughout the region.

Time constraints can be of various kinds. A graduate student investigating the development of children's mathematical-reasoning skills wished to follow the same group of pupils through their six years of primary education. However, the need to earn her degree within a reasonable time rendered such a plan impractical. Therefore, she abandoned the notion of a longitudinal investigation and substituted a cross-sectional design in which she could test children at all six grade levels within a period of a few weeks. Subsequently, when she interpreted the results of her investigation, she would need to assume that if she had followed a single cohort of children from first through the sixth grade, the development of their reasoning skills would have been much the same as that reflected in the cross-sectional approach.

Time was also a factor in a study of the tasks performed by school principals in school districts of different sizes. After the researcher discovered that many principals' schedules prevented them from being interviewed at the times he had available, he substituted mailed questionnaires for interviews.

CONCLUSION

The above set of four standards and conditions obviously fails to exhaust the considerations researchers may adopt as they decide how they will gather data. Additional factors can include a researcher's particular training and talents, distances to travel for collecting data, parents' willingness to have their children participate in research projects, government regulations about the right to privacy, pressures of political groups to prevent or to encourage certain types of research, and more.

4

Surveying the Professional Literature

The task of surveying the professional literature consists of locating books, periodicals, and reports that will be useful in conducting one's own research. It is not uncommon for an academic adviser or a manual on thesis writing to recommend that a single chapter of a student's thesis or dissertation be dedicated to a review of the literature related to the topic at hand. That chapter is often the one following the chapter in which the research topic has been introduced. Carrying out the literature review can be useful in acquainting the researcher with an array of theories and empirical studies bearing on the intended topic. However, if the student has not thought carefully about how such a survey can best contribute to the project at hand, that chapter may become no more than an extended recital of other people's studies whose function in the present project is not at all clear. The aim of the following pages is to explain how such a difficulty can be avoided. The twofold purpose is (a) to inspect the roles that the professional literature can play in research programs and to propose where in a research plan different items from the literature can make their contribution and (b) to suggest efficient ways of conducting literature reviews.

ROLES PLAYED BY THE PROFESSIONAL LITERATURE

Learning about what other researchers have done can be helpful at each stage of the research process—selecting and stating a topic, providing a supporting rationale, choosing methods of data collection, organizing and analyzing the data, interpreting the results, and reporting the outcomes. In searching the literature, an investigator can profit from using these stages as guides for determining what contribution, if any, a given item from the literature can make to the project at hand. A useful aid in the review process is a code sheet that lists the stages, with each stage symbolized by code letters. How code letters are used can be illustrated with an example focusing on a woman's proposed study of violence in schools.

The code sheet she prepared read as follows:

Code	Research Stage
TOPIC	Topic statement
DEFINE	Defining key terms
RATION	Rationale—where the topic fits into the field; what the topic contributes
METH	Methods and instruments of data collection
CLASS	Ways of classifying and analyzing data
INTERP	Ways of interpreting data
REPORT	Ways of reporting data

Guided by the key phrase *school violence*, she then conducted a computer-assisted search of journals in university libraries. An article she found in *JAMA, the Journal of the American Medical Association,* was entitled "Violence-related Attitudes and Behaviors of High School Students." It reported a comparison of students' attitudes in 15 New York City schools. She photocopied the two-page article and wrote code letters in the margin beside four paragraphs at different junctures of the report. She placed the letters RATION beside a paragraph describing the incidence of adolescent homicides in New York City and nationally. She also wrote RATION beside two paragraphs reporting the incidence of violence-related attitudes among the students participating in the study, because she thought those passages might be useful in preparing the supporting rationale for her study. She wrote METH next to a paragraph describing the questionnaire that high school students had filled out to express their attitudes about violence. She had flagged that passage on the chance that she might wish to use a similar type of questionnaire in her own project. In addition to thus marking the margins of photocopied articles, whenever she made handwritten notes about passages from books or articles she also placed relevant code letters in the margins of the note sheets.

By thus coding potentially useful passages, she later could easily find the reference materials she needed at successive stages of the research process without having to reread every photocopied article or set of notes she had collected. For example, in preparing to write her study's rationale, she could quickly gather all photocopies and handwritten notes that displayed RATION in margins. Later, when interpreting her compiled data, she could collect all materials that displayed the INTERP code.

Whenever she reviewed a book or article that yielded nothing helpful for her own study, she copied the author's name and the title of that source onto a note card so she could later recall that she had already inspected the item and had found it of no use.

The code-letter approach is thus a useful method for extracting needed material from the professional literature.

The question now can be asked: Where in the final research report should the results of the literature search be placed? In response, I suggest that the selections extracted from the literature are best distributed throughout the stages of the report relevant to the selections' code letters. This means that in a thesis or dissertation, all of the material taken from the literature review will not be placed in a single chapter. Instead, those selections that help delineate a context for the present research project will be in a *rationale* chapter, those describing data-collection methods will be in a *research-procedures* chapter, those bearing on data analysis will be in a *results* chapter, and so forth. Likewise, in a journal article, citations from the literature are best situated in the sections of the article pertinent to the code letters. Such a practice can be illustrated with segments of representative journal articles.

Defining Key Terms

In specifying the meaning of key words used in her investigation of students' responses to violence on television, Tulloch (1995, p. 95) adopted a definition employed by another author:

> Prosocial aggression has been defined as aggression 'used in a socially approved way for purposes that are acceptable to the moral standards of the group'. (Sears, 1961, p. 471)

Providing a Rationale

To furnish a context for their study of alcoholic parents of delinquent youths, McGraha and Leoni wrote:

> The relationship between divorce and delinquency has been extensively investigated by researchers. Most of the studies have found that delinquents do come from broken homes significantly more often than do nondelinquents. The Gluecks' classic 1950 study comparing 500 delinquents and 500 nondelinquents found that over 60% of the delinquents came from broken homes as compared to a little over a third of the nondelinquents. More recent studies by Haskell and Yablonsky (1982) and others have found clear evidence of the association between delinquency and broken homes. Many researchers, however, have questioned the real importance of the broken home and have focused instead on the quality of the relationships and general atmosphere in the home. Yablonsky and Haskell (1988) found that the internal patterns of interaction within the family were more important than the family structure in explaining delinquency. In a study of self-reported delinquency among 500 youth, Hindelang (1973) concluded that attachment to parents was inversely related to delinquency, while Cernkovich and Giordano (1987) in a survey of 900 youths found that it was the

quality of the relationships in the home, not the structure of the family, that was most important. (McGraha & Leoni, 1995, p. 473)

Adopting Data-Collecting Methods

Kerwin and her associates (1993, p. 222), in a study of racial identity in biracial children, introduced their research method in this manner:

> In the present study, we incorporated ethnographic analyses of semistructred interviews with Black/White biracial children and their parents. . . . [The] purpose of the study was to uncover the important variables for those who are directly involved with biracial identity development—Black/White interracially married parents and their biracial offspring (see qualitative methodology discussions of Brause, 1991; Hoshmand, 1989; Ponterotto & Casas, 1991; Taylor & Bogdan, 1984). Marshall and Rossman (1989) stated that the purposes of exploratory research include the following: "to investigate little-understood phenomena; to identify/discover important variables; [and] to generate hypotheses for future research" (p. 78). In attempting to reach these goals, we used the long interview method articulated by McCracken (1988), who described this method as "one of the most powerful methods in the qualitative armory. . . . [it] gives us the opportunity to step into the mind of another person, to see and experience the world as they do themselves." (p. 9)

Interpreting Results

As an aid in interpreting the outcomes of their study of delinquent youths' alcoholic parents, McGraha and Leoni (1995, p. 480) prefaced their statistics on runaway adolescents in their sample of delinquents with these references to previous studies:

> Family relationships have long been recognized as factors leading to runaway behavior. . . . In contrast to previous theories that characterized runaway children as emotionally disturbed or mentally deficient with poor impulse control (Bovvins & O'Neal, 1959), or as a normal part of growing up (Homer, 1973), the more popular explanation today is that running away is a response to problems and stress in the home (Johnson & Carter, 1980). Bennan, Huizinga, & Elliott (1978) found that runaways are beaten by their parents twice as often as nonrunaways, and that they experience long-term family conflicts. In [our] current study, 30 (83%) juveniles from alcoholic homes reported at least one runaway from their family, while only 13 (45%) of the youth from nonalcoholic homes reported running away.

In Tulloch's (1995, p. 109) interpretation of her students' attitudes toward violence on television, she referred to other researcher's explanations of comparisons between males and females.

The overall shift of older girls to greater endorsement of nonviolent options is in line with the claim of the importance of a principle of nonviolence in mature female morality (Gilligan, 1982). While social learning approaches to differences in male and female attitudes to violence (Dominick & Greenberg, 1972; Perry, et al., 1986) have focused on differential pressures on boys and girls to inhibit aggression, the present data have indicated that female students are more rejecting of aggression even when the initial aggression was male.

With the foregoing examples of how references from the professional literature can be incorporated into research projects, we next consider effective ways of performing literature surveys.

CONDUCTING A REVIEW OF THE LITERATURE

Technological innovations in recent decades have revolutionized the task of surveying the research literature. In the mid-20th century, investigators who wished to learn which books had been published in their field of interest were obliged to finger their way through a university's card catalogue and to inspect bibliographies published at the end of the books they found. To locate relevant journal articles, they not only perused bibliographies but also took advantage of such periodicals as *The Education Index, Psychological Abstracts,* and *Sociological Abstracts* which listed articles from a variety of publications and offered brief descriptions of the articles' contents. Once a useful publication was obtained, it became the researcher's task to copy by hand any passages that might prove useful. This process was not only laborious and extremely time consuming, but it resulted in people often failing to find worthwhile materials bearing on their research topic.

By the 1990s, all that had changed. Researchers now enjoyed the advantages of computerized library catalogues, personal computers in the office and home, and modems (modulate-demodulate devices) that linked personal computers into a world-wide network of library holdings via telephone lines and communication satellites. Just as leafing through library card catalogues was a thing of the past, so also was the need to copy by hand everything a researcher wished to extract from a publication. Now it was possible to photocopy passages of a book or of a journal article. As an alternative, it was not even necessary to have the original publication in hand, for it was possible with a home computer to print an abstract or the entire text of a recent newspaper, magazine, or journal article that was stored in a distant library database hundreds or thousands of miles away.

One useful way to view the process of surveying the literature is in relation to the location in which the search is carried out, that is, in a library or from a distance. But in either location, the search is guided by key words drawn from the statement of the research problem and by related terms. Consider, for example, the following research problem cast in the form of three questions.

What are the sources of financial support of schools in three advanced industrialized nations (Germany, Japan, United States) and in three developing nations (Argentina, Egypt, Philippines)? What are the similarities and differences among the six nations in their sources of school finance? What are the causes of the differences?

The underlined words in this example can be combined to furnish terms that direct the search. For example, combining *school finance* with the name of a country—such as *school finance in Japan*—provides a pertinent phrase to find in the index of a book, in a computerized catalogue of library holdings, or among the titles of journal articles. Related words that may also assist in a literature survey are either synonyms of key terms or else are other words closely associated with the research topic. In our example, useful related terms include *educational finance, school finance, education budgets, education costs, school fees,* and any such terms coupled with a country's name, such as *Philippines school fees.*

The methods of conducting a literature survey within a library itself differ somewhat from those appropriate for conducting a survey from a distance. Consequently, it is useful to inspect the two locations separately.

Searching in the Library

Being physically present in a library enables an investigator directly to examine the contents of books and journals—peruse a book's index, scan chapter contents, and copy out useful passages. If the library has an open stacks policy (allowing patrons to wander along the aisles of shelved books and periodicals), people are able to locate the call numbers of publications related to their research topics and then browse among all of the holdings in the section containing those call numbers. Libraries that maintain closed stacks are less convenient, since they require that a patron order a particular volume which then must be found by a library assistant and delivered to the user—a process that sometimes takes hours.

Hunting for useful materials in a book store is similar to browsing in an open stacks library. Customers are able to search among books in their field of interest and skim through the tables of contents and indexes to locate key terms.

In recent years, libraries have been changing from a card catalogue system to computerized catalogues. During this transition, patrons have been obliged to hunt for materials by means of both the traditional card drawers and computer terminals. Older library holdings are still listed only on cards, whereas newer ones appear only in the computer bank.

In the past, collections of abstracts of journal articles were available only in paperback report form, with a year's series of these monthly or quarterly periodicals bound together within a hardback cover. However, today such indexes are available in more than one form—as computer data banks and/or as compact discs that display their contents on a computer screen.

The easy availability of photocopy machines in libraries saves researchers time by permitting them instantly to reproduce pages of publications rather than copying the material by hand.

Searching from Afar

Surveying the professional literature from a distance assumes two principal forms—correspondence through the mails and a computer search by means of a modem that links an investigator's personal computer into libraries via the telephone lines.

The most common form of postal correspondence consists of an investigator writing to an author who has published studies in the investigator's field of interest in order to request a list of relevant bibliographic references or to ask for reprints of the author's articles. The typical way of locating such authors is to find citations of their works in the bibliographies at the end of journal articles or books. Most authors of published studies are associated with higher-education institutions. Their institutional affiliations and mailing addresses can often be found in a footnote attached to their journal articles or book chapters. Or, as another option, authors' addresses may be found in a library's reference volumes, such as in *Who's Who* or in a publication that identifies a nation's higher-education faculty members and their locations.

Writing to authors to request lists of their publications often enables a researcher to locate items that would not normally appear among references that accompany the writer's journal articles. Hard-to-find items include speeches, in-house reports, unpublished manuscripts, conference presentations, essays in esoteric journals, and works not yet in print. Some researchers make a practice of sending postcard requests to authors for reprint copies of particular articles.

Whereas postal correspondence is of some use, the personal computer is of far greater value for surveying the literature from a remote location. A home computer equipped with a modem that connects to a telephone line enables a researcher to gain access to a range of library holdings in a wide variety of locations—access to the titles of books, journals, newspapers, reports, dissertations, and other publications. A library's catalogue can be reached either via a telephone number specific to that library or by means of a computer network service to which the researcher subscribes (Compuserv, America Online, and others connected to the Internet and World Wide Web). University libraries, in order to limit their users to a reasonable number of individuals, often require that users enter their system with an assigned password. Passwords are ordinarily reserved for faculty members and qualified students of the particular university and for other individuals who make special arrangements with the library to use its facilities.

A few years ago library lists that were accessed from a remote computer offered only the titles of books and articles. Subsequently the lists of articles began to include an abstract of the entries' contents. More recently, the lists have provided complete journal articles for certain entries, enabling an investigator, at home or in the office, to read articles in detail without needing to have the journal itself in hand. It thus has become possible for researchers at home to reproduce with their computer-printer a copy of an entire article or of selected segments.

CONCLUSION

The purpose of surveying the professional literature is to improve the quality one's own research by discovering what other investigators have done in the area of one's interests. In this chapter I have suggested that literature searches are rendered more efficient if they are guided by code words that identify at which junctures in a research project citations from the literature will be most useful. In recent years, the rapid development of personal computers and of computer networks that provide access to libraries' holdings have greatly enhanced the ease, speed, and comprehensiveness of literature reviews.

RESEARCH PROJECT CHECKLIST

1. Which words and phrases will be useful in directing my search of the literature?
     List key words and phrases derived from the statement of the
       research problem._____

     List useful related terms that can also guide the search._____

---

2. Into what segments or sections will my study be divided? What code word will I use to signify each part?
     List code words and the part of the final research report that each
       represents._____

3. How do I plan to survey the professional literature?
     ___Visit libraries to locate books and journal articles.
     ___Write to authors to request lists of relevant publications.
     ___Write to authors to request offprints of their articles.
     ___Conduct a search of library holdings from a remote location by
          means of a personal computer equipped with a modem.
     ___Other (explain)_____

5

Approaches to Gathering Data

The purpose of this chapter is to describe six popular approaches to data collection in terms of (a) defining characteristics of each approach, (b) the types of research questions the approach is equipped to answer, (c) versions of the approach, including their advantages and limitations, and (d) common problems and their solutions that the approach involves. The six are case studies, historical analyses, ethnographies, surveys, correlational comparisons, and experiments. As will be demonstrated, these six are not mutually exclusive. A given research project may utilize more than one of them.

CASE STUDIES

A case study is an indepth analysis of a single entity. That entity may be a person, a group, an organization, a system, a method, or an event. Such studies assume a comparative character when two or more cases are considered in relation to each other or when the study of a single entity encompasses several time periods that are compared. Typical titles of case studies featuring description, explanation, evaluation, and prediction are:

Description—The Education of Theodore Roosevelt
   —Model English Universities: Oxford and Cambridge
   —A Day in Three Classrooms
Explanation—Alternative Causes of Autism
   —Environments and Genius: Einstein, Mozart, Michaelangelo
   —Contrasts in Teachers' Influences: Adolf Hitler's School Days
Evaluation—The Quality of Child Rearing in Three Innercity Families
   —Comparing Reinforcement Schedules in Four Cases of Attention Deficit
   —The Success of Two Counseling Techniques with Four Pakistani
   Immigrants

Prediction—School Budget Projections: A Rich District and Its Poor
            Neighbor
        —University Enrollment Prospects: Belgium and the Netherlands
        —Dim Future: Family-Planning Education in the Sudan, Uganda, and Zaire

The greatest advantage of a case study is that it permits a researcher to reveal the way a multiplicity of factors have interacted to produce the unique character of the entity that is the subject of study. If we can assume that every person, group, institution, or event is unique—unlike every other in at least some details—then the case study becomes the most suitable approach for delineating that uniqueness.

An important limitation of the case approach is that generalizations or principles drawn from one case can be applied to other cases only at great risk of error. Users of research studies are usually not interested in learning only the outcomes of a particular investigation; instead, they are interested in finding how a given case can help them understand other similar people, institutions, or events. The question they ask is: What knowledge derived from the present instance can validly be applied to explaining a broader collection of cases? This risk of error in assuming that other cases will somehow be the same as the one at hand can be reduced by studying more than one case in order to identify their likenesses and differences and thereby better recognize the level of confidence that can be placed in conclusions drawn about such phenomena.

However, researchers are not always hoping to generalize the results of a particular case to other situations. For instance, a teacher may study her pupils' use of the PLATO computer program for learning mathematics simply so she can better understand those children's motivations, skill improvement, social interaction patterns, and attitudes toward computers. Case studies can also serve to introduce readers to new ways of perceiving educational events, as in studies entitled:

        —The Role of Unstated Behavior Rules in Four High-School Classrooms
        —The Effect Over Time of Placing an Epileptic Child in a Fifth-Grade Class
        —Two Afro-American Teachers' Experiences in an All White School

Finally, it may be the methodology of a particular case study, rather than principles derived from its results, that people find most useful, as when researchers who read a case adopt the methods of that study for conducting their own investigations.

In planning a case study, a researcher can profitably begin with the questions, problems, or hypotheses that define the target variable. The research then becomes an investigation of the system of factors and the patterning of their transactions that explain how and why the target variable behaves as it does. The target definition is then analyzed to yield specific guide questions that identify the kinds of information to be sought, feasible sources of such information, and methods of collecting it. The set of guide questions, in effect, defines the case study's structure and content. It identifies the perspective from which the participants in the case are viewed.

The following examples illustrate the kinds of questions guiding the conduct of three quite different cases. The first example compares a successful publication project with a failed project, the second focuses on the politics of a nursery school over time, and the third compares the educational backgrounds two historical figures.

Publishing Ventures: One Succeeded, One Failed

In the Pacific island territory of American Samoa, a consultant was hired by the government's department of education to suggest methods of discovering the islanders' most pressing educational needs. After considering a variety of options, education officials adopted three approaches: (a) testing pupils' academic and psychomotor achievement, (b) collecting community members' opinions, and (c) surveying classroom problems. Over the following months, the three approaches were successfully implemented, the resulting data were analyzed, and reports were published (Thomas & Titialii, 1973a).

One unmet need discovered during the project was the lack of traditional Samoan cultural elements in the schools' curricula at all levels of the educational ladder. As the research team considered which aspects of culture might best be added to the course of study, it became apparent that a wide range of traditional forms of recreation—games, sporting events, amusements—were pursued in Samoans' daily life, but none of them were in written form. They existed only in people's memories. As older Samoans passed away, these elements of culture were gradually being lost. Thus, the research consultant suggested that the department of education sponsor a project aimed at collecting descriptions of types of recreation and publishing them in book form so they might be preserved and taught in school. The department's leaders agreed to the plan and assigned two seasoned Samoan educators to interview members of the community in order to collect the information required for the book. The consultant and the two Samoan staff members devised an interview guide sheet to ensure that complete information would systematically be gathered about each pastime. Then the consultant left the islands to return to his own institution, scheduled to come back to Samoa at the end of six months to aid with the final preparation of the book. When he did return, he learned that nothing had been done about the project during his absence (Thomas, 1976). In effect, the envisioned publishing effort had died, and there were no plans to revive it.

These two events—the successful publication of unmet educational needs and the unsuccessful attempt to publish traditional island pastimes—set the stage for a comparative case study aimed at explaining why one project had succeeded and the other had failed. Here, then, are the central questions to be answered by the case study and the specific guide questions that delineated the domain of the study by identifying the sorts of information needed, likely sources of the information, and methods of collecting it.

The target variable: What were the factors that caused the needs-study project to succeed and the recreational-activities project to fail?

Guide questions defining the domain of the case: How did the people in List A view the issues in List B?

List A:

The director of the department of education

The assistant director of the department

The director of curriculum development

The head of the unmet-educational-needs project

The head of the Samoan-language-and-culture program

The two staff members assigned to the traditional-recreation project

The off-island research consultant

List B:

What was the importance of the unmet-needs study as compared to the traditional-recreation project? If one was more important than the other, what made it so?

Is the curriculum content derived from Western civilization, which has dominated the school program, more important than traditional Polynesian cultural content? How desirable or necessary is it that descriptions of traditional culture be recorded in written form? (This question is posed in view of the fact that there was no written version of the Samoan language prior to the arrival of Christian missionaries in the islands in 1830, so records of Samoan culture were traditionally transmitted only in oral form.)

How might Samoan social traditions have influenced the behavior of the department of education's decision makers and the staff members' commit-ment to the two projects? In other words, did Samoan social etiquette affect the enthusiasm and sincerity with which individuals embraced the unmet-needs program compared with the forms-of-recreation project?

What professional or personal interests or commitments competed for the time and energy of the particular staff members assigned to implement the two projects? To what extent did those staff members command the skills needed to carry out their assignments? If the staff members needed help with performing their duties, was that help readily available?

What administrative machinery was available to ensure the continuing operation and monitoring of each project? If such machinery was not available, then why? If it was available but did not function, then why?

What would be the consequences expected from the success or failure of the unmet-needs study as compared to consequences expected from the success or failure of the forms-of-recreation project?

Sources of answers to the guide questions: The individuals in List A. Written communications regarding the two projects, including minutes of meetings, written directives, and progress reports.

Methods of collecting answers: Interviews with the people in List A. Content analysis of written communications about each of the projects.

Power Struggles in a Nursery School

Early childhood education was the major field of interest of a university graduate student who was the mother of a three-year-old daughter enrolled in a nursery school that was partially associated with the university's department of education. As a master's degree research project, the student chose to analyze the political maneuvers of competing groups that sought to control the operation of the nursery school. The study was carried out from the vantage point of a participant-observer, since the student herself was a member of one of the competing groups. Thus, one challenge she faced in conducting the study was that of maintaining some measure of objectivity in collecting and interpreting data.

The study assumed the form of a time series, since the researcher analyzed the pattern of relationships among participating groups at four junctures during a six month period. Each juncture represented an event that marked significant change in the power relationships among the rival groups.

The primary groups consisted of (A) the woman who directed the school and her supporters in the form of two assistant teachers and a few mothers of children enrolled in the school and (B) several mothers of nursery-school children. Each of these primary groups was loosely linked to background supporters. Group A counted on the support of the university's director of business services who provided part of the nursery school's funds. Group B counted on the backing of the head of the education department's early-childhood-education program.

The publicly visible issues at the heart of the struggle were the charges by Group B that the school's quarters were not kept clean, food was prepared in an unsanitary fashion, university students who visited the school were not properly supervised, and conflicts among children were handled badly. However, observers of the case noted that behind these stated issues were the political motives of strong-willed individuals vying for decision-making control of the school.

The question that identified the target variable and the constituent questions delineating the study's domain were as follows:

The target variable: At key transition points in the struggle for control of the nursery school, what was the composition of the rival groups, what were their goals, what were their strategies, how effective were their efforts, and what were the causes of their success or failure?

Guide questions defining the domain of the case: At each of the four critical junctures in the struggle for control:
     What contending groups or factions could be identified? Who were the members of each faction (core members and supporters)? What factors bound the group members together? What role did each member play in a

group's activities; what were the relationships of power and position within each group? How cohesive was each group in the sense of how much the group's members agreed with each other? What were the stated aims of each group? What unstated aims or motives did each group appear to harbor? What strategies did each faction adopt to achieve its goals? What was the nature and outcome of confrontations between the factions? How well did each faction achieve its stated and unstated aims?

Sources of answers to the guide questions: Members of each group. Outside observers who did not participate in the struggles between factions. Meetings conducted within a faction or conferences between individual members of a faction. Meetings between groups or between individual members of rival factions. Such documents as reports submitted by the nursery-school director to the university's head of business services, correspondence between groups, correspondence of individuals or groups with the head of business services or with the head of the university's early-childhood-education program.

Methods of collecting answers: Interviews with members of the rival factions. Observations of meetings about the nursery-school's affairs. Observations of conversations and discussions among members of a faction and between members of rival factions. Content analysis of documents.

After collecting answers to the guide questions at each of the four transition points in the six-month struggle for control of the school, the researcher compared the results at one point with the results at subsequent points in order to identify the dynamics of change that the case involved.

Moral Education: Nightingale and Franklin

Two historical figures often lauded for their moral convictions are (a) the English woman recognized as the inspiring pioneer of nursing education, Florence Nightingale, and (b) the American colonial publisher, inventor, and political luminary, Benjamin Franklin. The foci of interest for a comparative case study were the educational foundations of these two individual's moral development (Thomas, 1997a).

The target variable: What were significant causal factors in Florence Nightingale's and Benjamin Franklin's moral development?

Guide questions defining the domain of the case: Within what social environments did the central figure's (Nightingale's, Franklin's) early moral training take place? Who were important people in these contexts? What roles did each of those people play in the central figure's moral education? How was that influence exerted? In other words, what was the nature of each person's interaction with the central figure? What were the apparent moral effects of each of those persons' influence? What was the central figure's moral self-identity? In other words, how did the central figure perceive herself or himself as a moral being?

With the passing years, what new people or communication media (reading matter) affected the central figure's moral education? In what ways did these new experiences influence that individual's moral principles and behavior? To what extent did the central figure implement her or his own moral education, and how was this done? What were the central figure's apparent motives that directed her or him toward the moral commitments that she or he adopted? Did the individual's moral self-identity change over time; and if so, how and why?

In what ways were Florence Nightingale's and Benjamin Franklin's moral upbringing alike and different? How have Florence Nightingale's and Benjamin Franklin's moral natures been judged by historians?

Sources of answers to the guide questions: Biographies of Nightingale (Underwood, 1994; Strachey, 1933; Woodham-Smith, 1951) and of Franklin (Seavey, 1988; Van Doren, 1938), Benjamin Franklin's autobiography (Franklin, 1866/1941), Florence Nightingale's collected letters (Vicinus & Nergaard, 1990), and selected Nightingale publications (Nightingale, 1963).

Methods of collecting answers: Content analysis of the published documents.

Conclusion

Whereas the principal contents of case studies are determined by the guide questions that establish the investigator's focus at the outset of the study, researchers should take advantage of unexpected types of information that were not foreseen but are nevertheless valuable additions to the case. For instance, in the nursery-school study, a casual conversation with a homeowner whose property was adjacent to the nursery school might yield pertinent data. Or from reading biographies of Florence Nightingale and Benjamin Franklin, an investigator may be moved to add the following pair of guide questions to the original list: How may accidental events as compared to planned events affect a person's moral development? How may the places to which an individual travels influence that person's moral education?

HISTORICAL ANALYSES

Historical investigations often assume the form of case studies traced over time or located within a particular era of the past. The focus of historical accounts can be individual persons (Ghandi, Churchill, Bolivar), groups (team, religious denomination, ethnic entity), segments of society (the aristocracy, the middle class, the homeless), institutions (schools, museums, philanthropic foundations), geographic units (cities, nations, regions), educational philosophies (Deweyism, Hinduism, Marxism), educational practices (lecturing, field trips, aptitude testing), events (the establishment of schools, the passage of education laws, the appointment of ministers of education), and more. As noted earlier, descriptive accounts tell what occurred on particular occasions or else they trace the progression of successive events. Explanatory studies not only describe events, but also seek to explain why they happened as they did. Evaluative histories assess the desirability of the events.

Representative titles include:

Description—A Chronicle of Early Childhood Education in Japan
          —A History of the Montessori School Movement
          —The Sorbonne 1259-1959
Explanation—Educating the James Brothers: Henry and William
          —The Sources of Jesuit Educational Goals and Practices
          —Social Forces and Curriculum Change in Spain: 1898-1998
Evaluation—Consequences of a Civil-Service Examination System: The
          Ch'ing Dynasty
          —The Quality of Parents' Assessments of New York City Schools: 1930,
          1960, 1990

Four interacting variables that determine the nature of a historical study are: (a) the time span encompassed, (b) the aspects of education and/or of the society to be included and emphasized, (c) the theoretical vantage point from which those aspects are viewed, and (d) the availability of relevant historical information. Researchers can profitably have these four factors in mind as they plan their historical accounts.

The Time Span

The chosen time span can be either continuous or segmented. It is continuous when the historian traces the gradual development of an aspect of education or the society, as in *The Evolution of the Malaysian Ministry of Education—1965-1995* or *A History of Los Osos Middle School.*

The time span is segmented when the target variable is inspected at more than one discrete point in time: *Costs of a University Education—1940 and 1990.*

Aspects of Education and of the Society

As noted earlier, educational research can focus on some aspect of the process of education or on interactions of education with aspects of the surrounding society. Because both education and society in their entirety are far too complex to manage within a single historical account, investigators are obliged to select which facets of education and society they intend to include—and among the facets, which are to be emphasized. By making this selection, historians establish the boundary lines of their studies and identify the types of information needed to answer their projects' guide questions. The aspects to be emphasized in a study are usually featured in the statement of the target variable and oftentimes in the title of the work.

—A History of Main Street School's Parent-Teacher Association
—Political Party Influence on Moral-Education Legislation in Ohio and Florida
—The Changing Goals of Village Primary Schools in Wales
—Portrayals of Nationalism in Burmese Textbooks: 1930-1990

Theoretical Viewpoints

Just as three-dimensional objects in space cannot be seen from all sides at the same time, so also aspects of education and society are usually inspected from selected vantage points in the form of theoretical perspectives. Chapter 3 introduced a number of such viewpoints—structural-functionalist theory, Marxist theory, behaviorist theory, Darwinian theory, and more. A historian's theoretical stance affects which happenings from the past will be chosen as significant and what interpretation will be placed on those events.

For instance, a researcher using *conflict theory* to interpret the development of schooling in post-independence Tanzania (1961-1998) could be expected to collect data that reveal: (a) which factions in the society were in competition with each other for control of the schools, (b) the overt and covert goals held by each faction, (c) the source of each faction's power, (d) the strategies each adopted to achieve its ends, and (e) how successful those techniques proved to be. In contrast, an advocate of *neo-colonialist theory* would more likely collect information about: (a) the nature of schooling when Tanzania was under British colonial administration, (b) the colonial schooling background of Julius K. Nyerere, who became the most influential political figure in post-independent Tanzania, (c) sources of the educational structure planned by the new government so that the society might achieve self-reliance, and (d) vestiges of colonial education that forced adjustments in the government's plan.

Relevant Historical Resources

One of the greatest challenges authors of historical studies face is that of ensuring that the account they write is an accurate portrayal of what occurred. The challenge derives from the fact that historians are limited to the particular chronicle of the past that they happen to find. And how authentically those materials represent the events they depict is often open to serious question. Furthermore, the farther back in historical time the events occurred, the greater the question about the validity of the records that remain. For example, heated controversies continue today over the issue of who wrote the Jewish Torah and Christian Bible and about the authenticity of those books' contents (Friedman, 1987).

A variety of factors in the past have contributed to the distortion and loss of historical records. Over the centuries, valuable books and letters have been destroyed by fire and flood. In wartime, armies intentionally demolish the libraries and archives of the vanquished. The victors in revolutions and political elections replace the defeated forces' accounts of events with their own version of what took place. Manuscripts, letters, books, and newspapers are lost through the carelessness, neglect, or ignorance of people who fail to recognize the potential future importance of those materials. In addition, some significant social developments were never cast in written form for any of several reasons— the particular society had only a spoken form of language, or the developments occurred within a segment of the population that was illiterate, or those people who might have recorded the events did not consider them worth writing about. Hence, no documentation of such developments became available.

Finally, researchers themselves may be to blame for presenting an erroneous view of the past. They distort reality either because they have been incomplete in their search for source materials or else because they bring to their work a bias (religious, philosophical, ethnic, political, social-class) that predisposes them to favor certain materials and discount others.

In view of these risks to the authenticity and balance of knowledge about the past, conscientious historians adopt several safeguards to promote the accuracy of their work. One way is to obtain multiple accounts of a particular event or of a document in order to determine how closely different versions match. For instance, the minutes of a school board meeting can be checked against a newspaper report of the event or against a letter found in the effects of a participant in the meeting. Where there are contradictions between accounts of an episode, the researcher may choose to present both versions to readers, then offer arguments in support of each version or else adduce a line of logic that favors one account over the other.

Another method of testing the accuracy of a historical account is to locate the account within the sociopolitical atmosphere of its day. The historian attempts to find convincing evidence that a given description of an incident reasonably reflects what would be expected to occur in the context of those times.

A third avenue for judging the trustworthiness of historical records is through estimating the reliability of a source by its status as an official document or by the reputation of its author. A copy of an education law bearing a government seal is usually more to be trusted than a newspaper editorial about the law. The description of a controversial event by a political office holder or spokesperson for a government department is likely to be questioned more than a description of the episode by an ostensibly objective scholar whose professional fate does not depend on political approval.

To compensate somewhat for the risk of inaccuracy inherent in historical studies, the historical approach has much to offer for explaining the causes of educational conditions. That is, a traditional and much-practiced way to conceive of causation has been in terms of the chronology of events. Earlier happenings are seen as the well-springs of later ones. Past episodes are viewed as the causes of present effects. In like manner, present effects themselves will be the causes of future outcomes. Thus, the task faced by the historian who seeks to explain cause is that of: (a) identifying which factors from the past have contributed to the present state of affairs, (b) calculating how much influence each of the factors exerted, and (c) proposing how the factors blended together to bring about such a result.

Planning a Historical Study

As with case studies, planning historical research can profitably start with a statement of the target variable, then continue (a) with guide questions defining the realm of that variable, (b) with sources of answers to those questions, and (c) with methods to be used in searching through those sources. The following examples illustrate the planning that can be inferred from the contents of two representative historical accounts.

The first study describes the competition between Protestants and Catholics to determine the nature of schooling for American Indians during the quarter century 1888-1912 (Prucha, 1979). The second study analyzes the fate of progressive education in the Midwestern United States between 1930 and 1960. The analysis includes comparisons between traditional schools and their progressive-education counterparts (Zilversmit, 1993).

Protestants, Catholics, and American Indians

The Churches and the Indian Schools, 1888-1912, is a detailed study written by a Jesuit priest, Francis Paul Prucha, to explain the

tension and conflict between Protestants and Catholics over Indian mission schools at the end of the nineteenth century and the beginning of the twentieth. [This account] grows out of an earlier study of the Protestant humanitarian reform organizations that dominated American Indian policy in the late nineteenth century. The goal of those reformers was to Americanize the Indians, to destroy tribalism with its communal base, and to substitute the individualism which marked white society. Since the Americanism that they sought to impose upon the Indians was conceived in terms of the evangelical Protestant heritage of America from which the reformers came, the Catholic missionaries did not fit well into the proposed patterns.

The conflict between the two religious groups was perhaps inevitable and unavoidable, for the fundamental expectations of each of the antagonists clashed sharply with those of the other. There was no disagreement about the absolute necessity of religious (specifically Christian) influence upon the civilization of the Indians as they were prepared for assimilation into the white man's society.

The conflict rose, rather, over differing Protestant and Catholic views about the place of each other within American society. (Prucha, 1979, p. ix)

The contents of Prucha's book suggest that his research plan included the following elements.

The target variable: Over the quarter century 1888-1912, what were the issues involving Indian schools that Protestants and Catholics fought about, what were the aims that each of the combatants hoped to achieve, and how was the conflict ultimately resolved?

Guide questions defining the domain of the study: What was the condition of the Indian tribes in the latter 19th century; how and why did they arrive in such a condition? What provisions were made for Indian children's education? Who made such provisions and why? What religious practices did the Indians follow; what influences determined which practices they would adopt? What roles did Protestant and Catholic groups play in determining the curriculum and control of the Indian schools? What issues involving Indian schools produced conflicts between Protestants and Catholics, and why? What key events occurred in the struggles over those issues? What agencies and individuals played key roles in the events? What part did Indians play in the conflict? By 1912, how was the conflict resolved?

Sources of answers to the guide questions: Records of the Bureau of Catholic Indian Missions, the Indian Rights Association Papers in the Historical Society of Pennsylvania, and records of the U.S. government kept in the National Archives. Papers of individuals who participated in the controversy. Printed documents from all three branches of the federal government (administrative, legislative, judicial). Newspaper and periodical articles.

Methods of collecting answers: Content analysis of the sources as directed by the guide questions.

Progressive Education's Rise and Demise

Zilversmit's (1993) book-length account of the progressive education movement in the United States is titled *Changing Schools: Progressive Education Theory and Practice, 1930-1960.*

The target variable: When, where, and how have principles of progressive education been applied in representatives schools in the Midwestern United States?

Guide questions defining the domain of the study: How and when did the progressive education movement start? What were the key principles of the movement? In what ways were those principles similar to and different from traditional educational principles over the years 1930-1960? In representative schools in the Midwestern United States, when, where, and why were progressive methods applied in classrooms? How did progressive practices compare with procedures found in traditional classrooms? What sorts of evidence have been used by different authors to assess the impact of progressive philosophy on classroom practice? What were the historical trends in the adoption of progressive methods? What vestiges of the progressive movement could be found in classrooms in the 1990s, and how and why did those remnants become part of school practice near the end of the 20th century? What does the analysis of the rise and decline of progressive education suggest about the process of school reform?

Sources of answers to the guide questions: Books and journal articles about the history of American education, about progressive education, and about educational reform movements. Archives of records from progressive schools (minutes of meetings, curriculum guides, teachers' manuals, regulations, speeches). Newspaper accounts of educational developments during the 1930-1960 period. People who were personally involved with progressive education or with competing educational movements. Scholars who have studied progressive education and other reform efforts.

Methods of collecting answers: Content analysis of books, journal articles, newspaper accounts, and archival materials. Interviews and written correspondence with people who were involved in the progressive education movement or with competing movements, or ones who have studied such matters.

The theoretical position from which Zilversmit's analyzed progressivism includes at least three perspectives, those of: (a) *reformation theory* in which a philosophical ideal (John Dewey's child-centered school) is translated into classroom practices that are disseminated through books, professional journals, educational conventions, and teacher-education programs, (b) *conflict theory* in which innovators vie with conservatives for control of classroom practices, and (c) *inertia theory* in which traditional patterns of behavior within a massive social system, and the shortage of facilities and funding to achieve required alterations, prevent reform movements from effecting significant change in the majority of the system's components. From his vantage point, Zilversmit concluded that

> Despite the impassioned discussions of progressive education in the 1920s and 1930s, despite the marked progressivism of a few school districts and the increasing importance of progressive ideas in state education departments and teachers' colleges, it is clear that by 1940 progressive education had not significantly altered the broad pattern of American education. The call for a child-centered school had, for the most part, been ignored. (Zilversmit, 1993, p. 34)

ETHNOGRAPHIES

Ethnography is the chief investigative approach employed by cultural anthropologists. Here are three typical ways ethnography is defined.

Ethnography [is the] descriptive study of a particular human society or the process of making such a study. Contemporary ethnography is based almost entirely on fieldwork and requires the complete immersion of the anthropologist in the culture and everyday life of the people who are the subject of the study. (Ethnography, 1994, p. 582)

Ethnography means, literally, a picture of the "way of life" of some identifiable group of people. Conceivably, those people could be any culture-bearing group, in any time and place. . . . Particular individuals, customs, institutions, or events are of anthropological interest as they relate to a generalized description of the life-way of a socially interacting group. . . . Ordinarily an outsider to the group being studied, the ethnographer tries hard to know more about the cultural system he or she is studying than any individual who is a natural participant in it, at once advantaged by the outsider's broad and analytical perspective but, by reason of that same detachment, unlikely ever totally to comprehend the insider's point of view. The ethnographer walks a fine line. With too much distance and perspective, one is labeled aloof, remote, insensitive, superficial; with too much familiarity, empathy, and identification, one is suspected of having "gone native." (Wolcott, 1988, pp. 188-189)

Ethnography is that form of inquiry and writing that produces descriptions and accounts about the ways of life of the writer and those written about. (Denzin, 1977, p. 3)

In educational research, the societies on which ethnographies focus include those found within a classroom, a school, a community, an ethnic group, a neighborhood, a department in a university, a team, a club, a teachers' union, a school board, an administrators' organization, a ministry of education, or the like. Donning the analytical lenses of a cultural anthropologist, the investigator enters the society for an extended period of time to study how it functions. For instance, a graduate student assumes the position of a teaching aide in a primary-school classroom, thereby equipped to experience classroom activities from an assistant teacher's vantage point and to mingle with the children on the playfield and in the lunchroom. Or a researcher joins a teachers' union, attends its meetings, and talks with fellow members about union activities. Or an educator lives for a period of time in a foreign country to analyze mass communication media (television, radio, newspapers, magazines) that exert an educational influence on the populace and to observe ways members of the society respond to the media.

Since the purpose of ethnographic research is to depict a group's culture, it is important that investigators have a clear notion of what the term *culture* is intended to imply for their work. Not everyone defines *culture* in quite the same manner. However, most popular definitions contain similar core meanings, as indicated in these examples.

Culture or civilization, taken in its wide ethnographic sense, is that complex whole which includes knowledge, belief, art, morals, law, custom, and any other capabilities and habits acquired by man as a member of society. (Singer, 1968, p. 527)

Culture—the integrated pattern of human knowledge, belief, and behavior. Culture, thus defined, consists of language, ideas, beliefs, customs, taboos, codes, institutions, tools, techniques, works of art, rituals, ceremonies, and other related components. (Culture, 1994, p. 784)

The culture of any society is made up of the concepts, beliefs, and principles of action and organization that an ethnographer has found could be attributed successfully to the members of that society in the context of his dealings with them. (Goodenough, 1976, p. 5)

Whereas case studies are intended to reveal the individualistic attributes of a particular person or institution, the purpose of ethnographies is to identify beliefs and customs shared by members of a social system. In effect, case studies emphasize features that make one person or organization different from others, while ethnographies emphasize the commonalities that unify members of a society.

No society—whatever its size—is sufficiently simple to be analyzed completely within a single research project. Thus, as with historical research, it is necessary for an investigator to select the aspects of culture that will be the focus of the ethnography at hand. Those aspects in a particular project can be identified by questions that serve as guides to data collection. This point can be illustrated with three examples. In the first, attention centers on religious education in two widely separated cultural settings—a Navajo Indian community in the Southwestern United States and the island of Okinawa in the Western Pacific. The second example analyzes students' responses to teachers' classroom management techniques in an American high school. The third compares the role of physical punishment as a child-rearing tactic in the South Seas nation of Tonga with the role of physical punishment in Australia.

Navajo and Okinawan Religious Education

In this research effort, separate ethnographic field studies of life in Navajo and Okinawan societies provided the data for comparing the transmission of religious beliefs from one generation to the next in the two settings (Iverson, 1981; Lebra, 1966; Reichard, 1963; Shimabukuro, 1950; Yanagita, 1951). The guide questions identify the portions of those studies which provide material for the comparison (Thomas, 1997b).

The target variable: What are the important components of each of the two societies' religions, what means are used to propagate religion from one generation to the next, and in what ways are the two societies' religions and methods of religious education alike and different?

Guide questions defining the domain of the case: Answer these questions about the traditional religion in each of the two societies: What is the purpose of human life? What natural and/or supernatural forces control events in the physical and social universe? By what means, and to what extent, can people influence those forces? What rites and rituals are practiced? What are the purposes of those rites and rituals? What material objects are part of religious practices, and what are the functions of those objects? What moral rules or values should guide people's behavior? What are the sources of those values? What consequences can result from abiding by or from violating moral rules? What are the sources of such consequences? To what extent is there agreement within the society about the purpose of life, the forces affecting events in the universe, the means of influencing the forces, proper moral values, and the consequences of abiding by or violating moral rules? What controversies arise over the foregoing beliefs, and how do those controversies affect people's lives?

In each of the two societies, who teaches the foregoing religious beliefs and practices? In what settings does such instruction take place? At what times in people's lives are the beliefs and practices taught, and why at these times? What instructional methods and materials are used? How is the success of religious education evaluated?

In regard to the above aspects of religious education, how are Navajo and Okinawan religious beliefs and practices similar to and different from each other? What are likely reasons for these similarities and differences?

Sources of answers to the guide questions: Members of the society who occupy different positions in the political authority structure, in the social class system, and in the religious hierarchy—including informants of different ages and of both genders. Published histories, anthropological accounts, and sociological studies of each society.

Methods of collecting answers: Interviews with members of the society, observations of events bearing on religious matters, content analysis of published materials.

Students' Perspectives, Goals, and Strategies

A doctoral candidate in a university's department of education obtained permission from the principal of a nearby high school to attend high school classes for a semester in order to study how students perceived teachers' techniques of classroom management, particularly the teachers' ways of directing learning activities and maintaining order. The project included a description of students' academic and social goals, the strategies class members adopted for pursuing those goals, and how teachers responded to such strategies (Allen, 1982). The comparisons drawn in this research were between classes in different subject areas, between teachers, and between students who differed in their perceptions, goals, and strategies.

The target variables: What techniques of classroom management do teachers use, how do students interpret those techniques, what goals do students hope to achieve by their responses to teachers' management efforts, and what strategies do students adopt for pursuing those goals?

Guide questions defining the domain of the case: What tasks of classroom management do the teachers face? How do these tasks vary from one class to another? What techniques of classroom management do different teachers adopt? How successfully do these techniques achieve the teachers' apparent goals? What do students believe are the teachers' motives behind the management techniques? What strategies do students adopt for responding to those techniques? What goals do students hope to achieve by their strategies? How successful are the students' strategies for achieving their goals, and why? Which of the teachers' techniques are most successful in achieving the teachers' goals, and why?

How does the particular mixture of students in a given class influence the management tasks the teacher faces, the techniques the teacher employs, and the success of those techniques in achieving the teacher's goals? How does the mixture of students influence students' interpretation of the teacher's motives and management techniques, the strategies students adopt, the goals at which those strategies are directed, and the effectiveness of the strategies in attaining such goals?

In what ways do teachers vary in their goals and their management methods? In what ways do students vary in their interpretations of teachers' management techniques, in their own goals, and in the strategies they employ for pursuing those goals?

Sources of answers to the guide questions: Class sessions. Teachers' opinions. Students' opinions. Records of disciplinary actions relating to the classes, teachers, and students who are the subjects of the research.

Methods of collecting answers: Daily observations of class sessions. Informal observations of students' conversations outside of class. Interviews with teachers. Interviews with students. Content analysis of records of disciplinary actions.

Child Punishment as a Teaching Device

In a journal article entitled "Dealing with the Dark Side in the Ethnography of Childhood: Child Punishment in Tonga," Helen Kapavalu described the role of physical discipline as an instructional device in contemporary Tongan society (Kapavalu, 1993). The article also included occasional comparisons between Tonga and a typical Australian community. The content of Kapavalu's description implies that the following kinds of questions guided her research.

The target variable: What role does physical punishment play in traditional Tongan child rearing, on what rationale is such punishment founded, and what consequences result from that practice?

Guide questions defining the domain of the case: What is the authority structure (the system of controllers and the controlled) in Tongan society? How is this structure reflected in the broader community, the family, and the school? What characteristics determine a person's place in the authority hierarchies? What personal-social qualities are valued in Tongan culture? What methods are used by authority figures to foster those qualities in children and youth? Upon what rationale and perception of child nature are these methods founded? How do children and youths respond to such methods, particularly to the use of physical punishment? What significant consequences appear to result from physical punishment—consequences for individuals and for the conduct of Tongan society? What changes, if any, are occurring in the techniques used for socializing the young; what are the likely causes of those changes; and what are the probable consequences of such changes for the welfare of individuals and for the traditional Tongan social system?

How does the role of physical punishment as a child rearing device in Tonga compare with its role in a typical Australian community? What problems can occur for people from a Tongan background when they enter Australian society, and vice versa?

Sources of answers to the guide questions: Incidents of punishment in the daily routine of life in Tongan homes, schools, church sessions, markets, playgrounds, recreational events, and work sites. Tongans living in Tonga and ones living in Australia. Ethnographies and accounts of life in Tonga written over past decades by missionaries, anthropologists, and visitors to the islands. Descriptions of child rearing and of child abuse in Australia.

Methods of collecting answers: Observations of child-rearing practices in Tongan settings. Interviews with Tongans in Tonga to learn their perceptions of physical punishment as an instrument of child socialization. Interviews with non-Tongan observers of life in Tonga to gather incidents of physical punishment and the observers' assessments of the desirability of such punishment. Interviews of Tongans who have emigrated to Australia, with the interviews directed at discovering immigrants' views of the physical punishment of children. Content analysis of published accounts of Tongan culture and of child rearing practices in Australia.

SURVEYS

The purpose of survey research is to describe specific characteristics of a large group of persons, objects, policies, practices, institutions, or events. The process of conducting a survey involves *gathering information* about some *target variable* from a quantity of *sources of the same type,* then summarizing the information in a readily comprehended form. By analyzing each of the italicized items in this description, we can illustrate the multifaceted nature of surveys and the contributions they can make in comparative research (Babbie, 1990; Jallife, 1986; Rea & Parker, 1992).

Target Variables

Target variables are of many kinds, as demonstrated by the titles of studies focusing on the following dozen types of variables:

Knowledge—Mathematics Achievement among Nine-Year-Olds in 32 Nations
—Pupils' Misconceptions of Historical Events
Skills—Computer Keyboarding: Speed and Accuracy at Four Stages of Training
—Kinds of Practice Routines among Distance Runners
Habits—Girls' and Boys' Use of Leisure Time
—Health Effects of Four Weight-Reducing Diets
Attitudes, Opinions—Parents' Expectations for Children's Academic Success
—University Students' Opinions of Fee Increases
Evaluations, Judgments—How Teachers Rationalize Their Methods of Discipline
—Ratings of Teachers by Good and Poor Students
Objectives—What is Worth Learning? Humanists versus Pragmatists
—The Aims of Canadian Education, 1850, 1900, 1950, 1998
Policies—Legal Control of Private Universities in China and Japan
—Compulsory Schooling Regulations in Developing Nations
Practices—Changing Roles for School Inspectors in Remote Rural Regions
—Who Pays for the Village School? A Study of Sub-Saharan Africa
Teaching Methods—The Classroom Use of Computers in London and Paris
—The Popularity of Chalk-and-Talk versus Class Discussion
Equipment—The Availability of Textbooks in Saudi Arabia's Primary Schools
—Facilities for Preparing School Lunches in Small and Large Schools
Communication Media—Linking Violence on Television with Student
  Misbehavior
—Evidence of Racial Prejudice in Secondary-School History Books
Educational Contexts—Population Density and Achievement Test Scores
—Home Languages of Bilingual Students in Southern France

It should be apparent that this list of target variables is far from definitive. Among many additional types are: educational philosophies, teacher characteristics, student characteristics, curriculum designs, types of schools, community resources, administrative structures, laws and regulations, and sources of funds.

The titles of studies in the above list represent two general classes of surveys—the cross-sectional and the longitudinal. In cross-sectional studies, information about the status of the target variable is collected for one particular time. In longitudinal studies, information is gathered at successive periods of time as reflected in such entries as "Changing Roles for School Inspectors" and "Aims of Canadian Education, 1850, 1900, 1950, 1998."

In preparing to conduct a survey, an investigator can usefully begin with the research question that defines the target variables and then identify sources of information about those variables.

Sources of Information

The phrase *sources of the same type* refers to the kinds of entities from which data are to be collected. In our Chapter 4 description of ways to survey the professional literature, the source-type consisted of documents bearing on the particular target variable being studied. As a further example, in a study of parents' opinions of a city's schools, the source-type is comprised of adults who have children currently attending those schools. In a project focusing on the legal control of private universities, the type includes printed laws and regulations as well as records of court cases and government directives related to violations of rules.

Specifying the types of sources from which information is to be collected guides the researcher in selecting the methods and instruments to used for collecting the data.

Gathering Information

The following five examples illustrate typical options available for collecting information from the identified sources. From among the options, investigators select one or more that are feasible in the circumstances under which they are obliged to work.

1. *Topic*—A Nationwide Survey of Twelve-year-olds' Reading Skills
   Source—12-year-old pupils
   Data-gathering options—(a) Paper-pencil testing or (b) computerized testing in which pupils read passages silently, then offer answers to questions that assess how well they comprehended the passages. (c) Individual interview sessions in which a pupil reads a passage aloud, then orally answers questions about the content of the passage.

2. *Topic*—Changing Curriculum Patterns in Five Cities' Primary Schools
   Sources—(a) Printed materials: Curriculum guidebooks, courses of study, teachers' instructional manuals, records of curriculum-planning sessions, newspaper articles, minutes of legislative hearings, school laws, and administrative directives. (b) People: school principals, curriculum planners, teachers.
   Data-gathering options—(a) Content analyses of printed materials as guided by research questions and rating devices. (b) Interviews with people engaged in curriculum planning or implementation, or (c) questionnaires filled out by such people.

3. *Topic*—Types and Incidence of Behavior Problems in Representative Urban, Suburban, and Rural Secondary Schools
   Sources—(a) Printed materials: Schools' records of student disciplinary cases, individual students' cumulative record folders, juvenile-court

records. (b) People: Such school personnel as teachers, school counselors, school principals, and truant officers.

Data-gathering options—(a) Content analyses of printed materials, with the results compiled as anecdotal records, checklists, or rating scales. (b) Interviews with school personnel or questionnaires that personnel complete.

4. *Topic*—College Instructors' Distracting Mannerisms
   Sources—(a) classroom observations and (b) students' responses.
   Data-gathering options—(a) Classroom observations: Trained observers attend college classes to record (anecdotal record, checklist, rating scale) instructor mannerisms that distract learners from the content of the instruction; or a video camera records instructor behavior that is later analyzed by researchers to identify distracting mannerisms. (b) Students' responses: By means of individual or group interview sessions or else by means of written questionnaires, students report instructor mannerisms that divert attention from the content of the lesson.

5. *Topic*—Students' Opinions of Vocational and College-Preparatory Curriculum Tracks
   Source—Secondary-school students   .
   Data-gathering options—(a) individual interviews, (b) group interviews, (c) printed opinionnaires.

Researchers can choose the data-gathering methods they will use by (1) inspecting the options, (2) estimating how accurate the information will be, and (3) weighing the accuracy of data against the feasibility of the data-gathering process to arrive at the method of collecting needed information.

The Matter of Sampling

In some instances researchers intend the conclusions derived from their surveys to apply only to their sources of information (people, documents, events) that participated in the survey. For example, the headmaster of a secondary school canvassed all members of the student body to learn how many students wished to study a foreign language during the coming school year and which languages they would prefer to learn. As a second instance, a teacher solicited the opinions of her class members' parents about the disciplinary policy she intended to adopt as a means of encouraging more students to complete homework assignments. Another investigator analyzed the minutes of every meeting of a city's school board for the previous five years to learn which members of the board most often supported measures to increase services to the handicapped and which members failed to support such measures.

Although some researchers thus wish to draw generalizations only about the participants in their survey, far more wish to extend their survey conclusions beyond those participants. In effect, the survey's subjects are considered to be only a portion—no more than a sample—of the population to which the research conclusions will be applied. To illustrate, on the basis of testing the mathematics skills of 1,500 12-year-olds, researchers may draw conclusions about all of a province's 127,000 12-year-olds. From a review of 130 cases of students dismissed from school for breaking the law, investigators can extract generalizations that they assume are valid for the entire population of 1,600 such cases in juvenile-court files.

If researchers are to make extensions of survey results convincing, they need to furnish evidence that the sample of people, documents, or events accurately reflects key characteristics of the population which the sample is supposed to depict. It is thus important that researchers recognize the advantages and limitations of various methods of drawing samples and that they understand statistical procedures for estimating how faithfully samples of different sizes represent their envisioned populations (Barnett, 1991; Chaudhuri & Vos, 1988). A detailed discussion of those matters is provided in Chapter 9.

CORRELATIONAL COMPARISONS

A substantial proportion of comparative studies involve correlational analyses. In such studies, the investigator is interested in discovering the extent to which a change in one variable is accompanied by some degree of change in another. Consider, for example, the relationship between these variables:

—*School size and students' extracurricular participation*: Does the average student in large schools engage in more types of extracurricular activities than the average student in small schools? (No, quite the reverse, according to Barker & Gump, 1964.)

—*Teachers' reading habits and pupils' reading skills*: Do pupils whose teachers read extensively score higher on reading tests than pupils whose teachers spend little time reading? (Yes, according to a report of a 26-nation study by Postlethwaite & Ross, 1992, p. 35.)

—*Age and the motive of revenge*: Does revenge as a motive for punishing wrongdoers increase between late childhood and young adulthood? (No. Revenge as a motive was found to decrease with advancing age in a study by Divers-Stamnes & Thomas, 1995.)

Correlations can be either positive or negative. In positive correlations, an increase in one variable parallels an increase in the other. To illustrate, children in the United States have been found to be better readers if they attend schools that have more books per student, provide more hours of reading instruction, and have teachers with more years of teaching experience (Postlethwaite & Ross, 1992). As a second example, research on science instruction among 200,000 students in 23 countries revealed that:

In nearly all countries, 10-year-old and 14-year-old children from [socio-economically] higher status homes, from homes with more reading resources, and from homes with parents with more years of education performed better on science tests than children from poorer homes with respect to these characteristics. . . . The length of time students spent on homework also had a positive effect on achievement. (Postlethwaite & Wiley, 1992, pp. 157, 162)

In the case of negative correlations, an increase in one variable is accompanied by a decrease in the other variable, as in the above references to (a) school size and extracurricular participation and (b) age and the motive of revenge.

If, when one variable changes, nothing happens to the other, then the two are not correlated. For instance, the investigators conducting the 23-nation study of science instruction found that, on the average, neither the size of a school or of a class, nor the number of different subjects that students studied in their final year of secondary school, was related to how well students performed on standardized science tests (Postlethwaite & Wiley, 1992, pp. 160-161).

Obviously, not all variables are related to each other in the same degree. At the highest level of correlation, the extent of change in one variable is accompanied by the same extent of change in the other variable. In contrast, at the opposite extreme of correlation, change in one variable is associated with no change at all in the other. There are many methods of expressing degrees of relationship. One popular method, applied when the variables are expressed in quantities, is Pearson's product-moment correlation coefficient. In the Pearson system, the highest level of correlation is labeled 1.00, indicating that any change in one variable is always attended by the same extent of change in the other. The lowest level of correlation is labeled .00, meaning that change in one factor is never attended by any change in the other. In between these two extremes are graduated levels of relationship. For instance, the following are product-moment correlations reported for various sorts of comparison.

The relationship between:

Fourth-graders' scores on a standardized reading test and their scores on a mathematics test = +.82 (Slavin, 1984, p. 15).

High-school students' fear of failure and their fear of how their parents' would react to the students' failure = +.52 (Chung & Walkey, 1989, p. 150).

General intelligence and extroversion in girls = +.19 and in boys = +.21 (Duncan, Emslie, & Williams, 1996).

School achievement and self concept = +.35 (Follman, 1984).

Amount of psychotherapy and amount of patient improvement = +.32 (Smith & Glass, 1977).

Class size and amount of bullying among students in a group of English secondary schools = +.62. Affluence of a community and the frequency of bullying in the community's secondary schools = -.32 (Whitney & Smith, 1993, pp. 18-19).

Family size and Spanish-language achievement of secondary-school applicants in Mexico = -.16 (Palafox, Prawda, & Velez, 1994, p. 173).

Frequently correlations are offered in verbal rather than numerical form. This is particularly the case in historical studies where authors postulate relationships. Consider three examples. In the first, the proposed relationship is between (a) how nation-states were created and (b) European and African sociocultural settings. In effect, the author proposes that the way nations were formed differed between Europe and Africa.

> In Europe, the acknowledgment by ethnic communities of their common history and cultural identities served as a basis for the creation of nation-states. In certain cases, like the Italy of Cavour or Germany of Bismarck, unity was strenuously sought when there was sufficient conviction that a cultural nation already existed.
>
> In Africa, however, this process was inverted and essentially diachronic. Colonial states were created within artificial boundaries which hardly coincided with the limits of traditional politics. Irrespective of their historical past, social affinities, or long-standing feuds, various communities whose cultures, traditions, and languages differed considerably were brought together for the purpose of facilitating colonial administration. . . . Under such circumstances, the colonial state can be seen as a "proto state" within the limits of which Africans had to forge a new sense of solidarity and belonging, [an assignment borne by education systems]. (Adjangba, 1993, p. 195)

Researchers sometimes offer examples intended to suggest the intensity of a correlation. Here is a case in which the relationship is between (*a*) the extent of pain or inconvenience parents are willing to suffer to have their children succeed with school examinations and (*b*) the amount of assistance that parents hope the gods will provide for their children at examination time. The link between variables *a* and *b* is the religious ritual that many Japanese or Korean parents perform.

> The most desperate manifestation of Shinto devotion to exams is probably the "one-hundred-time homage" (*ohyakudo-airi*), which aims to win sympathy from the deity through self-inflicted torment. To perform *ohyakudo-airi*, parents or students climb stone steps leading to the shrine, pass through an archway representing the division between the secular and divine worlds, ring a bell that announces their visit to the god, and then pray. To fulfill this ritual, the procedure is repeated a hundred times. In Korea . . . mothers at a Buddhist temple bow 3,000 times a night for their children's success on exams. . . . (Zeng, 1996, pp. 266-267)

Additional ways to calculate relationships among variables are introduced in Chapter 9.

Correlations are extremely important in explanatory research, because all statements about causation are statements about correlations among variables. However, the fact that two variables are correlated does not necessarily mean that one contributed at all to the outcome of the other. Thus, it is critical that researchers recognize the difference between *casual* or *incidental* correlations and *causal* or *determining* correlations. An anecdote used to illustrate this distinction focuses on the relationship between the numbers of storks in communities of the lowland countries of Western Europe and the number of babies born there. Observers noted that communities which had larger numbers of storks also had more babies born. This correlation might then be cited in support of the theory that storks bring (are causes of) babies. However, doubters could contend that the positive relationship was no more than casual, derived from the fact that storks happened to prefer living in villages rather than in cities and that villagers traditionally bore more children than did urbanites. The relationship, according to skeptics, is incidental rather than causal.

Thus, simply demonstrating a positive or negative correlation is not sufficient evidence of cause. What is also needed is a convincing line of logic demonstrating that one variable was at least partially the result of the other variable's presence. Frequently the line of reasoning is designed to show that one variable (the cause) preceded the other (the effect) and that the two could not have occurred in the reverse order. Constructing a persuasive argument that links two variables in a causal relationship often entails proposing how the relationship is mediated by a chain of factors.

As explained in Chapter 9, a number of statistical procedures are available to buttress causal modes of reasoning.

EXPERIMENTS

An experiment usually consists of applying one or more specified treatments to an individual, group, or institution, then assessing what effects those treatments had (this is the step of description) and estimating why such effects occurred (this is the step of explanation). A key assumption underlying experiments is that events are the result of one or more causal factors. The purpose of an experiment is to manipulate the potential factors in a manner that reveals (a) which of them have indeed caused an event and (b) how much each factor contributed to the outcome.

Designs of experiments can assume a variety of forms that vary from the extremely simple to the highly complex, with each form bearing particular advantages and limitations. The simpler the design, the easier it is to carry out the research. The more complex the design, the better the experiment accounts for variables that affect the outcome and, as a result, the greater the confidence a researcher can place in the conclusions drawn from the results. In brief, ease and feasibility of application are bought at the expense of insecurity regarding conclusions drawn about cause. Confidence in conclusions is paid for by greater difficulty, time, and bother.

The following overview of experimental designs advances from the simple to the complex. The final matter addressed in the discussion is the question of which features of a design researchers can profitably consider when choosing the design most suitable for guiding a particular educational decision.

Ex Post Facto

The most elementary design involves (a) applying a treatment to an entity, (b) assessing how well the entity performs following the treatment, and (c) estimating how much the treatment contributed to that performance.   For example, a secondary-school science teacher used a new biology textbook with her class. At the close of a three week unit of study on genetics, she gave a final test to discover how much the students then knew about genetic inheritance. If the students received high scores on the test, the teacher might conclude that the textbook was a very efficient learning aid. If they received low scores, she might decide that the book were poorly suited to her class's needs and abilities.

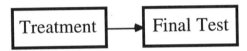

This form of experiment can be labeled *ex post facto* or *after the fact* because the teacher has drawn conclusions about the effect of the treatment—the effect of the particular textbook—solely on the basis of evaluating students after they had experienced the treatment. The main advantage of the ex post facto model is that it's easy to use. It involves little bother on the part of the experimenter. But it also leaves unanswered important questions about which factors contributed to the students' test performance. In particular, we know nothing about how much the students already understood about genetics before they read the book. It is even conceivable that some students had a more accurate knowledge of genetics before they studied the text, and that the text explained things in such a muddled fashion that it confused the readers, causing them to doubt what they already knew. Further, we do not know what other sources of information the students may have used during the three week unit of study.   And we are left wondering whether the class learned more using the new textbook than they would have learned from some other book or from the teacher's lectures.

Pretest-Treatment-Posttest

To provide a more convincing foundation for estimating the influence of the biology textbook, the teacher could replace her ex post facto plan with a pretest-treatment-posttest design.   In this case, at the outset of the study unit on genetics, she would have the students take a test (pretest) about genetics before she even discussed genetics or assigned the class members to read the genetics section of the text. Then, after the class members had completed the three week study of the book (treatment), she would test (posttest) their command of the material. In order to estimate how much the textbook had added to the learners' knowledge, she would subtract the students' pretest scores from their posttest scores and conclude that the obtained difference represented the contribution made by the book. In other words, the teacher's judgment would be based, not on the final test scores, but on the extent of change from pretest to posttest.

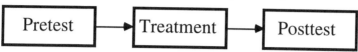

Compared Treatments

Although the pretest-treatment-posttest design clears up some questions that the ex post facto plan failed to answer, it leaves in doubt several other matters. Is the new textbook better than the old one? Would students have learned more by working on problems involving genetic inheritance? Would they have succeeded as well if the teacher had presented the material in the form of illustrated lectures or a series of videotaped television programs?

In an effort to answer such queries, the teacher could divide the class into two equal groups. One group would use the old textbook and the other group the new book. Or one group would study the new text while the other group viewed videotaped programs. But if the teacher arbitrarily assigned students to the two groups, it is possible that one group would end up with more adept science students than the other group. Subsequently, if the higher-ability group succeeded better than lower-ability group on the posttest, it would not be clear how much of their success should be credited to their greater aptitude and how much to the particular treatment they received. One way the experimenter could cope with this problem would be to pretest the students before assigning them to treatment groups, then pair up the students so that both members of each pair had nearly identical scores. One member of each of the matched pairs would be assigned to Treatment A and the other member to Treatment B. This process would help ensure that at the outset of the genetics unit the two groups were evenly matched in terms of their entry knowledge of genetics. When change scores were later computed between the pretest and posttest results, the researcher could be more confident that the treatment, and just the treatment, rather than variations in the individuals' prior knowledge, was the greater cause of any of the

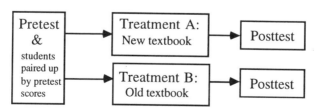

difference found between the groups' levels of success.   This compared-treatments design could be expanded to include more than two treatment options.   The experimenter could divide the biology class into three groups so as to permit comparisons among the new-textbook, old-textbook, and illustrated-lecture approaches.   As a further step, a videotape-program approach could be included by dividing the class into four groups.   However, adopting more treatment alternatives creates problems of sample size and logistical feasibility.

It is apparent that every additional division of the class reduces the size of each group.   In a class of 32 students, the average final-test score in a simple pretest-treatment-posttest plan is based on 32 participants.   In contrast, each group's average score in a four-treatment comparison is based on only eight students.   Obviously, the greater the number of students on which an average is founded, the more likely the average score will accurately represent the performance of a typical student.   In effect, small samples of participants are highly subject to the influence of a few deviant individual scores which may happen to be included in a sample, with such participants contributing to a distorted picture of the typical effectiveness of the treatment they experienced.   But in samples composed of large numbers of participants, the influence of individual deviant scores is diminished by the presence of far more scores from more typical participants.

In addition to causing problems of sample size, adding treatment options increases experimenters' logistical difficulties.   How can the biology teacher reasonably manage a class of students who are divided into groups that simultaneously study genetics via four different approaches?   Thus, the advantages of adopting increasingly complex compared-treatments designs must be paid for in reduced feasibility.   One obvious way to solve the problem of unduly small samples is to solicit larger numbers of participants.   In our present illustration, that would mean engaging more biology classes from more schools in the genetics-instruction experiment.   However, doing so would raise costs and increase the difficulty of coordinating and monitoring the study.   It would also add to the number of uncontrolled variables that could affect the test results, such variables as having more teachers with different levels of instructional skill and more students from diverse socioeconomic backgrounds.   As a result, investigators are obliged to choose an acceptable compromise between complexity of experimental design and the practical demands of their research setting.

Assigning Participants to Treatments

We have already inspected two ways of assigning people to different treatments.   The first and easiest way is to allocate people arbitrarily, paying no attention to how they might be similar to, or different from, each other.   The second way is to match participants according to some characteristic considered influential for the study at hand.   In our biology-class example, that characteristic was the students' scores on a genetics pretest.   In other studies the foundation for matching can be age, intelligence, language skill, muscular coordination, ethnic origin, socioeconomic status, religious affiliation, and the like, depending on the nature of the research project's target variable. As noted above, the problem of achieving a good match between participants increases with the number of treatment groups that the particular experiment involves. Pairing up students on the basis of similar intelligence-test scores for a two-treatment study is easier than matching them in quartets in a four-treatment design.

A third method of assigning subjects to treatment groups is by random selection. One popular way of carrying out the random-assignment method consists of a series of steps that can be illustrated with the case of a two-treatment experiment. First, each participant is assigned a number, which is written on a slip of paper. Second, all of the numbered slips are placed in a hat or bowl and thoroughly stirred around. Third, one slip is drawn randomly from the hat, and the person belonging to that number is assigned to Treatment A. Another slip is then drawn, with the person bearing that number assigned to Treatment B. This process is then continued, with the odd-drawn individuals relegated to Treatment A and the even-drawn to Treatment B, until the entire collection of slips has been exhausted.

As an alternative to the slips-in-the-hat procedure, the experimenter can assign each participant a number, then use a table of random numbers from a statistics textbook or a series of random numbers generated by a computer program to place the participants in their treatment groups.

The random-assignment method is based on the assumption that unrecognized factors which could inadvertently affect the outcome of the experiment will be distributed equally between the treatment groups. Therefore, if those factors do, indeed, influence the results of the experiment, the influence will be the same within each treatment group. In other words, the unrecognized factors in one group cancel out the same factors in the other group in their effect on the final results. It is thus assumed that any differences found between the groups in the final testing will be solely the consequence of the differences between the two treatments and not a result of extraneous variables.

The following example illustrates an experimental design for which the random assignment of learners to different treatments is especially appropriate. Imagine that a researcher wishes to discover the comparative effectiveness of two self-instruction methods of teaching introductory economics. The information gained from this experiment will help administrators of an open university decide which method they should adopt in their distance-learning program for students who are taking economics courses by correspondence. One of the methods employs a series of workbooks in which students solve problems. The other method utilizes step-by-step lessons provided on personal-computer diskettes.

A special feature of the researcher's experimental design is its provision for revealing a potential reactive effect. As Ball (1985, p. 4200) explains,

Reactive effects in measurement occur when the behavior elicited by the measurement procedures is not characteristic of the behavior that would have occurred in the absence of the measurement procedure.

Aware of the possibility of reactive effects, the researcher planning the introductory-economics experiment suspects that if students were given a pretest to show what they already knew before studying the workbook or computer program, the pretest itself might function as a type of treatment. In other words, students might learn something about economics during the process of taking the pretest, and that knowledge would later serve to improve their posttest scores. Hence, the posttest might not accurately reveal what students gained solely from the workbook or computerized lessons, because the students' scores could be a mixture of knowledge derived from both the pretest experience and the intended treatments. In an effort to determine the influence of these two sources of knowledge—the pretest and the planned treatments—the investigator randomly distributes the experiment's participants among four groups. Two groups—A and B—will study from workbooks and two—C and D—from computer programs. Group A will take a pretest before starting the workbook, while Group B will begin the lessons without having taken the pretest. In like manner, Group C will be pretested but Group D will not.

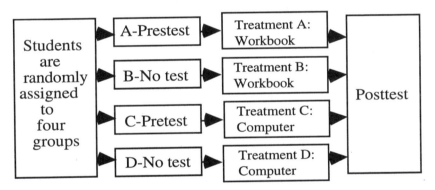

Let us now assume that 600 university students took part in the experiment so that there were 150 in each group. Finally, on the 100-item posttest, the groups' average scores were:

Group A = 84   Group B = 74   Group C = 92   Group D = 83

On the basis of these results, it would appear that the pretest did indeed function as a kind of treatment, since students who took the pretest in either a workbook or computer group earned scores about 10 points higher than students who were not pretested. It would also appear that the computer version of the economics course was somewhat more effective than the workbook version, since scores in groups C and D were higher those of students under the comparable A and B treatments.

It is useful to recognize that reactive effects may result not only from pretesting but also from a variety of conditions related to assessment situations. For instance, the presence of an observer taking notes in the back of a classroom may change the pupils' or teacher's behavior so that the events the observer records are not typical for that classroom. Likewise, the age, gender, or ethnicity of an interviewer may cause interviewees to respond in ways that are less than candid.

In the field of education and in other social-science disciplines, patterns of experiments are often referred to *quasi-experimental designs* to distinguish them from *authentic experimental designs* employed in the physical sciences. The term *authentic* in this context refers to the practice of randomly assigning people to different treatments. However, random assignment is often impossible in educational settings. Such is the case when a teacher must, for practical reasons, apply a particular teaching method to an entire class of students. Or a researcher must include all of the schools within a district in a study of a method of budgeting, because all of the schools are legally obligated to use that method. And the budgeting method is then compared to a different method used in another school district. Or an investigator is obliged to depend on those parents who are willing to be interviewed about their child-rearing methods, thereby leaving out all parents who are unwilling to be interviewed. In these instances, since the resulting experiments lack the randomization feature, they do not qualify as true or authentic experiments. However, since in all other respects they are indeed experiments, their designs can be deemed at least *quasi-experimental.*

Time Series

In addition to the designs described above, many others are available, each incorporating characteristics required for solving particular research problems. For example, when investigators study a teaching method, they often wish to know not only the immediate effects of that method but also how stable those effects will be with the passage of time. In other words, after a few weeks or months, how much have students forgotten of what they learned from the method? Has their long-term memory of the lesson contents been distorted in any way? To answer such questions, one or more posttests can be added to the experimental design.

However, some people are not content with knowing the condition of the target variable only at periodic intervals following the application of a treatment. They also want to know the variable's condition over a period of time leading up to the treatment's intervention. Their purpose is to learn whether the apparent change at the point of intervention was actually caused by the treatment or, in contrast, was no more than a segment of a trend that had been going on for some time prior to the intervention. The research design necessary to fulfill this requirement is one that involves the periodic collection of data substantially before and after the treatment's initial application. The trend line established by the periodic measurements reveals what effect the treatment apparently exerted on the target variable. To illustrate what such a design can reveal, let us assume that a high school mathematics teacher institutes an incentives plan aimed a stimulating students to better performance on weekly algebra tests. The teacher's plan consists of awarding students points for improving their test scores. When students have accumulated enough points, they can exchange the points for ice cream at the school cafeteria, for tickets to a nearby theater, or for reduced prices on tape cassettes at a local music store.

Next, assume that the teacher instituted this plan last February. It is now May, so the scores students have earned on weekly tests over several months can suggest how well the incentive program achieved its purpose. Our attention focuses on the performance of three students—Albert, Bart, and Candice. First, consider some simple pretest-treatment-posttest data from February. The test given the week before the incentive-plan was introduced serves as the pretest. The test given two weeks after the plan appeared acts as the posttest. Figure 5-1 displays the three students' scores on these occasions.

From these results, it appears that the incentive plan worked very well indeed for Bart, had slight effect on Albert, and had very little, if any, influence on Candice. However, when these results are cast within a time series extending from September to May, our conclusion about the effect of the incentive program can be quite different. Figure 5-2 represents the trend line drawn from

Figure 5-1

Pretest-Treatment-Posttest Design

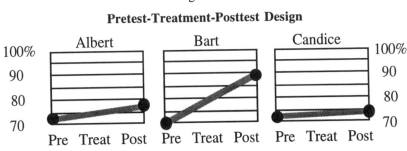

Figure 5-2

Interrupted-Time-Series Design

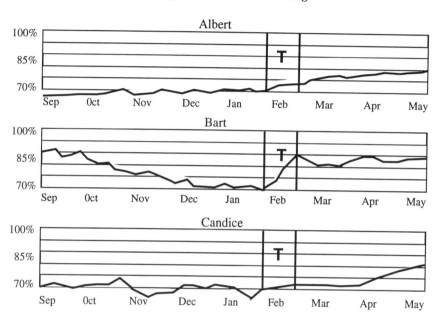

the students' test scores, September through May, with the **T** in the graphs indicating the point at which the incentive plan was introduced.

It is apparent that the three time-series in Figure 5-2 furnish a more complete foundation for estimating the effect of the incentive program than do the simpler pretest-treatment-posttest data in Figure 5-1. In Albert's case, there is a question of whether the program actually did interrupt the time series reflected in his performance, since the gain during the initial weeks of the incentive plan could well be no more than a continuation of an improvement trend that had begun some months earlier, a trend due to factors other than the enticement of the new incentives. For Bart, the incentive program may well have aided in getting him back on track after his test scores had been slumping over the past several months. The pattern of Candice's scores brings up the question of whether the incentives had no effect on her performance or, on the other hand, the effect was substantial but was delayed. To settle this question, we might ask Candice how she accounted for her improvement in April and May. Perhaps she would say, "A few weeks after the teacher was giving prizes for doing better on tests, I decided I'd like to get some prizes too, so I started working harder on my homework." Such a response would support our *delayed-effect* hypothesis. However, assume that instead she says, "In April I got my new reading glasses, and that made it easier for me to do my written work." On the basis of this information, we might conclude that the incentives did not alter Candice's achievement in algebra class.

In summary, time series are useful in revealing the role that a treatment apparently has played in the behavior of individuals or groups by showing how the intervention fits into, or interrupts, an extended pattern of behavior. The time-series design is particularly useful when the researcher has only one or two individuals to study rather than a large group. "The simple logic of the time-series experiment is this: if the graph of the dependent variable shows an abrupt shift in level or direction precisely at the point of intervention, then the intervention is a cause of the effect on the dependent [target] variable" (Glass, 1988, p. 449). However, a considerable amount of subjective judgment is involved in deciding how much of a change in a trend line warrants a conclusion that a treatment has indeed been an effective cause of an individual's or group's performance.

Choosing among Experimental Designs

The foregoing overview of experimental designs has introduced some of the most common types but certainly has not exhausted the options. Other alternatives are described in the following sources listed among the references at the end of this book: Campbell & Stanley, 1966; Glass, McGaw, & Smith, 1981; Miles & Huberman, 1994.

The task of selecting a suitable design for a particular study involves at least three steps: (1) considering the characteristics of the available experimental designs, (2) deciding whether an experiment will be the most appropriate mode of investigation to answer the research question (or will some other form—historical, ethnographic, correlational—be more appropriate), and (3) selecting a design that will produce the most convincing evidence within the context of the study at hand. Significant features of "the context of the study at hand" include: (a) the magnitude of the educational consequences that can potentially result from the outcome of the study, (b) how much the experiment will interfere with normal events, and (c) the availability of the time, funds, facilities, and participants that the experiment requires.

When judging the likely magnitude of consequences, researchers can consider how greatly decisions derived from an experiment will influence people's welfare and how many people will be affected. A way of arriving at this judgment can be illustrated with two kinds of decisions, the first involving science videotapes and the second involving drug treatments for hyperactive pupils.

In the first example, a high school teacher wishes to assess the comparative effectiveness of two introduction-to-geology videotapes as the basis for deciding which tape the school should purchase. He intends to derive his assessment from an experiment in which one group of students views Tape-A and the other group views Tape-B. In terms of the welfare of students, it likely makes relatively little difference which tape is judged more effective. In other words, one tape will probably not have much more impact on the students' academic progress than the other. Furthermore, a relatively small number of people will be affected by whichever tape is chosen as the better one, for the number will be limited to students who enroll in that particular school's geology classes over the next few years. Thus, the teacher is not taking a great risk with students' lives if he adopts a simple, rather than complex, experimental design. Probably a two-group pretest-treatment-posttest form will be sufficient to suggest which tape is the preferred instructional tool. It is true that such a design will fail to account for a number of variables that might influence students' test scores— such as sample size (the two groups to be compared will be relatively small), distractions during the videotape viewing, and memory loss over coming weeks. However, adopting a design that would accommodate all such variables would entail more bother and expense than the choice between tapes is worth. The simple pretest-treatment-posttest seems to represent an acceptable compromise between feasibility and precision. The results of the experiment will not be foolproof, yet they should be sufficient for the teacher's rather modest purpose.

In the second example a psychiatrist from a university's medical college is cooperating with a large city's schools in studying the effects of three drugs in the treatment of hyperactive elementary-school pupils. The aim of the study is to determine which of the drugs reduces distractibility in pupils, enabling them to concentrate on their school work without suffering such undesirable side effects as drug addiction, lethargy, depression, and long-term memory deterioration. The research team intends to conduct an experiment that can reveal which of the three drugs is best. In this case, the choice of a research design is far more crucial than in the case of the geology videotapes. The final decision about which drug, if any, should be administered to hyperactive pupils could critically affect the academic success and general health of large numbers of children—not only children in this one city's schools, but hyperactive pupils throughout the nation if the experiment's results are widely disseminated. Hence, it will not suffice to employ a simple pretest-treatment-posttest design that includes four groups of hyperactive pupils (one group taking no medication and each of the other groups taking one of the three drugs). It will be more appropriate to adopt a time-series design that includes large numbers of participants that are randomly assigned to the treatments. Adequately assessing the outcome of the experiment will also require a far more complex evaluation system than the one called for in the videotape study. Whereas the science teacher's pretest and posttest instruments could reasonably consist solely of paper-pencil tests of the content of the videotapes, the psychiatrist's drug study requires a variety of measures, including appraisals of hyperactivity (types and levels), pupils' concentration skills, conditions of distractibility, mood (depression, optimism, self-confidence), speed and accuracy in acquiring knowledge, study habits, and long-term memory.

In summary, there is no experimental design that is superior to all others for all research situations. The choice of a design requires balancing costs (time, energy, participants, facilities, funds, bother, undesirable side effects), the gravity of decisions that are based on the outcome of the experiment, and the benefits that could derive from the research results.

CONCLUSION

For convenience of discussion, the approaches to data collection reviewed in this chapter have been presented as six separate types. However, it is clear that in practice those types are not mutually exclusive. One type often merges with another. A case study conducted over an extended period of time becomes historical research. Most ethnographies are essentially case studies. And correlational information, survey results, and experiments can be embedded in a historical account.

Furthermore, each of the approaches may include a variety of specific information-gathering techniques and instruments. Commonly used techniques, along with their advantages and disadvantages, are described in Chapters 6 and 7.

RESEARCH PROJECT CHECKLIST

1. What is the target question or series of questions that my research is intended to answer?_____

2. Which approach or combination of approaches will I employ in my research?
       ___1. Case study
       ___2. Historical analysis
       ___3. Ethnography
       ___4. Surveys
       ___5. Correlational comparison
       ___6. Experiment
       ___7. Other (explain)_____

3. If I plan to include an experimental approach in my research, what form of experimental design will I employ? (Describe and diagram the design.)

(Note: Answer questions 4, 5, and 6 for each approach that will be used.)

4. What specific questions will guide my search for answers to the target question? (List questions.)

5. What sources of answers to the guide questions do I intend to use? (List sources.)

6. What instruments and techniques do I plan to use for gathering information from those sources of data? (List instruments and techniques.)

6

Data Collection Techniques I: Content Analysis, Interviews, and Observations

This chapter introduces three techniques often used in educational research—content analysis, interviews, and observations. The purpose of the chapter is not to analyze each technique in detail but, rather, to describe each type's basic nature, to illustrate typical occasions for which that type is well suited, and to suggest guidelines for each technique's efficient use. Two further data-collection devices—tests and questionnaires—are inspected in Chapter 7.

CONTENT ANALYSIS

As explained in Chapter 1, the process of content analysis entails searching through one or more communications to answer questions that an investigator brings to the search. Content analyses are not limited to written or printed documents but extend as well to audio recordings, still photographs, motion-picture films, video recordings, and the like. In comparative versions of educational research, content analysis involves (a) focusing on educational institutions and their relationships to individuals' lives or to society in general and (b) inspecting not just a single communication but, rather, studying two or more so as to identify likenesses and differences among them. Comparisons can involve documents from different times, different places, different authors, and more.

Investigators typically analyze communications in order to answer two levels of questions—the descriptive and the interpretive. Descriptive questions focus on what a communication contains. Interpretative questions focus on what those contents likely mean. Our concern in the present chapters is limited to techniques of descriptive analysis. Ways of interpreting the content of communications are addressed in Chapter 11.

Qualitative, Quantitative, and Patterning Studies

The three principal descriptive-analysis questions concern qualities, quantities, and patterning. The qualitative question is: Does this document contain the characteristic for which I am searching? The quantitative question is: In what amounts does the intended characteristic appear? The patterning question is: Which relationships among the characteristics interest me?

The Qualitative

Three typical aspects of quality that analysts can choose to study are field-of-focus, reflected attitude, and discursive style.

The field-of-focus of a communication is the aspect of education it discusses. Examples of broad fields are curriculum, school finance, personnel administration, evaluation, and achievement standards. However, the topic of interest is usually only a portion of a broad field. In the area of curriculum, a document may deal solely with the contents of primary-school social studies, with ways of selecting mathematics learning objectives, or with textbooks for college classes in music theory. The analyst's task can involve inspecting two or more documents to determine how they compare in the way they treat the field of interest. The documents may represent different times, different places, or different authors. Titles of studies of this type can be:

—*Different Times.* Changes in the Contents of Chicago's Teachers' Contracts—1936-1996.
—*Different Places.* General-Education Requirements in Four Ivy League Universities
—*Different Authors.* The Objectives of Literature Education à la Steinbeck, Michener, and Stegner.

The term *reflected attitude* refers to a communication's general emotional or judgmental tone. An analyst's purpose is to reveal attitude similarities and differences among the documents being compared. The types of attitudes on which the researcher's attention centers can be reflected in such contrasting terms as optimistic/pessimistic, critical/uncritical, antagonistic/supportive, prejudicial/nonjudgmental, positive/negative, and the like. Studies of this sort can bear such titles as:

—Contrasting Opinions of School Integration Schemes
—Decentralizing Curriculum Development: New Life or Suicide?

The phrase *discursive style* means the pattern of logic by which an author seeks to convey his or her message. The content analyst's task consists of comparing the communication modes of two or more documents. Products of such studies might be entitled:

—Speeches about School Reform: Politicians' Tricks of the Trade
—The Writing Styles of History Textbooks in Peru, Morocco, and Spain
—The Rhetoric of Deception: Rationales Offered in Support of Schooling
  Legislation, 1978-1998

The Quantitative

As conceived in this book, quantitative methods are not in conflict with the qualitative. Instead, the quantitative are simply extensions of the qualitative, representing an effort to determine with some precision (1) the amount or frequency of existing characteristics (incidence) or (2) the degree of relationship among characteristics (correlation).

In way of illustration, the amount of a characteristic could be the aim of a study in Switzerland that compares the quantity of time devoted to instruction in foreign languages (French, German, Italian, English) in the country's various school districts (*cantons*). Or, an instance of cross-national analysis can be a survey of curriculum descriptions in 60 countries in order to determine "official curricular emphases in eight primary-level subject areas (as measured by average annual hours of instruction)" (Benavot, 1992, p. 150).

Relationships within an educational setting can also be rendered more precise when cast in quantitative form. For instance, observers of educational development in Germany have noted that certain alternative, competing types of secondary schools have been more highly favored than other types by different political groups (Weiler, 1983). A researcher wishing to derive a more accurate picture of this apparent link between school types and political positions could do so by analyzing the contents of five German newspapers that represent different political preferences. The analysis, conducted over a period of months, would be designed to reveal (a) the number of articles in which a given type of school is mentioned, (b) the total amount of space devoted to each school type, and (c) the articles' evaluative remarks about each school type (neutral, favorable, unfavorable). These quantitative data could then be manipulated statistically to provide a numerical assessment of the relationship between each newspaper's political stance and its treatment of the two varieties of secondary education.

Patterning

Sometimes investigators are interested in discovering patterns of relationships among characteristics found in a communication. A historian may study the minutes of a school-board's meetings in order to establish the chronology of events in a community's educational development. A sociologist may peruse students' cumulative folders to learn the extent of correlation between students' academic success and such home-background characteristics as parents' education, housing, family size, and available reading matter in the home. A political scientist may compare a ministry of education's administrative-organization chart with a collection of memoranda from different offices in the ministry in order to trace the flow of ideas about a new curriculum plan. A social psychologist may inspect biographies published in *Who's Who* to find the sorts of post-secondary institutions that had been attended by prominent business executives as compared to ones attended by eminent artists, authors, and scientists.

Conducting Content Analyses

A typical process of content analysis consists of five steps: (1) stating the general question that the research project is intended to answer, (2) decomposing the general question into its constituent subquestions, (3) finding communications that will likely answer the subquestions, (4) inspecting communications to locate passages pertinent to the subquestions, and (5) recording and organizing the results of the inspection.

Two common ways of conducting content analysis are demonstrated in the following examples. The first illustrates how educational planning related to the political concept of *self-reliance* evolved over time in the East African nation of Tanzania. The second focuses on references to ethnicity in secondary-school American history textbooks.

A Qualitative Analysis Over Time

The United Republic of Tanzania was established in 1964 as a union of two former British colonies—Tanganyika and Zanzibar. The new nation's first president, Julius K. Nyerere, became the chief architect of Tanzania's development plans. A central feature of the plans was the goal of making Tanzania not only politically independent of other nations—and particularly of former colonial powers—but also economically and culturally independent. The term adopted to rally the populace to this mission was *self-reliance*, with the role of education in achieving the goal depicted in the president's paper entitled *Education for Self-Reliance* (Nyerere, 1968).

Let us now consider the steps to be taken by a researcher who wishes to trace the evolution of the notion of self-reliance in Tanzania over the period 1964-1994 by means of analyzing the content of selected communications during that 30-year span.

STEP 1: *State the general question to be answered by the study.* The general question delineates the principal domain of communications that can profitably be analyzed.

> In Tanzania over the years 1964-1994, how were educational plans and the implementation of such plans influenced by the goal of achieving self-reliance?

Hence, the relevant communications will be ones mentioning the concept of self-reliance and its connection with education in Tanzania during the 1964-1994 era.

Sometimes the initial question is sufficiently specific to serve as the complete guide to the precise information sought during the inspection of communications. Frequently, however, the initial question is too broad to suggest the precise information that should be extracted from documents. In such instances, a second step is recommended.

STEP 2: *State subquestions that identify components of the general question.* The subquestions not only indicate the precise information to be sought in the process of inspecting documents, but they also clarify the investigator's conception of which topics should make up the final research report.

> When did the aim of self-reliance first appear in communications issued by Tanzanian political leaders, particularly by Nyerere in his speeches and writings? How long did the aim of self-reliance persist over the 1964-1994 period? Was the aim emphasized more at one time than at another?
>
> How were the characteristics of self-reliance defined? In other words, what would distinguish a self-reliant Tanzania from a dependent Tanzania? Did the conception of these characteristics change over the 1964-1994 era? If so, in what way?
>
> What role was assigned to the education system for achieving self-reliance? In other words, how would education be expected to contribute to a self-reliant society? What changes would be needed in the existing education system to foster self-reliance?
>
> How effectively was the education system changed into the form that would ostensibly promote self-reliance?
>
> By 1994, to what extent had Tanzania achieved the political, economic, and cultural self-reliance the nation's leader had envisioned? How much could the education system be credited with the success of the plan or could be blamed for any lack of success?

This list will serve as the guide to which contents of communications will be included in the final research report. However, it is also the case that, in the process of an investigator's perusing documents, the documents' contents might suggest additional subquestions that can help answer the researcher's initial general query. Those new questions will then be added to the list.

STEP 3: *Identify communications that likely contain answers to the subquestions.* Guided by the key words *Nyerere, self reliance,* and *Tanzania*, the investigator searches libraries' listings of books, journal articles, magazine articles, and newspaper reports to locate resources pertinent to the research questions. The bibliographies and references at the end of relevant books also provide titles of additional useful resources. The ultimate collection of communications to be inspected includes speeches, articles, books, and conference deliberations written by Nyerere, by other Tanzanian officials, and by outside observers of Tanzania's efforts to achieve self-reliance.

STEP 4: *Analyze the contents of the chosen communications.* Analyzing the collected documents involves keeping a list of the subquestions at hand to guide the process of scanning the pages of a book chapter or an article in order to locate passages bearing on any of the subquestions.

STEP 5:   *Record and organize the findings.*   The researcher prepares 5-by-8-inch cards on which to record notes about useful passages of each document inspected. To facilitate the task of later organizing the cards in useful sequences, the investigator assigns a code to each question. For example, 1stSR refers to the question: When did the aim of self-reliance first appear in communications issued by Tanzanian political leaders, particularly by Nyerere in his speeches and writings?   TraitsSR refers to: How were the characteristics of self-reliance defined? And EdChange is the code for the question: What changes would be needed in the existing education system to foster self-reliance?   As these examples suggest, codes are typically easier for the researcher to recall if they are cast as concise mnemonic reflections of the essence of the subquestions to which they refer. To illustrate, the connection between such a code number as 4 and its intended subquestion is more difficult to remember than is the code word EdEffect (How effectively was the education system changed into the form that would ostensibly promote self-reliance?)

At the top of a note card, the analyst writes the code that identifies the type of material treated on that card's notes.   The code letters are followed by the bibliographic source of that card's material. Usually the name of the author, the publication year, and the page numbers of the selected passage will be sufficient, since a separate card will be prepared with the complete bibliographic reference that will appear in the list of references at the end of the final research report. Beneath the identifying information, the researcher either (a) summarizes the essence of the relevant passage in her or his own words and/or (b) directly quotes an entire passage or a segment of it. Here is a sample note card:

EdChange   Nyerere, 1967, p. 282

Primary school should focus on all the pupils, not just the ones most academically apt.   School should stress skills and values needed in village life so children will learn

"to live happily and well in a socialist and predominantly rural society, and contribute to the improvement of life there."

The bibliography card relating to this note card reads:

Nyerere, Julius K. (1967).   Education for self reliance.   In J. K. Nyerere, *Freedom and socialism: A selection from writings and speeches 1965-1967.* Oxford: Oxford University Press.

Note cards prepared in such a manner can later be organized in a sequence that facilitates the researcher's writing about each of the subquestions. In effect, all cards bearing the same code can be organized in a chronological sequence to reflect the way the concept of self-reliance and its educational applications changed—or perhaps did not change—with the passing of time.

There are several variations of the above procedure. For instance, some authors prefer to take notes on a lined tablet rather than on cards and to place the code words and each passage's page numbers in the left margin adjacent to the notes and quotations.

A Qualitative/Quantitative Comparison of Textbooks

The Tanzania study was concerned entirely with qualitative concerns—the definition of self-reliance and educational provisions intended to foster self-reliance. However, some content analyses center attention on both qualitative and quantitative aspects. Such is the case in a study of allusions to ethnicity in secondary-school American-history textbooks over the three decades 1965-1995.

The five steps in content analysis described for the self-reliance study are the same as those adopted for the textbook investigation. But while none of the steps in the Tanzania example involved the use of computers, the procedures adopted for the textbook project make heavy use of computer technology. As noted at the end of this section, numbers of software programs have been designed specifically for content analysis, each with its own special features. However, the following history-textbook example illustrates a computer application that requires no more than an up-to-date word processing program, along with a scanner and optical-character-recognition software.

STEP 1: *State the general question to be answered by the study.*

> Which ethnic groups were mentioned in successive editions of three popular American-history high-school textbooks published between 1965 and 1995, how much attention was accorded each group, and what was the tenor of the attention?

STEP 2: *State subquestions that identify components of the general question.* As a guide to what constitutes an ethnic group, the researcher first stipulates seven ethnic classes that are defined in terms of groups' ancestral origins, then poses questions to answer about the groups.

> In each edition of the selected textbooks:
> (1) How much space (in terms of words and pictures) is dedicated to each of the following ethnic groups—those of: (a) Native-American ancestry (American Indians), (b) European ancestry (not limited to Anglo ancestry), (c) Latino ancestry, (d) Subsaharan African ancestry (Black Africa), (e) Arab and Middle-East ancestry (North Africa and East of the Mediterranean Sea), (f) Asian ancestry, (g) Pacific Island ancestry.
>
> (2) To what extent is the mention of an ethnic group solely descriptive, with no negative or positive implications regarding the group's rights, abilities, or roles in the society?

(3) To what extent does the attention to an ethnic group include negative, condemnatory evaluations of the group's rights, abilities, or roles in the society?

(4) To what extent does the attention to an ethnic group include positive, complimentary evaluations of the group's rights, abilities, or roles in the society?

In comparisons among successive editions of the same textbook, to what extent did the answers to questions (1)-through-(4) change? If they did change, then in what manner?

In comparisons among contemporaneous editions of the three different publishers' textbooks, to what extent did the answers to questions (1)-through-(4) differ from one book to another? If they did differ, then in what manner?

STEP 3: *Identify communications that likely contain answers to the guide questions.* The investigator telephones several school districts to learn which American history textbooks (a) they currently use and (b) they have used in the past. From the results of this survey, the researcher selects three textbooks that appear to be widely used, then borrows copies of present and past editions from school districts or from a nearby university's curriculum-materials center.

STEP 4: *Analyze the contents of the chosen communications.* To implement the process of analysis, the researcher first enters representative chapters of each book into a personal computer by means of a scanner and optical-character-recognition (OCR) software. The scanner photographs one page at a time as the OCR translates the page's words into the same form that would result if the words had been typed into the computer from the keyboard. However, such a procedure uses a large quantity of computer memory. (If a scanner and OCR program were not available, the researcher could still copy the book's contents into the computer by typing from the keyboard, but that would be a laborious and time-consuming task, susceptible to typing errors.) The textbooks' contents can now be read from the computer screen rather than from the books themselves.

Analyzing a textbook chapter involves keeping a list of the subquestions at hand to guide the process of examining the pages to locate passages bearing on subquestions (1) through (4).

STEP 5: *Record and organize the findings.* There are several ways that the textbook contents, as viewed on the computer screen, can be analyzed and recorded. Which method is best depends on such considerations as the amount of the computer's available random-access memory (RAM), the types of research questions to be answered, and the researcher's preferred way of working. One of these possibilities is presented here. It consists of five phases:

Phase 1: For each ethnic category, subquestions (2), (3), and (4) are assigned code identifications. For instance, the codes for the Native American group are:

NAm-0 refers to passages mentioning Native Americans with no negative or positive implications regarding the group's rights, abilities, or roles in the society. [Subquestion (2)]

NAm— refers to passages mentioning Native Americans that include negative, condemnatory evaluations of the group's rights, abilities, or roles in the society. [Subquestion (3)]

NAm+ refers to passages mentioning Native Americans that include positive, complimentary evaluations of the group's rights, abilities, or roles in the society? [Subquestion (4)]

The same three types of codes are assigned for the other six ethnic groups, so there are Euro-0, Euro—, Euro+, Lat-0, Lat—, Lat+, and the like for each group.

Phase 2: The book chapter in the computer will be analyzed for each ethnic group in turn. First, following the end of the computer's version of a chapter, the researcher places the three codes for the particular ethnic group that is currently the focus of attention. Then the investigator begins perusing the chapter contents. A quick way to locate each mention of the ethnic group consists of using the "find" function from the word-processing program's "edit" menu. When the "find" rectangle is brought onto the screen, the name of the desired ethnic group is typed in, so that each time the "return" key is pressed, the computer will find the next use of that name. The researcher can then read the passage containing that ethnic designator in order to discover how much space is dedicated to the group and whether the contents are solely descriptive [subquestion (2)], or are negative [subquestion (3)] or positive [subquestion (4)].

Phase 3: After evaluating the nature of a passage [in terms of questions (2), (3), and (4)], the researcher employs the "copy" function from the "edit" menu to copy the words, phrases, or sentences that comprise the reference. Once again the "find" function is brought onto the screen, and the code appropriate for the copied passage is entered. For example, when the Native-American passage is complimentary, the code NAm+ is entered, and the computer cursor jumps to the NAm+ location at the end of the textbook chapter. At that location, the researcher enters the copied passage.

By repeating phases 2 and 3 throughout the chapter, the researcher accumulates under each code all of the passages that allude to the particular ethnic group, with the passages organized according to whether they are descriptive, negative, or positive. To make space in the file containing the chapter for the next ethnic group, all of the material under the codes can be copied and transferred to a separate file designated for the group that has just been analyzed. The coded material following the chapter is then erased, leaving room for new codes that refer to the next ethnic group whose passages will be extracted and placed under that new set of codes. This same process is repeated for all ethnic categories, so each group ends up with its separate file containing all references to it in the textbook chapter.

(Note: It is apparent that at phase 2 the investigator may need to make more than one pass through the chapter, with each pass guided by a different "find" word since more than one designator may be used in the chapter to identify a given ethnic group. For instance, it would be well to make one trip through the chapter guided by the term *Native American* and another trip guided by *Indian*. Likewise, in locating references to people of European heritage, it would be desirable to try a variety of designators—*Anglo, German, Scandinavian, Swedish, Italian, Irish,* and more.)

Phase 4: When phase 3 has been completed for all seven ethnic categories, the researcher has seven separate files, each containing all of the chapter material referring to that file's particular group. It is now a simple matter to compute the quantity of chapter space dedicated to each group. For instance, opening the Latino file, the investigator selects (highlights or blackens) all of the material under the code Lat-0 and activates the "word count" function, which yields the total number of words describing Latinos. The same procedure furnishes an instantaneous word count for any other set of material under a given code. By this means, the researcher promptly and accurately answers subquestions (1) through (4). And when phases 1 through 4 have been completed for each of the textbooks under review, the material is available for answering the questions regarding (a) trends in the treatment of ethnic groups over time and (b) comparisons of one textbook series with another.

Phase 5: When writing the final interpretation of the study's findings, the author selects illustrative passages from the separate ethnic-group files to demonstrate the qualitative differences in the treatment of ethnic matters that appeared at different time periods in the three textbook series.

Specialized Content Analysis Programs

As noted earlier, a variety of computer software programs have been developed to facilitate the process of content analysis (Weitzman & Miles, 1994). Examples of programs that systematically organize text for search and retrieval are *askSam, FolioVIEWS,* and *Orbis.* Such programs facilitate searching for and retrieving various combinations of words, phrases, coded segments, and memos. Others not only include code-and-retrieve capabilities, but also permit analysts

> to make connections between codes (categories of information)); to develop higher-order classifications and categories; to formulate propositions or assertions, implying a conceptual structure that fits the data; and/or to test such propositions to determine whether they apply. They're often organized around a system of rules, or are based on formal logic. Examples are *AQUAD, ATLAS/ti, HyperRESEARCH, NUDIST,* and *QCA.* (Miles & Weitzman, 1994, p. 312)

(Addresses for distributors of the aforementioned programs are listed in the section titled Content Analysis Computer Programs near the end of this chapter.)

INTERVIEWS

Interviews are often employed in case studies, ethnographic research, and surveys. Their use in historical studies and experiments is less frequent. The following discussion addresses alternative interview strategies, advantages of interviews, and guidelines for the conduct of interviews.

Alternative Interview Strategies

Researchers with little experience planning interviews are often prone to devise their interview questions in a haphazard fashion, when they would be better advised to design the questions to fit an intentional strategy. The forms and purposes of different strategies can be illustrated with examples of four types labeled *loose, tight, converging,* and *response-guided.*

Loose Question Strategy

The aim of a loose or broad question approach is to reveal the variable ways respondents interpret a general question. Consider, for instance, a proposed study conducted to answer this query:

What diverse meanings do students attach to words commonly used in classroom teaching, and what implications does such diversity hold for the accuracy of students' learning?

Because the purpose of the study is to expose the extent of variability among students' interpretations, the interviewer plans to pose questions in a very general form, offering respondents unrestricted freedom to tell what a particular word or phrase means to them.

What does the word *discipline* mean to you?
People sometimes talk about *democratic methods of decision making.* What do you think those methods would be? How would democratic methods work?
What do you think about *marijuana?*
When you hear the expression *human rights,* what does that mean? Could you give examples of human rights?

Sometimes the issue at hand is not the variability in meanings of terms but, rather, it is the diversity of respondents' evaluations of people, events, policies, or practices.

What's your opinion of Jesus?
What do you think about the American military dropping an atom bomb on Hiroshima in World War II?
How would you like to have a woman as president of our country?

In pursuing a loose strategy, interviewers resist respondents' attempts to have questions rephrased in greater detail, since the intent of the approach is to expose the variety of interpretations.

Tight Question Strategy

The purpose of a tight or restricted strategy is to discover which selections respondents prefer among several limited options. Thus, while a loose strategy features open-ended queries, a tight strategy usually involves multiple-choice questions. This type is typical of the questions asked in public opinion surveys, such as the Gallup poll.

Questions sometimes focus on people's activities, traits, or habits. For instance, a survey of college students' drinking habits may include such items as:

> How often do you have at least one drink of an alcoholic beverage? Daily? Two or three times a week? Two or three times a month? Never?
> What form of alcohol do you most often drink? Beer or ale? Wine? Hard liquor?
> Have you ever driven a car after drinking?

In other studies, the questions concern respondents' opinions.

> Which candidate do you favor in the upcoming state senate election? Drake? Lopez? Martinelli? Johnson?
> Which political party's agenda do you find most appealing? Democratic? Republican? Reform? Libertarian?
> Do you approve of affirmative action policies that provide special opportunities for college admission to students from disadvantaged minority groups?

On occasion, the answers obtained in a tight-question approach are enriched by the interviewer asking respondents to support their decision with a rationale, that is, with reasons for selecting the answer they chose.

> Why do you think Drake would make the best state senator?
> Why do you feel affirmative action admission policies should be continued?

One of the appealing advantages of a tight-question approach is the ease with which the results of the study can be compiled. The researcher's job of organizing the answers merely requires that the percentage of people selecting each option be reported. In contrast, organizing the answers to open-ended questions (including respondents' rationales) is often a complex, demanding task.

Converging Question Strategy

A converging approach is intended to incorporate the advantages of both the loose and tight strategies. The interviewer first asks broad, open-ended questions to discover what seems uppermost in the respondent's mind in relation to the topic at hand. Then, following the respondent's answer, the interviewer asks one or more limited-choice questions. The label *converging question strategy* refers to this funnel-like approach—broad queries followed by one or more sharply focused questions.

Such a tack can be illustrated with the pattern of questioning adopted for a study of adolescents' opinions about what sanctions should be applied to people who had violated rules, laws, or customs (Diver-Stamnes & Thomas, 1995). Each interview began with the description of an incident. The interviewer then asked two general questions: (a) whether the incident involved wrongdoing and (b) what should be done about the wrongdoer. Following the respondent's replies to these open-ended queries, the interviewer asked additional questions focusing directly on specific sanctions that could be applied to the wrongdoer.

Interviewer describes the target incident and asks the first broad question: Here's the case: "In a jury trial, a 23-year-old man was convicted of killing a woman who caught him trying to rob her house in the middle of the night. A police officer who was a witness at the trial of the 23-year-old man reported that the man had also been stealing from other homes over the past several months."—So that's what happened. Do you think the man did anything wrong?

Respondent—14-year-old boy: Yeah, he stole and he killed.

Interviewer asks the second broad question: What do you think should be done about him?

Respondent: I think stealing should be a crime not punished by prison as it is now, but he should give back what he took, or something equal. Like if someone stole a car, and the people didn't get it back for two months, then the thief would have to pay all expenses—like bus transportation—that the people incurred over that period of time. That sort of equals what he took.

As far as killing goes, I think life in prison would be best. I don't believe in the death penalty. Really, the only thing prison should be used for is something serious, like when you kill a person.

Interviewer follows up the respondent's answer: How do you think compensating victims for robbery and sentencing killers to life in prison would help? What would be the aim?

Respondent: For compensation? Well, it's like if they steal a whole bunch of money and hide it and they just go to prison, then get out five years later, and they still have the money they stole. So you shouldn't be able to have what you took. Compensating is better than prison.

As for killing, I think life in prison would teach the person not to do it again. Maybe he'll get some time off for good behavior, but I don't think the time in prison should be less than 15 or 20 years. I think life in prison is good punishment for killing, since he took somebody's life.

Interviewer asks first focused question: Okay. Now, some other people we've interviewed had different ideas about the consequences for the robber. I'll read them, and you can decide whether these are as good as yours. Just say whether or not you would agree with these. Here's the first one: "He should be put to death."

I realize you've kind of commented on that already, but would you want to comment a little more?

Respondent: Well, it's really much more expensive to put someone to death than to keep them their whole life in prison, because of all the appeals. I know some people would like to be put to death instead of go to prison because they'd have such a bad life in prison. Life imprisonment is really like taking someone's life away. Besides, I don't believe in capital punishment.

Interviewer asks second focused question: The next suggestion by others is: "We don't have to decide what to do, since God will take care of it."

Respondent: Well, that's sort of a hard one. (*long pause*) I believe in a sort of creator, but I don't believe that—if there is a God—that God takes that active a role. It seems that the world isn't perfect, and it never has been. If God fixed things, then everything would be better than it is now. So if we just left it all up to an idea—the idea of God—the world would be much worse. We have to decide for ourselves what to do. (Diver-Stamnes & Thomas, 1995, pp. 8-9)

By starting with broad questions, the interviewer optimizes the likelihood of eliciting diverse opinions. If the process were conducted in reverse, with specific multiple-choice options (yes/no on the death penalty and on God's intervention) posed first, followed by general open-ended questions, respondents' answers to the open-ended queries might be influenced by the options suggested in the multiple-choice phase.

Response-Guided Strategy

A response-guided approach consists of the interviewer beginning with a prepared question, then spontaneously creating follow-up queries relating to the interviewee's answer to the opening question. This technique enables the researcher to investigate in some depth the respondent's detailed comprehension of issues related to the initial question. Perhaps the best known version of such a strategy is the *clinical method* popularized by the Swiss child psychologist, Jean Piaget (Inhelder & Piaget, 1964). Piaget defended his deviation from using a single, standard set of questions by explaining that all children do not interpret a given question in the same way. Thus, the experimenter probes the child's understanding and may then cast the problem in a different form to help ensure that the problem situation is the same for each child, even though the wording of it may not be identical each time. In effect, the child's initial answer guides the interviewer in devising additional questions to pose.

A typical interview of this type is illustrated in the following passage in which eight-year-old Per is being asked about some flowers—primulas (primroses) and other varieties—that the interviewer placed before the child. The interviewer's purpose was to discover how Per classified objects into a general set (flowers) and into subsets within the general set (primulas, violets, tulips).

At the point we enter the discussion, Per has already responded to th question that asked her to order the flowers into three levels of classes: ˴ᴄᴜᴏw primulas, primulas, and flowers (adapted from Inhelder & Piaget, 1964, p. 107).

Interviewer: Can one put a primula in the box of flowers (without changing the label)?
Per: Yes, a primula is also a flower.
Interviewer: Can I put one of these flowers (a tulip) in the box of primulas?
Per: Yes, it's a flower like the primula. . . .
Interviewer: Suppose I remove all the primulas, will there be any flowers left?
Per: Oh, yes, there will still be violets, tulips, and other flowers.
Interviewer: Well, suppose I pick all the flowers, will there be any primulas left?
Per: No, primulas are flowers. You're picking them, too.
Interviewer: Are there more flowers or more primulas?
Per: The same number. Primulas are flowers.
Interviewer: Count the primulas.
Per: Four.
Interviewer: And the flowers?
Per: Seven.
Interviewer: Are they the same number?
Per (astonished): The flowers are more.

It is apparent that the experimenter in this example not only was interested in gathering information about Per's reasoning processes, but also had a didactic aim in mind—that of advancing Per's command of logic by confronting her with inconsistencies resulting from her initial mode of classifying the flowers.

As the foregoing examples of strategies demonstrate, it is important for researchers to design their interview techniques carefully to suit the particular aims of the research project at hand.

Advantages of Interviews

It should be apparent that many of the questions in the foregoing examples could be presented to respondents in questionnaire form rather than as part of a personal interview. Distributing questionnaires to a group of participants enables a researcher to save the time that interviewing would require. In addition, a far larger number of people can participate in a questionnaire survey than would be possible through individual interviews. Nevertheless, substantial advantages that interviews provide make interviewing the preferred data-gathering technique for certain kinds of research.

An investigator's taking the time and trouble to conduct personal interviews rather than simply pass out questionnaires to a classroom of students or send forms through the mail suggests to respondents that the researcher particularly values their opinions. This display of sincere interest in respondents' views can enhance the diligence and care with which respondents answer questions.

Furthermore, the interview setting enables a researcher to clarify questions that respondents may find confusing. Interviews also make it easy for participants to amplify their answers or to digress from the central topic in ways that prove useful to the investigator. And interviews can provide an in-depth understanding of a respondent's motives, pattern of reasoning, and emotional reactions not possible with questionnaires.

Guidelines for the Conduct of Interviews

The interview can profitably begin with the researcher explaining the kind of information being sought, the reasons for collecting it, and what use will be made of the interviewee's replies. It is also appropriate to describe for interviewees the method being used to record their responses and to tell why such a method has been adopted. In addition, participants will frequently be more candid in their replies if they are confident that their identity will not be revealed in a published report of the research. Hence, the interviewer's method of maintaining the anonymity of a respondent's answers can be explained. This introductory portion of the session can also include a brief summary of the interview process so the respondent will know what to expect and therefore not be distressed by unwelcome surprises during the session. In summary, then, such an opening portion of the interview (a) honors respondents' right to know what is expected of them and what use is to be made of their statements, (b) attempts to place respondents at ease, dispelling fears about how the interview might threaten their sense of security and adequacy, and (c) seeks to encourage forthright, honest answers to the interview questions.

Here is an example of the way researchers sought to accomplish such goals in the introductory stage of the interview used for gathering data in the earlier-mentioned study of adolescents' proposed sanctions for wrongdoers.

> *Interviewer:* We're trying to learn how young people of different ages think about the consequences people should face when they've done something wrong. So we're asking you to help us as one of the 14-year-olds that we are interviewing. We plan to report the results of these interviews in a book we are writing.
>
> Here's the way it goes. I'll read you a short description of a case of somebody doing something wrong, and then I'll ask a few questions about the case. This isn't some kind of test. It's just a way to collect people's opinions, so you can say whatever you think. We just want your opinion.
>
> I'll tape-record what you and I say so that later I can write down your exact ideas and not make any mistakes. We won't be using your name, so you can feel free to say anything you like and not be worried about who might hear it.
>
> Do you have any questions about how this goes?
>
> *Interviewer answers subject's questions, then turns on the tape recorder and records the following information: the interview number and the age and gender*

of the interviewee. Example: "This is interview number 12 with a 14-year-old boy." (Diver-Stamnes & Thomas, 1995, p. 214)

In conducting the interview itself, researchers obviously wish to elicit the most truthful answers possible from respondents. To maximize the accuracy of those answers, interviewers can try to ensure that they are forthright in explaining their research goals.

Offering Candid Explanations of Research Goals

In some studies that employ interviews, a researcher faces an ethical problem that may not be easy to solve. Such is the case when an interviewee's answers are likely to be less than truthful if he or she knows the full objective of the research. Consider, for example, the following questions that research might be designed to answer:

> In formal conversation, to what degree do students use conventional (i.e. *proper* or *correct*) grammar and avoid repetitious, unnecessary interjections such as "you know" and "like, man"?
>
> To what extent do students reflect ethnic stereotypes in their comments about their fellow students?
>
> How consistently do students apply the same moral values in judging the behavior of their own nation's government as they apply in judging the behavior of other nations' governments (a) in wartime, (b) in peacetime, (c) in times of intense international economic competition, (d) in matters of immigration, and (e) in matters of espionage (spying)?

Because people's replies might well be constrained or distorted if they knew the purpose of the research was to answer such questions, the likelihood that participants will respond in a truthful, unguarded manner is increased if they are unaware of the actual aim of the interview. However, withholding such information violates the principle that subjects of research studies have the right to know what the investigator is seeking to discover. To resolve this dilemma, researchers sometimes adopt such a policy as the following:

> The subjects in an investigation have the right to suffer no harm, including no social embarrassment or criticism, as a result of opinions they express in an interview. This aim can be achieved if (a) information that might identify individuals (such as their names, addresses, or occupations) is kept confidential and (b) in reports of the research, pseudonyms are substituted for institutions, clubs, or locations that might offer hints about the identity of the participants.

Implying Which Answers Are Most Respected

It is not unusual for some respondents to fashion their replies to suit what they guess will please the interviewer. In other words, they say what they think the interviewer wants to hear rather than what they themselves truly believe.

This may happen when a participant estimates that the researcher holds a socially approved or stereotypical notion about the interview question being asked, so the participant casts his or her response to match that notion. Questions of this sort include:

Do you think teenagers should take up smoking cigarettes? (The expected socially approved answer would generally be *no*.)

Should some students be given special opportunities to enter college—opportunities that other applicants don't receive? If so, who should get those special privileges and why? (The expected socially approved answer could be either *yes* or *no*, depending on the apparent ethnic or socioeconomic status of the interviewer.)

One way an interviewer can attempt to elicit forthright answers is to frame questions in a manner that makes each potential answer appear reasonably defensible. In other words, the defense for each competing answer is built into the question in order to conceal which answer the interviewer might favor.

Some people say teenagers should not take up smoking cigarettes because it's bad for their health. But others say cigarettes are enjoyable and help people relax; and smoking isn't harmful to teenagers if they stay physically active, so it's all right for teenagers to smoke. Which of these opinions do you agree with?

Not all colleges use the same policies for deciding which applicants they will admit as students. One policy, aimed at admitting the students who are most likely to succeed in college, is that of accepting applicants solely on the basis of their high-school grades and entrance-test scores. So students with higher grades and test scores are admitted and those with lower grades and scores are not. But a different policy permits a college to accept students who may have lower grades or test scores but who are from an ethnic group that has suffered discrimination in the past. The purpose of this policy is to compensate people from the ethnic group for past disadvantages by giving them a chance for higher education. Which of these policies do you think is better—using just grades and test scores or giving some consideration to applicants' ethnic or social-class background?

OBSERVATIONS

Gathering research data by observation involves watching and/or listening to educational events. The aspects of observations discussed in this section are those of (a) specifying what to look for, (b) determining the observer's most suitable relationship to the observed, (c) deciding when to observe, and (d) adopting an appropriate method of recording the results of observations.

Specifying What to Look For

Sometimes investigators contend that they view each new educational setting with a completely open mind, unencumbered by preconceptions, thereby fitting themselves to comprehend the setting "entirely on its own terms." Such may be the assumption behind the intention to observe a classroom of students "just to see what life is like in such a setting." However, I doubt that anyone can ever validly claim to enter any setting, no matter how familiar or how exotic, without bringing along expectations about what to look for and how to interpret what is seen and heard. The notion that observers do bring preconceptions to each new environment can easily be demonstrated by asking an observer, "What did you see there? What was it like?" The answer reveals the mental set—the type of expectation—that determined which aspects of the environment attracted the visitor's attention. The observer has selected only a few of the myriad variables that could have been noted, such variables as the cleanliness of the pupils' fingernails, the types of wood used in constructing the desks, germs carried by the dust in the air, the size printing type used in the pupils' textbooks, the teacher's instructional methods, and far more.

Thus, it appears desirable for observers to decide ahead of time which features of a setting they intend to appraise and then to formulate questions that target those features. This does not mean that, once in the setting, investigators should ignore other characteristics they find salient—characteristics that can be the source of questions that deserve investigating in their own right. It does mean, however, that observers should recognize that they do not enter educational environments free from expectations, and that is it well to identify what those expectations may be.

The extensive variety of questions that can be answered through different forms of observation can be illustrated with the following eight examples. Each example includes (a) the research question that guides the observation, (b) a suitable method of observing, and (c) a theory or body of information that was at least partially the source of the questions and that will be useful for interpreting the results of the observation.

1. What percentage of class time do third-grade pupils in the Linwood School District spend directly on academic studies as compared to the percent spent in other ways?

   Observation method: Over a period of 15 school days, in a series of observations throughout each school day, randomly selected children are each watched for a 10-minute time interval.

   Body of information: Time-on-task studies (Fisher & Berliner, 1984; Harnischfeger, 1985; Karweit & Slavin, 1980; Moore, 1985).

2. What levels of mental development and initiative are displayed by 10-year-old boys and girls as they solve science problems in five-member discussion groups?

Observation method: On successive occasions, the researcher observes each of 12 discussion groups as they attempt to solve six science problems. The observer tape-records and graphically charts the contributions of each pupil in the five-member group.

Theory: Models of cognitive development (Piaget, 1930, 1969, 1973a; Case, 1992).

3. To what extent do high school teachers hold different academic expectations and standards of acceptable classroom behavior for girls than for boys?

Observation method: Video recordings (taken by inconspicuous, stationary cameras rather than cameras operated by technicians) are made of 32 class periods distributed among eight classrooms (four in charge of women teachers, four in charge of men teachers). The recordings are later analyzed to answer the research question.

Body of information: Gender stereotyping in educational settings (Bennett, Gottesman, Rock, & Cerullo, 1993; Billigmeier, 1985; Mboya, 1995; Shepardson & Pizzini, 1992; Yogev, 1985).

4. How does the cultural history of a people influence classroom activities in Japan, Russia, Scotland, and Zambia in terms of unwritten educational objectives and of teacher-student and student-student interaction patterns?

Observation method: In each country, observers sitting in 15 junior-secondary-school classrooms (five days in each class) take notes on (a) educational objectives implied in teacher and student behaviors and (b) styles of social interaction between teachers and students and between one student and another.

Theory: Children's sociohistorical development (Luria, 1976; Vygotsky, 1978).

5. In their attempt to reach decisions about controversial issues, what tactics do school board members use for imposing their preferences on fellow board members who may disagree with such preferences?

Observation method: While attending meetings of three school boards at times that controversial issues are being discussed, the researcher takes notes about (a) the positions adopted on the issues by different board members and (b) the tactics pursued by different members to impose their will on the group.

Theory: Conflict theory (Blalock, 1989; Burton, 1990; Crozier, 1975; Foucault, 1984).

6. What instructional techniques do mothers of primary-grade children use when trying to teach their children arithmetic and reading skills?

Observation method: In an elementary school associated with a university's department of education, a conference room is used for small-group meetings and tutoring sessions. An adjacent observation booth equipped with a one-way-vision mirror enables observers in the booth to watch what takes place in the conference room without the occupants of the conference room being aware of the observers' presence. Twenty mother-child pairs are recruited to participate in the research on parents' instructional techniques. During each observation session, a mother and her first-grade daughter or son meet in the conference room so the mother can practice helping the child learn simple arithmetic and reading skills. At the opening of each tutoring session, a member of the research staff meets with the mother and child to furnish an arithmetic worksheet and reading book. The staff member then leaves the room. Meanwhile, in the observation booth, a researcher watches the tutoring session though the one-way-vision mirror in order to take notes about the mother's instructional approach and the child's responses.

Theory: Instructional theory (Coker & White, 1993) in mathematics (Baroody, 1989; Cruikshank & Sheffield, 1992) and in beginning reading (Schwartz, 1997; Wagner, et al., 1997).

7. In an elementary school located in San Francisco's Chinatown district, what is the nature of bilingual education; how do bilingual classes fit into the overall social system of the school and of the community?

Observation method: Ethnographers observe classes for bilingual students and classes for monolingual students and they interview students, teachers, administrators, and parents to learn those individuals' perceptions of the school's bilingual-education practices. The approach to conducting observations is explained by the principal ethnographer in the following manner:

> Ethnographers differ from other social science researchers in that they tend to follow a cyclical rather than linear pattern of investigation. A linear design begins with a well-defined problem and specific hypotheses [and] . . . research instruments are designed before the researchers go out to the field to collect data or test subjects. . . . Ethnographers, on the other hand, work more like explorers of a new territory. They enter the frontier territory with only a . . . general goal—to understand and chart the territory. They can only plan their course of investigation in a preliminary way. They may follow a certain direction at first but change course after having evaluated the initial data. They analyze the information they gather to discover new questions and directions for the next phase of field work. Thus the research process moves in a cycle that is repeated again and again until the project nears completion. (Guthrie, 1992, p.178)

The way specific questions are generated from classroom observations in the midst of the study can be illustrated with the observations of recent immigrant children who have come to the school with little or no command of English. As the ethnographers gradually participate more actively in classroom life, they notice that non-English-speaking (NES) pupils often form an isolated group, usually seated together in one corner of the classroom and instructed by a teacher's aide. This observation leads to the creation of specific questions focusing on whether the NES pupils' self-concepts are affected by their segregation, whether they can ever transfer into a regular reading group, and whether they fare better in their segregated group than they would if integrated into the regular program (Guthrie, 1992, p. 191).

Theory and body of information: Ethnographic theories and reports (Bauman, 1972; Malinowski, 1922; Spradley, 1979, 1980; Trueba, Guthrie, & Au, 1981).

8. How do the procedures for reaching decisions in faculty meetings of a typical U.S. American university compare with the procedures found in a typical Indonesian university?

Observation method: An American psychologist, spending a year as a visiting professor in an Indonesian university, is intrigued by the conduct of the first faculty meeting he attends. He decides to avail himself of this opportunity to carry out a study comparing the Indonesian institution and his own university in the United States in terms of (a) the types of issues addressed in faculty meetings, (a) faculty members' styles of participation, and (c) the manner in which decisions are reached. To accomplish this purpose, at each monthly faculty meeting throughout the academic year he takes notes about these three features of Indonesian meetings. At the end of the year, when he returns to the United States, he takes notes about the same features at the monthly faculty meetings he attends in his own university.

Theory: Group-dynamics and decision-making theory (Bacharach & Hurley, 1991; Bess, 1988; Plante, 1987; Uhlfelder, 1997).

The Observer's Relationship to the Observed

When researchers have the opportunity to determine how far they will distance themselves—physically and social-psychologically—from the events they observe, they can profit from recognizing the advantages and disadvantages of different degrees of relationship with the happenings they intend to witness. The above eight examples of observation situations can serve to illustrate linkages between the observer and the observed. As shown in Figure 6-3, the examples can be ordered along a scale ranging from the remote to the intimate. Among the eight, the most remote relationship was found in the case of the unmanned videotape cameras in high-school classrooms (Case 3—Gender expectations). No researchers were present in the classrooms as the activities were recorded, nor did the researchers learn what had occurred until they later analyzed the tapes. At the opposite end of the remote/intimate scale is the instance of the university professor who analyzed faculty meetings in U.S. and Indonesian institutions (Case 8—Faculty meetings). Not only was he immediately and conspicuously present in the meetings, but he was also an intimate participant, directly able to affect the nature of the events he was observing.

Next to the faculty meeting case, the second most intimate relationship is found in the study of bilingual education in a school in San Francisco's Chinatown. Here the ethnographers inhabited the classrooms of the people being observed and conversed with them over an extended period of time. This example qualifies as *participant-observation*, a typical method used by cultural anthropologists. However, it is useful to note that a significant distinction can be drawn among different varieties of participation. That distinction can be illustrated with the Indonesian and Chinatown examples. In the faculty meeting case, the participant-observer was an integral actor in the social system he studied. In the Chinatown project, although the researchers participated in class-room life, they did so as tolerated—perhaps welcome—visitors, but without any rights or responsibilities for the conduct of the social system. In effect, the ethnographers were more observers than participants and thereby would be expected to have less influence on events than would the foreign professor as a member of the Indonesian faculty. But it is also true that the professor was not entirely equal to his Indonesian colleagues, for he did not share their cultural history and thereby would likely bring somewhat different meanings to events than would indigenous Indonesians. Yet, back home in his own university, he would be equal to his fellow faculty members in cultural understandings.

The second most remote relationship appeared in Case 6 where mothers tutoring their children were unaware that they were being seen by observers from behind a one-way-vision mirror. Thus, the behavior of mother and child would be unaffected by the presence of researchers. However, the relationship between observers and the observed was a bit less remote than in the gender-expectations case, since the people observing the mother-child pairs were witnessing the event at the time it took place, rather than later only viewing a videotape of the scene.

The remaining four cases are located near the center of the remote/intimate scale. In each of those situations, the observer was a visitor visibly present in the room with the observed and thus could potentially influence the behavior of those being observed. In Figure 6-1, Case 2 (science discussion groups) has been placed slightly closer to the intimate end of the scale, because the observer of a small group would need to be nearly within the group itself in order to record and chart the verbal exchanges among the group members.

Figure 6-1

Relation of the Observer to the Observed

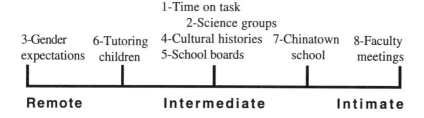

Consider, now, the advantages and disadvantages of the relationship conditions illustrated in the eight cases. The more remote the connection between observers and their subjects, the less likely the observers will influence the incidents they are witnessing. Remoteness increases the probability that participants in the incident will act in their typical fashion. Thus, the observed events will be an accurate sample of the participants' usual behavior. However, in being remote, an observer is apt to miss subtle aspects of events or to misinterpret what occurs. This is where intimacy makes its chief contribution. The closer the observer's relationship with the observed, the more likely the observer will see, hear, and feel the inconspicuous but significant features of an event and will have the background knowledge required for deriving an insightful interpretation of what those features mean. But too much intimacy—too close an emotional identification of the observer with the observed—can damage the objectivity that is valued in scientific investigations. Hence, researchers' hearts may come to control their heads, so the report of their observations may reflect what they wish the world were like rather than what the world really is.

In sum, when selecting a method of observation, researchers can properly include in their considerations the degree of remoteness/intimacy that best suits the conditions of their project.

When to Observe

To maximize the efficiency of the observation process, researchers can usefully weigh the advantages of different times to observe. The available options include event sampling, social-interaction charting, focal individual sampling, time sampling, multiple-scan sampling, behavior-type sampling, and sequence sampling (Hinde, 1983, pp. 37-38).

In event sampling, the observer waits until a target event appears before recording what occurs. For instance, in a study of teachers' discipline techniques, the investigator takes notes about teacher-student interactions only at the time a student breaks a rule and the teacher responds to the infraction. Or in an investigation of pupils' methods of settling disputes on the playground, the observer attends only to occasions of disagreement or debate among participants.

Social-interaction charting involves the researcher filling out a matrix or chart of people's social transactions so as to reveal the relative social positions of individuals within a group of two or more participants.

Focal individual sampling involves recording in detail all behavior of one individual over a specific period of time. Responses of others to that individual may also be noted. Such information is valuable in studies of the pace and variety of the target person's activities, permitting comparisons among individuals as well as across situations in which the person participates.

Time sampling (also known as *instantaneous sampling*) involves the investigator recording every act carried out by an individual during a predetermined time interval. For example, in a nursery school a researcher may observe a particular child at three five-minute time periods during the morning. Time sampling is particularly useful for estimating the percentage of time individuals spend in rather common activities.

Multiple-scan sampling is an extended form of time sampling in which the observer records all the behaviors of one person within a group for a specified interval, then does the same for another individual, continuing in this fashion until all members of the group have been observed. The sequence may then be started over with the initial subject and continued through another cycle of group members. Such a method is appropriate when time sampling for a single student is inadequate for revealing the behavior shown (since it fails to reflect the group's influence on the individual) and when the researcher wants information about a number of students within that same time frame.

With behavior-type sampling, the investigator records observations only when subjects exhibit a particular kind of action. To illustrate, in studying teachers' styles of question asking, the observer takes notes only at the time a teacher directs class discussion or orally tests students' comprehension of what they were assigned to learn. In an investigation of children's humor at different age levels, the researcher records only instances of children telling jokes, teasing, acting silly, or playing tricks on each other.

Sequence sampling involves tracing the series of actions that comprise a given behavior pattern. The observing begins with the initial act of a behavior episode, such as when a teacher begins to explain how to write a business letter or a student at the blackboard starts to solve a mathematics problem. Recording each subsequent step in the sequence continues until the episode is over. Results of sequence sampling enable an investigator to compare different individuals' modes of addressing the same kind of life situation, or comparisons can be made of the same person's modes over time.

Methods of Recording Observation Results

Ways of recording the outcomes of observations include field notes, audio and video recordings, checklists, matrices, and rating scales.

Field notes are either summaries or detailed accounts of events as written during the events or shortly afterwards. In order to facilitate rapid note taking, observers sometimes employ a standard variety of stenographer's shorthand or else a symbol system of their own devising. The notes taken at the time of an event may later be expanded with increased detail and interpretation while the observer still has the incident clearly in mind.

Using audio or video recording equipment can significantly increase the accuracy of observation reports. Easily transported, battery-operated audio tape-recorders enable a researcher to capture interviews in their original form. Battery-operated television cameras (camcorders) reproduce the sights and sounds of classroom activities, faculty meetings, altercations on the playfield, and the like. With the resulting recordings at hand, a researcher can review conversations and scenes time and again in order to verify what occurred and to extract nuances of people's remarks and reactions.

A simple way to record the extent to which selected features appear during a witnessed incident is to prepare a checklist. The investigator's recording task consists of placing a tally mark beside the appropriate item on the list each time the particular behavior appears during the event. Checklists are useful not only for reporting features of incidents but also features of products, such as students' compositions, science projects, social-studies maps, personal-history journals, and art works.

A checklist cast in the form of a two-dimensional matrix can serve for reporting interactions between two variables. In one form of matrix, the names of the individuals in the setting can be listed across the top (columns) and down the side (rows) of a chart. Then interactions between pairs of individuals can be tallied in the cell that is the intersection of the two individuals' names. The number of tallies in a cell indicates the frequency of the pair's interactions. Special tally symbols can be used to indicate particular characteristics of the interaction, such as friendliness versus antagonism. A horizontal tally may signify an antagonistic exchange between two pupils, while a vertical tally may reflect a friendly exchange. Sociometric maps can also be constructed to display the amount, direction, and quality of participation of different members of the group.

Whereas the typical checklist tells only whether an aspect of an event did or did not appear, a rating scale permits the observer to report the degree of a feature in terms of either its quality or quantity. The professional literature in the fields of education, psychology, and sociology contains descriptions of many types of rating scales that have been tested in numerous studies so that their advantages and disadvantages are well known. The professional literature also offers detailed descriptions of how different varieties of scales can be constructed, such as Likert and Thurstone types (Aiken, 1996; Dawes, 1972; Fishbein, 1967). In addition, researchers often devise scales of their own to suit the particular conditions of the observations they intend to make.

Figure 6-2 displays two forms that items can assume on a researcher-constructed scale. The first example illustrates two items from an eight-item device for judging students' speaking skills. The second shows two items from a six-item instrument for assessing the quality of an individual's sportsmanship while playing games.

With this illustration of rating devices, we close our discussion of observation techniques useful in educational research.

Figure 6-2

Two Types of Rating Scales

TYPE A: Described levels of performance

Directions: Write an **X** at the point along each scale line that best describes the speech behavior of the student who is giving an oral report to the class.

1. Logical sequence of thought

|--|

Talk moves easily	Occasionally neglects	Continually begins
from one idea to	to include all ideas	at illogical place.
another. No ideas	needed by listeners.	Omits important
out of sequence.	Sometimes wanders	ideas. Often
	from topic.	departs from topic.

2. Mannerisms and gestures

|--|

Gestures nicely empha-	Sometimes hand, face,	Hands play with objects.
size speech. No distract-	body movements draw	Posture awkward.
ing mannerisms	attention away from	Facial movements
	speech.	continually distract.

==

TYPE B: Frequency of behaviors, plus typical actions

Directions: On each scale line, check the percentage that best reflects the frequency of the behavior identified for that line. Beneath each line are phrases telling how players may act during a game. Write an X in the blank before every phrase that is typical of the player who is being rated.

1. Plays hard whether winning or losing.

|---------|---------|---------|---------|---------|---------|---------|---------|---------|---------|
0%   10   20   30   40   50   60   70   80   90   100%
___Plays hard only when winning.   ___Plays hard only when losing.
___Cries, pouts, or complains when losing.

2. Willingly follows rules.

|---------|---------|---------|---------|---------|---------|---------|---------|---------|---------|
0%   10   20   30   40   50   60   70   80   90   100%
___Makes up own rules.   ___Changes rules during game.
___Angry outbursts about rules.   ___Quits game if dislikes rule decision.

DISTRIBUTORS OF CONTENT-ANALYSIS SOFTWARE

In the following list, the underlined title of the software is followed by the name and address of the creator and/or distributor of the program.

AQUAD: Günter Huber, University of Tübingen, Department of Pedagogical Psychology, Munzgasse 22-30, D-72070 Tübingen, Germany.

askSam: P. O. Box 1428, 119 S. Washington Street, Perry, FL 32347.

ATLAS/ti: Thomas Muhr, Trautenaustarsse 12, D-10717 Berlin, Germany.

FolioVIEWS: Folio Corporation, 2155 N. Freedom Blvd., Suite 150, Provo, UT 84604.

HyperRESEARCH: Researchware, Inc., 20 Soren St., Randolph, MA 01268-1945.

NUDIST: Tom and Lyn Richards, Qualitative Solutions and Research Pty. Ltd., 2 Research Drive, La Trobe University, Melbourne, Victoria 3083, Australia.

Orbis: XYQuest, The Technology Group, Inc., 36 S. Charles St., Baltimore, MD 21201.

OCA: Kriss Drass and Charles Ragin, Center for Urban Affairs and Policy Research, Northwestern University, Evanston, IL 60208.

RESEARCH PROJECT CHECKLIST

1. Do I plan to include any content analysis in my research? If so:

   1.1 What questions will I attempt to answer?

   1.2 What kinds of communications do I intend to analyze?

   ____Books
   ____Journal and/or magazine articles
   ____Newspaper accounts
   ____Organizations' reports or minutes
   ____Personal letters
   ____Television programs or motion pictures
   ____Others (identify)_____

   1.3 For each kind of communication that I plan to analyze, how and where will I obtain the items I need?

2. Do I plan to include interviews among my data-gathering methods? If so:

   2.1 Whom do I intend to interview? How and where will I find such people?

2.2 What interview forms do I plan to use?

____Loose

____Tight

____Convergent

____Response-guided

____Other (identify)_____

2.3 What research questions do I hope the interviews will answer?

3. Do I intend to include observations in my data-gathering techniques? If so:

3.1 What people, events, or products do I plan to observe?

3.2 What relationship do I intend to establish with the observed?

____Remote (from a vantage point so the observed do not see me)

____Intermediate (visible, in the same location but not directly involved in the subjects' activities)

____Intimate (participant-observer)

3.3 What observation sampling forms will I adopt?

____Event sampling

____Social-interaction charting

____Focal individual sampling

____Time sampling

____Multiple-scan sampling

____Behavior-type sampling

____Sequence sampling

____Other (identify)_____

7

Data Collection Techniques II: Tests and Questionnaires

Testing consists of giving people tasks to perform, then judging the adequacy of their performance. The skills that tests are designed to assess can be primarily physical (running, throwing a ball, lifting weights), psychomotor (driving a car, typing information into a computer), or mental (defining words, solving algebra problems, memorizing a poem). Questionnaires consist of sets of questions people answer about their personal attributes, knowledge, or attitudes. Tests and questionnaires are both widely used in educational research, especially in surveys and experiments.

The first section of Chapter 7 describes types of tests and their typical functions in comparative studies. The second section illustrates popular kinds of questionnaires.

TESTS

Tests can be divided into categories according to their sources and their intended functions. The two chief sources of tests used in educational research are formal test publishers and researchers themselves.

Tests issued by publishers are typically of a standardized variety, designed to assess aptitudes or knowledge that educators frequently wish to measure. However, when no available published instruments are deemed suitable for a given study, researchers create tests that precisely fit their needs.

Published Standardized Tests

Broadly speaking, a standardized test is one which has been taken by a large number of people so that the test-makers have been able to determine rather accurately how well a typical student of a particular age, grade-in-school, or type of educational program will succeed on the test. Standards are usually reported in terms of how well "average six-year-olds" or "average 11th-graders" or "average college applicants" answer the test questions. The items on well-constructed standardized tests have been analyzed statistically to eliminate poorly phrased questions and to ensure that only valid, discriminating ones are included. Such tests require a standard method of administration. That is, they should be administered to students in exactly the same manner each time so the results will be comparable.

Standardized tests are available to serve diverse functions, such as those of measuring general intelligence, specific aptitudes or abilities, patterns of thought, levels of achievement, and such personality characteristics as personal-social adjustment, interests, and attitudes. A wide range of tests and related assessment instruments have been created to perform such functions. For example, the Educational Testing Service's test-collection library contains well over 16,000 tests and measurement devices gathered from a wide variety of sources (Educational Testing Service, 1990).

Some tests are of the paper-pencil variety and can be administered to a group. With others, the tester poses questions for an individual to answer during an interview, or else the tester observes the individual perform a task, such as that of speaking before a group or participating in a game.

The title of a test often suggests which function the instrument is intended to measure. Such is the case with the *Wechsler Intelligence Scales for Children, Kaufman Brief Intelligence Test, Modified Vygotsky Concept Formation Test, Scholastic Abilities Test for Adults, Strong-Campbell Interest Inventory, Preschool Language Assessment Instrument, Music Achievement Tests,* and *Kindergarten Readiness Test.*

As a guide for investigators in their search for a standardized test to match their current data-collection needs, the following discussion focuses on what to look for when choosing a published test and where to look.

What to Look for When Choosing a Test

In the process of selecting a published test for use in a research program, three characteristics that warrant attention are the test's validity, reliability, and norms.

Test Validity. *Validity* means the extent to which a test accurately measures the factors that the researcher wishes to assess. Methods of judging validity vary with what the researcher hopes the test will reveal. The following examples illustrate four of those methods.

Achievement. Assume that an investigator wishes to measure how well students have mastered the content of the science class they recently completed. To determine if a particular published science test will be a valid measure for his purposes, the researcher needs to compare the items on the test with the specific content the students studied. By this process of matching test items to the specific class objectives, the investigator judges the *content validity* of the test. The closer the match, the more valid the test for assessing student achievement.

As one option, an investigator could choose to administer one form of the test at the beginning of the semester (pretest) and a different but equivalent form (same content, but different specific questions or problems) at the end (posttest). Then, at the close of the semester, by subtracting each student's pretest score from the student's posttest score, the researcher would be in a better position to decide how much the class learned during the semester than if he had based his judgment only on the final examination scores.

Aptitude. Whereas achievement testing focuses on the past, intelligence or aptitude testing focuses on the present and future. The investigator's intent is to use a test for predicting how well individuals are likely to succeed in some present or future endeavor. The term *general intelligence* is commonly used to identify a measuring instrument whose purpose is to reflect how adequately a person might perform in nearly any situation requiring mental or psychomotor skill. The words *aptitude* and *ability* typically refer to how adept an individual will likely be in performing a particular kind of mental or psychomotor task—or at least how adept the person will be at learning how to perform the task.

Estimating the validity of intelligence or aptitude tests calls for different information than that required for judging the validity of an achievement test. What is needed here is evidence of the test's accuracy of prediction. For instance, an estimate of the *predictive validity* of a college aptitude test can be obtained by computing the relationship between college applicants' entrance-test scores and their later success in college classes. To perform this comparison, researchers first test the applicants, then wait until the applicants have been in college three or four years and have thereby compiled a record of the grades they earned in their classes—a record summarized in the form of a grade point average. The grade point average is called the *criterion measure.* Then the extent of correlation between students' aptitude test scores and their grade point averages can be computed. The result of this computation is reported as a *correlation coefficient,* a single number representing the predictive accuracy of the college aptitude test. (See Chapter 9 for an explanation of correlation coefficients). The higher the correlation between test scores and grade point averages, the more valid the test—that is, the better the test predicts how well students will fare in their college studies. The predictive validity of other types of aptitude tests is established in a similar manner. A mechanical ability test's validity is determined by a comparison between candidates' test scores and their later on-the-job performance as mechanics. A test that correlates +.85 with job performance is a far better predictor than one that correlates only +.35.

Intelligence. The term *general intelligence* typically implies that people with a greater quantity—or a higher quality—of a general mental talent will be more skillful at understanding concepts, analyzing problems, and memorizing facts in virtually all fields of knowledge than will people with less general mental ability. (However, the dominant belief today among psychologists is that what appears to be general intelligence is actually composed of subgroups of mental aptitudes that are only loosely correlated with each other [Gardner, 1983; Guilford, 1967; Razel, 1989]). Among children and young adolescents, a traditional method of establishing the validity of such tests has been to utilize test problems which older children solve more adequately than do younger children, on the conviction that intelligence improves rather regularly with age over the first two decades of life. The test items are graded by age levels— several items at each level are ones that have been passed by the majority of children of that particular age. The assumption is that a child who passes all items up to her age level, plus some items above that level, has above-average intelligence. A child who passes all items up to and including her age level is judged to be of average intelligence (average mental age). Children who fail some items below and at their age level are considered below average in intelligence. A single number, called the *intelligence quotient* (IQ), reflects the relationship between the child's chronological age and mental age. The IQ is calculated by dividing a child's mental age (as judged by the particular test's items) by the child's chronological age (and that quotient is multiplied by 100 to eliminate decimal fractions). Thus, an average IQ will equal 100. Any IQ notably beyond 100 is judged to reflect above-average intelligence and any IQ notably less than 100 is regarded as below-average intelligence (Terman & Merrill, 1960a, 1973).

Interest. The most popular types of interest tests are those designed to reveal which vocations people find most appealing. One method of estimating the validity of a vocational-interest test is to compile the patterns of interests expressed on the test by people who are already successful in their occupations. The assumption then is made that the closer the match between the pattern of test answers of a youth who takes the test and the pattern of successful people in a particular vocation, the more likely the youth would be content to pursue such an occupation in terms of lasting interest (Campbell & Hansen, 1985).

The extent to which a test validly measures what it is supposed to measure is affected by several variables—how clearly the test directions and test items are worded, the time allowed for completing the test, distracting sounds and sights when the test is administered, and more. Certain of these disturbing elements can be reflected in a test's reliability statistics.

Test Reliability. In everyday language, the words *validity* and *reliability* are often used as synonyms. However, in the field of evaluation, the two terms carry different meanings. Whereas *validity* means how accurately a test measures what it is supposed to measure, *reliability* means consistency. There are three main forms of consistency—test-retest, alternate-form, and split-half. One or more of these forms can be reported for a standardized test.

In the test-retest variety, the same testing instrument has been administered to a group on two occasions. The purpose is to determine the similarity between students' scores on the first and the second occasions. Thus, the test-retest method reflects consistency over time. If the students' scores deviate significantly between one testing and another a short time later, the test cannot be trusted as a valid measure of their knowledge or skill. Test-retest reliability is usually reported as a correlation coefficient. Perfect correspondence between a student's success on the first and second testings would be reflected in a coefficient of +1.00. Some slight deviations in students' relative positions from one testing to the next might result in a reliability coefficient of +.91 or, for greater deviation, +.85. Any test-retest correlation below +.85 or so casts doubt on the test's ability to yield consistent results.

Frequently test publishers issue alternate forms of the same test. This can be a convenience for researchers who wish to test subjects on more than one occasion but do not want to use exactly the same form of the test both times, since students sometimes remember specific test items from the initial testing session. An alternate-form reliability coefficient tells how comparable two or more forms proved to be when the forms were administered to a large number of subjects. As with the split-half approach, correlation coefficients above +.90 are most desirable, since they indicate that the students' performance on one form of the test was very similar to their performance on the other form. The two forms apparently measure the same characteristics equally well.

The *split-half* method produces a coefficient reflecting the degree of a test's internal consistency. A split-half correlation coefficient is computed by comparing students' scores on the first half of the test with their scores on the second half. Or, as another option, students' scores on the even-numbered test items can be compared with their scores on odd-numbered items. Thus, a split-half coefficient suggests how consistently a test's parts (halves or odd-even items) measure a particular characteristic.

In summary, the term *test reliability* can refer to any of three different forms of consistency—consistency over time (test-retest), comparability of forms (alternate-form), or internal consistency (split-half). The manual that accompanies a standardized test will often report one or more of these measures in the form of correlation coefficients. In addition, books and journals that review tests will frequently provide data about reliability that goes beyond the information in test manuals. (See Conoley & Kramer, 1989; Kramer & Conoley, 1990; Mitchell, 1985.)

Test Norms. A test becomes standardized by being administered to a relatively large group of people whose scores are recorded and analyzed. This group is usually called the *normative group* or sometimes the *standardization group*, the *sample*, or the *sampling group*. The record of the group members' levels of success on the test are called *norms*. Norms can include such characteristics of a group's performance as average scores by (a) age levels or grade levels, (b) gender, (c) subsections of the test, and (d) special aspects of the individuals' performance (such as speed and comprehension on a reading test or problem-solving and computational accuracy on a mathematics test).

Whenever researchers intend to use norms for interpreting the results obtained in their own study, two questions are of particular import. First, to what extent are the people in the normative group comparable to the intended participants in the research project in terms of characteristics that would likely influence their performance—such characteristics as age, level of education, gender, and cultural background? The expression *cultural background* in this context refers to such features as the participants' command of the language in which the test is written, their familiarity with printed tests, and perhaps their socioeconomic status. The closer the match between the normative group and the people in the intended study, the greater the investigator's confidence that the norms can be meaningfully used in the analysis and interpretation of the scores achieved by the study's participants.

Second, how many people were included in the normative sample? Generally, the larger the number of persons in the normative group, the more faith one can place in the norms as accurately reflecting the characteristics of the population from which the sample was drawn.

Therefore, when selecting a test whose norms will be used in the interpretation of the results of an intended study, investigators can search the test's administration manual or consult assessments of the test in journals and books in order to learn the size and relevant demographic features of the group on which the norms were based. (See Conoley & Kramer, 1989, 1992; Conoley and Impara, 1994, 1995; Kramer & Conoley, 1990; Mitchell, 1985.)

An excellent guide to judging the quality of published tests is the volume entitled *Standards for Educational and Psychological Testing* (AERA, APA, & NCME, 1985).

Where to Look for Standardized Tests

The most useful descriptions of tests are found in compilations of testing instruments, test publishers' catalogues, library holdings, and journal articles relevant to the aims of the researcher's proposed study.

Probably the two most valuable compilations of test descriptions are those found in the periodic editions of the *Mental Measurements Yearbook* and in the six volumes of *The ETS Test Collection Catalogue*.

For several decades the most helpful guide to standardized tests has been the series of *Mental Measurements Yearbooks* initiated by Oscar Buros and, since his demise, have been continued by the Buros Mental Measurements Institute at the University of Nebraska (Conoley & Kramer, 1989, 1992; Conoley and Impara, 1994, 1995; Kramer & Conoley, 1990; Mitchell, 1985.) The yearbooks contain reviews of achievement, aptitude, intelligence, and personality tests written by analysts who have no connection with the publishers of the tests. Thus, the yearbooks' descriptions and appraisals are likely to be more objective than are the contents of publishers' catalogues, advertising brochures, and manuals that accompany the tests.

An even more extensive survey of published tests and related measuring devices is provided in descriptions compiled by the Educational Testing Service's test collection staff. Unlike the *Mental Measurements Yearbooks*, the ETS volumes include no assessments of the strengths and limitations of the listed tests but, rather, confine their treatment to each measuring instrument's name, purpose, contents, types of people for whom the test is intended, and its source. Each volume in the ETS series concentrates on a particular variety of test— achievement, vocational, cognitive aptitude and intelligence, attitudes, affective measures, and tests for special populations. The breadth of coverage is impressive, as suggested by the fact that the volume treating cognitive aptitude and intelligence measures contains descriptions of over 1,300 assessment devices (Educational Testing Service, 1990).

Further sources of test descriptions are the catalogues issued by such publishers as the Educational Testing Service (Princeton, NJ), Psychological Corporation (555 Academic Court, San Antonio, TX 78204), and Psychological Assessment Resources (P. O. Box 998, Odessa, FL 33556). The catalogues frequently offer more detailed information than that found in the Buros yearbooks and ETS volumes. Publishers' materials also include information about new tests or recent revisions of established instruments that does not appear in the above-mentioned compilations of tests.

The appearance of computerized university library catalogues has greatly facilitated the hunt for information about tests. A computer search for names and descriptions of tests can be conducted by the investigator's bringing the library's catalogue onto the computer screen, then entering key words to locate pertinent books and journal articles that likely offer assessments of tests or else contain descriptions of studies in which standardized tests have been used. Key terms that serve this purpose can combine (a) the field knowledge, the behavior, or the personal traits that the researcher wishes to assess and (b) a word that either refers to the act of assessing or identifies the time-focus of the assessment. Examples of words designating fields of knowledge are *reading, mathematics, geography, astronomy,* and *economics.* Behaviors include *verbal fluency, computational speed, problem analysis,* and *eye-hand coordination.* Examples of words reflecting traits are *personality, attitude, self-concept, aggressivity,* and *submissiveness.* Terms referring to the act of assessing include *evaluating, measuring, appraising, assessing,* and *judging.* A time focus is suggested by such words as *achievement* (what has been learned), *aptitude* and *ability* (present performance suggesting future potential), and *prediction* (future performance). Permutations of key words to use in searching library holdings can assume such combinations as *reading aptitude, science skills, appraising aggression, mathematics achievement, assessing self-concept, history tests, attitude measurement, ability testing,* and the like.

As investigators peruse journal articles retrieved by a library catalogue search, they not only learn which tests the authors of the articles used in their own work and how well those tests performed, but they may also learn of other tests that the writers discuss and list among the references at the end of the article.

Researcher-Created Tests

Researchers and classroom teachers produce their own tests when no suitable standardized variety is available. The main advantage of self-created tests is that they can be designed precisely to fit the conditions of the present research project —the project's objectives, the kinds of people taking the tests, and the testing context. Since the most common type of researcher-created test is one aimed at assessing how well learners have reached instructional goals, the following discussion focuses on achievement tests. The presentation is organized around four principles of test construction, with each principle accompanied by examples of how it should be applied or might be violated.

Content Validity

Principle 1: Each test item should focus on a stated objective that learners are expected to master.

The content validity of an achievement test is determined by the extent to which (a) all test items assess the learners' mastery of defined objectives and (b) an accurate balance is established between the array of test items and the array of objectives (the largest number of test items are provided to assess for the most important objectives).

When this principle is adopted, the first step in test construction become that of clearly stating the learning goals. An efficient way to word an objective is in terms of *learner behavior*, that is, in terms of the way learners will respond when they have properly mastered that objective. This point can be illustrated with the social-studies learning goal of "Understanding the U.S. Constitution's Bill of Rights."

The concept of *understanding* can be quite complex, since there are different types of understanding; and the form in which test questions are most profitably cast differs from one type to another. Because the term *understanding* does not describe an observable behavior, it is useful to identify which kind of understanding is intended by wording objectives in the guise of observable acts or products. Consider, for example, the following observable acts, each of them representing a slightly different kind or level of understanding the Bill of Rights.

As a result of their learning, the students can:
1. Select from a list of human rights the ones included in the Bill of Rights.
2. Recite the Bill of Rights, word for word.
3. In their own words, tell which rights are provided in the Bill.
4. Give examples of the application of each right to everyday living.

5. Describe various ways that each right can be interpreted and tell how each interpretation might influence the outcome of court cases that involve those rights.

That these five do, indeed, represent different sorts of understanding is shown by the fact that a given student may be able to perform some of the behaviors satisfactorily but not others.

As illustrations of behavioral objectives representing different varieties of *understanding* in three other subject-matter areas, note the following examples:

Mathematics. Mixed numbers and fractions. Pupils demonstrate their understanding of mixed numbers and fractions by correctly:
1. Changing mixed numbers into their equivalent fractions and vice versa.
2. Discriminating between mixed numbers and fractions.
3. Solving word problems that involve mixed numbers and fractions.

Science. The water cycle (the hydrologic cycle in which the amount of water remains the same but its form changes as water evaporates into the atmosphere, condenses, then falls as precipitation—mist, rain, sleet, or snow). Students show how well they comprehend the water cycle by:
1. Drawing a diagram of the hydrologic cycle, labeling the diagram's parts, and tracing the progression of one part of the cycle to another.
2. Defining the terms *evaporation, precipitation, condensation,* and *run-off,* and explaining how each term is related to the others in the water cycle.
3. Describing the temperature, humidity, and wind conditions that influence the different stages of the water cycle.

Language. Adjectives. After studying adjectives, students can:
1. Offer a definition of the term *adjective* and contrast that meaning with the meaning of *noun, verb,* and *adverb.*
2. Identify which words in sentences are adjectives.
3. Change the form of other parts of speech (nouns, verbs) so they function as adjectives in illustrative sentences.
4. Give examples of common errors that people make in the use of adjectives, such as their confusing adjectives with adverbs and nouns.

The usefulness of casting objectives in the form of observable student behavior can now be demonstrated with the principle of item appropriateness.

Item Appropriateness: Objectives

Principle 2: The kind of test item selected to evaluate for a specific objective should be as appropriate as possible to that objective.

Most test items can be classified as one of the following types: (1) multiple-choice, (2) completion or fill-in, (3) short-answer, (4) essay or narrative, or (5) mixed. Some types of items are better suited to testing for certain objectives than are other types. The following discussion illustrates each of the five item types and suggests the conditions under which a particular type is appropriate for measuring progress toward a particular kind of objective.

Multiple-choice questions. These require test-takers to select the best answer from among a set of proffered options. Objectives for which multiple-choice items are well suited are ones that begin with such verbs as *identify, recognize, select, choose, match,* and *discriminate between.*

Sometimes there are only two options from which to choose:

Directions: If a statement is true, circle the letter **T.** If a statement is false, circle the letter **F.**

    T   F   1. A *felony* is a more serious crime than a *misdemeanor.* [testing for a fact]

    T   F   2. When Indians made villages and grew corn on small farms, they were at the culture level called the *formative stage.* [testing for a concept]

Other times the choice is among three or more alternatives.

Directions: From among the words under each question, find the best answer to the question. Write an **X** on the line in front of that answer.

    1. Margie put $20 in the City Savings Bank. When she took the money out of the bank one year later, the bank gave her $22. What is the extra $2 called?

      ____stock

      ____bond

      ____principal

      ____interest

Instructions: Draw a line under every adjective in each sentence.

    1. The small, blue car was parked near the last tall tree.

    2. The pretty girl who owned the sheep dog really should have won first prize.

Another type of multiple-choice item is the matching variety.

Directions: At the left of each item in Column I, place the letter of the best answer from Column II. Some answers in Column II may be appropriate more than once, and some may not be appropriate at all.

    ____1. Largest city in the United States   a. Washington

    ____2. Capital of the United States   b. New Orleans

    ____3. Largest seaport on the East Coast   c. San Francisco

    ____4. Home of the Mardi Gras   d. New York

    ____5. At the foot of the Rocky Mountains   e. Denver

    ____6. Largest seaport near the end of the   f. Boston

          Mississippi River   g. Los Angeles

    ____7. Largest city in the Western United States

Completion questions. Completion or fill-in items call for the student to provide a word or brief phase that accurately completes a statement or answers a question.

Directions: In the blank space in each of the following sentences, write the word that best completes the sentence.

1. The title for the chief executive officer of the United States government is
   _____.

2. The title for the chief executive officer of the British government is
   _____.

Completion questions are more demanding than multiple-choice items because the options from which test-takers choose fill-in answers must come solely from the test-takers' minds rather than being provided on the test itself. The kinds of objectives for which fill-in items are appropriate include ones beginning with such verbs as *cites, names, furnishes, mentions,* and *quotes.*

Short-answer items. Test questions that require an answer consisting of a few phrases or sentences are typically called short-answer items.

Give the names of the main divisions into which geologists classify rocks.
What is the difference between an improper fraction and a mixed number?
What requirements must foreigners fulfill to become citizens of Canada?
Which rights are provided in the Bill of Rights.

Short-answer items are usually more challenging than completion questions, since the short-answer variety involves providing more information or more of an explanation than do fill-in items. Objectives calling for short answers are those that start with such words as *define, propose, list, state,* and *briefly describe.*

Essay or narrative questions. Essay items call for one or more paragraphs of description or explanation. Thus, they require greater skill than do the multiple-choice, completion, or short-answer varieties because (a) all of the answer options must come from the student's own mind rather than from alternatives that appear on the test and (b) the narrative needs to represent a coherent, logical succession of ideas. Objectives for which essay items are well suited begin with such words as *analyze, compare-and-contrast, describe in detail, defend, evaluate, explain,* and *illustrate.*

Frequently the statement of a behavioral objective can serve directly as an essay item.

Define the terms *evaporation, precipitation, condensation,* and *run-off,* and explain how each of these terms is related to the others in the water cycle.
Give examples of common errors that people make in the use of adjectives, as in their confusing adjectives with adverbs and nouns.
There are three main parts to our national government. Each part has a particular job to do. Tell the name of each of these three parts. Then tell the main job or responsibility given to that part of the government.

In summary, some types of test items measure more directly for certain kinds of objectives than do other types. Describing each learning objective in the form of desired student behavior can serve as a useful guide to the kind of test item that will be most appropriate for measuring progress toward that objective.

Item Appropriateness: Test-Takers

Principle 3: The types of test items employed should be appropriate to the level of test-competence of the people taking the test. The items should be so constructed that the student clearly understands the question asked or the problem to be solved.

Two factors that researchers can profitably consider as they create tests are the test-takers' likely mental maturity and their prior acquaintance with the types of test items they will face.

In regard to mental maturity, it is clear that younger respondents should have simpler forms of test items than do older respondents. Whereas 14-year-olds can adequately deal with multiple-choice items that involve four or five answer options, two-option choices are more appropriate for six-year-olds. Essay questions suitable for 18-year-olds will not provide a fair assessment of the abilities of eight-year-olds whose reasoning abilities and written-composition skills are relatively undeveloped.

If the test features types of items that respondents have not met before, the initial item can be used to illustrate the proper way to answer questions.

Directions: Under the title "Kinds of Trial" you see four ways that accused persons can be tried. Under the title "Examples" you see some examples of different people being accused of crimes and being tried. In the blank in front of each example, write the name of the kind of trial you think the example shows. As a sample, we have already answered the first item for you.

Kinds of Trial

Trial by jury	Trial by ordeal
Trial by a judge	Trial by battle

Examples

judge   1. The king said, "Tell me what the prisoner did. I will decide whether he is guilty."

_____2. A peasant was accused of robbing a knight. To decide if the peasant was guilty, the crowd made him walk over hot coals. If the peasant's feet were not burned, he was not guilty.

_____3. In a basketball game, Harry said that Kent fouled him. Kent said he had not fouled Harry. To decide who was right, the boys decided to have a fist fight.

_____4. In a Girl Scout troop, a girl named Laura broke several troop rules. To decide whether Laura should be put out of the troop, the scout leader chose five girls who were to talk with Laura and then vote on whether to keep her in the troop or get rid of her.

Item Discrimination Power

Principle 4: Test items should discriminate between learners who have met the objectives and learners who have not.
Item types differ in the degree to which students can guess the correct answer without having mastered the knowledge or skill that the item is designed to assess. The chance of simply guessing an answer is reflected by a fraction in which the numerator is 1 and the denominator is the number of options available to the test-taker. Thus, with true-false items and other dual-choice types, the chance of guessing is 1/2 or 50%. A test-taker can, on the average, earn a score of at least 50% simply by blind guess. With four-option multiple-choice items, the chance of guessing correctly is reduced to 1/4 or 25%. With completion, short-answer, and essay questions, the possible answer options are innumerable, so that test-takers can rarely, if ever, guess correctly.

The discrimination power of a test is also reduced if the phrasing of an item, such as a grammatical clue, gives away the correct answer.

____In biochemistry, a particle composed of electrons, protons, and neutrons is called an: (a) quark, (b) molecule, (c) atom, (d) cell.

Other characteristics of a test can also affect how well it differentiates between learners who have and who have not achieved the objectives. Clumsily worded items may be answered incorrectly by students who know the required information but have been confused by the way the questions are phrased.

T F 1. It is not possible never to elect a person to public office who will represent the welfare of the many and the desires of the few.

Completion questions that fail to suggest the focus of the desired answer or that contain too many blanks can also confuse students who have mastered the material.

Poor item: The man who wrote the U. S. Declaration of Independence was
_____.

Better item: The name of the man who wrote the Declaration of Independence was _____.

Poor item: The water cycle_____from _____, to _____, and   finally to _____, then starts _____.
Better item: The water cycle progresses from evaporation, to condensation, and finally to_____, then starts over.

Summary

The foregoing brief introduction to researcher-created tests has addressed only a few of the important features of high-quality tests. Other aspects that warrant attention include reliability, detailed item analysis, testing contexts, test administration, piloting the test, and the morality of testing. These additional aspects are treated in such publications as those prepared by Hambleton and Zaal (1991), Heaton (1990), Hopkins and Antes (1989), Oosterhof (1996), Roid and Haladyna (1982), Thorndike (1971), and Wiggins (1993).

QUESTIONNAIRES

A questionnaire is a research instrument consisting of a series of questions people answer about their life condition, beliefs, or attitudes.

The term *life condition* refers to characteristics of people that identify their status in regard to gender, age, place of residence, vocation, income, education, religious affiliation, ethnic background, and the like.   Such information is typically used by researchers to place respondents in categories that are easily compared, on the assumption that the categories may be associated with the study's target variables. In a project focusing on students' attitudes toward birth control methods, the investigator may estimate that girls' and boys' attitudes could differ significantly.   Thus, it is important to know the gender of each student who completes a questionnaire. But if there is no reason to suspect that a particular aspect of the respondents' status—gender, age, religious affiliation, or such—might be correlated with a target variable, there no good reason to include information about that aspect on the questionnaire.   Questions about aspects of respondents' lives that will not enhance the interpretation of the study's results simply waste the time and effort that participants must use in completing the questionnaire.

The word *beliefs* refers to respondents' convictions about a topic, such as students' rights, laws that govern compulsory schooling, what occurred during a schoolboard meeting, typical child-rearing practices of an ethnic group, or the average cost of attending a college.

Attitudes are underlying tendencies for people to act in certain ways. The tendencies derive from the individuals' collection of values, which can be of various kinds, including those bearing on moral behavior, etiquette, fair play, human rights, financial responsibility, job efficiency, artistic taste, protecting the environment, and more.   Questionnaires are designed to reveal people's attitudes through the opinions they express. A researcher asks for opinions on the assumption that information about people's preferences can help explain and predict their behavior in decision-making situations.   In the realm of education, investigators collect opinions about a wide range of issues—religion in the schools, sex education, how to finance schooling, contents of the curriculum, homework policies, school athletics, ways of disciplining students, methods of selecting school personnel, sexual harassment, public and private schools, and the like.   Questionnaires designed solely for gathering people's opinions are sometimes called *opinionnaires.*

A questionnaire can be administered either as a printed document that respondents fill out or as a list of queries posed by an interviewer, who then compiles interviewees' answers either by writing on a printed form or by recording the respondents' replies on audio or video tape.

The following presentation describes (a) types of questionnaires and questionnaire items and (b) guidelines for creating effective questionnaires.

Types of Questionnaire Items

For convenience of discussion, questionnaires can be analyzed in terms of four item types: (1) dual-choice, (2) multiple-choice, (3) short-answer, and (4) narrative or essay.

Dual-Choice Items

Dual-choice items offer respondents two options from which to choose—yes/no, agree/disagree, like/dislike, approve/disapprove, ever/never. Two advantages of the dual-choice questions are that the items can be quickly answered and the results easily compiled. In research reports, the results are typically reported as percentages—"53% of parents favored the school-bond assessment" or "19% of students reported that they had never tried any form of alcohol." A further advantage is that researchers can include more items on a two-choice questionnaire than is generally the case with instruments that pose a greater number of potential answers to each item, as in multiple-choice items and in open-ended questions that require a narrative response.

One limitation of dual-choice items is that they fail to reveal graduated levels of belief that would be discovered if respondents were able to show where their opinions belonged on a scale ranging from extremely high to extremely low. A second potential disadvantage is that the very ease with which two-level items can be marked may encourage a hasty person to check off answers carelessly without thoroughly considering each item's implications.

Multiple-Choice Items

Respondents can be offered multiple options either as a list of discrete answers from which to choose or as a dimension or scale extending from one extreme to the other.

Discrete options. The discrete-answers type is best suited to situations in which the options are distinctly different from each other rather than degrees of judgment along a single dimension. The first of the following examples is intended for polling high school students' opinions prior to their student-government election. The second is for obtaining parents' attitudes about priorities in the expenditure of funds earned by a school district's parents' association.

Directions: Place an X on the line before the one candidate you would prefer to have as president of the senior class.

____Sherry Bender

____Mavis Clark

____Marquis Lenton

____Cornell Jefferson

Seven uses have been suggested for spending the money collected from the parents' association bazaar, lottery, and solicitation of funds from business organizations. Place a *1* beside the item you think is the best way to use the money, a *2* beside the way you consider second best, and a *3* beside the way you think is third best.

____Cheerleader uniforms

____Computers

____Football uniforms

____Library books

____Resurface driveway

____School newspaper

____Senior prom

Scaled options. Frequently people's opinions are most accurately reported as positions along a dimension whose divisions represent sequential qualities, frequencies, or amounts. The choice alternatives can be represented as degrees along a scale line, as proportions, or as successive discrete items.

Degrees along a scale line. The following examples illustrate two typical forms of researcher-constructed rating scales.

The first, a semantic-differential type (Osgood, 1952), features diametrically contrasting adjectives at the opposite ends of each scale line (Figure 7-1). This example displays the first four lines of an assessment instrument designed to elicit early-childhood-education students' judgments of how mothers interacted with their preschool children as shown in scenes recorded on videotape. The "favorable" end of scales is randomly changed from left to right on successive lines so as to combat any tendency of participants to carelessly mark the same end of all scales on the basis of the response-set they bring to the task, such as a tendency to generally approve or disapprove of the mother in the scene. In effect, students must study every scale line individually in order to produce a coherent overall judgment of the mother-child modes of interaction.

A researcher can later convert the students' judgments into numerical form for purposes of analysis by weighting the seven spaces from 1 (least favorable rating) to 7 (most favorable rating).

The second example (Figure 7-2) shows the early lines of a rating device for collecting parents' estimates of their children's academic potential in comparison with their estimates of the children's academic performance. The researcher's purpose is to discover parents' conceptions of any discrepancy between the parents' opinion of the child's ability and the child's actual accomplishment.

Figure 7-1

Mothers' Styles of Interacting with Preschoolers

Instructions: As you watch the videotape, use this rating sheet to show your opinion of the pictured mother's way of relating to her child. Along each scale line, mark an X in the space that reflects your judgment of the mother's approach to the child.

Warmhearted		___	___	___	___	___	___	___	___		Coldhearted
Patient		___	___	___	___	___	___	___	___		Impatient
Demanding		___	___	___	___	___	___	___	___		Accepting
Supportive		___	___	___	___	___	___	___	___		Critical

Since such a scale yields numerical scores representing parents' judgments, the investigator is able to provide quantitative summaries of perceived discrepancies between ability and potential for individual children and for groups.

To achieve greater precision in the scales they create, researchers sometimes adopt one of the scaling procedures developed by such attitude-measurement pioneers as L. L. Thurstone and E. J. Chave (1929), R. Likert (1932), and L. Guttman (1950). Each procedure requires a considerable amount of work, and each has its own advantages and limitations. Which method an investigator adopts can depend on the aim of the research project at hand.

If we wish to study attitude-patterning or explore theories of attitudes, then probably the Likert procedure will be the most relevant. If we wish to study attitude change, or the hierarchical structure of an attitude, then Guttman's method might be preferable. If we are studying group differences, then we'll probably elect to use the Thurstone procedure. (Oppenheim, 1966, p. 123)

Proportions. Sometimes a scale is not graphically represented as divisions along a line but, instead, as assumed proportions of some total amount. Figure 7-3 offers three versions of the proportion style.

Successive discrete items. What sometimes appear to be discrete items are actually successive degrees along a scale. The items are simply organized as a list or as separate states rather than as segments of a continuous line. Figure 7-4 illustrates two ways such choices can be displayed.

Figure 7-2

Ability Compared with Performance

Directions: Parents usually have an idea of how much ability their children have to succeed with their school work. Parents also have a some idea of how well their children are actually doing in their school work. To show what you think about how closely your child is performing up to his or her ability level, please mark each of the following lines to show your ideas. Each line has 25 spaces representing 25 children in the classroom. Each space stands for one child. Child #25 is the highest in the class in the subject area of that scale line. Child #1 is the lowest. The rest of the pupils are ranked between the lowest and the highest.

Now, to show your idea of your child's ability in the subject area of a scale line, write the letter **A** in the space that you think best reflects your child's ability. Then, to show how well you think your child is currently performing in that subject area, write the letter **P** in the space you think best reflects how well you think your child is actually succeeding in that subject as compared with the other children in his or her class.

The first scale is a sample of how one parent might mark her child on reading.

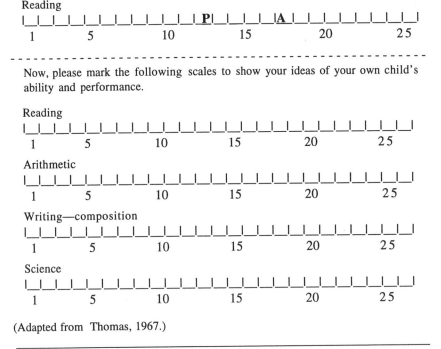

Reading
```
|__|__|__|__|__|__|__|__|__|__|__|__| P|__|__|__| |A |__|__|__|__|__|__|__|
 1        5          10         15        20         2 5
```

- -

Now, please mark the following scales to show your ideas of your own child's ability and performance.

Reading
```
|__|__|__|__|__|__|__|__|__|__|__|__|__|__|__|__|__|__|__|__|__|__|__|__|
 1        5          10         15        20         2 5
```

Arithmetic
```
|__|__|__|__|__|__|__|__|__|__|__|__|__|__|__|__|__|__|__|__|__|__|__|__|
 1        5          10         15        20         2 5
```

Writing—composition
```
|__|__|__|__|__|__|__|__|__|__|__|__|__|__|__|__|__|__|__|__|__|__|__|__|
 1        5          10         15        20         2 5
```

Science
```
|__|__|__|__|__|__|__|__|__|__|__|__|__|__|__|__|__|__|__|__|__|__|__|__|
 1        5          10         15        20         2 5
```

(Adapted from Thomas, 1967.)

Figure 7-3

Recommended Committee Composition

On the school district's 12-member student-discipline committee, how many committee members do you think should be:

_____school principals?

_____teachers?

_____counselors?

_____students?

_____parents?

- -

High School Students' Use of Time

Over the 24-hour period of an average weekday, how may hours do you spend:

_____in school?

_____doing homework after school?

_____looking at television or videos?

_____listening to music on the radio or on tapes or compact discs?

_____working at a job or doing chores at home?

_____sleeping?

_____playing sports?

_____hanging out with friends?

_____eating meals?

_____other (describe)_____

- -

Students' Assessments of Instructors

During what percentage of the time that you spend in your world history class do you feel that the instructor:

_____is truly an expert in the subject-matter of the day.

_____presents material in an easily comprehended sequence.

_____speaks clearly.

_____has distracting mannerisms.

_____holds your attention.

Figure 7-4

Discrete Items Representing Successive Degrees

1. Listed choices:

How often do you come to school without having eaten breakfast?
_____Always—I never eat breakfast.
_____Very often—three or more times a week.
_____Half the time.
_____Seldom—I nearly always eat breakfast.
_____Never—I never miss breakfast.

2. Separate states:

People worry about different things. To show how much the situations in the following list worry you, in the space to the right of each item write an X in the column that best describes the amount of worry that situation causes you.

	Worry a lot	Worry some	Rarely worry
Won't do well in school			
Won't be popular			
May disappoint my parents			

Short-Answer Items

Short-answer items require respondents to offer a word or phrase in reply to a question. One advantage of such items is that they do not restrict respondents' answers to a set of options presented by the researcher but, rather, they permit participants to reply in any way they wish. A disadvantage is that the range of answers may be so diverse that the responses are difficult to classify into categories that are easy to compile and interpret. Yet such diversity may be necessary if people's answers are to accurately represent their opinions and knowledge.

Here are five short-answer questions from a study of teachers' interests.

What are the names of three books that you have particularly enjoyed reading?
Do you read any magazines regularly? If so, which ones?
What are your three favorite television programs?
Do you enjoy listening to music? If so, what kind of music?
What are the names of three of your favorite songs?

Narrative/Essay Items

Some questions require replies in the form of extended descriptions or explanations.

Items calling for descriptions often concern past experiences in respondents' lives or their predictions about the future. The first of the following examples is designed for a survey of school principals' perceptions of their jobs. The second is intended for a study of the risks high school teachers perceive in a proposed policy about expelling students from school.

(1) Describe two difficult decisions and two easy decisions that you were obliged to make during the past school year.

(2) What do you see as disadvantages or dangers in the suggested rules for expelling disobedient students? What do you see as advantages?

Items calling for explanation are of the "why" variety, aimed at discovering the line of reasoning behind respondents' preferences and actions. Such questions are typically asked as follow-ups to another kind of item.

(A) Of the four textbooks you inspected, which one do you prefer?
_____*The World of Mathematics*
_____*Modern Math*
_____*Applied Mathematics*
_____*Mathematics in Daily Life*
(B) Why do you prefer that book over the others?

In contrast to multiple-choice and short-answer questions, narrative items enable respondents to identify in detail a variety of factors that have influenced their experiences and opinions. As a result, narrative responses can reveal the unique patterning of different people's knowledge and attitudes. However, the individualistic nature of narrative answers increases the difficulty of classifying responses into categories that are readily compared.

Methods of Questionnaire Administration

As already mentioned, questionnaires can be administered in several ways. When respondents can be collected in the same location for a period of time, as is the case of students in a classroom, then a questionnaire in printed form can conveniently be given to the entire group simultaneously. This approach not only enables the researcher to collect a quantity of data in a brief period of time, but also to monitor the activity, ensuring that respondents complete their questionnaires independently and that everyone returns a completed form to the investigator. Obviously, people can also fill out printed instruments at their own convenience, as when students take questionnaires home for parents to complete or a researcher mails inquiries to respondents. Mailed questionnaires have the advantage of reaching a large number of potential respondents in distant locations at relatively low cost. However, respondents may feel no obligation to fill out the instrument or else they may indefinitely postpone completing it so that the percentage of completed questionnaires the researcher ultimately receives may be quite limited. This means that the investigator runs the risk of drawing invalid conclusions from the compiled results if the response rate has been low. Furthermore, when people fill out questionnaires at home, they cannot ask for clarification of puzzling items, as would be true if the researcher were present. In addition, the researcher has no way of knowing whether the person who has been sent the questionnaire actually completed it independently. Nevertheless, such limitations often need to be accepted, as many types of studies must necessarily depend on distributed questionnaires since there is no practical way to collect the respondents in the same location at the same time.

The task of gathering questionnaire data by means of interviews can assume several forms. The interview may be conducted via a face-to-face conversation between one interviewer and one respondent. Or there can be two or more respondents present, each asked the same question in turn. However, in any multiple-respondent setting, the answers given by one subject can readily influence the answers offered by another, so that the data collected from one person is not independent of the data collected from another. When several people are present, there may be only one person answering the questions with the others functioning solely as observers. Such is the case when the parent or teacher of a preschool child insists on sitting nearby as the child is interviewed. The parent may then feel constrained to prompt the child, interpret the child's answers, rephrase the researcher's queries, or object to certain questions. As a result, the investigator, in the final research report, is obliged to mention these occasions and to estimate how the observer's presence may have influenced the obtained answers.

During the interview, the researcher may immediately record the subject's answers on a questionnaire form or as written notes. Or the session can be recorded on audio or video tape, thereby obviating the need for the researcher to write down the subject's remarks, since the task of classifying the answers can be performed later when the tapes are replayed. Audiotapes offer the advantage of revealing how respondents phrase their answers, suggesting the feeling tones and sense of conviction conveyed in their voices. Videotapes, in addition, can help researchers interpret interviewees' facial expressions and body language.

Interviews need not be limited to face-to-face encounters but can also be conducted over the telephone or by electronic-mail (computer e-mail), thereby extending the number and locations of people who can be interviewed.

Certain types of questionnaire items are better suited for use in interviews than in printed, self-completed questionnaires. For instance, questions that call for an extended description or explanation are easier to answer orally than in writing. However, multiple-choice questions that pose three or more alternatives from which to choose are easier to answer when in printed form than when presented orally. This is because respondents who have a printed questionnaire before them can simultaneously view the entire array of choices rather than hearing them one after another and having to keep them all in mind while reaching a decision. On the other hand, dual-choice and short-answer items are appropriate in either printed or interview form.

Guidelines for Constructing Questionnaires

Two matters researchers can profitably consider when creating a questionnaire are how to sequence items and how to improve the initial version of a questionnaire by conducting a pilot study.

Sequencing Items

The opening portion of an interview or printed questionnaire is usually dedicated to life-condition information that permits respondents' answers to be placed in categories useful for comparing one class of respondents with another. Kinds of information that will be meaningful can vary from one study to another. One researcher may consider age and gender data helpful, another may value evidence about respondents' ethnic backgrounds and education, whereas a third may deem people's religious and socioeconomic status important.

The patterning of the questions that follow the life-condition information can significantly affect the questionnaire results. Thus, attention should be given to the likelihood that placing a question early in the sequence may exert an undesirable influence over the way respondents answer later questions. Consider, for example, a study of students' opinions of discipline methods used in schools (Diver-Stamnes & Thomas, 1995). The researchers wished to learn (*a*) whether students judged certain acts (such as a nine-year-old cheating on a test) to constitute wrongdoing; (*b*) if that act was indeed wrong, then what consequences would they propose for the transgressor; and (*c*) would they agree with a selection of particular sanctions (such as warning, spanking, dismissing, or humiliating the pupil in front of her classmates) that might be imposed on the transgressor. The researchers then needed to determine the order in which these three issues should be presented during an interview. They decided it would be best to address issue-*a* first, issue-*b* second, and issue-*c* third because:

—If a student in answer to issue (*a*) said there had been no wrongdoing, it would be unnecessary to ask about issues (*b*) and (*c*).

—If the specific sanctions (*c*) were described before issue (*b*) was posed, the specific sanctions might be interpreted by the respondent as representing a correct answer to issue (*b*). In that event, the respondent's answer to issue (*b*) would not represent the consequence that he or she would spontaneously have proposed for the wrongdoer.

As noted in Chapter 6, the term *funnel approach* has been used to describe a question sequence that begins with a very broad query, then progressively narrows the scope of questions to address specific points. For example, in a study of students' health practices, an interviewer may adopt the following pattern:

> In order to have good health, what are the most important things you think
>   people should do? What things should they pay attention to?
> What part do you think the food you eat plays in maintaining good health?
> What kinds of food do you think are most important for good health?
> What kinds of food do you believe are most damaging to health?
> How do you think drinking alcohol influences health?
> What about eating chocolate candy—what effect does that have on health?
> How about french fries and hamburgers—are those good for your health?
> How about milk? How about carrots?

Conducting a Pilot Study

After the questionnaire has been cast in what appears to be a satisfactory version, it can be tested on a sample of respondents that will not be participating in the final survey. The purpose of the pilot study is to discover weaknesses in the questions and in the method of administration.

A typical piloting procedure consists of five steps:

(1) Selecting a group of 15 to 30 respondents whose characteristics are similar to those of the individuals who will be the subjects of the research project. The characteristics are ones the researcher believes may affect the kinds of answers subjects offer. For example, if the researcher estimates that respondents' ages will influence their answers, then the pilot group should reflect the age range to be found among the people who will participate in the final survey.

(2) Explaining to pilot-study subjects that the researcher is asking for their help in refining the questionnaire or interview. The subjects' responsibility will be two-fold: (a) to complete the questionnaire in the manner intended for the final-survey group and (b) to inform the researcher of any problems they encountered in carrying out the task.

(3) Administering the questionnaire to the pilot subjects.

(4) Asking the subjects about problems they may have encountered, such as inadequate instructions for completing the questionnaire, items worded in a confusing manner, questions they found offensive, or too little time to finish the activity.

(5) Revising the questionnaire items and method of administration on the basis of the pilot-study results.

In the final report of the research project, it would be appropriate to describe the pilot study and the contribution it made to the final version of the questionnaire process. However, when the investigation's results are reported, it would be wrong to combine the questionnaires from the pilot subjects with those obtained in the final survey, since the questionnaires and the conditions under which they are administered will usually differ between the pilot phase and the final study.

Pilot studies can also be used to generate the answer options for multiple-choice questions. How to accomplish this can be illustrated with a survey of teachers' opinions about which moral issues are suitable topics for moral-education programs (Lin, et al., 1998). In the pilot phase of the investigation, 25 teachers were provided a list of 20 topics and asked (a) which of the topics they would recommend for use with sixth-grade pupils and (b) their reasons for either accepting or rejecting each topic. The range of issues treated in the list included crime, religion, health, functions of government, sexual behavior, business practices, intergroup conflicts, gender equality, and personal rights. Each topic was phrased in the form of a question or statement, such as:

—Should ordinary citizens have the right to own guns and to carry guns in their cars?
—Women and men should have equal rights in occupations, in religious positions, and in marriage.

When the research team analyzed the responses from the pilot study, they selected nine of the most popular reasons for accepting a topic and nine for rejecting a topic. These reasons were printed in two columns in the opening section of the final version of the questionnaire. Each reason was identified by a code letter. The following directions explained how respondents should fill out the opinionnaire.

If you think a topic *should* be taught, circle **Yes.** If you think a topic *should not* be taught, circle **No.** Then show the reasons for your decision by writing the *code letters* of your reasons on the line labeled **Code Letters.** If you do not find all your reasons in the lists of **Supporting Reasons**, then write your extra reasons on the line labeled **Other Reasons.** You can give *one reason* or *more than one* for each topic.

Three of the reasons supporting a decision to reject a topic were:

A—The topic is too complex for pupils to understand.
F—Teaching this topic would be against the law.
G—Students would find this topic too emotionally upsetting.

Three of the reasons supporting a decision to accept a topic were:

O —The topic helps students make good decisions.
W—The topic is important for the nation's welfare.
Z —The topic is easy for students to understand.

The research team adopted such an approach because they recognized that in previous studies of similar issues, asking only an open-ended question about reasons ("What are your reasons that you would accept or reject this topic?") elicited only a segment of the wide range of people's reasons that could be revealed through the probing that a list of "reason options" could provide. The belief that furnishing lists of likely reasons would be worthwhile was supported by the results of administering the final questionnaire to 140 teachers in the United States and 94 in Taiwan. When offering reasons in support of their choices, respondents did not indiscriminately list the same reasons for the entire set of their decisions. Instead, they provided different rationales for selecting different topics, thus suggesting that they did not hastily judge the topics but seriously weighed the various kinds of values that guided their decisions. It was also the case that respondents seldom cited only a single reason in support of a given choice. On average, across all 20 topics, 85% of the participants gave two or more reasons (Lin, et al., 1998).

RESEARCH PROJECT CHECKLIST

1. Do I plan to include any standardized tests in my research? If so:

1.1 What research questions will I attempt to answer with those tests?

1.2 What kind of test do I need for each type of question?

1.3 Where will I hunt for suitable tests?
_____ *Mental Measurements Yearbooks*
_____ *ETS Test Collection Catalogue*
_____Journal articles in the area of my project's topic
_____Test publishers' catalogues
_____Other (describe)_____

1.4 What kinds of information will I seek about tests I find?
_____Validity
_____Reliability
_____The kinds of people on which the norms were based
_____Other (describe)_____

2. Do I plan to create any tests of my own? If so:

2.1 What research questions will I attempt to answer with such tests?

2.2 If I am preparing an achievement test, how will I state the objectives that serve as guides to the sorts of test items I should create?

2.3 Which kinds of items will be most appropriate for such objectives and for the levels of maturity of the people who will be tested?

____Dual-choice

____Multiple-choice (3 or more choices)

____Matching

____Completion, fill-in

____Short-answer

____Essay, narrative

____Other (identify)_____

3. Do I plan to use one or more questionnaires in my study? If so,

3.1 What research questions will I attempt to answer with questionnaires?

3.2 In what form will I cast the questions?

____Dual-choice

____Multiple-choice

    ____Discrete items

    ____Scaled items

____Short-answer

____Narrative or essay

____Other (identify)_____

3.3 In what form will the questions be administered?

____Face-to-face, one-on-one interview

____Face-to-face group interview

____Telephone interview

____E-mail interview

____Printed questionnaire filled out in a group session (such as a class in school)

____Printed questionnaire that individuals fill out at home

____Printed questionnaire mailed to respondents

____Other (identify)_____

3.4 Do I plan to pilot test the questionnaire? If so,

    3.4.1 What should be the characteristics of the people who make up the pilot sample?

    3.4.2 How many people will be in the pilot study?

Stage III:

Organizing and Summarizing Information

Three ways of organizing and summarizing research data are described in the chapters that make up Part IV. Chapter 8 focuses on classification schemes, such as taxonomies and typologies. Chapter 9 describes statistical techniques useful in synthesizing quantitative data and in drawing inferences from a sample that is assumed to be representative of a population of people, institutions, or events. Chapter 10 illustrates a variety of graphic methods of displaying information.

8

Classifying Data

One of the most important activities in the conduct of research is that of classifying the collected information so as to render the research outcomes understandable. Classifying consists of placing data into categories that can be compared. The purpose of this chapter is to introduce key features of classification schemes and to illustrate the application of different schemes in various research projects. The early portion of the chapter addresses: (a) characteristics of classification systems, (b) how and when, in the process of conducting research, classes are established, and (c) how data can be reliably assigned to categories. The latter portion of the chapter contains examples of diverse classification schemes employed in typical research projects.

CLASSIFYING INFORMATION

One of the most fundamental attributes of human thought is people's propensity to arrange their experiences in terms of categories or classes. By assigning happenings to categories, we render events comprehensible by revealing how they are similar to, and different from, other events. Classifying people, objects, and incidents enables people to compare and contrast experiences and thereby construct an orderly mental map of reality that assists them in coping with the demands of their lives. And certainly classification is the essence of comparative education.

The tendency—indeed, the necessity—for people to classify experiences derives at least partly from the limited capacity of the human mind to simultaneously contemplate a multitude of variables.

How many comparisons can be assimilated by those who seek an understanding of the patterns of comparisons? Writers on psychology such as Nobel laureate Herbert Simon believe that humans can simultaneously consider only a few items of information, perhaps fewer than four (depending partly on [how much is compressed into a comprehensible "chunk" of information]). For this reason, humans employ categorical ideas to think efficiently about what would be overly complex. (Walberg, Zhang, & Daniel, 1994, p. 80)

It appears that most of the classifying people do is automatic and subliminal rather than conscious and intentional. In other words, the act of relegating the content of events to mental categories usually is performed below the threshold of consciousness. However, as children grow up, and especially as they pursue formal education, the task of classifying becomes increasingly deliberate. Formal education to a great degree consists of teaching diverse styles of classifying so that happenings can be compared in useful ways.

Every comparative-education study involves classes, whether intuitive—and perhaps hardly recognized as classes by the researcher—or intentionally designed. Intentionally designed categories are much to be preferred, since they are under the investigator's conscious control. In contrast to intuitive and unrecognized categories, intentional classes can be precisely defined, the nature of the categories can be readily explained to the researcher's audience, and a system can be devised for accurately determining what sorts of data should be placed in which categories.

The practice of mentally categorizing observations has apparently been a natural human function from earliest times. However, the business of rationally devising formal systems for classifying events is of more recent vintage. The science of classification, often called *taxonomy* or *systematics*, probably originated with the ancient Greeks, brought to fruition during the fourth century B.C.E. in the works of Plato and his student Aristotle. The product of systematics can be referred to as a *taxonomy* or, alternatively, as a *typology, classification scheme,* or *codification system.* In the field of biology, the theory of evolution proposed by Charles Darwin (1809-1892) is a taxonomy for codifying the patterns in which the earth's multitude of life forms descended from common beginnings over eons of time. In chemistry, Dimitri Mendeleyev (1834-1907) created the periodic table, a taxonomic system that not only equips chemists to classify known chemical elements but also to predict properties of as-yet-undiscovered elements. In education, the taxonomy of educational objectives described in this book's opening chapter allows researchers to compare educational aims in terms of selected distinguishing features (Bloom, 1956). The cube introduced in Chapter 2 enables people to classify any educational-research proposal in terms of its geographical/locational level, nonlocational demographic features, and influential aspects of the education system and of the society (Bray & Thomas, 1995).

Three characteristics of classification systems discussed in the following pages include (a) their sources, (b) decisions about when to establish classes, and (c) assigning data to categories.

Sources of Typologies

The sources of a researcher's classification scheme can be (a) someone else's theory or typology, (b) someone else's scheme as modified by the researcher, or (c) a system created entirely by the researcher herself or himself.

Adopting Someone Else's Scheme

The taxonomy of children's stages of intellectual development proposed by the Swiss psychologist, Jean Piaget, is an example of a classification scheme subsequently applied by scores of other researchers. Piaget identified four major stages of mental growth between early infancy and later adolescence—sensorimotor period (birth to age 2), preoperational-thought period (ages 2-7), concrete-operations period (ages 7-11), and formal-operations period (ages 11-15). He also located substages within certain periods (Piaget & Inhelder, 1969). A host of other researchers have found Piaget's system useful for classifying the intellectual performance of diverse kinds of children in different societies, on different tasks, and under various experimental conditions.

Modifying a Scheme

Frequently an investigator alters an existing taxonomic system to suit the needs of a particular research question or population of subjects. For instance, Piaget's four-stage classification system was changed in several ways by Case (1992), by Fischer (1980), and by Mounoud (1986) as they analyzed children's performance on the tasks posed in those three authors' own studies.

An even more radical alteration of Piaget's development hierarchy was introduced by Kohlberg when he created a taxonomy of the development of moral reasoning among children and adolescents. In Kohlberg's typology, three major stages of development were each divided into a pair of substages so as to form a six-step hierarchy (Kohlberg, 1984). The steps ranged from reasoning at the lowest stage (as founded on self-centered hedonism) to reasoning at the highest stage (as founded on principles of objective, even-handed justice).

Creating a New Scheme

Investigators can devise their own classification plan if they fail to find an existing system that fits the requirements of their research question. An example is the taxonomy created to guide the selection of curriculum content regarding indigenous Samoan culture for use in the schools of American Samoa. The research question was: What will be the most appropriate curriculum contents for teaching Samoan culture to Samoan children and youths in a school system that has focused mainly on curricula imported from the United States? To answer this question, a team of seven Samoan educators and a research consultant from the United States pored over books about Samoan culture and discussed daily life in Samoan villages. From their analysis of the resulting material, they extracted eleven categories of culture that they believed would provide students with a multifaceted view of traditional Samoan life. The eleven concerned (1) the society's long-established, chieftain-centered social system, (2) methods of governance in the islands over the past two centuries, (3) material culture (housing, tools, boats, etc.), (4) occupations, (5) the oral arts, music, and dance, (6) religious beliefs and practices, (7) ceremonies, (8) games, sports, recreation, entertainment, (9) land animals, birds, fish, sea animals, (10) plant life, and (11) significant non-living elements of the environment (the ocean, mountains, rain, etc.).

Within each of these major classes, three principal subcategories were defined: (a) types of products or activities under a particular major class, (b) significant characteristics of each of those types, and (c) how the types changed with the passing of time. As a further substep, significant types were identified. The form of the resulting scheme can be illustrated with the items under major-category 5: oral arts, music, and dance.

5.1 Types of artistic expression
    5.1.1 Stories and legends
    5.1.2 Poems
    5.1.3 Songs
    5.1.4 Proverbs
    5.1.5 Riddles
    5.1.6 Recitations of chieftain-title lineage (*faalupega*)
    5.1.7 Instrumental music
    5.1.8 Dances
5.2 The following characteristics of each type listed under 5.1
    5.2.1 Its name and varieties
    5.2.2 Its likely origins
    5.2.3 Its function in Samoan society and in the lives of individuals
    5.2.4 Who created it
    5.2.5 Occasions on which it was performed
    5.2.6 Who performed it, and how performers obtained their training
    5.2.7 What standards were used to determine the:
        5.2.7.1 Structure or form of the particular type
        5.2.7.2 Quality of such an art work or its performance (For example, what characteristics cause a story to be judged excellent or of poor quality?)
5.3 How the art types under 5.1 have changed over time (such as by the influence of foreign cultures or local innovators, when, and why) (Thomas, 1974, pp. 51-52)

When to Establish Classes

For convenience of presentation, I have located this chapter on codification systems to follow the data-collection chapters. However, it should be apparent that the choice of classes can also occur at other stages of the research process. In fact, class selection begins with the initial statement of the research question when the investigator delineates the phenomena that come within the purview of the intended study. Proposing to compare methods of financing education in France, Germany, and Italy implies that those three nations will form one set of classes, and alternative methods of finance will comprise a second cluster that interacts with the three nation categories. In addition, a further set of classes focusing on causes is implied if the research question is stated as: What are the similarities and differences in the methods of financing education in France, Germany, and Italy, and what factors account for such similarities and differences?

Whereas certain ways that data will be codified can be specified in the early stages of a project, others will not be identified until during or after the data have been collected. Consider, for instance, Johnston's (1988) investigation of the moral reasoning of adolescents who were asked to offer solutions to the central problems in two of Aesop's fables (*The Porcupine and the Moles* and *The Dog in the Manger*). The intent of the study was to gather evidence for assessing the validity of Gilligan's contention that Kohlberg's six-stage hierarchy of moral development, which focuses on *justice* as the basis for moral decisions, is appropriate for males but not for females. Gilligan's research (1982) had led her to conclude that while males tend to base their moral decisions on concepts of *justice*, females tend to found their judgments on concepts of *compassionate caring*. Kohlberg's justice-and-rights orientation holds that everyone should be treated the same under the law. Gilligan's care-and-response orientation holds that feelings of compassion for the plight of the people involved in moral conflicts should take precedence over even-handed justice in solving moral dilemmas. As Johnston prepared to test Gilligan's proposal, she already had two sets of classes into which adolescents' responses to the fables would be placed: (a) the two gender categories (girl/boy) and (b) the two moral-orientation categories (justice/care). Then, to obtain 60 adolescents to participate in her study, she recruited a group of volunteers from the sixth grade of two elementary schools and another group from the sophomore class of a high school. Thus, she had now added two age categories (11-year-olds and 15-year-olds) to her classification system. Subsequently, after collecting all 60 students' solutions to the fables' dilemmas, Johnston discovered that not all of the participants' answers fit neatly into either the justice category or the caring category. Some answers included an equal measure of justice and caring, so Johnston created a new category to accommodate answers focusing on both justice and caring. Furthermore, a few responses failed to fit any of the three categories, so those answers were relegated to another class entitled *uncodable,* "which meant the answer did not clearly represent any identified logic" (Johnston, 1988, p. 54).

So it is that decisions about how to classify information can be made at various junctures of the research process, from the very beginning through the act of placing the collected data into appropriate categories.

Assigning Data to Categories

If the research outcomes are to provide accurate answers to research questions, then the classification categories must be defined precisely enough to enable any reasonably-informed judge to place data in their proper locations. Some types of categories are easy to define and recognize. Such is the case with divisions based on gender, age, time interval (year, decade, century), place (school, city, nation), and measures that result in definite quantities (heights, test scores, days absent from school). Any errors made in placing data in their proper categories are the result of carelessness of the people doing the placing, not the result of imprecise definitions.

However, the distinctions among categories designed for certain other variables are not so obvious, so that codifiers are quite apt to disagree about where a particular response or observation deserves to be located. Consider, for example, the task of assigning students' answers to the justice and caring categories in Johnston's Aesop's fables study. When students were asked about the moral problem embedded in each fable, they could reply in any way they chose. It then became the researcher's task to extract from students' replies (some of which were quite complex) the portions that seemed to reflect either a justice attitude or a caring viewpoint—or both, or neither. Such judgments on the part of the researcher could involve a substantial measure of subjectivity which might result in one person coding data into different categories than did another. The greater the amount of subjective opinion involved in the coding process, the less trustworthy are the reported outcomes of the research. Three of the ways investigators seek to increase the accuracy of assigning data to categories are those of (a) defining each class in a manner that clearly distinguishes it from any other class, (b) accompanying each definition with examples of the sorts of data (such as the students' replies in the Johnston study) that belong in that category, and (c) conducting training sessions for the people who will do the coding.

Thus, just as researchers should be concerned about the reliability of tests (internal, split-half, alternate-form consistency), so also they should be concerned about consistency in classifying data. The issue of interest here is reflected in two questions.

The first question concerns the *successive-judgments reliability* of researcher decisions. Specifically, to what extent does the researcher place a particular kind of observation or response consistently in the same category? Imagine that a teacher is judging how logically students' argue their case in essays they have written about human rights. The teacher has established five categories of logic in which to locate students' arguments—*superior, above average, moderate, below average,* and *very poor.* Her appraisal technique is deemed perfect in terms of successive-judgments reliability if, when she reevaluates the essays this week, she gives each one exactly the same rating that she gave it last week. In effect, her method is 100% reliable. However, such an outcome would be quite unusual. Studies of such matters have shown that raters' successive judgments of narrative data (essays, letters, descriptive oral responses, and the like) are often quite inconsistent.

The second question concerns *interrater reliability:* To what extent do two or more judges agree on where to locate a particular observation or response? If multiple judges are in substantial agreement about the placement of data, then the definitions of categories and the training of judges are considered trustworthy. A typical way to assess interrater reliability is to have two or more raters independently classify the same data (narrative answers to questions) into the study's categories. The interrater reliability is then reported as the percent of times the coders' judgments matched. In the Aesop's fables project, Johnston reported intercoder reliability for two raters as 100% agreement on coding students' solutions to *The Dog in the Manger* story and of 90% agreement on coding solutions to *The Porcupine and the Moles* fable (Johnston, 1988, p. 54).

We would hope that when Johnston's coders received copies of students' responses, the copies did not include information about each student's gender, because providing gender information could conceivably bias the raters' judgments. It seems likely that when Johnston launched her project, she was already favorably disposed to Gilligan's hypothesis about differences between females and males, for Johnston conducted her project in Boston, adjacent to Gilligan's academic base (Harvard University) and Johnston's study was published in a book edited by Gilligan and associates. Hence, if Johnston's coders did know the gender of a student whose protocol they were judging, they could be inclined—intentionally or not—to make the coding of answers support the Gilligan hypothesis. Consequently, if raters' assignment of data to classes is to be not only reliable but also valid, it is important that the raters be obliged to make "blind" judgments, that is, to reach decisions unmarred by information that could compromise the objectivity of those decisions.

ILLUSTRATIVE CATEGORIES

The purpose of this second section of the chapter is to identify diverse modes of classifying information found in representative studies. The studies illustrate seven different bases for classifying data. It should be clear that these seven represent only a few among many classification systems that researchers have used.

To render the studies convenient to compare, I have described each in terms of its central theme, sources of data, types of data collected, and classification scheme.

Chronological Categories

The most common way of ordering information in historical studies is by successive time periods; and within each period, subcategories may be identified. Sometimes the subcategories are identical from one epoch to another. For example, within each period an author may provide data on the numbers and types of schools, their enrollments, their sponsoring organizations, and relevant economic and political conditions in the society. In other instances, the subcategories in one era will differ somewhat from those in others. One period may feature the effect on education of a current war and economic problems whereas another may stress student unrest and new curricula in the schools.

In the first of two illustrative cases, each chronological period focuses on key people and events in the development of international comparisons of educational achievement. In the second example, values education in Russia is described for two time periods: (a) the 70-year era of communist hegemony and (b) the recent period following the introduction of *perestroika.*

CASE 1: The opening chapter of a volume entitled *Monitoring the Standards of Education* furnishes a historical background against which the contents of the remainder of the book can be viewed (Husén & Tuijnman, 1994).

Sources of data: (a) Content analyses of books, journal articles, and government reports of international assessments of educational achievement and (b) the authors' personal recollections as participants in international evaluation projects.

Types of data: Names and contributions of individuals, groups, and organizations that played key roles in the development of international evaluation activities from the 1930s into the 1990s.

Classification scheme: The five major categories are labeled "the early days" (1930s-1950s), "the 1960s," "the 1970s," "the 1980s," and "prospects for the 1990s and beyond."

CASE 2: In a journal article entitled "Russian Education after Perestroika: The Search for New Values," the vice president of the Russian Academy of Education, Nikolai D. Nikandrov, described changes in values education before and after the demise of the USSR's communist regime (Nikandrov, 1995).

Sources of data: (a) Content analyses of newspaper articles, history books, and government directives bearing on education, (b) public opinion surveys, and (b) the author's direct observations of events from his key position in the Russian education system.

Types of data: Educational policies regarding the aims and methods of values education, the political sources of such policies, the effects of those policies on students' learning, changes in people's attitudes since the end of the USSR, and effects of such changes on enrollments in different types of higher education.

Classification scheme: The author divided his presentation of data into three categories: (a) the historical background of values and education in the USSR—1920-1989, (b) changes in value commitments in Russia during and following the period of perestroika introduced by Mikhail Gorbachev in 1989, and (c) post-1989 attitude changes in Russian society along with educational implications of those changes.

Process Categories

The process through which an educational activity or social event progresses can provide categories into which data are placed.

In *Monitoring the Standards of Education*, one chapter inspected ways of checking on the performance of education systems in a variety of nations (Postlethwaite, 1994).

Sources of data: (a) Personal observations as a consultant to diverse nations' ministries of education and (b) content analyses of journal articles and books reporting evaluations of education systems in different countries.

Types of data: Reports of methods used in periodic assessments of how well nations' schools and their students have met performance criteria.

Classification scheme: The researcher divided the schooling process into three phases: (a) inputs into schools, (b) processes in schools, and (c) outcomes and outputs. Each of these major categories was defined in terms of its constituent subcategories. For example, the subcategories under "processes in schools" were: teacher time (teacher work load or time spent in class), curriculum, opportunity for students to learn, time allocation (number of hours each week devoted to each subject), how the school is organized, and methods of school inspection (supervision).

Stage Categories

The development of people, institutions, and social movements is often conceived as a series of progressive stages to be used in classifying individuals, institutions, social movements, or socio-political systems. Piaget's portrayal of children's intellectual growth and Kohlberg's version of moral-reasoning styles are both ways of categorizing human development. Karl Marx proposed a three-stage scheme for classifying the evolution of societies' political-economic systems (feudalism, capitalism, state socialism) and of those systems' educational institutions. Walberg, Zhang, and Daniel (1994) performed a complex statistical analysis of 139 variables—"world education indicators"—for 164 countries in order to generate a taxonomy that permits nations' education systems to be "parsimoniously and discretely clustered into three major groups" that reflect stages in societies' socio-political development.

Group A consists of 49 underdeveloped countries, largely in Africa.

Group B is composed of 79 functional democracies, mostly in Asia, Europe, Oceania, and North and South America.

Group C includes 36 post-industrial democracies in Northern Europe and North America.

A further development example is Beeby's (1966) evolutionary taxonomy for analyzing the nature of change in education systems:

In *The Quality of Education in Developing Countries,* Beeby asserted that school systems pass through four discrete qualitative stages whose identifying characteristics are determined to a great extent by teachers' levels of general education and by their professional training.

Sources of data: (a) The analysis of books and journal articles that describe education in developing nations and (b) the author's direct observations of educational practices in a variety of nations in which he conducted research and served as a consultant on educational matters.

Types of data: Descriptions of teaching practices in the schools of developing societies, analyses of change processes in such schools, and information about the levels of teachers' general education and professional training.

Classification scheme: Four stages of development and the teacher and school-system characteristics that Beeby identified are summarized in Table 8-1.

Problem-Centered Categories

In problem-centered research, the chief classes of data are the problems the author has identified. Frequently the problem categories are accompanied by solution categories, as in the following example.

The book *Lives in the Balance—Youth, Poverty, and Education in Watts* describes the living conditions and educational experiences of students in a Los Angeles inner-city high school (Diver-Stamnes, 1995).

Sources of data: (a) Observations of students and their living conditions, (b) interviews with students and school personnel, and (c) content analyses of books, journal articles, newspapers, and television news reports.

Types of data: The author, a high school teacher and counselor, assumed the role of participant-observer as she witnessed her students' behavior, talked with them about events in their lives, and maintained a log of what she learned from those encounters. From her notes she extracted a series of problem conditions that seemed to contribute to adolescents' academic and personal-social difficulties. To provide a comparative context within which to interpret her observations, she analyzed the contents of books and journal articles bearing on the identified problem conditions.

Table 8-1

Stages in the Evolution of Schools' Approaches to Instruction

Stage Title	Instructional Mode	Teachers' Characteristics
Dame school	Unorganized, meaningless symbols, very narrow subject content, very low achievement standards	Limited education, no training in teaching methods
Formalist school	Highly structured, symbols with limited meaning, rigid syllabus, rote memorization	Limited education, but some training in teaching techniques
Transition school	Highly organized, less restrictive syllabi and textbooks, more emphasis on meaning	Better general education, more training in methods of teaching
Meaningful teaching	Stress on meaning and understanding, richer curriculum offerings, wider range of methods, problem solving and creativity emphasized	Good general education, well trained in teaching methods

(Adapted from Beeby, 1966)

Classification scheme: The author adopted two sorts of categories—problems and potential solutions. The problem categories into which she fitted data (events from students' lives) were: academic performance, family life, street gangs, substance abuse, malnutrition, and unsanitary and unsafe environments. The solutions categories were similar: academic performance, family life, gangs, substance abuse, stress, premature mortality, joblessness, and needed services.

Paired-Contrasts Categories

Researchers frequently classify data in terms of two contrasting attributes—male/female, public/private, urban/rural, developed nation/developing nation, and such. Sometimes more than one pair of contrasting viewpoints are adopted by an author, as demonstrated in Ishumi's (1992) choosing two pairs of opposing viewpoints for organizing his analysis of ethnocentrism in African schools.

The book chapter entitled "Colonial Forces and Ethnic Resistance in African Education" is a historical study of conceptions of culture in colonial and post-colonial Africa.

Sources of data: Content analyses of selected historical accounts from the 19th century through most of the 20th century.

Types of data: Historical materials reflecting different authors' perceptions of indigenous African culture.

Classification scheme: The chapter's first pair of categories contrasts (a) opinions about African culture as drawn from an outsider's (European) perspective and (b) opinions drawn from an insider's perspective (African's or sympathetic Muslim scholar's view). The second pair examines ethnocentrism as displayed (a) within African schools and (b) outside the schools.

Causal Categories

Often the classes that researchers employ represent potential causes of the study's target variable. The purpose of such research is to determine if, and to what degree, the characteristics represented by the categories have likely contributed to the target variable, as determined by computing correlations between the characteristics and the target variable. Sometimes only one or two such categories are identified, in the belief that the characteristics of the target are the result—entirely or mainly—of the operation of one or two causes. Other times a large number of potential causes are cited, under the impression that the condition of the target variable could be the consequence of multiple components. Such is the case in the following example in which the target was students' tested reading skills and the categories of potential causes were characteristics of teachers and of the teaching context. The study involved 93,049 nine-year-olds and 100,365 fourteen-year-olds in 32 countries as well as the 4,992 teachers of the nine-year-olds and 5,526 teachers of the fourteen-year-olds (Lundberg & Linnakylä, 1993).

In their book *Teaching Reading Around the World,* Lundberg and Linnakylä reported correlations between students' tested reading skills and 17 variables estimated to be possible contributors to reading competence.

Sources of data: (a) Achievement tests of students' reading skills. (b) Questionnaires completed by teachers and by students.

Types of data: (a) Test scores reflecting students' ability to comprehend narratives, documents, and expository writing. (b) Student-completed questionnaires reflecting students' voluntary reading habits. (c) Teacher-completed questionnaires reflecting teachers' characteristics, their teaching methods, and the context in which they taught reading.

Classification scheme: Three clusters of categories offered information about 17 input variables, while a fourth cluster focused on students' reading abilities and habits.

Three sets containing a total of 17 input (likely causal) variables:

Cluster I: Teacher characteristics: (1) education, (2) experience, (3) gender, (4) readership (amount and type of reading done by teacher), (5) teacher's aims in reading instruction.

Cluster II: Teaching strategies: (1) time allocation, (2) assignment of homework, (3) skill orientation, (4) strategy orientation, (5) literature orientation, (6) functional orientation (practical use of reading), (7) assessment for accountability (providing reports for the school's administrators), (8) assessment for instruction (providing information to improve teaching methods).

Cluster III: Proximal teaching conditions: (1) class size, (2) instructional time, (3) percentage of students speaking a language other than the reading-test language, (4) number of textbooks per student.

One set of four categories offered information about the target variable—that is, the output variable of pupils' reading competence:

Cluster IV: Students' reading skills and habits: (1) narrative comprehension, (2) expository comprehension, (3) document comprehension, (4) frequency and types of voluntary reading.

Line-of-Logic Categories

Many research reports are organized as a sequence of categories representing what authors believe forms a line of reasoning that readers will find comprehensible and convincing. The following instance illustrates the set of categories adopted by a coalition of researchers to depict the legislative and policy environments of adult education in ten nations.

A special issue of the *International Review of Education* featured articles designed to account for the legal status of adult education in Australia, Brazil, England and Wales, the Ivory Coast, Hungary, India, Morocco, the Philippines, Switzerland, and the United States (Haddad, 1996).

Sources of data: Content analyses of national-history books, of legal documents bearing on educational opportunities for adults, of government publications focusing on adult education and employment, and of critiques of the nation's educational provisions.

Types of data: Historical background and demographic information about levels of literacy and education in the society, legal provisions and policies relating to education for adults, descriptions of adult-education programs, and analyses of the strengths and weaknesses of adult-education provisions.

Classification scheme: The five principal categories adopted by the authors were ordered in this sequence: (a) the historical background of adult education, (b) the legislative and policy framework, (c) the structure and amount of adult education, (d) current contextual problems, and (e) trends in providing adult education. Within each main category, authors were free to define subcategories that would accommodate special conditions in the nation whose adult-education system they described.

RESEARCH PROJECT CHECKLIST

1. What kinds of categories do I plan to use in my study?
   ____Chronological
   ____Stage
   ____Process
   ____Problem-centered
   ____Paired-contrasts
   ____Causal
   ____Multiple-causal
   ____Line-of-logic
   ____Other (identify)_____

2. For each of the identified kinds of categories:
   2.1 What will be the source of data?
   2.2 What will be the type of data?
   2.3 What classification system will I employ?

9

Statistical Analyses and Sampling

Statistical treatments of educational information have two purposes. The first is descriptive—to summarize information in an easily comprehended, quantitative form. The second is inferential—to provide an estimate of how likely a sample of people or events accurately represents a broader population of people or events. The following discussion first identifies a variety of descriptive statistics that are useful in research, then turns to matters of inference. The aim of the chapter is to suggest which types of statistics are most suitable for answering different kinds of questions. However, the aim does not include explaining the mathematical foundations underlying those statistical procedures nor to tracing in detail their methods of computation. Such foundations and computational techniques will be found in the kinds of books listed at the end of the chapter.

USING DESCRIPTIVE STATISTICS

The descriptive statistics included in this section are percentages, percentiles, measures of central tendency, measures of variability, measures of skewness, and correlation techniques. The presentation of each type opens with questions that the statistic is designed to answer. The discussion then continues with an explanation of the statistic's nature, its advantages and limitations, and examples of its application in comparative studies.

Percentages

The research question: What proportion of a variable (such as students, schools, equipment, events, or the like) display a particular characteristic?

Among the 300 female students surveyed, 35% would condemn the war criminal to death. Among the 114 males surveyed, 49% would put him to death.

The annual urban population growth rate in Argentina is 1.65%, in Afghanistan 4.84%, and in Tanzania 9.59%.

Nicole's test scores were: 86% in language usage, 68% in mathematics, 72% in science, and 93% in social studies.

The annual school budget allocated 67% of the funds for personnel salaries, 13% for equipment and supplies, 8% for transporting students, 7% for administrative expenses, and 5% for miscellaneous costs.

A valued feature of percentages is their ability to translate disparate measures into a common coin that permits easy comparisons among the measures. For instance, in the case of students' opinions about a war criminal, 105 females and 56 males would put the man to death. But the question of whether females were more prone than males to recommend execution cannot be answered until we know the number of each gender in the survey (300 females, 114 males). Even then we are unable make an accurate comparison until the figures are translated into a common denominator. Translating the quantities into percentages provides the solution—35% of the females and 49% of the males advocated executing the man.

Another advantage of percentages is that they are a familiar part of the general public's everyday living, so research results expressed in percentages can be readily understood by a very broad audience.

As Figure 9-1 shows, pie-shaped charts are often useful for graphically conveying the meaning of percentages.

Figure 9-1

Pie Charts for Displaying Percentages

Student Opinions of Death Penalty

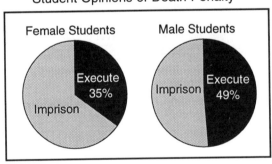

Percentiles

The research questions: What proportion of a variable falls below a designated point on a 100-unit scale? Within a collection of items (people, institutions, objects, events, or the like) where does one item rank in comparison with the others?

The meanings of *percentage* and of *percentile* are closely linked but not identical, which is a distinction sometimes missed by people not well acquainted with the two terms. Whereas a *percentage* tells the proportion (on a 100-unit scale) of a variable that displays a given characteristic, a *percentile* is the point on the scale below which a given percentage of people, objects, or events are located. Thus, a percentile tells where a particular person, object, or event stands in relation to the total number of other persons, objects, or events in terms of some specified feature. Let us say that Nicole was in a class of 33 students. Of the 50 items on the language-usage test, Nicole answered 43 (86%) correctly. However, 16 of Nicole's classmates did better than she by answering 44 or more items correctly. This meant that in the class of 33 students, 16 of them (48.5%) scored higher than Nicole and 16 (48.5%) scored lower. Hence, Nicole was in the middle, at the 50th percentile—the point below which nearly half of the students' scores fell. In like manner, we could determine Nicole's percentiles in the other three subject areas by computing where she ranked in relation to her classmates on the math, science, and social-studies tests. Furthermore, by learning the annual urban-population growth rates of an additional 17 countries, we could determine the percentile ranks of Argentina, Afghanistan, and Tanzania in comparison to the others. We could then conclude that:

Nicole's percentile ranks in the four tested subjects were: 50th percentile in language usage, 15th percentile in math, 67th percentile in science, and 88th percentile in social studies.

In urban-population growth rate for 20 developing nations, Argentina is at the 10th percentile, Afghanistan at the 65th percentile, and Tanzania at the 95th percentile.

Percentiles thus provide a convenient way to show one unit's (person's, school's, nation's, or such) position on some measure in relation to the other units in the group under consideration. Like percentages, percentiles allow a researcher to compare disparate rankings in terms of a single, readily comprehended scale.

Graphic Comparisons

As Figure 9-2 demonstrates, bar charts—sometimes called *histograms*—are convenient devices for graphically comparing groups and for comparing individuals within groups. Even a brief glance at the distributions of reading-test scores in the three rural schools shows that students in School B generally performed better than students in Schools A and C. Furthermore, those in School C were distributed somewhat more evenly across the range of scores than were students in either School A or School B. The bar charts also aid us in comparing students. When we learn that Anne earned a score of 68 in School A, we recognize that she was one of the better readers among her classmates. But if she were in School B, she would be slightly below average. And judging from the test results, one of the two best readers was in School B and the other was in School C, since each of them earned a score of 75.

Although we can derive a good deal of information from the bar graph, we are left without detailed answers to several questions: Precisely, which school was the better overall, A or C? In which school were the scores most bunched together, A or B? In which school were the scores balanced better around the average, A or C?

Figure 9-2

Distributions of Reading-Test Scores in Three Rural Schools

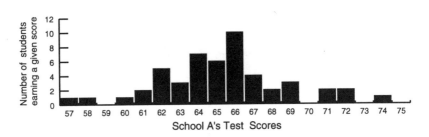

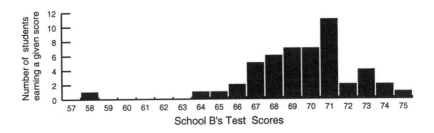

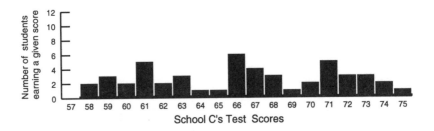

To answer these queries, we can turn to statistics describing central tendencies, variability, and the balance of score distributions that is referred to as skewness.

Measures of Central Tendency

The research question: What single number can show the level reached by a group in terms of some measure? The measure in question can be any one of many kinds—achievement-test scores, per-pupil costs for school supplies, numbers of days teachers were on sick leave, incidence of students' illicit drug use, football team scores, and much more.

The three most commonly used central-tendency statistics are the *arithmetic mean,* the *median,* and the *mode.* Each is designed to answer a particular central-tendency question.

The Mean

The research question: What was the average among the measures of some characteristic?

> Ratings on sportsmanship among pupils in the discussion groups were 17.3 points higher on average than ratings of pupils in the lecture groups.
> Textbook costs throughout the school system this year rose $13.56 over last year.
> The average class size in Monarch City is 25.7 students, in Desert Wells is 30.8, and in Langston 33.7.

The arithmetic mean is computed by adding together all of the measures attained by the members of a group, then dividing the sum by the number of members. Groups can then be conveniently compared in regard to how well they performed *in general* or *in the main* or *on the average.* For the three rural schools in Figure 9-2, the mean reading scores were 65.30 in School A, 69.5 in School B, and 66.26 in School C. Earlier, by inspecting the bar graphs we were unable to judge whether students in School A earned higher scores than the ones in School C. However, after computing the means we now recognize that School C students scored higher on the average than those in School A, and we know precisely how much higher.

The Median

The research questions: What score separated the upper half of the group from the lower half? Which score fell in the exact middle of the group's distribution of scores?

Whereas the mean for a group of students that took a test is computed by totaling their scores and dividing by the number of students, the median is determined by listing the students' test scores from the highest to the lowest, then counting up this list to find the halfway point. The median is that halfway score (if there is an uneven number of students) or it is the space between the two scores that lie just above and below the middle (if there is an even number of students). The median obviously is the same as the 50th percentile.

The median income of Preston High School graduates is $41,000, and of Marline High School graduates is $57,000.

The median times spent on homework assignments by sophomores over the past month were: mathematics 25 hours, science 16 hours, foreign language 22 hours, and history 19 hours.

In Figure 9-2, the medians for the rural students' reading performance fall at score 65 in School A, 70 in School B, and 66 in School C. Thus, the comparative success of the students in the three schools as pictured by the medians is quite the same as that furnished by the means. Hence, either the mean or median in this case would answer our research question equally well. The median is the easier to compute from inspecting the distribution of scores in a bar chart—we simply begin counting individuals from the bottom of the distribution (or from the top) until we reach the halfway point. Thus, for sake of convenience, the median might well be the statistic we would choose to calculate. However, sometimes the mean and median give rather different impressions of what occurred, as will become clear when we discuss skewness.

The Mode

The research questions: Which is the most popular score in a distribution of scores? Which is the maximum number of items required to fill some educational need?

The term *mode* identifies the score or amount that appears most frequently in a distribution. Thus, in an array of test results, the mode is the score the greatest number of students earned. In the rural-school example, the modal score for each of the schools is shown by the tallest bar. For School A the mode is 66 (9 students earned that score), for School B it is 71 (11 students), and for School C it is 66 (6 students).

Consider, also, how the mode serves to identify the maximum number of items required for some educational function. If the school librarian learns that the modal class size in the school is 37 (the class with the largest number of students), then she knows that 37 chairs are needed in the library to accommodate an entire class at one time. Obviously, if there are enough chairs to seat all members of the school's most populous class, there will be quite enough to seat all students from any class. Likewise, if the athletic instructor learns the size of the largest physical education class, he can order enough jerseys to outfit all members of any class that arrives.

As a measure of central tendency, the mode is less helpful than either the mean or the median, because the mode might occur at any place in the distribution other than near the middle.

Measures of Variability

For many research interests, it is not sufficient to learn only the average of an array of measurements. It is also important to learn how much the measurements are bunched together or spread out. For this purpose, we need statistics that summarize the extent of variability or dispersion in a distribution. Several kinds of variability measures are available. Those described in the following pages include the total range, distance between percentiles, interquartile range, standard deviation, and variance.

Range

The research question: What is the distance between the highest score and the lowest one?

The *range* or *total range* is calculated by subtracting the lowest quantity in a distribution from the highest quantity.

At first glance, it might appear that the range is a desirable measure of dispersion, since it is easy to compute and understand. However, the range is determined entirely by the two scores at the opposite ends of a distribution. Consequently, it fails to show whether the bulk of the scores between those extremes are bunched together or spread out. For example, in Figure 9-2, the arrays for the three rural schools all have the same range (17 points), yet the picture of variability of scores from one school to another is very different. Most of the scores in School B are clustered within a 7-point spread, whereas most scores in School C are distributed across 11 points. The fact that one student in School B scored far below his classmates on the reading test accounted for the range in that school matching the ranges of the other two schools.

When people ask for a report about the variability within a group's performance, they typically want to know about the group in general, not simply about the two extreme individuals at the opposite ends of the array. Thus, in educational research, the range is rarely useful. Unlike the range, the following statistics depict the variability of the bulk of the items in a distribution, not just the two items at the extreme ends.

Distance Between Percentiles

The research question: How many units of measurement or of scores lie between a selected percentile in the upper half of a distribution and another selected percentile in the lower half?

As explained earlier, along a 100-point scale, a percentile is the point below which a specified fraction of the measurements or scores are located. A girl who is taller than 78% of her agemates is at the 78th percentile in height. A boy who runs faster than 43% of other 9-year-olds is at the 43rd percentile in speed.

The distance between selected percentiles can be used to describe the extent of variability among measurements in a distribution. To choose which percentiles to use, we need to estimate what portion of extreme scores at the opposite ends of the scale we wish to disregard in order to report how much the majority of the scores were spread out or clustered together. If we decide that eliminating 10% at each end would be sufficient to prevent extreme scores from affecting the impression of group variability, then our measure of dispersion will consist of reporting the distance between the 10th percentile and the 90th percentile, thereby encompassing the middle 80% of the scores in our report. Or if we think it best to disregard 15% at each end, we will report the distance between the 15th percentile and the 85th percentile, thus focusing on the middle 70% of the measurements. In choosing which pair of percentiles to adopt, we wish to (a) prevent extreme measurements—outliers or deviants—from distorting the picture of variability for the group in general, but at the same time (b) avoid cutting off so many measurements that we end up telling more about central tendency than about dispersion. For instance, reporting the distance between the 45th and 55th percentiles would focus on only the central 10% of measurements and would ignore how the remaining 90% clustered together or spread out, thus failing to reflect the extent of variation within the group as a whole. The effects of such choices are illustrated in Figure 9-3, which displays the array of science test scores for students at Bay City High School and Linvale Preparatory Academy. (So there will not be an excessive number of intervals across the baseline of either bar graph, each interval along the baselines represents two adjacent scores, thereby forming a sequence extending from the lowest score that any student achieved [48] to the highest [84]. Consequently, the interval labeled "48" includes students who earned scores of 48 and 49, interval "50" includes students who had scores of 50 ad 51, and so on across the scale.)

In the Bay City distribution, the middle 80% of students fell between scores 56 (10th percentile) and 76 (90th percentile), a distance of 20 points. In the Linvale distribution, the middle 80% fell between scores 60 (10th percentile) and 72 (90th percentile), a range of 12 points, thereby reflecting a considerably tighter bunching of scores at Linvale than at Bay City. The distances between the 15th and 85th percentiles likewise depict less variability among the Linvale students—18 points at Bay City and barely 12 at Linvale.

One popular version of distance-between-percentiles is the interquartile range, which reports the distance between the 25th percentile (first quartile) and the 75th percentile (third quartile). The interquartile range, therefore, reflects the extent of dispersion among the middle 50% of a distribution's measurements. Sometimes the interquartile range is divided by 2, producing the *semi-interquartile range*.

The interquartile range for the Bay City High students is 14 points (75th percentile minus 25th percentile), so the semi-interquartile range is 7 points.

Figure 9-3

Distance-Between-Percentiles as a Measure of Variability

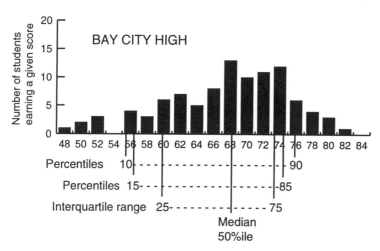

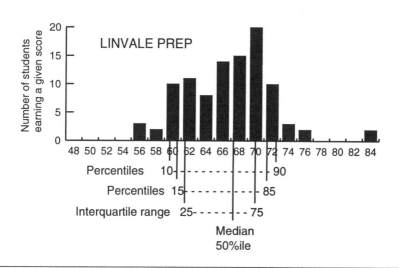

It is useful to note that the principal types of central-tendency and variability measures form two families of statistics. First, in the percentiles family the measure of central tendency is the median (50th percentile), while variability is determined by some version of distance between percentiles (including the interquartile and semi-interquartile ranges). Therefore, if the median is used to report the general success of a group of students, the accompanying measure of variability can reasonably be a version of distance between percentiles.

We turn now to the second family of variability measures.

Standard Deviation and Variance

The research question: How much do measurements or scores in a distribution stretch above and below the mean?

As noted above, calculating the median and allied percentiles consists of counting the number of scores extending from the lowest and highest. In contrast, computing the mean involves totaling all the measurements or scores, then dividing the sum by the number of measurements or scores. Three measures of dispersion related to the mean are ones determined by calculating how far a distribution's scores deviate from the mean. These measures are named the *average deviation, variance,* and *standard deviation.* The hypothetical example in Figure 9-4 of 36 students playing a dart game at a party will serve to illustrate the nature of each of the measures.

Although the average deviation is rarely used in statistical analyses, inspecting its computation can be helpful in explaining the meanings of variance and standard deviation. The average deviation tells how far, on the average, all the scores or measurements in a distribution are located above and below the mean. To calculate the average deviation for the dart-game data in Figure 9-4, we first need to recognize that each of the scores in the left column represents an interval. The score number is the center of that interval. Therefore, the number 4 identifies the center of an interval extending from 3.5 to 4.5. The number 3 interval extends from 2.5 to 3.5, and so on with the rest of the scores. When we add all of the dart-game scores together and divide that sum (132) by the number of students (36), we find that the mean of the distribution is 3.67. Thus, the mean falls in the lower portion of the 4 interval—exactly .12 above the lower limit (3.5) of that interval. To calculate the average deviation for the dart-game distribution, we need to determine how far each student's score deviates from 3.67. So, if a student earned a score of 4, we find how much that differs from the mean by subtracting 3.67 from 4 (4 - 3.67 = .33). In the same way we find that a student's score of 5 deviates from the mean by 1.33 points (5 - 3.67 = 1.33). And a score of 2 deviates from the mean by 1.67 points (3.67 - 2 = 1.67). By carrying out these calculations for all 36 scores, and summing the results, we obtain a total of 46.66, which is then divided by the number of students (36) to yield the average deviation (1.30) of scores from the distribution's mean. This 1.30 might then be used to compare the 36 students with students from other classes in order to determine which group demonstrated greater variability in throwing darts. Assume, for instance, that the average deviation for a second class was 1.78 and for a third class was 0.92. It is thus apparent that the scores in the second class spread out far more than did the scores in either the Figure 9-4 group or the third class. The tightest bunching together of scores appeared in the third class with its 0.92 average deviation.

In contrast to the average deviation, which is seldom employed in research, the variance and standard deviation are very popular, since both provide important advantages. The method of computing the variance is similar to that used for the average deviation—except with the variance, each score's deviation from the mean is squared before the deviations are added together. The squaring process increases the weighting of deviations as their distance from the mean increases. Thus, the variance is the average of the scores' squared distances from the mean.

Once the variance has been calculated, the standard deviation is easy to determine. You simply find the square root of the variance. Note in Figure 9-4 that the standard deviation of 1.77 is the square root of the variance of 3.14. The conventional symbol for the standard deviation is the small Greek letter sigma (σ), and for the variance it is sigma-squared (σ^2).

Figure 9-4

Students' Scores in a Dart Game

Scores   *Number of Students Earning Each Score*

Scores	Tally	Statistics
9		N = 36 students
8	/ /	Mean = 3.67
7	/	Average deviation = 1.30
6	/	Variance = 3.14 = σ^2
5	/ / / /	Standard deviation = 1.77 = σ
4	/ / / / / / / / / / /	
3	/ / / / / / / / / /	Range = 8
2	/ / /	Median = 4
1	/ / /	Mode = 4
0	/	

The Normal Distribution Curve

Over the years, large numbers of people have been measured to determine their status on such physical characteristics as height and weight or their relative standing on a test of some mental ability—general intelligence, academic aptitude, or the like. The results of such measurements have shown that the

...utiibutions of scores have tended to assume nearly the same configuration. The bulk of the group cluster around the middle, with the remaining people's scores gradually diminishing as they deviate farther above and farther below the majority. Because so many human characteristics seem to result in such a configuration, this common arrangement of measurements has been called the *normal distribution curve.* (It is also called the *bell-shaped curve* or the *Gaussian* curve after Karl Friedrich Gauss, a German mathematician and astronomer who developed procedures related to it.)

As shown in Figure 9-5, the relationship of the standard deviation to the normal curve provides researchers with useful information. The area of the curve lying one standard deviation above the mean contains slightly more than one-third (34.1%) of the scores or measurements reported in a given research project. The same proportion of scores is found in the area within one standard deviation below the mean. Hence, slightly over two-thirds (68.2%) of the scores lie in the area between +1σ and -1σ from the mean; 95.4% of the measurements will be found in the area +2σ and -2σ from the mean; and nearly all (99.7%) will be within +3σ and -3σ from the mean. The closer a distribution approximates the form of a normal curve, the more these proportions can be trusted.

Figure 9-5

Standard Deviations and the Normal Curve

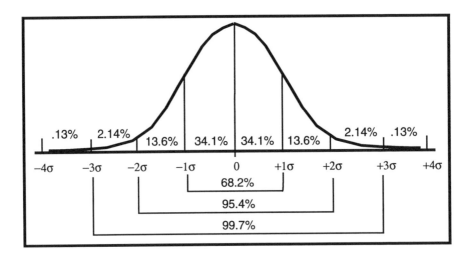

The standard deviation and the variance are not only convenient statistics to report for portraying the comparative variability of several distributions of scores or measurements, but they offer particular advantages for the inferential use of statistics, as we will see later in this chapter.

Skewness

Research questions: How symmetrical is the array of measures? In other words, how closely does the shape of the lower half of the distribution match the shape of the upper half?

The statistical concept reflected in these questions is *skewness*. Figure 9-6 shows two distributions of scores. In the one labeled *normal distribution*, the form of the lower half of the array of scores is a mirror image of the form of the upper half. In the example labeled *skewed distribution*, the lower half of the array is rather like a tail, whereas the upper half is humped. When the tail-like form is in the lower half of the scale, the distribution is said to be *negatively skewed*. When the tail is in the upper half of the scale, the array is called *positively skewed*.

Measures of skewness report how much a distribution deviates from perfect symmetry. The degree of skewness of the normal distribution in Figure 9-6 is 0.0, because the scores are not skewed at all. However, such is not the case with the reading scores for the three rural schools in Figure 9-2. There, the distribution of scores is least symmetrical in School B, where the students tended to bunch toward the top of the scale (-1.16) The closest to symmetry is School C (-0.01). School A is between the other two, with scores slightly skewed toward the high end of the scale (+0.18).

Figure 9-6

Normal and Skewed Distributions

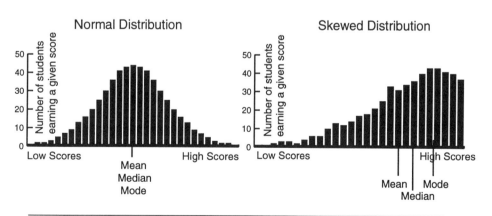

In Figure 9-6, the skewed distribution depicts Samoan high-school students' performance on a Samoan-language reading test (Thomas & Titialii, 1973b). The degree of skewness is -0.78. The abundance of students bunched together at the high end of the distribution suggests that the reading test did not sufficiently challenge the best readers' skills.   It seems likely that the students who earned perfect or near-perfect scores were actually not all alike in ability.   Probably some of them were better than others, but the test lacked a sufficient number of difficult items to separate the very good readers from the superior ones.   In the future, the test constructors would be advised to put more *top* on the test by including some items that demand more subtle reading interpretations than do the questions on the existing test.

Figure 9-6 illustrates the way skewness influences the relationships among the mean, median, and mode. In a symmetrical array, the mean, median, and mode are all at the same location.   However, in a typical skewed distribution, the median will lie between the mode and the mean. The mean is tugged toward the tail end of the scale by the extreme scores that lie in that direction. The greater the skewness, the larger the separation among the three measures. In a markedly skewed array, the median is likely the best of the three statistics to represent the central tendency of the distribution.   In the skewed display in Figure 9-6, students' scores range from a low of 2 to a high of 27, with 27 representing a perfect score. The median is 21 and the mean 19.87. The standard deviation is 5.31, and the interquartile range is 7.

Correlation Techniques

The research question: The general question that correlation statistics are designed to answer is: When a change occurs in one variable, how much change—if any—occurs in another variable?

The general question, when recast in terms of particular variables, results in such queries as the following:

Ethnic status and academic achievement: Are students from certain ethnic groups more successful at academic studies than students from other ethnic groups?

Television viewing and violent behavior: What is the relationship between the amount and kinds of television programs children watch and the amount and types of violent acts in which children engage?

Mothers' intelligence and daughters' intelligence. How closely do mothers' IQs (intelligence quotients) correspond to their daughters' IQs?

Identical twins' academic achievement. In pairs of identical twin girls, how does the level of academic achievement of a typical girl compare with the academic achievement of her twin sister?

Administrative style and teacher satisfaction: Are school principals' administrative styles related to the degree of satisfaction expressed by teachers who serve under those principals' supervision?

A variety of statistical procedures are available for answering such questions. Which procedure will be appropriate in a given case depends on the kind of data found in the variables that are being compared. Variables appear in three principal forms: (a) as a *series* of scores or measurements ranging from low to high, (b) as a series of rankings extending from first to last, or (b) as a dichotomy, pitting two or more separate categories against each other. Table 9-1 indicates which correlation process is suited to which pattern of data. Each of the correlation procedures listed in the right-hand column of Table 9-1 is described briefly in the following pages.

Table 9-1

Kinds of Data and Correlation Procedures

Variable A	Variable B	Correlation Technique
Measurement series	Measurement series	Pearson product-moment (r)
Ranks	Ranks	Spearman rank-order (*rho* or ρ)
Measurement series	Dichotomy	Biserial (r_b)
Dichotomy	Dichotomy	Phi coefficient (ϕ)

Pearson Product-Moment Correlation

The research question: What is the degree of relationship between two variables if each variable consists of measurements along a scale that consists of a series of equal intervals?

In judging whether the Pearson product-moment method (symbolized by the letter r) is appropriate for a given study, the researcher needs to decide whether both of the variables being compared represent equal-interval scales. Strictly speaking, an equal-interval scale is one in which the distance from one step to the next step is precisely the same throughout the entire length of the scale. Measures of height fulfill this equal-interval requirement, since the distance from 25 centimeters to 30 centimeters is exactly the same as from 60-cm to 65-cm or from 105-cm to 110-cm, and so on. Measures of temperature, of weight, of time, of speed, of dollars, and of distance on a running track also involve equal-unit scales. In contrast, some scales used in the field of education and in the social sciences may appear at first glance to be composed of equal intervals, but upon closer inspection it becomes clear that they are not. The scoring of intelligence-test results in terms of IQ levels is a familiar example. The difference in intellectual ability between an IQ of 100 and one of 105 is not the same as the difference between 120 and 125, because the questions that make up the test are not all of equal difficulty. Test items that differentiate between IQs 120 and 125 are probably more demanding than those that distinguish between

IQs 100 and 105. Likewise, a distribution of scores on a test of English usage or of science facts does not produce an *equal-interval scale* in the strict meaning of the term, because the items that differentiate between scores 80 and 90 are likely more difficult than those that differentiate between scores of 30 and 40. In effect, a 10-point difference in one segment of the scale is not equal to a 10-point difference in another segment.

This distinction between truly equal-interval scales and scales that contain intervals that are only approximately equal has caused some critics to condemn the use of the Pearson method in a great many of the studies that have employed the procedure. (More than 90% of all correlation coefficients reported in the research literature within the behavioral sciences are Pearson r's.) However, Heermann and Braskamp's (1970, pp. 30-110) analysis of a host of investigations suggests that using Pearson's technique with variables involving intervals that are no more than approximately or partially equal is still warranted. Glass and Hopkins (1984, p. 9) have observed that the critics' "disenchantment with the classical methods was premature." Thus, it is generally acceptable to apply Pearson's r in studies whose variables consist of test scores or involve ratings of performance or of attitude.

Our purpose in this section is not to detail the technique involved in calculating r. Such information is found in the statistics books listed at the end of the chapter. Here we confine our attention to a brief description of what different magnitudes of r can mean.

The size of r can range from 0 to 1.00. An r of 0 means that change in one variable is associated with no change in the other. For instance, it seems likely that the r between college students' political attitudes and their shoe sizes is 0.0, meaning that there is no link between the two variables. Hence, knowing a student's shoe size offers no clue at all about the student's political views, nor will information about a student's political attitudes aid us in estimating that individual's shoe size. However, r's that approach 1.00 can aid us a great deal in estimating a given individual's position on one variable from knowing his or her position on the other. But before demonstrating that point with some illustrative r's, we should note that two variables can be related in either a positive or a negative manner.

A positive r means that high scores on one scale are accompanied by high scores on the other. Likewise, low scores on one variable are associated with low scores on the other. In contrast, a negative r means that low values on one dimension are related to high values on the other.

For example, a study of the IQs of identical twins raised in the same home has yielded an r of +.91, so that if we know the IQ of one member of the pair, we can safely judge that the other member's IQ will be nearly the same. However, for identical twins raised in separate homes, the r found between their IQs was only +.67. This means that, whereas there is still a tendency for the twin of a person with a high IQ to have an above-average intelligence-test score as well, our estimate of what that score will be is less accurate than if the *r* were +.91 or even +.80 or +.75. Still less confidence can be placed in predicting a child's IQ if we know the IQs of the child's brothers or sisters, because evidence about the *r* between siblings raised together suggests a relationship of only +.50. And if the siblings have been raised apart, the *r* descends to +.40. There is even less connection between the IQs of unrelated children who are reared in the same home (*r* +.23), and no connection at all between unrelated children who are reared in separate homes (*r* 0.00) (Newman, Freeman, & Holzinger, 1937). Hence, in the case of two unrelated children who have been raised apart, estimating one child's IQ from knowledge of the other's IQ is no more than a wild guess.

Negative correlations can also range from 0 to -1.00. But in this case, low scores along one scale are associated with high scores along the other. Among people from ages 50 to 90, there is a negative relationship between age and muscle strength, because with advancing age, people's strength diminishes. As in the case of positive *r*'s, the closer a negative *r* approaches -1.00, the more accurately a score on one variable can be predicted from knowing a given score on the other variable.

Consider these two examples of *perfect* correlations, one positive and the other negative.

Pearson *r*	Variable 1	Variable 2
+1.00	Centigrade temperatures	Fahrenheit temperatures
-1.00	Students' correct answers on a science test	Students' incorrect answers on a science test

Spearman Rank Correlation

The research question: What is the degree of relationship between two variables if each variable consists of ranks along a scale rather than measured intervals?

Frequently research data are not in the form needed to compute a Pearson *r*, because one or both of the variables consist of ranks instead of measured amounts. Sometimes the data are originally collected as rankings, as when teachers are ranked in terms of popularity with students, basketball players ranked by overall ability, and nations ranked by the prestige of their higher-education systems. Other times the data are collected as quantities which are then converted into ranks for convenience of computation. Thus, provinces can be ranked by per-pupil expenditures, colleges by their graduation rates, and students by their grade point averages.

The most popular method of computing correlations between pairs of ranked data is the Spearman procedure, symbolized by the Greek letter ρ (rho). Spearman coefficients, like Pearson *r*'s, can range from 0 to 1.00 in either a positive or negative direction. Interpreting magnitudes of ρ is much like interpreting similar magnitudes of r.

Biserial Correlation

The research question: What is the degree of relationship between two variables if one is measured in a graduated fashion so as to produce a sequence of quantities and the other variable is in the form of a dichotomy?

Two computational techniques for determining the association between such variables are the *biserial* and *point-biserial* methods. Each method yields correlation coefficients that are estimates of what the Pearson r would be if both variables were normally distributed arrays rather than one of them being in the form of a dichotomy.

Deciding whether the biserial technique is appropriate in a given research situation depends on the researcher's assumption about the nature of the dichotomous variable. The biserial method is not appropriate in cases of *true* dichotomies, such as sex (male/female) or students' class attendance on a particular day (present/absent). However, it is applicable when the dichotomy appears to be an artifact of crude measurement. For instance, in a survey of parents' opinions about teaching birth control methods in high school, data may be collected in the form of a dichotomy (*agree/disagree*). But it is likely that parents' opinions are actually far more varied than the resulting data suggest—some parents will have strong objections to birth control instruction, some will disagree moderately, others will object mildly, some will agree but with serious reservations, and so on. If a more precise scaling approach had been used in gathering opinions, the results would have assumed the form of a distribution of graduated steps. In effect, the dichotomous variable in this instance was not truly discrete. Therefore, it is this latter type of spurious, crude-measurement dichotomy for which the biserial correlation technique is designed. Because coefficients resulting from biserial computations are estimates of Pearson r's, the interpretation of biserial coefficients is similar to the interpretation of r's.

On the other hand, if the dichotomous feature is truly discrete (male/female, citizen/alien, fourth-grade pupil/non-fourth-grade pupil), an estimate of r can still be obtained by applying the *point-biserial* method.

Phi Coefficient and Contingency Coefficient

The research question: What is the degree of relationship between two variables if both of them are dichotomous?

The phi (r_ϕ) coefficient is the product-moment correlation between two variables when each variable is scored as discrete points rather than as a series of measured steps. For example, imagine that we wish to determine among students in a junior high school the direction and degree of relationship on a given school day between two variables: (a) family type and (b) homework diligence. We identify two types of families (single-parent and two-parent) and two levels of homework diligence (homework completed and homework not completed). For convenience of computation, we arbitrarily assign the score 0 to students in one-parent families and the score 1 to those in two-parent homes. Likewise, we assign the score 0 to students who failed to hand in their completed homework on the particular day and a score of 1 to those who completed their assignment. Then we can locate in a 2-by-2 contingency table the number of students who fit each of four conditions: (a) 1-parent family and missing homework [0-0], (b) 1-parent family and completed homework [0-1], (c) 2-parent family and missing homework [1-0], and (d) 2-parent family and completed homework [1-1]. Assume that we collect family-type and homework-completion information from 200 students and enter the data into a contingency table (Figure 9-7). We see by the totals at the bottom of table that there were 90 students from 1-parent homes and 110 from two-parent families. By applying a standard formula for computing the phi coefficient, we learn that in this case of our fictitious junior high school the $r_\phi = +.06$. The positive value of r_ϕ indicates that students with 1's on home-type were a bit more likely to have 1's also on completing homework. In effect, there was a slightly greater tendency for students in 2-parent families to complete their homework than for those in 1-parent families. But the magnitude of the phi is so small that its usefulness for drawing generalizations about the relationship of family type and homework diligence would be of no practical value.

For sake of comparison, let us now assume that we next collect information about a different set of 200 students on a different day's homework assignment, then enter those data into Figure 9-8. The resulting phi coefficient is $r_\phi = +.17$, showing a somewhat higher tendency than in Figure 9-7 for students from 2-parent homes to hand in homework in comparison to students from 1-parent families.

The data used in contingency tables need not be restricted to two discrete positions on each of the variables. For instance, a table comparing high school students' grade levels (10th/11th/12th) and those students' use of alcohol during a given week (did drink vs. did not drink) would produce a 3-by-2 table. In like manner, other variables represented in discrete types or steps could produce larger size contingency tables—4-by-4, 3-by-6, and such.

Other Correlation Options

The correlation methods described in the above paragraphs are only four of the more commonly used techniques. Numerous other approaches found in statistics textbooks and journal articles are designed to suit additional conditions of the data that a researcher has at hand. For instance, in some situations the relationship between two series of measures may not assume the shape of a straight diagonal line. As scores on one variable increase, the scores on the other do not increase regularly in a similar manner. Such a relationship results if

Figure 9-7

Family Type and Homework Diligence—Example 1

Type of Home

Homework Completed?		1-parent [0]	2-parent [1]	Totals
	No [0]	36	38	74
	Yes [1]	54	72	126
	Totals	90	110	200

Figure 9-8

Family Type and Homework Diligence—Example 2

Type of Home

Homework Completed?		1-parent [0]	2-parent [1]	Totals
	No [0]	42	33	75
	Yes [1]	48	77	125
	Totals	90	110	200

people's ages over the life span are compared with their eye-hand coordination scores. Whereas age increases in regular steps, eye-hand skills do not; instead, such skills increase in early life, remain at a high level for much of adulthood, then decline in old age, thereby rendering their progression *curvilinear.* In such cases, an eta (η) coefficient should be computed to reflect the association between the variables.

As a second example, under certain conditions a tetrachoric coefficient (r_t) rather than a phi coefficient can usefully be calculated to determine the magnitude of the relationship between two variables, each of which is a dichotomy.

The term *factor analysis* identifies several alternative procedures for estimating which features are common to a series of correlations that have been computed from a variety of measures of a group of individuals. For example, a large number of students can be administered tests intended to assess their mental abilities. Correlations can then be computed to determine which test items are highly related to each other and which ones appear to be mainly independent of each other. The assumption is that when certain items are closely associated (so that students who do well on one item in the cluster also do well on the others, and vice versa), a particular mental ability or mental *factor* underlies that group of items. Typically, a label is assigned to that cluster of closely related items, with the label intended to reflect the cognitive skill—or *factor*—that binds the cluster together. For example, the labels applied to factors found in such test batteries as the Primary Mental Abilities (Thurstone, 1938) and Differential Aptitude Tests (Bennett, Seashore, & Wesman, 1952) are: number comprehension, verbal reasoning, verbal comprehension, abstract reasoning, clerical speed and accuracy, mechanical reasoning, space relations, language usage, and word fluency.

> In applications in education, factor analytic studies have been undertaken in such diverse areas as prose style, administrative behavior, occupational classification, attitudes and belief systems, and the economics of education. The technique is still in extensive use in the exploration of abilities, in the refining of tests and scales, and in the development of composite variables for use in research studies. Its most promising applications in recent years, however, have been concerned with the testing of explicit hypotheses about the structure of sets of variables, as in the study of growth models. . . . It has also facilitated the comparison of the factorial structure of different subpopulations, allowing investigators to determine whether the factorial structure of a given set of variables varies, for example, with sex, age, ethnicity, socioeconomic status, or political affiliation. (Spearritt, 1985, pp. 1822-1823)

For steps to follow in calculating the correlation coefficients mentioned in the foregoing pages, and for explanations of the conditions under which each method is appropriate, readers can consult such books as those listed at the end of this chapter.

DRAWING INFERENCES FROM SAMPLES

As mentioned earlier, descriptive statistics summarize in a concise form the results of measurements of a group of individuals or events. Sometimes researchers are interested only in what such statistics tell about that group. However, other times they want to apply the group's results to a larger population. In other words, the measured group is considered to be a sample of a larger population that has not been measured. Hence, from testing the reading ability of 200 nine-year-olds, an investigator may intend to draw inferences about the reading skills of all of a city's or state's nine-year-olds. From a statistical summary of 350 college students' expressed attitudes about the use of marijuana, a researcher may hope to estimate the attitudes toward illicit drugs of all students in that particular college—or perhaps of all students in all of the nation's higher-education institutions. However, extending the conclusions about a tested group to a larger population always entails a risk of error, since the sample group may not truly represent the larger population. In effect, the sample may be biased. Therefore, it is important for researchers to have ways of judging how likely the statistics gathered about a sample will accurately portray the features of an intended population. Or, stated as a question, what is the probability of making an error when using descriptive statistics as the basis for drawing inferences about a population? The procedures for answering such a question are called *inferential statistics.*

It is useful at this point to consider the sources of errors that may distort the conclusions drawn from assessing people or events. In the case of descriptive statistics, inaccurate conclusions derive from measurement errors. For instance, the purpose of having students take a history test is to discover precisely their knowledge of historical facts, concepts, trends, theories, and the like. However, various kinds of errors can render the assessment inaccurate. The directions for taking the test may be unclear, some test items may be badly phrased, noises in the classroom may disrupt students' attempt to concentrate, the time to complete the test may be too short, the tester's method of correcting the students' answers may be faulty, and more. Such measurement errors can be reduced by careful attention to the preparation of the test, to the manner of administering it, and to the method of correcting it. However, if the results of testing a sample of students are used as the foundation for drawing inferences about the broader population of students from which the sample was drawn, another source of inaccuracy can distort the inferred picture of the population's knowledge of history. That source is *sampling error,* meaning the degree to which inferences about a population likely deviate from the true characteristics of that population.

The following discussion of sampling error is presented in two parts. Part 1 describes two popular statistical procedures for estimating the magnitude of sampling error. Part 2 introduces alternative ways of drawing samples from populations.

Estimating Sampling Error

A researcher can never know for sure how accurately one sample drawn from a population reflects the characteristics of that population. The only way to know positively how closely the mean of 100 pupils' test scores represents the mean that would be achieved by all 50,000 pupils in a county's school population would be to test all 50,000. But since testing the entire population would likely be considered impractical, the best an investigator can do is to estimate the probability that the sample mean is close to the population's true mean. Inferential statistics are designed to furnish that estimate. We will briefly inspect two of the ways to arrive at such estimates—the *t*-test and the analysis of variance.

The *t*-Test

Researchers often compare two groups in terms of their means. If the means are found to differ, the question arises: Does each group represent a different population in relation to the characteristic that was measured, so the difference in these sample means reflects an actual difference in the means of the underlying populations? Or are the two groups simply two slightly biased samples from the same population, whose true mean we really don't know? To illustrate, imagine that 50 women and 50 men are enrolled in a college class entitled "Methods of Logic." On the final test at the end of the semester, the mean for the women is 83.6 and for the men 78.9. We may now ask whether these scores reflect a difference only between female and male members of that particular class, or is the population of the kind of college women who enrolled in the class generally more adept at learning the methods of logic taught in the class than is the population of the kind of college men who enrolled? The *t*-test provides an estimated answer to this query.

To perform a *t*-test, we first compute the standard deviation for the women's and men's distributions of final-test scores and find that the women's $\sigma = 6.7$ and men's $\sigma = 6.3$. Next, by applying the appropriate computation procedure (found in nearly any statistics textbook, a procedure requiring the two groups' means and standard deviations), we learn that there apparently is less than 1 chance in 1000 that the two groups represent the same population and that the obtained means are different simply because of bias in drawing the samples. In other words, our results support the conclusion that the population of women (of the kind enrolled in the logic class) is on the average somewhat more skilled at learning the methods of logic taught in the class than is the population of men (of the kind that enrolled). There is a 999 chance in 1,000 that this conclusion is warranted.

However, if the means for women in our hypothetical logic class had been 81.0 and the men 83.6 (with the standard deviations still $\sigma = 6.7$ and $\sigma = 6.3$), we would learn that there are likely 5 chances out of 100 that there is no real difference in the means of the populations from which these women and men were drawn. In effect, there are 5 chances in a 100 that the difference between 81.0 and 83.6 is simply the result of sampling error—the men's sample just happened to include more adept logic learners—and that both the men and women represent the same population in terms of ability to master the logic techniques taught in the class. But there are 95 chances in 100 that the obtained differences actually do reflect a difference that would be found in the mean scores of the two populations of the kinds of women and men who took the test.

Thus, the *t*-test is designed to help researchers estimate the probability that measures of a sample of people or events accurately portray the broader populations of people or events from which the sample was apparently drawn. In addition to testing the representativeness of obtained means, there are *t*-tests for pairs of percentages, standard deviations, correlations, and measures of skewness.

In the above brief sketch of the *t*-test procedure, I have not taken the space to point out several important assumptions about the way samples are drawn from populations, assumptions that significantly affect the appropriateness of *t*-tests in particular studies. For explanations of those assumptions, readers are directed to the suggested readings at the end of this chapter.

Analysis of Variance

As explained earlier, *variance* (σ^2) is a description of how much measurements spread away from the center of a distribution.   Specifically, the variance is the average of the squared measurement-deviations from the mean.

We have seen that the *t*-test is used to estimate whether the means from two samples represent the same population or two different populations.   The analysis of variance (ANOVA) is a statistical procedure for simultaneously testing how likely three or more means represent samples drawn from the same population or, in contrast, are means representing different populations.   One example of comparing three or more means is found in a study of attitudes toward a 10-o'clock curfew law as expressed by parents, teachers, police officers, and teenagers.   Another example is found in a study of mathematics test scores of high school students representing six ethnic groups—Anglos, Latinos, Afro-Americans, Asians, Native Americans, and Pacific Islanders.

Not only does ANOVA permit the simultaneous comparison of multiple means, but the results are more accurate than if *t*-tests were applied to each pairing of the multiple means being studied. Glass and Hopkins (1984, p. 324) point out that "ANOVA is the most common of all inferential statistical techniques in education and the behavioral sciences."

ANOVA results are interpreted in much the same way as those of the *t*-test, that is, in terms of the probability that a difference between sample means are the result of sampling error rather than the result of a difference in the true means of the populations from which the compared samples were drawn.   Thus, a difference among sample means that could occur by chance (by sampling error) at a probability level of only 1 time in 100 gives the researcher more confidence in believing that the means of the represented populations are truly different than does a difference among sample means that could occur by chance 5 times in 100 or 10 times in 100.

ANOVA can also be extended to test the likelihood of interactions among factors. For instance, one researcher used ANOVA to discover whether teachers' ethnic status affected their perceptions of how adaptable Anglo and Latino students were. The results showed that there was indeed interaction between teacher and student ethnic types. Latino teachers more often judged Latino students as more adaptive, whereas Anglo teachers more frequently considered Anglo students more adaptive (Glass & Hopkins, 1984, p. 404).

Ways of Drawing Samples

The types of research in which concerns about sampling are most important are experiments and surveys. Among numerous methods of drawing a sample to represent a population, five are described in the following paragraphs. They bear the titles *simple random, multistage, cluster, systematic,* and *convenience.*

Simple Random Sampling

In the field of education, the populations that investigators choose to study can usually be defined in terms of their (a) content, (b) units, (c) extent, and (d) time (Kish, 1965). For instance, in a study of the reading habits of Canadian college freshmen, the population can be specified as: (a) all first-year college and university students, (b) in all higher-education institutions, (c) in Canada, (d) in 1998. Or, in an investigation of the student-discipline policies in Philippine private secondary schools, the population can be described as consisting of (a) all discipline regulations, (b) in all private secondary schools, (c) in all of the Philippine Islands, (d) in 1998.

Consider, then, how we might proceed to compile information about Canadian college students' reading habits. We quickly recognize that the task of gathering data from all Canadian freshmen is well beyond the resources we command. Thus, we decide to study only a sample of Canadian freshmen. To help ensure that our sample truly represents the pattern of reading habits of the student population, we decide to use a random sample. The basic rule in drawing a random sample is that every individual in the population must have an equal chance of being selected. One way to fulfill this requirement would be to obtain the names of all 1997 first-year college students and assign each an identification number, starting with 1 and continuing until we reach the total number of students. We then decide what size sample will (a) provide a sufficiently large group to offer a trustworthy estimate of the population characteristics and (b) at the same time will fit our budget, staff, and time constraints. On the basis of these considerations, we choose to gather data from 300 respondents. Our next step is to obtain a list of random numbers, either from a table in a statistics book or from a computer program that generates random numbers. The first 300 numbers in that list identify which students (in terms of their assigned identification numbers) from throughout Canada would be included in our survey.

The advantage of drawing a simple random sample of the population is that we can now make a good estimate of sampling error (by such techniques as the *t*-test or ANOVA) and thus know how well the results of our sample likely reflect the reading habits of the nation's entire population of first-year college students. The disadvantage is that carrying out such a sampling plan would entail far more expense and difficulty than the results of the study would warrant. I doubt that all of the nation's post-secondary institutions would be willing to send us the names of their freshmen. In addition, drawing students randomly from across the nation would necessitate our collecting reading-habit information (by mailed questionnaires, phone calls, or face-to-face interviews) in many different sections of the country. Therefore, unless a population is quite limited in size and distribution, direct random sampling is usually not practical.

Multistage and Cluster Sampling

One way to simplify our problem of drawing a random sample of students would be to carry out the selection process in stages. That is, a population often can be described in terms of a hierarchy of sampling units of different sizes and types. In the case of our reading-habits study, the hierarchy could consist of two stages or levels: (1) colleges and universities and (2) first-year students within those institutions. First, we list the names of all colleges and universities. Then by a random-selection process, we choose five institutions. Next, we obtain the names of all first-year students in those five institutions, and from that list we randomly select 300 students to be surveyed. This procedure meets the basic requirement for random sampling (each student has had an equal chance to be chosen) and has much simplified our task of conducting the survey. A number of variations of multistage sampling are available to accommodate the conditions of different studies and different types of populations (Ross, 1985).

Cluster sampling is similar to multistage sampling. In both methods, the first step is the same—the population to be investigated is divided into groupings referred to as clusters. For the Canadian example, each college or university would be a cluster. In both multistage and cluster sampling, the number of clusters to be included in the sample would first be chosen by random selection. But the two methods differ at the second step of the process. Whereas in the multistage procedure, the second step consists of randomly selecting units (students) within each of the clusters, in cluster sampling all of the units in a selected cluster become members of the sample. In effect, every first-year student in a selected college would be interviewed.

Techniques for estimating sampling error for the multistage and cluster approaches are provided in such sources as Kish (1965) and Henry (1990).

Systematic Sampling

Within relatively small populations, a systematic sample usually will represent a population's characteristics as accurately as will a random sample. Consider, for example, a secondary school with an enrollment of 1,400 students. The dean of students wishes to collect students' opinions of the new dress code that the school is proposing to adopt—a code requiring students to choose their garb from among two styles for boys and three styles for girls. Rather than soliciting the opinions of the entire population of 1,400, the dean plans to interview only 35 students or 2.5% of the total. To select the 35 who will participate in the study, he assigns each student in the school a number, ranging from 1 to 1,400. Then he writes numbers 1 to 20 on a sheet of paper and, with his eyes closed, touches a pencil point to the sheet. The pencil points to number 7. That number identifies the first student to be included in the sample. And because 2.5% of 1,400 is 20, the 20th student from 7 (student 27) is the second one to enter the sample. The 20th student beyond 27 (student 47) becomes the third. And in like manner, each subsequent 20th student is chosen until the desired 35 have been identified.

Because only chance errors, rather than other sources of bias, are apt to affect how closely the interview results approximate the population's opinions about the dress code, the statistical techniques described earlier for estimating sampling error (*t*-test and ANOVA) can be appropriately used with systematic sampling.

Convenience Sampling

A great many studies in the field of education involve what have been called *available, convenience,* or *accidental* samples. Such is the case when teachers in an elementary school test sixth-graders' mastery of computer keyboarding, when a graduate student assesses a group of kindergarten children's methods of settling disputes, or when an anthropologist analyzes the instructional roles played by members of three families. In these instances, the particular elementary school, kindergarten, and families were chosen because they were convenient to study, not because they were randomly selected representatives of a defined population. Therefore, the value of such studies resides in what they tell about the people who participated directly in those investigations rather than in generalizations that might be proposed about a population of sixth-graders, kindergarten children, or families. In effect, there is no available statistical procedure for estimating how well convenience samples reflect the pertinent characteristics of whatever population a researcher may wish to speak about.

The best a researcher can do in such situations is to (a) identify the features of the sample that seem to be causal factors (factors that influence keyboarding, ways of settling disputes, and family members' roles), then speculate about whether those same factors might obtain in other groups (representing a population) that could be studied. For instance, the teachers who evaluated the keyboarding skills of their school's sixth graders might suggest that results similar to the ones obtained in their research would perhaps be found in other schools that displayed similar—and apparently influential—conditions, such as, (a) the same computer facilities, (b) the same computer-literacy instruction, (c) teachers with similar training, and (d) pupils from similar socioeconomic backgrounds. However, such generalizing from an available or convenience sample to an assumed population is a very risky venture, since there is no clear way of identifying and measuring the factors that may have biased the sample's results.

CONCLUSION

The purpose of this chapter has been to describe some of the more popular ways to summarize quantitative research results, to estimate how accurately a sample of people or events represents a population about which the researcher wishes to speak, and to draw samples from populations. The chapter's presentation of these matters has admittedly been cursory at best. For more complete treatments of statistical and sampling techniques, readers can consult the sources listed in the Suggested Readings.

SUGGESTED READINGS

Babbie, E. R. (1990). *Survey research methods* (2nd ed.). Belmont, CA: Wadsworth.

Barnett, V. (1991). *Sample survey principles and methods.* New York: Oxford University Press.

Chaudhuri, A., & Vos, J. W. E. (1988). *Unified theory and strategies of survey sampling.* New York: Elsevier.

Glass, G. V., & Hopkins, K. D. (1996). *Statistical methods in education and psychology* (3rd ed.). Boston: Allyn & Bacon.

Gravetter, F. J. (1988). *Statistics for the behavioral sciences.* St. Paul, MN: West.

Hays, W. L. (1994). *Statistics* (5th ed.). Fort Worth, TX: Harcourt Brace.

Henry, G. T. (1990). *Practical sampling.* Newbury Park, CA: Sage.

Kish, L. (1965). *Survey sampling.* New York: Wiley.

MacNeill, I. B., & Humphrey, G. J. (1987). *Applied probability, stochastic processes, and sampling theory.* Boston: Klumer.

Popham, W. J., & Sirotnkik, K. A. (1992). *Understanding statistics in education.* Itasca, IL: Peacock.

Rea, L. M., & Parker, R. A. (1992). *Designing and conducting survey research.* San Francisco: Jossey-Bass.

Sirkin, R. M. (1995). *Statistics for the social sciences.* Thousand Oaks, CA: Sage.

RESEARCH PROJECT CHECKLIST

In planning their investigations, researchers can profit from answering the following queries. "In my research project, do I plan to—."

1. Use any graphic displays of quantitative information? If so, what types of displays will I provide?
   ___Pie charts
   ___Bar graphs (histograms)
   ___Other (describe)_____

2. Use any descriptive statistics? If so, which ones?
   2.1 Proportions
      ___Percentages
      ___Percentiles
   2.2 Measures of central tendency
      ___Mean
      ___Median
      ___Mode
   2.3 Measures of variability
      ___Range
      ___Interquartile range
      ___Distance between percentiles _____&_____
      ___Variance
      ___Standard deviation
      ___Other (describe)_____
   2.4 Measures of skewness
      ___Type (identify)_____
   2.5 Correlation measures
      ___Pearson product-moment (r)
      ___Spearman rank-order (ρ)
      ___Biserial (r_b)
      ___Phi coefficient, contingency coefficient (r_ϕ)
      ___Eta coefficient (curvilinear relationship) (η)
      ___Factor analysis
      ___Other (identify)_____

3. Use any inferential statistics? If so, which ones?
   ___t-test
   ___ANOVA
   ___Other (describe)_____

4. Apply the conclusions I draw from my research results to encompass a population of which my data are apparently a sample?   If so, what method of sampling will my study employ?

     ___Simple random
     ___Multistage
     ___Cluster
     ___Systematic
     ___Convenience (available)
     ___Other (describe)_____

10

Tables and Graphs

An economical method of presenting a summary of complex information is to cast it in tabular or graphic form. Narrative descriptions of data necessarily arrange ideas in linear order, one idea after another in single file. In contrast, tables and graphs are able to display a quantity of information concurrently, enabling readers not only to view a variety of items simultaneously but also to grasp the items' interrelationships. In the present chapter, strengths and limitations of these two modes of organizing data are illustrated with comparative examples.

DISPLAYING DATA IN TABULAR FORM

Tables consist of lists of items arranged in rows and columns. Some lists are quite simple, involving only one variable (Table 10-1—moral values). Others are complex, involving multiple variables (Table 10-2—world regions' illiteracy rates and per-inhabitant expenditures on education). Various methods can be used for ordering the items in a list. They can be arranged randomly (Table 10-1), alphabetically (Table 10-2), chronologically, quantitatively, or as steps in a process.

Not only can tabular information be presented as a single list (Table 10-1), but it can also be organized as a matrix whose individual cells show the interaction of the row and column variables (Table 10-2).

Several dimensions can be accommodated in a matrix if, along each of the axes, subcategories of variables are included. By such a device, Table 10-3 accommodates four variables on the horizontal and vertical axes (grade level and sex on the x axis, district and school on the y axis) plus a fifth variable within the cells (average mathematics test scores). As suggested by Table 10-3, using the rows (the vertical axis) to represent the more extensive series of variables (districts and schools) makes more efficient use of page arrangement in a research report than does assigning those variables to the columns.

Table 10-1

Moral Values in Textbooks—Taiwan and Indonesia

The Moral Values	Taiwan	Indonesia
Diligence in study—Try hard in school.	X	X
Politeness—Follow rules of social intercourse.	X	X
Patriotism—Support the nation.	X	X
Public-mindedness—Protect the environment.	X	
Honesty—Tell the truth, never cheat.	X	X
Godliness—Honor and obey God.		X
Thrift—Save money, do not waste materials.	X	
Tolerance—Respect others' social status and opinions.		X
Courageousness—Be brave, do not fear difficulties.	X	
Freedom—Freely organize and express opinions.		X
Filial piety—Respect and obey parents.	X	X
Persistence—Never stop trying.	X	

(X = The value appears in textbooks.)

Sources: Lin (1985, pp. 74-77); *Pendidikan moral pancasila* (1982-83).

Table 10-2

World Regions' Illiteracy Rates and Per-Inhabitant Expenditures

Region	1995—Percent of Illiterates in Population: Age 15 and Over			Public Expenditure on Education Per Inhabitant in U.S. Dollars	
	Total	Female	Male	1980	1993
World Total	22.6%	28.8%	16.4%	$129	$229
Africa	43.8	54.0	33.5	48	36
America	8.3	8.9	7.6	310	597
Asia	27.7	36.6	19.1	41	92
Europe	1.5	1.8	1.2	417	782
Oceania	5.2	6.5	3.9	467	743
Developing Countries	42.0%	53.2%	31.1%	$32	$43
Developed Countries	1.3%	1.6%	1.1%	$500	$1,089

Source: UNESCO, 1995, pp. 2-8, 2-28.

Table 10-3

Average Math Test Scores in Two School Districts*

	Grade 3			Grade 6		
	Boys	*Girls*	*All*	*Boys*	*Girls*	*All*
District 3						
J. Q. Adams School	62	72	67	81	79	80
M. L. King School	58	64	61	84	82	83
J. F. Kennedy School	67	69	68	82	84	83
District 3 Average	**62.3**	**68.3**	**65.3**	**82.3**	**81.7**	**82**
District 7						
Oakdale School	51	47	49	64	60	62
East Lane School	48	41	45	58	64	61
Central School	57	61	59	73	70	72
El Monte School	61	58	60	76	74	75
District 7 Average	**54.3**	**51.8**	**53.3**	**67.8**	**67.0**	**67.5**
District 8						
Carlton School	73	73	73	84	82	83
Elm Grove School	70	76	73	86	87	87
Bayside School	56	60	58	70	66	68
District 8 Average	**66.3**	**69.7**	**68.0**	**80.0**	**78.3**	**79.3**
Districts Combined	**61.0**	**63.3**	**62.2**	**76.7**	**75.7**	**76.3**

*Potential scores ranged from 0 to 100. More advanced mathematical operations were required on the sixth-grade test than on the third-grade test.

A narrative accompanying Table 10-3 can direct readers' attention to significant features of the data. For example, girls tended to score slightly higher than boys at the third-grade level in districts 3 and 8. However, at the sixth-grade level in all three districts, boys scored slightly higher than girls. In addition, the lowest (Bayside) and the highest (Carlton and Elm Grove) scores occurred in the same district (District 8) at both the third-grade and sixth-grade levels.

DISPLAYING DATA IN GRAPHIC FORM

Graphs are diagrams that communicate multiple variables and their interrelationships in a way that would be difficult to convey in a narrative. Whereas tables are generally superior to graphs in summarizing multiple, precise quantities, graphs are usually more effective for showing complex interactions among variables. The types of graphic displays illustrated in the following section are time lines, trend graphs, path analyses, maps, organization charts, flow charts, and theory-structure charts.

Time Lines

A time line portrays chronological relationships among events. Compared with verbal descriptions, time lines are more effective in delineating the length of periods between events and in presenting all events simultaneously.

Figure 10-1

Time Line of Nations' First Universities

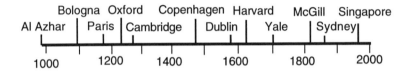

A description accompanying the time line can offer details about the pictured data. For instance, the specific years in which the universities in Figure 10-1 were established can be furnished in this sort of verbal summary:

The dates that various nations' earliest universities were founded are as follows:
    Egypt's Al Azhar University—970 by the Fatimid Islamic dynasty
    Italy's University of Bologna—around 1100
    France's University of Paris—late 1100s
    England's Oxford (1249) and Cambridge (1284) Universities
    Denmark's Copenhagen University—1479
    Ireland's University of Dublin—1591 by Queen Elizabeth I
    The United States' Harvard (1636) and Yale (1701) Universities
    Canada's McGill University—1821
    Australia's University of Sydney—1850
    Singapore's National University—1980

Trend Graphs

Depicting the pace of change over time is illustrated in Figure 10-2, which shows the estimated growth in the world's population by year 2050. When trends for a variety of variables are displayed, it is appropriate to apply a different style to each line (solid, dotted, dashed, dash-dot lines) so as to distinguish clearly among the variables. The following type of explanation can suggest educational implications of the trend.

Figure 10-2

Projected World Population Increase

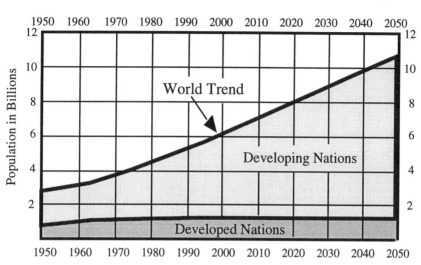

Virtually all of the next half-century's population increase will occur in developing nations, since the advanced industrial societies have by now nearly reached a steady state of growth due to family-planning practices and other social conditions that cause the developed countries to produce hardly more than enough children to replace their elders in the population. This means that the most serious educational problems associated with population growth will be suffered by developing societies. (Thomas, 1990b, p. 304)

Path Analysis

The statistical procedure known as *path analysis* equips researchers to estimate the route through which causal factors influence outcomes. The procedure involves calculating the correlations among variables that are measured in a research project. An example is a study by Hoy, Tarter, and Witkoskie (1992) in which the authors assessed five variables relating to the attitudes of school personnel and the effectiveness of a school—(a) how supportive the school principal appeared as a leader of the faculty, (b) teachers' interactions with their peers (collegiality), (c) teachers' trust in the principal, (d) teachers' trust in their colleagues, and (e) the effectiveness of the school (Figure 10-3).

Figure 10-3

Path Analysis of School Principals' Influence

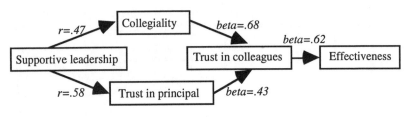

Source: Hoy, Tarter, & Witkoskie, 1992, p. 42.

The authors explained that:

The results demonstrated the complexity of the relationships. Supportive principal leadership produced colleagiality and trust in principals, but not trust in colleagues. Teacher trust in colleagues, not leadership behavior of the principal, explained effectiveness in schools. (Hoy, Tarter, & Witkoskie, 1992, p. 38)

Maps

Maps offer readers an instant impression of the comparative locations of regions, nations, districts, institutions, or events that are the subjects of educational research. Maps are helpful in explaining such matters as the places from which samples were drawn for a survey or experiment, transportation routes to schools, the effect of population concentration on the location of educational facilities, the historical development of different types of schools, and the boundaries of various educational authorities' jurisdiction. Maps also aid in portraying relationships between schools' curriculum content and the geographical distribution of regions' languages, religions, vocational opportunities, and social-class structures.

Maps are useful as well in space comparisons of limited scope—floor-plan designs for a new school, ways of arranging tables and desks in a classroom, and alternative traffic patterns for moving students efficiently between class periods in a crowded high school.

The ability of maps to offer readers concise visual summaries is illustrated by one that accompanied research focusing on bilingual education programs in the United States (Figure 10-4). In this case, the investigator included the map to show the sections of the country in greatest need of programs to serve learners from homes in which Spanish was spoken.

Figure 10-4

Concentrations of Spanish Speakers

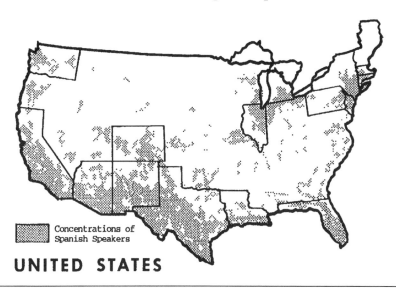

UNITED STATES

Organization Charts

Diagrams depicting the components of an organization are useful in delineating how the various parts of a social structure are related to each other. Two of the more popular kinds of charts are those that picture the institutions that compose a formal education system (Figure 10-5) and those that show power and communication relationships within an authority structure (Figure 10-6).

The comparison in Figure 10-5 is between the formal education systems of a typical industrialized society (Nation A) and a representative developing society (Nation B). For both nations, each level of the schooling hierarchy is cast in the form of a box whose width represents the total population of school-age children or youth in the society. The shaded portion within each box shows the proportion of an age group that is enrolled in the formal education system. Although both nations have compulsory school-attendance laws (age 6 to 16 in Nation A, age 7 to 14 in Nation B), it is apparent that Nation B has been unable to enforce compulsory attendance, as shown by the progressive rate of dropouts throughout the years of basic schooling. Additional variables summarized in the chart are the range of each formal education system in terms of years of schooling, the title of each schooling level, and the length of each level (in years).

Figure 10-5

Organization Structures of Two School Systems

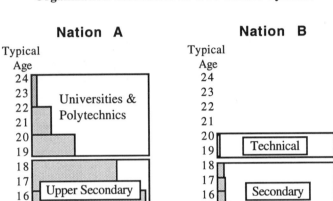

= Percentage of age group enrolled in school.

Diagrams are also often used for picturing the intended authority and communication patterns within an organization. It is the case, however, that the intended patterns may not entirely represent the way the organization actually operates. Figure 10-6 shows how discrepancies between a formal structure and informal reality can be conveyed in a single diagram. The intended operation of a hypothetical small city's administrative hierarchy is shown in the lines connecting the rectangles. Authority (decisions and power) is expected to flow from the board of education at the top, down through the administration's officers and bureaus, to the school principals, and to the teachers. Decisions are to be communicated along those same routes. However, an inspection of events

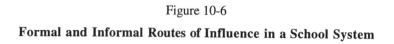

Figure 10-6

Formal and Informal Routes of Influence in a School System

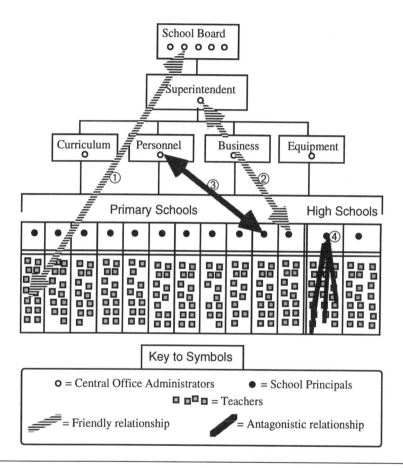

in the schools shows that power and communication often flow along channels other than those pictured in the system's formal structure. Four such exceptions to the formal plan are identified by the shaded arrows superimposed over the formal diagram. Arrow ① connects a school board member with a primary-school teacher who happens to be the member's sister. Because brother and sister maintain a close, friendly relationship and frequently discuss school business, the sister is able to wield greater influence over educational policies and practices than can the typical teacher. Arrow ② signifies an informal relationship between the superintendent of schools and a primary-school principal who is the superintendent's golf partner. Their weekly game of golf provides the principal information about school affairs before other principals learn of such matters through official channels. Arrows ③ and ④ identify antagonistic relationships that detract from the smooth operation of the administrative system. Link ③ represents a feud between a school principal and the director of personnel services—a feud affecting the appointment of teachers to the school. Link ④ signifies a conflict between a high school principal and a group of teachers who frequently refuse to carry out the principal's directives.

Flow Charts

The step by step operation of some aspect of education can be summarized in the form of a flow chart. The example in Figure 10-7 shows the phases through which a research proposal in a university's educational research bureau will pass from the initial introduction of the project to its final review stage.

Figure 10-7

Routes Followed by Projects in an Educational Research Bureau

I: INITIAL PROPOSAL STAGE			II: TENTATIVE ACCEPTANCE STAGE	
Proposals solicited	General proposal received	General proposal appraised	Detailed proposal (steps, personnel, equipment, budget)	Funds solicited

III: OPERATIONAL STAGE				
Personnel selected	Assignments given	Data collected	Data Analyzed	Interpretations & implications drawn
Equipment obtained	Staff trained			

IV: REPORT AND DISSEMINATION STAGE		V: PROJECT REVIEW STAGE		
Reports written	Reports distributed	Efficiency criteria determined	Project steps assessed	Recommendations offered

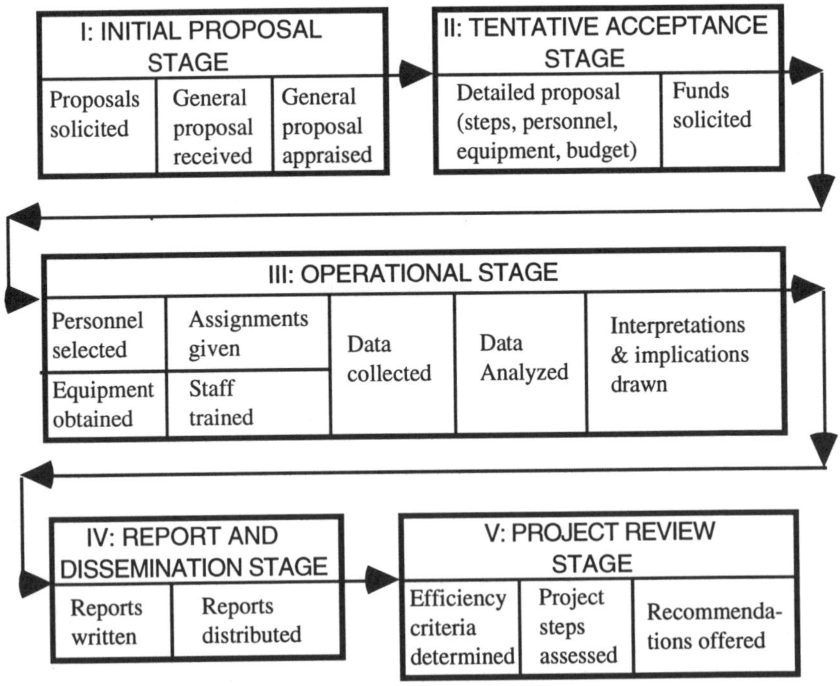

In a similar manner, diagrams can effectively summarize a wide range of other educational processes, such as the steps to be taken in planning and constructing a new school building, in dismissing an unsatisfactory teacher, in passing a law bearing on education, in teaching reading to young children, in publishing a textbook, and far more.

Theory-Structure Charts

A theory relating to a research project is often easier for readers to grasp if the verbal description is accompanied by a diagram identifying the theory's components and the interactions among the components. Figure 10-8 illustrates such a diagram.

I devised Figure 10-8 while conducting a study of (a) the conception of human personality embedded in Hindu religious doctrine and (b) educational implications of such a conception (Thomas, 1997b, Chap. 11). I was unable to find a consolidated Hindu description of personality structure and thus was obliged to collect elements of such a structure from diverse writings and to combine the elements in the following description, which was then cast in the graphic form shown in Figure 10-8.

Hindu theory divides the human being into two general parts—the physical (the visible body) and the nonphysical (consisting of mind, soul, will, and karma). When a person dies, the physical aspect gradually disintegrates and the mind and will disappear, but the soul that contains the karma continues to exist, ready to inhabit a new body for another sojourn on earth. The soul and karma, in effect, transmigrate into a new body upon the demise of the present body.

The term *karma* identifies both a product and a process. The process is founded on the following convictions:

(a) People's actions can be either morally good (faithful to the revered rules), or morally bad (in violation of the rules), or neutral (unrelated to the rules).

(b) Good behavior produces a positive effect or residue in the soul, bad behavior produces a negative effect, and neutral behavior produces no effect.

(c) Karma, as a product, consists of the algebraic sum of the positive and negative effects in a person's soul up to the present time. Karma is thus a kind of moral bank balance, with the bad deeds subtracted from the good deeds to yield a total which can be either dominantly negative or dominantly positive.

Hindu authorities agree that key features of the body-soul configuration include the senses, which vary in different accounts from eight to ten in number. Each sense is a seeker or grasper (*ghraha*) of a particular sort of experience (*atigraha*). In contrast to Western conceptions, the senses in Hindu theory include both receptors, such as the eyes, and executors of deeds, such as the hands. The senses and their external experiences form pairings, like the following from the *Kausitaki Upanishads*: Ear is paired with sound, tongue with taste, eye with visible form, smell with odor, speech with name, hands with action, feet with

Figure 10-8

Summarizing a Theoretical Model in Graphic Form

THE PERSON

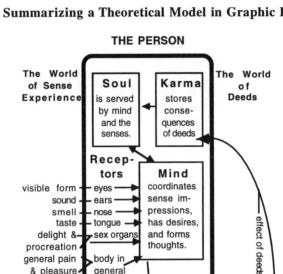

movement, the body in general with pleasure and pain, the sex organs with delight and procreation (Keith, 1925, p. 556).

A typical way Hindu theory interrelates these pairings is to envision the mind as the integrating center for the senses and to assign the mind the tasks of governing "desire, judgment, belief, doubt, unbelief, firmness, weakness, modesty, knowledge, fear . . . . Mind, therefore, is responsible for forming into ideas the impressions of the senses (sight, hearing, taste, smell, touch), which mind then—in the form of *will* motivated by *desire*—transforms into resolves that are carried out by the organs of action" (Keith, 1925, p. 554-555).

One way that the components of personality change with the passing of time is in the maturation of the mind—the accumulation of knowledge cultivated by the study of holy texts, by daily experiences, and by introspective meditation. In addition, a person's karma is expected to change as thoughts and deeds add to, or subtract from, the existing sum of karma.

A single diagram, such as the one in Figure 10-8, enables readers to compare the interrelationships among the elements of a theory. A display can assume an additional comparative dimension if two or more diagrams are juxtaposed to reveal likenesses and differences among theories—as when the Hindu model is placed beside models of Buddhist, Christian, and Freudian beliefs.

CONCLUSION

The tables and graphic displays reviewed in this chapter obviously fail to represent all of the kinds that researchers use to clarify their studies. Other forms can be found in books and journals that publish studies of educational matters.

RESEARCH PROJECT CHECKLIST

1. Do I plan to include tables in my research report? If so, for each table, what variables will I place on the x axis (columns) and what variables on the y axis (rows)?

2. Do I plan to include any charts, diagrams, or graphs in my research report? If so, which type or types will I use?

    ___1. Time line
    ___2. Trend graph
    ___3. Path analysis
    ___4. Map
    ___5. Organization chart
    ___6. Flow chart
    ___7. Theory-structure chart
    ___8. Other (describe)_____

Stage IV:
Interpreting the Results

The task of interpreting research outcomes involves answering the question: What does it all mean? The three chapters comprising Stage IV focus on ways of assigning meanings to content analyses (Chapter 11), to observations (Chapter 12), and to tests, questionnaires, and interviews (Chapter 13). The conception of *meaning* adopted in those chapters holds that different kinds of interpretation can be imposed on research outcomes, and each kind is reflected in the answer to a particular question. The following paragraphs identify a series such questions and the ways data can be interpreted to provide answers from descriptive, explanatory, evaluative, and predictive vantage points.

DESCRIPTIVE MEANINGS

As noted earlier, comparative descriptions involve telling how two or more entities are similar to and different from each other, without attempting to explain what has caused the similarities and differences or to evaluate whether one entity is better than another.

The emphasis in descriptive comparisons can be on analysis, synthesis, or both. *Analysis* means dissecting an educational event, organization, or practice into its constituent parts. The question that guides analysis is: What are the components of the entity being studied, and what significant relationships exist among those components?

Synthesis refers to the act of drawing together disparate entities to form a combined entity. Synthesizing typically produces an overarching set of principles or generalizations that can link together the constituent entities. The guide question becomes: What do the different educational phenomena have in common? How are they alike?

Interpreting a comparison in terms of both analysis and synthesis involves answering the three-part question: What are the constituent parts of each of the compared educational phenomena (analysis), how do the parts and their interrelationships differ between the two phenomena (contrast), and what generalizations can be drawn about what the compared phenomena have in common (synthesis)?

In short, the meaning of descriptive investigations lies in the recognition of their comparative similarities and differences. Such descriptive interpretations can be either brief and synoptic or lengthy and complex.

EXPLANATORY MEANINGS

The word *explanation* refers to proposals of how and why two or more educational phenomena came to their observed condition. Thus, an explanation identifies probable causes for the described likenesses and differences between educational entities. The question that guides explanatory interpretations becomes: Which factors account for the similarities and contrasts between educational phenomena, how much does each factor contribute to the phenomena's condition, and what is the nature of interaction among those factors that brings about such an outcome?

As noted in Chapters 1 and 2, the term *theory* or *model* is often used to identify the collection of ideas advanced for explaining cause. Thus, structural/functional theory and conflict theory serve as two different ways of accounting for how a particular set of educational outcomes arrived in their present state.

EVALUATIVE MEANINGS

The perspective represented by evaluative interpretations is guided by the question: Which of two educational entities is the better in terms of specified criteria of desirability? Or, in what order can several educational entities be ranked in regard to a particular set of standards of efficiency, propriety, cost/benefit, or the like?

Evaluative interpretation, therefore, calls not only for a description of the compared entities' characteristics, but also a set of appraisal criteria and a rationale in support of why those particular criteria are proper guides to evaluation.

PREDICTIVE MEANINGS

As mentioned in earlier chapters, predicting typically involves a description of the past and current states of entities, plus an estimate of what causes have been responsible for those past and present states. On the basis of such information, an estimate of the future condition of the entities can be constructed. Hence, drawing predictive interpretations can be directed by the question: What trends in the condition of the compared entities have developed from the past into the present, what causal factors apparently account for the direction and pace of those trends, how will those factors likely continue to operate in the future, and therefore what condition will the entities probably display on some specified future date?

RESEARCH PROJECT CHECKLIST

1. What kinds of interpretation do I intend to include in my study?
   ____1.1 Descriptive
       ____1.1.1 Analysis
       ____1.1.2 Synthesis
       ____1.1.3 Analysis and synthesis
   ____1.2 Explanatory
   ____1.3 Evaluative
   ____1.4 Predictive

11

Interpreting Content Analyses

Rarely is the purpose of content analysis simply that of describing one or more characteristics of a communication. Instead, the purpose is to use the description as the foundation for a proposal about what the described results mean. This chapter offers a sample of 15 types of interpretation organized under two divisions. The first nine types are general forms. The last six can more precisely be viewed as varieties of hermeneutics.

GENERAL FORMS OF INTERPRETING THE CONTENT OF COMMUNICATIONS

Researchers can offer various meanings of documents. The kinds illustrated in the following paragraphs are not intended to represent an exhaustive list but merely to show that a number of different meanings can be constructed from the results of descriptive analyses. The first three represent attempts of authors to express the essence of communications. The next three involve researchers' efforts to identify causes of depicted events. The final three perform confirmative, hortatory, and evaluative functions. As the discussion progresses, it will become apparent that the types are not mutually exclusive. Frequently, two or more modes are combined.

Expressing the Essence of Communications

Three ways researchers attempt to portray the essential nature of messages are by suggesting the documents' key themes, identifying personal qualities of the communications' subjects, or offering synopses of the documents' contents.

Key Themes Interpretation

In this variety, the investigator tries to capture in a few phrases the essence of a communication in respect to the themes it treats. The question guiding this effort is: What core ideas does the document contain? The task of interpretation assumes a comparative form when it sets the themes of one document—or one set of documents—against the themes of another, as in Gerbert's comparison of Japanese and American elementary-school reading books.

> Cultural diversity, so absent in the Japanese reader, is everywhere present in the American reader. So varied are the characters and experiences depicted in [American books] that one is often left wondering what nation their audiences might be living in. By contrasting the Japanese textbooks with American textbooks, I hope to show how Japanese materials are designed to create a common singular consciousness in their youth, . . . a sense of belonging to the Japanese nation. (Gerbert, 1993, p. 153)

An example from a more distant historical setting is Boorstin's (1948) view of the contrasting purposes of higher education in Thomas Jefferson's writings and in the Harvard University curriculum of Jefferson's day.

Boorstin points out in his book *The Lost World of Thomas Jefferson* that Jefferson's notions of modernity and usefulness tended to leave an educational legacy that was essentially "uncritical and conservative," whereas Harvard's more traditional emphasis on metaphysics and pure science made it "a center of intellectual ferment, a breeding ground for potent and revolutionary ideas, for new and pregnant systems of philosophy" (Bailey, 1978, p. 7).

Extracting key themes is not simply an objective act. As with all interpretation, it involves a substantial measure of personal judgment. In an effort to convince their audience, key-theme analysts may describe in some detail the line of reasoning that led to the themes they put forth. However, this effort may still leave some doubt in the reader's mind, as implied by Bailey's slightly guarded reaction to Boorstin's conception of the themes embedded in Jefferson's writings and the Harvard curriculum.

> Whether Boorstin is right or wrong, Jefferson's notion of educational utility was far removed from the emerging concepts of educational utility today. (Bailey, 1978, p. 7)

Personal Qualities Interpretation

Often an analyst endeavors to abstract from documents prominent features of an individual's or a group's personality. The documents that frequently serve this purpose are biographies, letters, speeches, and regulations that the individual or group has formulated. The question guiding such inquiry is: What characteristics typify this individual's or group's thought and behavior?

One variety of this sort of interpretation consists of a researcher comparing the personal qualities of different individuals who interact in an educational context. A case in point is Kyle's examination of the life of Cara Mallet, an English-woman who served in Australia as principal of a teacher-training college for women over the period 1883-1885. In her synthesis of information from a variety of archival materials, Kyle characterized Mallet and three other women who succeeded her as:

> well-educated, interested in promoting academic excellence for female trainees, and active in pursuing curriculum change and new teaching practices. . . . [They were] ambitious and adventurous, and they actively pursued professional gains and better training within the real constraints of the times. They were also the first tertiary-trained women professionals in Australia. This characteristic alone marks them out as especially interesting compared to their contemporaries. (Kyle, 1992, p. 485)

In contrast, a male principal of another institution, who took offense at Ms. Mallet's criticism of the way he taught English literature, was pictured in Kyle's analysis as having "penned a bitter response" to Ms. Mallet's reproach; "his apologia for his program proved less than convincing" and he "scorned her suggestion that studying 'two books' would be more appropriate." He stated that "'we are not disposed to commend any departure'" from his traditional mode of instruction. Kyle's analysis then continued with:

> One wonders at his use of the royal "we"! Perhaps he felt he was speaking for the department and other male teachers and administrators. Nonetheless, his use of the word "safe" is illustrative of his caution and opposition to change. (Kyle, 1992, p. 483)

Synoptic Interpretation

In synoptic interpretation, the analyst endeavors to provide a concise version of a longer communication. The analysis is guided by the question: How can I best prepare a brief version that is true to the spirit and content of the original document?

A synopsis goes beyond just identifying key themes in that it provides considerable detail, and in some cases it attempts to maintain a sense of the original author's writing style. In the comparative form of synoptic interpretation, summaries of two or more communications are placed side by side, with the analyst usually pointing out what could be regarded as significant similarities and differences. An example is the book *Models of Moral Education* in which each chapter represents an abridged version of a particular theorist's moral-education program—Shaver's rationale-building model, McPhail's consid-eration model, Raths' values-clarification model, Kohlberg's cognitive-moral-development model, and more (Hersh, Miller, & Fielding, 1980).

The researcher's challenge in synoptic interpretation is to decide what to take from the original documents and what to leave out. To do this properly, the investigator needs to be guided by selection criteria which identify comparable features to be derived from each document. For instance, the team of analysts who wrote the book *Oriental Theories of Human Development* used a series of questions to determine what they would distill from authoritative writings of five philosophical/religious traditions—Buddhism, Confucianism, Hinduism, Islam, and Shinto (Thomas, 1988). The questions concerned such issues as (1) the origin of the human species, (2) the goals of development, (3) causes of development, (4) the structure of human personality, and (5) implications of the theory for child rearing and education. Each religion's answers to the questions formed the content of the particular chapter of the book focusing on that philosophical tradition.

Causal Interpretations

The process of causal analysis involves two steps (1) identifying a correlation between two or more phenomena and (2) providing a line of logic which suggests that one of those phenomena is the result—at least partially—of the other. The first step—demonstrating a correlation—is descriptive; it consists of showing that as one factor changed, the other also changed, at least to some degree. The second step—establishing a causal link—is speculative, representing the analyst's estimate of how one of the factors has caused, or could cause, a related one.

Three versions of causal interpretation can be called the explanatory, the predictive, and the implicative.

Explanatory Interpretation

Explanatory analysis is concerned with the past, focusing on events that have already occurred. In one form of explanation, the researcher's purpose is to detect the influence of earlier documents (the antecedent or independent variable) on subsequent events (the outcome or dependent variable). The connection the analyst is seeking to establish can be expressed as a question.

> In what ways did changes in the university's sexual harassment rules alter faculty-student relationships?
> In terms of compulsory-education regulations, what differences are found among the Thai, Singaporean, and Malaysian school systems, and how have these differences affected school enrollments?

Another form of explanatory interpretation reverses the order of documents and events. Past events are viewed as responsible for the characteristics of subsequent documents. A familiar version of this approach involves an analyst identifying differences between an earlier document and its later counterpart, then proposing that particular events occurring in the time between the two publications are responsible for those differences. A case of Japanese school books illustrates this point. In 1993, new history textbooks approved by Japan's ministry of education (*Mombusho*) replaced existing texts in the nation's schools. Observers noted that a significant difference between the old and new books was their description of Japan's occupation of Korea (1905-1945) and invasion of China (1931-1945). According to Greenlees:

> The ministry has traditionally preferred to overlook some of the uncomfortable facts of Japan's wartime history. Details of atrocities such as the notorious massacre of Nanking in 1937, when the Japanese army raped and murdered thousands of Chinese civilians, have repeatedly been deleted from school textbooks. Existing history texts describe the 1937 invasion of China as "an advance" and largely ignore unpalatable events such as the infamous Bataan Death March [in the Philippines]. The new textbooks . . . are intended to provide a more honest picture of Japan at war. (Greenlees, 1993)

To account for the reasons behind such changes, Greenlees proposed that:

> The whole revision of history texts, the first in 12 years, is partly a response to the barrage of complaints from South Korea, China, and other East Asian states about the way Japanese children are presented with "sanitised" versions of their country's wartime history. (Greenlees, 1993)

As support for his analysis, Greenlees noted: "In a recent statement, the Japanese ministry of education agreed that consideration must be given to events in modern history that concern both Japan and its neighbours." He then provided his own estimate of motives behind the ministry's move.

> The Japanese hope that a fairer, franker account will lead to improved political and economic relations between Japan and its neighbours. The South Korean embassy in Tokyo has already welcomed the acknowledgement of the forced use of Korean women as "comfort women." (Greenlees, 1993)

In contrast to the people who analyze documents to explain causal influences, there are critics who play the role of debunkers, disputing the validity of such analyses. Debunkers operate either by doubting that the investigator truly understood the documents or by disputing the line of logic with which the investigator has connected the contents of documents to events. An example is Walford's quarreling with the argument put forward in a book focusing on connections between education and poverty.

> The authors claim that the first of [their] chapters uses data from up to 40 countries to investigate the effect of education on reducing poverty. . . . What the chapter actually does is provide some interesting correlations between various factors for the countries selected. . . . But it is positively misleading for the authors to infer causation from correlation. . . [in that] they do not overcome

the simple problem of untangling whether, for example, more equitable income distributions are caused by improvements in education or vice versa. The reality is probably a lot more complex than either possibility. (Walford, 1993, p. 84)

Predictive Interpretation

Predictive analysis addresses the future. Its aim is to estimate the influence that presently existing or newly proposed communications will exert on events in the days or years ahead. A predictive interpretation is essentially an inference about a likely causal connection between particular communications and specified future events. As in the case of explanatory interpretations, the connection the analyst is postulating can be expressed as a question. Here are three examples:

Will the newly proposed school-attendance voucher system result in higher levels of student performance than the levels found under present school-funding policies?

What changes can be expected in the contents of science textbooks if religious groups' criticisms of humanistic secularism replace prevailing publishing guidelines?

Will statistics on immigration trends affect regulations governing the language of instruction to be used in schools?

Implicative Interpretation

Implicative analysis is similar to the predictive variety in the sense that both of them focus on the future. However, the two differ in their emphasis. Predictive interpretation consists of speculating about what *will likely occur* as a consequence of a communication, whereas implicative interpretation concerns *potential applications* of a communication. Two subtypes of implicative interpretation involve comparing (1) different analysts' educational applications of the same document and (2) an analyst's proposing applications of two different documents.

Same Author, Different Analysts. Although the Swiss psychologist Jean Piaget wrote voluminously about child development, he seldom proposed educational implications of his theories (Piaget, 1970, 1973a). That job was left to his host of disciples, whose opinions sometimes differed regarding the types of applications that should reasonably derive from Piaget's writings (Elkind, 1976; Furth & Wachs, 1975; Kamil & DeVries, 1980; Murray, 1979; Varma & Williams, 1976).

Same Analyst, Different Authors. Whenever a single researcher infers educational practices from documents deriving from different authors, the results of this inquiry may form the contents of a book bearing such a title as *Models of Moral Education* (Hersh, Miller, & Fielding, 1980).

Confirmative Interpretation

Content analysis performs a confirmative function whenever the comparison of communications is intended to corroborate a belief the analyst wishes to advance. One sort of confirmative analysis is the manifold-support type, guided by the question: How much documentary evidence can I compile in support of my position? Another is the conflicting-version variety, derived from answering the question: Which of several contradictory accounts of an event is most convincing?

In the manifold-support type, multiple documents are interpreted as all substantiating the hypothesis, viewpoint, policy, or practice the analyst is advocating. In other words, the analyst seeks to convince others of the soundness of his or her stance by offering not just one, but a multitude of materials in support of that position. In way of illustration, Cremin (1970, p. 657) cites 12 "recent works" that represent the "serious and systematic study of characteristic family life" on which he based his own rendition of family influences on education in colonial America.

In the conflicting-version mode, a researcher compares two or more contradictory accounts of a policy or an event, then offers a line of argument to show that the particular account which supports his or her position is the most logical of the lot or, perhaps, is the one best supported by empirical evidence. For instance, Walberg compared policies urging school district consolidation with more recent studies of school district size and proposed that:

> the consolidation of districts into larger units that has been taking place for the past half century may have been a move in the wrong direction. Generally, it appears that the smaller the district, the higher the [student] achievement when the socioeconomic status and per-student expenditures are taken into account. Why? Superintendent and central staff awareness of citizen and parent preferences, the absence of bureaucratic layers and administrative complexity, teacher involvement in decision making, and close home-school relations—these may account for the apparent efficiency of small districts in North America. (Walberg, 1989, P. 162)

Hortatory Interpretation

A central motive behind this kind of analysis is to use the comparison of communications as a means of urging a reading audience to act in support of a particular educational philosophy, policy, organization, or set of practices. It is a form of advocacy research. An illustration is Ross's essay reviewing five books treating feminist themes. The advocacy nature of the essay is reflected in such observations as:

> further research on gender and education must not only reflect the complexity of the relationship between gender and education but analyze the sociopolitical

contexts in which these relationships are forged. . . . The subversive challenge of such a "morally engaged" enterprise "means facing questions of power and conflict that disrupt a comfortable academic world still heavily influenced by the myths of harmony and meritocracy". . . . [These books] suggest the possibilities for creating new knowledge from our educational disorder. (Ross, 1992, pp. 353-354)

Evaluative Interpretation

Evaluative analysis is concerned with judging whether one communication is better or worse than others in terms of specified characteristics, such as cost, social equity, clarity, user convenience, functional efficiency, aesthetic appeal, and far more. For example, several colleges' student-admission policies can be compared in terms of both cost and racial-group equity. Or two versions of a regulation governing the treatment of experimental animals in university psychology laboratories can be analyzed for the documents' clarity of explanation and provisions for protecting the experimental subjects' welfare. Alternative landscape-architecture plans for a high school can be reviewed for their visual charm and their efficiency in routing student traffic. Descriptions of several teacher-education programs can be examined for their balance between theoretical studies and practical classroom experiences.

Oftentimes the comparison is not based on a single document that is intended to represent a given educational practice but, rather, is founded on a series of related documents. This is illustrated in Castro's comparison of five models of vocational education that have been associated with four nations and one region—France, Germany, Japan, the United States, and Latin America (Castro, 1993). From a variety of materials describing vocational education in these countries, Castro extracted "defining characteristics" of each model. He used the resulting characteristics for assessing the models along several dimensions— cost, how well they suited their nation's sociocultural traditions, the extent of labor mobility in the nation, the coordination of schooling with work experience, and the balance between academic and vocational studies.

HERMENEUTICS

Hermeneutics, in its most general sense, can be broadly defined as the art or science of interpretation. Although the word *hermeneutics* has been around for centuries, its present-day heightened popularity in education and in the humanities and social sciences is of rather recent origin, dating principally from the early 1960s. Along with this heightened interest has come a fair amount of puzzlement arising from a lack of consensus among writers about precisely what the aim and methods of hermeneutics are. This lack of agreement even extends to the pronunciation of the term itself. (Is it best as *her-me-NOO-tics, her-me-*

NYOO-tics, or *her-me-NOY-tics*?) One result of the confusion is that potential users of hermeneutics fail to understand when or how to apply its methods.

A search of the literature on hermeneutics to learn how the procedure is defined yields a harvest of mixed worth. Wilhelm Dilthey (1833-1911), the German philosopher most often credited with stimulating the modern-day movement, defined hermeneutics as "understanding social phenomena in terms of the motives of the participants and the meanings [that such motives] give to institutions and events" (Macsporran, 1982, p. 47).

Less clear than Dilthey's statement is Bubner's assertion that: "For hermeneutics, understanding means a fundamental apprehension of truth which takes place in intersubjective processes of communication and in the mediation through history" (Bubner in Mannien & Tuomela, 1976, p. 69).

Equally elusive seems the meaning Giddens intended when writing that hermeneutics involves "grasping frames of meaning contextually as elements of the practice of particular forms of life—and not only consistencies with frames, but also inconsistencies and disputed or contested meanings" (Macsporran, 1982, p. 48).

In view of this murky condition of much of the discourse about hermeneutics, my problem in composing the following presentation was that of determining more precisely what roles hermeneutics might perform in educational research. I attacked the problem by reviewing key writings bearing on document interpretation in various disciplines, then extracting from those writings six functions that might reasonably qualify as hermeneutic activities applicable to educational research (Bozarth-Campbell, 1979; Gadamar, 1975; Garfinkel, 1981; Habermas, 1972; Held, 1980; Macsporran, 1982; Mazzeo, 1978; Odman, 1985; Palmer, 1969; Ricoeur, 1976; Thomas, 1987; von Wright, 1971). The six functions are those of *contextual interpretation, verification interpretation, data-accuracy interpretation, alternative interpretation, clarifying interpretation,* and *symbolism interpretation.*

Contextual Interpretation

In content analysis, *contextual interpretation* most often refers to how a document's meaning is affected by the historical or sociocultural context within which the document was composed. An example is Bailey's comparing the sociocultural environment of Thomas Jefferson's time with Bailey's own late-20th-century environment, implying that if Jefferson were living today he would likely offer quite different educational proposals.

> Most of Jefferson's specific educational assumptions and recommendations are, if taken in their appropriate historical context, starkly irrelevant to our present age. His task was to design an education system to undergird political freedom in a wilderness. Ours is to design an education system to preserve political freedom in a wildly elaborated technology. His task was to fashion an education

suitable for national independence. Ours is to fashion an education suitable for a condition of global interdependence. His task was to construct an educational curriculum that would assist citizens in unlocking and exploiting natural resources. Ours is to remind citizens, through education, that, first, our natural resources are precious gifts that need prudent conservation, and, second, that we must live not as exploiters of nature, but in loving symbiosis with other life and with nature generally. (Bailey, 1978, pp. 6-7)

Verification Interpretation

Verification analysis is aimed at determining the authenticity of a communication. The purpose is to help the analyst decide whether a communication is actually what it is purported to be.   Verification interpretation, in its comparative version, usually involves ascertaining which of two or more communications is the most authentic. This mode of analysis can result in such appraisals as Cremin's conclusion that "The literature on Horatio Alger, Jr., is replete with legend and even some fraudulent biography based on a nonexistent diary. Edwin P. Hoyt, *Horatio's Boys: The Life and Works of Horatio Alger, Jr.* appears to be authoritative" (Cremin, 1980, p. 565).

Perhaps the most common sort of verification analysis is reflected in the question: When there are two somewhat contradictory accounts of an event, which account is the more accurate? In attempting to answer this question, the experienced investigator will typically depend on both internal and external sources of evidence. The word *internal* refers to characteristics of the documents themselves, such things as factual consistency, completeness of presentation, chronological accuracy, and writing style. The word *external* refers to evidence from outside the document that either corroborates the account or casts doubt on it. External evidence usually consists of information about the same events as provided by other documents or witnesses.

Data-Accuracy Interpretation

Sometimes an investigator wonders whether the data and portrayal of events in a document are accurate. The researcher's guide questions become: To what extent are the episodes or information in the document complete, or at least representative of conditions at the time? What other information should have been included in the document to ensure that the data were accurate? Techniques for answering such queries include:

1. Reviewing the apparent sources of the original author's data to estimate whether the author had extracted from them a balanced description of conditions at the time.

2. Searching for new sources of information so as to check the contents of these new sources against the contents of the original author's work to learn

whether adding the new information warrants changing the conclusions drawn in the original work.

3. Estimating reasons for any data inaccuracies that have been discovered in the communication.

Alternative Interpretation

Frequently a critical reader will accept at face value a document's descriptive content but will question the author's interpretation of the material and then will suggest a different meaning for the data. Thus, the comparison the reader draws is between the existing document and an alternative version that the reader either has in mind or actually produces. A case in point is Shields' reaction to Schoppa's book *Education Reform in Japan* (1991).

> The data Schoppa presents, however, do not provide a totally convincing case for *immobilist* politics. The reform agenda he explores appears to originate more from players on the margins of the educational policy process than from the government in its fullest definition. Also, a contrary argument could be made that the government has dynamically moved away from many U.S. occupation democratic reforms toward more historically conservative Japanese practices. The strength of the Schoppa book is the root of its weakness. His data are so comprehensive that it is difficult to find theoretical constructs to give his descriptive detail coherent explanatory power. An obvious first step for Schoppa to consider for dealing with this challenge in future work is to develop more rigorous definitions of such key terms used in his arguments as: *conservative, policy process, immobilist,* and *government.* (Shields, 1992, p. 546)

The researcher's guide questions for conducting such a reappraisal can be: What is the political, moral, social-class, ethnic, or gender vantage point from which the original author viewed the events depicted in this document? To cast the issue in a comparative form, the investigator asks: How might the account have been different if the author had assumed a different vantage point?

This type has been most prominent in recent decades in formerly colonized nations whose people have sought to revise, from their own viewpoint rather than from that of the colonialists, the history of education during colonial times. But such revisionism is not limited to cases of newly independent peoples. It can occur as readily whenever the political control of a state falls into new hands, and the leaders of the new regime choose to recast historical accounts by reinterpreting the previously presented evidence. The resulting revised interpretation typically attributes ignoble motives to the people involved in the original account or else suggests that the educational practices of those earlier times produced different consequences than the ones described in the original document.

The researcher's methods for determining the accuracy of a work's interpretation can involve:

1. Estimating the way political, economic, and social motives of various groups in the society would likely have influenced their explanation of the educational events depicted in the original document, then
2. Comparing the analysis found in the document with the explanation that might derive from each groups' motives in order to determine whether the document's interpretation was biased or else was a balanced representation of different groups' viewpoints.

What often stimulates a scholar to initiate an alternative interpretation is the philosophical or theoretical persuasion to which the scholar subscribes, a persuasion different from that of the original author of the documents under question. For example, Marxist theory may be used for reinterpreting an account of 19th-century schooling in the Pacific Islands that had been written by a Christian missionary who founded schools there. Or conflict theory may be used to reassess changes in Eastern German education as described by a Russian historian after the Soviet Union took political control of Eastern Germany after World War II. When researchers thus intentionally bring a different theoretical perspective to interpreting a communication, they add further items to their list of guide questions: What were the philosophical assumptions and investigative methods of the original author, and how do those compare with the ones I bring to the reinterpretation of the work? What additional kinds of information do I require for my reappraisal, and why are these new kinds needed?

Clarifying Interpretation

The aim of this type is to render the meaning of a communication more easily understood than it was in its original form. In attempting to create a more lucid version of a work, the analyst is essentially saying, "What the author *really* meant was this." The rationale behind producing a clarifying interpretation is that the original version would be inordinately abstruse for potential readers. In other words, phrasings and concepts in the original work would be unduly archaic, foreign, technical, or ambiguous for the audience that the analyst hopes to reach. Examples of clarifying versions are Wadsworth's book *Piaget's Theory of Cognitive and Affective Development* (1989) and the critical reviews that comprise Cahn's edited volume *New Studies in the Philosophy of John Dewey* (1977).

Symbolism Interpretation

Much of language is symbolic, in the sense of words being used to convey meanings that differ from the literal meanings originally attached to those words. For example, the sequence of levels through which children advance in school have been called "the schooling ladder." A politician who wildly launches irrational accusations at a school system may be deemed "a loose cannon." A secondary school teacher whose mode of leading class discussions is reminiscent of Plato's dialogues may be referred to as "the Socrates of the tenth grade."

Not only do authors use individual words and phrases symbolically, but they sometimes speak in parables, describing an event or telling a tale whose meaning is not to be accepted literally but, rather, viewed symbolically as a representation of similar conditions at a different time or place. One of the best known parables in modern-day educational literature is Harold Benjamin's small book entitled *The Sabertooth Curriculum* (1939), which ostensibly describes educational practices in prehistoric times but actually is a parody intended to convey Benjamin's observations of how curriculum change operates in modern times. Jonathan Swift's *Gulliver's Travels* (1726) is one of the best known parables from the past that holds implications for educational practice. Jean Jacques Rousseau's *Emile* (1773), although cast as a novel, is a broad ranging treatise on child rearing and education.

We can thus suggest that when researchers hunt for a communication's symbols and seek to interpret them, they can be led by such questions as: Is the entire document symbolic—a fable, parable, or analog, so that its literal meaning is not the one intended by the writer? Or does the document offer two meanings, one literal and the other symbolic? Is most of the meaning of the document intended to be direct and literal, but within the work there are symbolic meanings found in proverbs, aphorisms, or allusions? How can a researcher recognize symbolic contents?

The investigator can seek answers for these queries through the use of such tools as dictionaries that trace word etymology, collections of proverbs, and literary and professional-education works from the time the document was written. In societies that have depended more on oral rather than written history and literature, clues to symbolic meanings may be sought through interviewing elderly members of the society. Essays, letters, or diaries that the original author produced may address themselves to matters of writing style, including how symbols are employed. If the document under consideration is a translation of a work originally produced in another language, then bilingual dictionaries can prove useful.

CONCLUSION

The varieties of interpretation described in this chapter are no more than a sample of the diverse sorts of analysis authors can apply to the contents of communications. It should be apparent that the types reviewed are not entirely separate but, rather, are intertwined. For instance, the tasks of verifying the authorship of a document and of interpreting a writer's use of symbols are both related to understanding something of the author's motives and the social and intellectual climate of the author's time and place.

It is also clear that content-analysis interpretations may be appropriate at several junctures of a research program. As authors review the published literature related to their research topic, they may summarize the results and significance of previous research in the form of a *synopsis* or identification of *key themes*. In the methods section of a research report, a writer may explain how the present-day social or technological *context* calls for different methods than those used in similar studies of the past. In the interpretation portion of a report, an author may explain how his or her theoretical stance requires an *alternative* to the interpretation offered by the producer of an earlier document.

RESEARCH PROJECT CHECKLIST

Which (if any) of the following types of interpretation of content analyses should I include in my research project?

___key themes
___synoptic
___causal (predictive)
___confirmative
___evaluative
___verification
___alternative
___symbolism
___predictive
___other (describe)_____

___personal qualities
___causal (explanatory)
___causal (implicative)
___hortatory
___contextual
___data accuracy
___clarifying
___implicative

Where in my research report should each (if any) of the selected modes of interpretation be placed?

12

Interpreting Observations

As explained earlier, the term *observation* refers to an investigator's (a) directly witnessing the actions of individuals, groups, institutions, and environments or (b) inspecting products created by individuals, groups, or institutions. Observers can either be bystanders who play no role in the witnessed events or be participants, as happens when they are active members of an organization they are studying. The things that people say in conversation—when giving orders, making requests, lecturing before a class, engaging in debate, and the like—are included among the observed actions that are the focus of Chapter 12. However, respondents' replies to questions that researchers ask in direct interviews are considered in Chapter 13 along with people's answers to written questionnaires.

This chapter offers a motley collection of ways that results of observations can be interpreted. The dual purpose is to suggest something of the diversity of available approaches and to illustrate the approaches with examples of specific educational investigations. The approaches are offered under the following topics: (a) behavior summaries, (b) inferred constructs, (c) learning environments, (d) person-context interactions, (e) instrument validation, (f) alternative cause estimates, and (g) behavior and attitude explorations.

BEHAVIOR SUMMARIES

At the outset, we can usefully examine the distinction drawn in the following pages between behavior summaries and inferred constructs.

A *behavior summary* is a concise description of some aspect of one or more observations. Consider, for example, an interpretation drawn about a four-year-old girl's ability to follow simple directions. The researcher makes the following three-part request, then observes the child's behavior.

Marsha, would you please do this? Pick up the flower that's on the table, put the flower in that glass, then bring me the book that has the picture of the cat on it.

After the child does indeed perform the three steps in the desired sequence, the observer interprets her behavior as reflecting a form of language competence—that of remembering and executing in proper order three requests of the type issued on this occasion. Behavior summaries are thus essentially nondebatable, since they are conclusions any reasonable person would reach. They are instances of "what you see is what you get."

In contrast, *inferred constructs* are often debatable, for they consist of interpretations an observer makes about unobservable abilities, traits, attitudes, values, or motives that are assumed to underlie the observed behavior. The overt behavior, in effect, is interpreted as signifying a general feature of the observed individual's personality. For instance, a spectator watching an informal basketball game on a school playground draws interpretations not only about which participants are the most skillful players (summaries of players' dribbling, passing, and shooting behavior) but also about personality characteristics that presumably underlie certain of their actions, such characteristics as *sense of fair play, desire to win,* and *team spirit.* None of these characteristics consists of observable actions. Instead, each is a psychological construct inferred from what was seen and heard.

The four types of behavior summaries reviewed below are those of specific competencies, likenesses/differences, trends, and time allotments.

Specific Competencies

To decide whether the subjects of a research project command particular types of knowledge or skill, an investigator can observe and summarize how well:

—each kindergarten child skips, hops on one foot, hops on two feet, jumps over a six-inch barrier, and plays a game of hopscotch according to the rules.
—each student in a high school choir sings in tune, keeps in time with the music, and sight-reads a simple song.
—each pupil from an inner-city junior high school exhibits standard American language usage when in conversation (a) with an agemate, (b) with a parent, and (c) with a teacher.
—each basketball player accepts referees' decisions without complaint.

Likenesses and Differences

Frequently researchers interpret data in terms of likenesses and differences among individuals or groups. For instance, observers recorded the contents of the humorous remarks and messages of 208 children ranging from age three to age 14 (Socha & Kelly, 1994). Children between ages three and eight were alike in producing mostly prosocial humor, that is, "courteous" or "clean" jokes and comments that conformed to decorum and politeness. From around age nine to age 14, children tended to be alike in producing proportionately more antisocial than prosocial humor, with antisocial jokes and remarks featuring mutilation, scatology, "dirty" sexual messages, and disparagement of people's appearance, gender, race, and social class. As for differences between groups' humor productions, boys indulged in more antisocial humor than did girls, and boys expressed more antisocial humor among their friends than in the presence of their teachers.

Trends

A series of behavior episodes that change gradually in a given direction can be interpreted as representing a trend. To be considered a trend, the series need not involve each succeeding episode progressing another step toward an identified end state. In other words, on some days there may be no advance or the behavior may actually regress. For example, when people are learning a skill, the chart of their improvement typically forms a jagged line of progress, a line reflecting periodic starts and stops, advances and retrogressions rather than continuous, smooth progress. Thus, to qualify as a trend, only the general pattern across the entire series need progress in the identified direction.

Researchers often depict trends by contrasting the past and present conditions of an event or institution by means of a narrative that focuses on qualitative rather than quantitative change. Consider, for instance, the annual children's parade in Aracana, a small town in the Andalusian region of Spain. In the past, following the adults' yearly Holy Week processions, boys and girls ages six through 12 would conduct their own spontaneous parades over a period of several days.

In constructing their *pasos* (floats), the children . . . would begin with old tables or cardboard boxes, cover each with a cloth that extended to the ground, mount their favorite possessions on top—with GI Joe, for example, pressed into services as Christ and with Barbie assuming the role of Virgin Mary—and surround the images with wild flowers. . . .

Thanks to the recent efforts of the teachers, however, the *pasos de los niños* have lost their character as an autonomous children's activity. . . . Prizes are awarded for the best *paso*, the best procession, and so forth. . . . In addition, parents are enlisted to help their children construct permanent and much more elaborate *pasos* and to sew the traditional costumes of penitents, clergy, and matrons, which many of the children now wear instead of ordinary street clothes. . . . In sum, the processions have been largely taken out of the children's hands and turned into a well-disciplined and competitive event. (Maddox, 1994, pp. 105-106)

Time Allotments

Observations of how much time a person spends in different activities are useful in suggesting the amount of experience a person has with assigned tasks or the amount of attention a person dedicates to different interests.

The matter of task experience is illustrated in a study comparing the effectiveness of four methods of improving the reading performance of first-grade pupils who lagged behind their classmates in reading skill. One of the methods, labeled the *reading recovery* approach, was of particular interest to the researchers who wanted to discover how closely teachers adhered to the recommended time allotments for this mode of instruction and, consequently, how much experience children had with each task. Teachers' time-allotment behavior was summarized in the following manner:

> A total of 18 RR [reading recovery] lessons were videotaped (2 lessons for nine teachers). Lessons in RR averaged 33 minutes, 21 seconds (slightly more than the 30 minutes designated for the instruction, indicating that the teachers exceeded allotted time). Average proportion of time devoted to reading was 60.2%. The lesson activities also included 25.3% of time spent on writing and 14.5% of time spent on the category called "other." The 14.5% "other" can be further broken down into: talk about books (63.2%); letter-sound work, or phonics (15.0%); word fluency practice (12.4%); letter identification work (3.9%); teacher reading to the child (3.5%); and general (2.0%). It can be seen that the greatest proportion of the "other" category involved teachers and children talking about the books read. (Pinnell, et al., 1994, pp. 21-22)

INFERRED CONSTRUCTS

The four varieties of inferred constructs addressed in the following paragraphs concern cognitive functions, attitudes, estimated meanings, and social interaction styles.

Cognitive Functions

The task attempted by researchers is often that of identifying types of thinking in which people engage in educational settings. The teacher who asks a student to "Think out loud as you work the next problem" is interested in understanding the student's cognitive functions, as is the counselor who asks, "What did you think would happen if you got caught driving after drinking?"

The matter of inferring cognitive functions is illustrated in a study by Dufresne-Tasse and Lefebvre designed to answer the question "What do people think as they view exhibits in a museum?" To gather data for the investigation, a member of the research team, equipped with an audiotape recorder, accompanied each of 45 visitors through a set of museum exhibits with the request that: "As you walk along, I would like you to communicate to me what you see, what you think, what you feel, and what you imagine, in short, everything that happens to you" (Dufresne-Tasse & Lefebvre, 1994, p. 473). Later, as the researchers listened to the tapes, they assigned each of a visitor's remarks to a cognitive-function category within their system of categories that bore such labels as *expressing, taking note of, identifying, comparing, explaining, justifying, solving, modifying, suggesting, anticipating, verifying,* and *judging.*

Attitudes

The term *attitudes,* as intended here, refers to ways a person perceives life events, ways that influence how the person will behave. An attitude, in effect, functions as a mental lens that colors how individuals interpret, and react to, their encounters with the environments they inhabit. Thus, a person's attitude is not something that others see directly but, instead, it is a construct inferred from observing what the person says and does. For convenience of communication, people assign labels to these assumed propensities to act, and researchers often employ the notion of attitudes in their studies of educational phenomena. The following two examples illustrate attitudes deduced from researchers' observations of people's behavior in educational settings.

In the nation of Malawi, Davison and Kanyuka saw a contrast between the ways parents and teachers treated girls and the ways they treated boys. Their observation led them to apply the labels *gender structuring* and *gender bias* to the attitudes they assumed underlay such differential treatments. The concept *gender structuring* referred to "Culturally determined ways of defining women and men and their roles in a given society at a particular historical time period [to] shape gender-specific opportunities and constraints" (Davison & Kanyuka, 1992, p. 455). *Gender bias* referred to people's tendency to provide more favorable educational opportunities to boys than to girls. After the authors described a host of observed behaviors that they interpreted as indicators of gender structuring and bias, they reflected their own attitudes toward such treatment in their proposal about what activists in Malawi society should do to alter conceptions of gender.

> Changing societal attitudes is not an easy task, particularly in rural areas where traditional gender beliefs and norms persist. However, an active campaign to change stereotypes about females, through the use of media at the national level, can provide a beginning. Similarly, institutional interventions to guarantee that girls showing academic promise be assured financial support—possibly through a government affirmative action program—will increase [girls'] staying in school. (Davison & Kanyuka, 1992, p. 466)

The second instance of attitudes inferred from observed behavior appears in Resnick's analysis of the failure of an educational program in Israel. In the early 1990s, the Israeli ministry of education's ability to finance schools diminished, resulting in a reduction of the variety of subjects in the curriculum. To counter this trend of curtailed learning opportunities, parents in one public school (grades one through eight) introduced an after-school curriculum enrichment program (CEP) that students could attend following the close of the regular school session at noon. Enrollment in the range of subject fields in the afternoon was voluntary and paid for by parents. However, the program barely lasted one year, its death due to a host of problems that included a student drop-out rate of 44%, disorderly learners, teachers often late to class, inadequate supervision by part-time administrators, a shortage of funds for supplies, and more. According to Resnick's analysis, much of the cause of the program's failure could be attributed to the contrast in attitudes that participants (students, teachers, administrators, parents) held about the regular school and the CEP. Resnick labeled this contrast the *Jekyll/Hyde syndrome.*

> What was "wrong" with CEP is that it took "Dr. Jekylls" from the morning classes, mostly well-behaved, achieving students, and turned them into afternoon "Hydes": unruly, dissatisfied children who did things in CEP in the afternoon, like cutting classes, that they would never consider doing even for the worst subjects in the morning hours. . . .
>   What had changed was the cultural context of CEP—the unarticulated "rules of the game." The essence of the school climate literature points precisely to the cultural variables of the school—peer norms, the level of expectation of academic behavior, and consensus about expectations and discipline—as determining, to a large degree, the success of the school. These were precisely the dimensions on which there was a reasonable degree of clarity and consistency in the mornings at the school, but which evaporated with the arrival of CEP in the afternoons. (Resnick, 1996, p. 235)

Thus, in his interpretation, the researcher inferred three sorts of constructs. The first focused on the elements of the school program, a construct that Resnick labeled *cultural context* or *school climate.* The second focused on attitudes implied in the description of students' behavior (obedient versus disobedient, responsible versus irresponsible, serious versus frivolous). The third reflected the connection between the first two constructs by means of a literary analogy—the *Jekyll/Hyde syndrome.*

Estimated Meanings

Researchers often speculate about what observed events mean to the people engaged in those events. An example is Mcguire's study of fifth-and-sixth-grade Canadian pupils who were under the tutelage of two teachers who employed different pedagogical approaches. After Mcguire systematically observed children's story-writing lessons in the two teachers' classrooms, she first inferred the intentions on which each teacher seemed to found her instructional approach. She then inferred the meaning that pupils would derive from their experiences under those approaches. In effect, Mcguire abstracted two estimates from her observations—one estimate of the teachers' conceptions of suitable writing lessons and another of the pupils' interpretations of those lessons.

Although both teachers appeared to value literacy and story writing as a set of social practices and to set up collaborative writing environments, they had different ideological views about the functions of literacy events and stories in their classrooms. Mrs. G. was more an enabler and responder to children's ongoing efforts; [Ms. M. J.] was more a linguistic resource for the children to draw on for vocabulary and spelling and a corrector of their written texts after a story-writing event. Consequently, the children are caught—somewhere among [1] perceiving story making as a constraint; a school chore of writing something down; reporting how things are for someone who . . . "already knows how things are"; and [2] perceiving it as a playful symbolic act—a free play of language and consciousness. (Mcguire, 1994, p. 122)

Mcguire also speculated about the meanings children attached to storytelling as influenced by the cultural context in which they were raised within a bilingual society (Quebec). She then bolstered her interpretations with detailed descriptions of two particular children's writing activities and of the children's comments about their work.

Social-Interaction Styles

A series of observations of people in social situations can lead a researcher to propose styles of social interaction exemplified by the behavior, to label each style, and to estimate the attitudes or motives underlying such actions. For example, from observing classrooms in South Korea, Sorenson concluded:

In the elementary grades I would characterize the student-teacher relationship as one of "warm authoritarianism"—demanding respect and compliance from students but at the same time convincing them that they care about them as human beings and have their best interests at heart. Such authoritarianism is not punitive, though later on, in middle and high school, less warm and more punitive forms are common. Almost half of middle and high school students, for example, report having received corporal punishment. (Sorenson, 1994, pp. 27-28)

LEARNING ENVIRONMENTS

Recent decades have witnessed increasing attention to the way characteristics of environments affect individuals' behavior. Such labels as *ecological psychology* (Bronfenbrenner, 1979, 1993) and *contextualism* (Ford & Lerner, 1992) reflect viewpoints about how environmental conditions influence learning that takes place under particular environmental conditions. The following three studies illustrate alternative ways scholars used their observations to infer how environments affect learning outcomes. In the first example the environment is a mother's style of teaching her child, in the second it is the presence of deviant students in a classroom, and in the third it is the assortment of sounds in a classroom.

Mothers' Instructional Styles

To investigate how parents' styles of instructing their children might affect children's intellectual development, Portes (1991) observed sessions in which each mother taught her elementary-school child an assigned learning task. The observations were guided by a style sheet that divided mothers' actions into a variety of types, such as (a) mother asks open-ended question or prompts child, (b) mother uses positive reinforcement, encourages, agrees with child, (c) mother interrupts child, (d) mother influences the child's response with obvious cue or statement, and (e) general comments not related to task. Different patterns of parental teaching styles were then correlated with the children's tested achievement in reading, language skills, mathematics, and ability to use reference sources. Correlations were also computed between children's academic performance and their gender, race, parental marital and socioeconomic status, and parental expectations for the child. By means of factor analysis, Portes was able to identify a cluster of parents' teaching behaviors that appeared to be the most important of the inspected variables in accounting for the differences among the children in achievement—particularly achievement in math and reference skills. He envisioned this cluster as a construct that could be labeled *the maternal verbal guidance factor* (MVG).

> The mother's use of positive reinforcement, encouragement, and agreement with the child is important. However, she also provides guidance by asking open questions and [offering] statements without giving obvious information to the child. . . . Sex, race, and parental marital differences were analyzed and not found to be significant for this factor. . . . The MVG factor may represent an active ingredient of the home environment that supports children's development in general, and perhaps more in some zones of development [such as math and reference skills] than others. (Portes, 1991, p. 34)

Deviant Students in the Classroom

Over a four-year period, Stevenson (1991) observed two dozen first-grade classrooms in order to discover the functions of deviant pupils within a classroom society. Most studies of classroom behavior problems have focused either on teachers' methods of maintaining order or on individual children's characteristics. In contrast, Stevenson adopted the construct *collective-resource perspec-*

tive, a viewpoint from which he sought to identify functions that deviant students (ones who test and break rules) perform as an aggregation.

> Even though deviant students are often viewed as disruptive and as challenging the teacher's authority, they also may promote order in the class in several indirect ways. One way is to clarify the rules and procedures of the classroom. . . . The constant struggle between teachers and deviant students serves to articulate publicly the classroom rules and procedures and their spheres of jurisdiction. . . . [Furthermore,] deviant students make the distribution of rewards more meaningful, since it is the constant contrast between the rewarded and unrewarded that gives value to being rewarded. (Stevenson, 1991, p. 128)

One finding of this investigation was that the size of the collection of deviant students in a class was established early in the school year and remained stable throughout the year. Stevenson then used his data to test two competing interpretations of such stability: (a) a particular teacher's methods of classroom management determined the size of the collection of deviants or (b) certain characteristics of students (cognitive and emotional skills or such social identities as "class clown") accounted for the size of the deviant group. However, he was obliged to reject both of these explanations because (a) the size of the cluster of deviants in a given teacher's classroom varied from one year to the next and (b) the membership in the cluster changed somewhat during the year. In other words, pupils who qualified as deviant during one period of time did not qualify at another time but were replaced by classmates who were newly considered deviant. Thus, the cause of the size stability of the ranks of deviant students required a different interpretation from either the teacher-method or student-characteristic explanation. Perhaps, Stevenson implied, the stability resulted from a complex of factors as yet unknown, so that more research would be necessary to reveal how the ranks of deviant students are established, how the ranks are maintained, and how deviant students contribute to keeping order in the classroom.

In summary, the researcher inferred that students who tested and broke class regulations formed an aggregation that qualified as a collective resource in promoting the operation of a classroom. Observations of 96 first-grade classrooms appeared to support this inference. The observations also revealed that the size of a deviant collectivity remained stable over the school year, but two possible interpretations of this stability (teacher-method, student-characteristic) were not supported by the data.

Classroom Sounds

In comparing kindergartens in Israel with some in West Germany, Kalekin-Fishman (1991) inferred that a teacher's conception of what constitutes good teaching will determine many of the sounds heard in the teacher's class, and that a particular pattern of sounds will affect what pupils learn.

To gather data, the researcher interviewed teachers and observed the sounds heard during kindergarten sessions. Her interviews were designed to discover the learning goals that teachers held for their children and the classroom-management methods teachers believed would best foster those goals. Her system for charting the sources, types, and quantities of kindergarten sounds enabled her to "map patterns of kindergarten events, as well as to characterize the environment" (Kalekin-Fishman, 1991, p. 219). She concluded that the patterns of sounds differed significantly between the two countries' kindergartens, and she inferred that this difference was the result of the different conceptions of what constituted good teaching that the teachers in the two countries expressed.

> In Haifa [Israel], the teachers pressed for achievement and group solidarity by enforcing a crowded schedule with a relatively strict time framework and an authoritarian distribution of activities. The focus of their messages was on naming activities and imposing recipes of behavior to induce socialization. This focus was reflected in the acoustical environment; sounds produced by different sources were highly differentiated, and teachers' sounds were often dominant. . . .
>
> Interviewees in Konstanz (Germany) asserted that their aim was to help the children develop their unique personalities. The teachers were guided by the notion that if they avoided putting pressure on the children, they were helping the children develop self-confidence and autonomy. . . . The acoustical environment reflected their intentions. In these kindergartens, there was a flow of relatively undifferentiated "white noise" throughout the sessions. (Kalekin-Fishman, 1991, pp. 219-220)

To interpret what the contrasting sound environments could mean for children's learning, Kalekin-Fishman adopted a strategy sometimes used by researchers as they seek to support the educational implications they draw from their studies. That is, she did not evaluate what children actually learned in the two sets of kindergartens. Instead, she depended on other people's studies for identifying the learning outcomes that she would expect to result from the acoustical environments she found in her investigation. To identify the learning consequences that she believed would derive from the Israeli teachers' methods, Kalekin-Fishman cited "findings from laboratory experiments" which showed that:

> Frequent variations of sounds and frequent cuts in the flow of sound (as in the salient teachers' talk) . . . promote alertness, concentration, persistence, and success in learning. (Kalekin-Fishman, 1991, p. 219)

She also referred to others' studies to support her belief that the kind of "white noise" observed in the German kindergartens worked against children's reaching the self-confidence and autonomy goals to which the German teachers subscribed.

Exposure to constant noise has been shown to lead to increased aggression or anger, as well as to learned helplessness and passivity . . . [It] detracts from sensitivity and contributes to a reduction of sociability and helping behavior. (Kalekin-Fishman, 1991, p. 220)

It should be apparent that the practice of using other people's theories and research findings as the sole basis for drawing implications from one's own findings can involve a considerable risk of error. Researchers who adopt such a strategy can properly caution their readers about the tentative and disputable nature of those interpretations. In Kalekin-Fishman's study, direct assessment of changes in the children's self-confidence, autonomy, alertness, concentration, persistence, and improvement in cognitive, social, and physical skills would have been a far sounder basis for her interpretation of the learning effects of acoustical environments than was her extrapolating implications from others' investigations.

PERSON/CONTEXT INTERACTIONS

Whereas such theoretical positions as environmentalism, ecological psychology, and contextualism have usually emphasized how environments affect people's behavior, the concept *interactionism* (Hewitt, 1994) has been used to focus attention on the reciprocal influence of person and of context. Hence, research from an interactionist perspective goes beyond estimating the effects of environments on learning by giving attention as well to how learners influence the settings they occupy. A notable example of interactionist interpretation is the substantial body of *interpersonal-expectations* and *self-fulfilling-prophecy* research (Babad, 1993) produced since the publication of Rosenthal and Jacobson's pioneering book, *Pygmalion in the Classroom* (1968).

In the typical classroom case of interpersonal expectations, the mutual influence between person and context:

(a) Begins with observable characteristics of a student, such as racial or gender indicators, influencing the teacher (as a component of the student's environment) to assume that those characteristics are necessarily accompanied by certain personality, attitude, aptitude, or behavior attributes. Thus, the student's skin color or facial expression may be connected, in the teacher's opinion, with either inferior intelligence or superior intelligence, with either eagerness to learn or disinterest, with a propensity either to violence or to submissiveness, or the like. Other observable features—such as a student's grooming, dress style, posture, or use of language—may likewise be interpreted by the teacher as indicative of character or ability. Consequently, according to *interpersonal-expectations theory*, the teacher will likely treat the student as if those assumed attributes were true.

(b) The student, in response to the teacher's treatment, may accept the teacher's appraisal as valid—or at least inevitable—and may subsequently act in ways that seem to confirm the teacher's opinion, thereby fulfilling the teacher's implied prophecy.

Such interpersonal interaction, with teacher and student influencing each other's behavior, sets off a cycle of reciprocal causes and effects that help establish the climate of the teaching-learning context.

As researchers plan studies to reveal person-environment interactions, they can profitably recognize the complexity of classroom interpersonal relations. Not only are the teacher's overtures to students affected by the teacher's beliefs about connections between students' observable characteristics and their personalities, but students' observations of the teacher's characteristics likewise help determine how students will act toward the teacher. Furthermore, students' perceptions of classmates can also significantly affect the learning environment. Therefore, research designs need to provide for the collection of information from the multiple vantage points of the persons who compose the social environment.

INSTRUMENT VALIDATION

Questionnaires are often intended to serve as short-cut techniques for learning about people's habits, preferences, and decision-making patterns. However, there is always a question about how accurately answers on questionnaires represent people's actual habits, preferences, and decision-making practices. In other words, do questionnaire responses truly mean what they say? To answer this query, investigators sometimes use direct observation as the basis for judging how closely people's behavior matches their questionnaire answers.

To illustrate, Ashley (1992) observed children's playtime behavior in order to judge the validity of the children's social status as charted on a sociogram constructed from the subjects' questionnaire answers. He first asked a group of 15 boys, ages eight through 11, to write down the names of the three classmates with whom they would most like to share a dormitory during a forthcoming field trip; the boys were also given the option of naming any classmates they would particularly wish to exclude from their dormitory. The results of their choices were plotted as a traditional sociogram—as a diagram of who chose whom. The diagram enabled the researcher to categorize boys as *stars* (chosen many times), as *average group members* (chosen by several classmates), and as *isolates* (chosen by no one).

To estimate the validity of the sociogram as a measure of the pupils' actual patterns of social interaction, Ashley observed each boy during a total of seven 15-minute sessions on the playground over a period of several months and coded each subject's social behavior on an observation schedule. The observation results were then compared with the original sociogram to show how well the data from the two sources matched. Ashley interpreted this comparison to mean that

> As a source of information about behavior, sociometry, like any other form of
> asking people what they do, is unreliable. . . . Popular children in sociometry
> do tend to have more interactions at playtime, but 'isolate' children are
> nevertheless engaged in fairly extensive interactions with groups and
> individuals—the range or number of such groups differing little from that of the
> popular children. . . . However, there are certain factors and patterns which can
> render sociometry useful. A child's *own* sociometric choices are a poor guide to
> the existence of friendships, but *mutual* choices are usually confirmed by
> observation and therefore considerably more reliable. (Ashley, 1992, p. 153)

ALTERNATIVE CAUSE ESTIMATES

After describing the outcomes of their study, researchers often speculate about why such results occurred, with such speculation frequently including several alternative cause possibilities. In effect, interpretation takes the form of posing a variety of possible explanations of the results.

For instance, in an investigation of ways to teach children how to react to potential abductors, 62 preschool children were divided into three groups. The first group viewed five brief videotaped scenes, each involving an adult stranger seeking to lure a child to accompany the adult. After every scene, a teacher directed the group members in practicing ways of avoiding and retreating from strangers who sought to lead them away. The second group did not view the videotape but, rather, had a teacher read them an oral description of the five incidents and then practice how they should respond to strangers' overtures. The third group had no training in ways to react to such overtures (Carroll-Rowan & Miltenberger, 1994).

The researchers adopted two methods of testing the effectiveness of the training procedures—*self report* and *in situ*. For the self-report appraisal, each child was interviewed at home by a research assistant who described one of the five abduction scenarios, and the child reported how he or she would react in such a situation. For the *in situ* assessment, each child was in a public place, such as the child's front yard or a nearby store, and was there confronted by a stranger (a research assistant) who chatted briefly with the child, presented an abduction lure, and asked the child to go with him. In each situation, an observer rated the child for how appropriately he or she responded.

A comparison of children's verbal and *in situ* reactions revealed "low verbal/nonverbal correspondence, with over half of the children's verbal reports differing from their actual performances" (Carroll-Rowan & Miltenberger, 1994, p. 125).

However, the results of both the self-report and *in situ* evaluations showed that the two training groups—video and oral-description—reacted more suitably than did the no-training group. Furthermore, the oral description was more effective than the video, an outcome that prompted the researchers to propose two alternative—perhaps mutually supportive—causes for such a result.

> First, children in the [oral-description] group listened to verbal scenarios about children in abduction situations and had to imagine the scenarios and the appropriate prevention responses. This imaginative responding was not required of children in the video group because the scenarios were visually presented to them. In part, children in the video group were engaged in passive learning. In contrast, the manual training method required a more active, possibly imaginative learning process. Second, it may be that [oral-description] training was more effective because more teacher-student interaction was involved. . . . Presumably the teacher's attention was an established social reinforcer and therefore the children may have been more motivated to attend and respond correctly. (Carroll-Rowan & Miltenberger, 1994, p. 125)

Such speculations about cause could then serve as hypotheses to be tested in future research projects.

BEHAVIOR AND ATTITUDE EXPLORATIONS

Some studies qualify as exploratory investigations because the researchers are guided only by very general questions rather than by specific hypotheses to test or precise questions to answer. As a consequence, interpretations of exploratory studies often include unanticipated conclusions. Such was the case in a study of the way a computer program, which functioned as students' personal tutor, altered teachers' and students' roles in high school geometry classes. The stimulus for conducting the study was the investigators' observation that there was a paucity of research exploring the impact of intelligent-computer-assisted instruction on classroom social processes.

> The two methods of data gathering were intensive qualitative classroom observations and repeated interviews with students and teachers. This approach was selected because our knowledge of the likely effects of intelligent computer-based tutors is so rudimentary that a flexible exploratory methodology seemed called for. (Schofield, Eurich-Fulcer, & Britt, 1994, p. 585)

In analyzing data collected in eight geometry classes over a two-year period, the authors discovered a paradox—students claimed that a teacher provided better help than an artificially intelligent computer-based tutor, yet those same students preferred to use the tutor rather than study by traditional methods, and they appeared to learn more while doing so. The researchers concluded that three factors could account for the seeming paradox.

First, rather than replacing the teacher, the tutor provided an additional resource for students. Second, using the tutors allowed teachers to provide more individualized help. Third, students using the tutors had more control over the kind and amount of help they received from the teacher, with helping interactions becoming more private and potentially less embarrassing. None of these changes were envisioned by the tutor's developers, highlighting the importance of exploring unintended effects of technology on classroom functioning. (Schofield, Eurich-Fulcer, & Britt, 1994, p. 579)

RESEARCH PROJECT CHECKLIST

In my research report, do I intend to gather data by means of observations? If so, which forms of interpretation do I intend to employ?

___1. Behavior summaries

    ___1.1 Specific competencies. Identify which competencies.

    ___1.2 Likenesses and differences. Specify the kinds of variables to be compared.

    ___1.3 Trends. Specify which variables will be traced across time.

    ___1.4 Time allotments. Describe the activities that will be compared.

    ___1.5 Other (explain)_____

___2. Inferred constructs

    ___2.1 Cognitive functions. Tell which functions will be studied.

    ___2.2 Attitudes. Tell what sorts of attitudes will be studied.

    ___2.3 Estimated meanings. Identify whose meanings will be inferred.

    ___2.4 Social-interaction styles. Identify whose social-interaction styles will be investigated.

    ___2.5 Other (explain) _____

___3. Influences of learning environments. Describe which environments, or aspects of environments, will be studied.

___4. Person-context interactions. Identify which people, or which kinds of people, will be studied and in what kinds of contexts.

___5. Instrument validation. Explain which instrument will be analyzed, and what kinds of observation will serve in the analysis.

___6. Alternative cause estimates. Tell what educational phenomena are being studied, and what theories or hypotheses may be useful in estimating the cause of the phenomena.

___7. Behavior and attitude explorations. Identify the kinds of behaviors or attitudes to be explored, and tell what observations will be made.

___8. Other (explain)_____

13

Interpreting Tests, Questionnaires, and Interviews

Tests, questionnaires, and interviews are the principal methods researchers use to obtain respondents' answers to questions. As the following potpourri of interpretations demonstrates, the distinction among tests, questionnaires, and interviews is often imprecise. Achievement and aptitude tests do, indeed, measure respondents' answers against accepted standards of right and wrong information, so those instruments qualify as tests in the traditional sense of the term. However, devices described as *attitude tests* or *personality tests* do not yield results in terms of correct and incorrect answers. Instead, they locate respondents' answers in categories which reflect inferred constructs like *self-concept, race prejudice, submissive personality, introversion, Christian viewpoint*, and more. Thus, such "tests" are essentially questionnaires that are sometimes referred to as *inventories* or *rating scales*. Their purpose is to classify people by means of the researcher's system of descriptive categories. Those devices are discussed in the questionnaire section, whether or not they officially bear the title *test*.

Nor should the distinction between interviews on one hand and tests and questionnaires on the other be regarded as absolute, since oral questions addressed to individuals can serve either to measure their status against a standard or to place them in a classification category. Consequently, the chapter has been divided into three sections—tests, questionnaires, and interviews—chiefly for convenience of discussion. Overlap among the sections can be expected.

TESTS

The interpretation of test results can serve numerous functions. Six of the functions involve (a) displaying individuals' and groups' levels of aptitude or achievement, (b) revealing individuals' and groups' strengths and weaknesses across a series of performances, (c) estimating the causes of correlations between characteristics of people's lives, (d) challenging conventional beliefs, (e) revealing the dynamics of the testing process, and (f) exposing limitations of research projects.

Comparative Levels of Aptitude or Achievement

The most common way to interpret test results involves either judging how individuals or groups compare in performing mental and physical tasks or judging how closely their performance approaches a selected standard.

An example of comparisons among groups is the earlier-mentioned survey of the reading skills of 210,059 children in 32 nations conducted during the period 1988-1990 by the International Association for the Evaluation of Educational Achievement (IEA). Of the total number of participants, 93,039 were age nine and 117,020 age 14. The tests were designed to measure students' skills in reading narrative prose (stories—fact or fiction), expository prose (factual description or explanation), and documents (tables, maps, graphs, instructions).

The principal results of the study were reported as mean test scores and standard deviations for the sample of students from each country. For instance, among nine-year-olds, the five top-scoring nations (and their overall average scores) were Finland (569), United States (547), Sweden (539), France (531), and Italy (529). The five lowest-scoring nations were Portugal (478), Denmark (475), Trinidad/Tobago (451), Indonesia (394), and Venezuela (393) (Elley, 1992, p. 14). (The mean score for all nations combined was 500.)

In brief, the meaning to be directly extracted from the test results was that some countries' nine-year-olds—as a group—were significantly more skillful readers than other countries' nine-year-olds.

Comparing students' test performance against a standard was illustrated in the study of pupils' reading ability in Zimbabwe mentioned in Chapter 1. The performance criterion consisted of 33 reading-test items that a committee of reading specialists and teachers had decided that pupils would absolutely need to answer correctly if they were to profit from instruction in grade 7. Two standards or levels were stipulated—a minimum level (mastery of 50% of the 33 items) and a desirable level (70% of the items). When a representative sample of sixth-grade pupils were tested, 38.1% reached the minimum level and 13.8% the desirable level. The obvious interpretation was that the great majority of students performed much lower than expected by the committee of experts and that relatively few students were prepared to succeed in grade 7 (Postlethwaite, 1994, pp. 35-36).

Different Patterns of Aptitude and Achievement

Tests are frequently used for revealing the patterning of people's aptitudes and achievements across various mental and physical skills. Particularly in the field of counseling, information derived from a battery of measures of different abilities is often useful in planning students' educational and vocational futures.

An expanding quantity of research in this area of such differential diagnosis addresses questions like: Which tests serve as the most valid measures of which aptitudes and achievements? To what extent does one test measure the same abilities as another test? What combination of different tests is most effective for revealing an individual's status across a broad range of aptitudes and subject-matter fields? How closely will a student's level of performance on one test match his or her performance on other tests—and why?

An illustration of a research project aimed at investigating the last of these questions is a study by Achter, Lubinski, and Benbow (1996) of the performance of intellectually gifted 13-year-olds on a series of tests and inventories. The research was conducted to help settle a controversy in the professional literature about the patterning of talents among the highly gifted. The conflict has centered on the concept of *multipotentiality* in reference to students who earn uniformly high scores across ability and achievement tests and who display multiple educational/vocational interests at high levels of intensity. In other words, the assumption behind the multipotentiality belief is that the aptitudes of the highly gifted do not vary much from one type of talent to another. Rather, the profile of their test results is high and "flat" across all types of tests. A further assumption apparently common among counselors is that multipotentiality confronts the gifted with a daunting array of equally attractive career options so the gifted themselves are at a loss in deciding which opportunities to follow.

Achter, Lubinski, and Benbow's search for studies empirically demonstrating multipotentiality led them to decide that "the notion of multipotentiality seems to rest primarily on unsystematic anecdotal evidence from counseling settings" (Achter, Lubinski, & Benbow, 1996, p. 66). Consequently, the aim of their own study was to measure the incidence of multipotentiality, particularly as it might be found among highly gifted adolescents. The results of administering a variety of aptitude/achievement tests and of interest/values inventories to more than 1,000 adolescents caused the researchers to conclude that:

> Empirical analyses based on data collected over 20 years from more than 1,000 intellectually gifted participants . . . revealed profound individual differences among gifted individuals in every class of variables . . . relevant to educational-vocational choice. . . . Fewer than 20% of the students [had] flat ability-interest or ability-value profiles and only 4.8% [had] flat ability-interest-values profiles.

Thus, the authors interpreted their results to mean that the belief in widespread multipotentiality among the gifted is ill founded.

Estimated Causes of Correlations

As noted in Chapter 5, finding that two variables are correlated does not necessarily mean that *variable A* has been the cause of *variable B* or vice versa. For instance, primary-school children in Swaziland whose fathers are absent from the home have been found to earn lower scores on vocabulary and drawing tests than do children whose fathers are present (Zoller Booth, 1995). This does not necessarily mean that a father's absence causes children to perform poorly or, on the other hand, that fathers leave home because of their children's inferior vocabulary and drawing ability. Perhaps the observed correlation is the result of some combination of other factors that are responsible for both the father's absence and the children's diminished performance, such factors as the family's economic status, parents' educational levels, and more. In effect, correlation does not inevitably mean causation. Although researchers usually recognize this fact, they are still tempted to speculate about how one variable in a comparison is responsible for the status of the other variable. Their speculation, often cast in cautious terms, is accompanied by a line of logic intended to convince readers that the suggested causal link is tenable. Frequently the authors buttress their speculation by citing similar studies reported by other researchers.

A typical form of such logic is illustrated in a study from Mexico showing the relationship between secondary-school applicants' achievement-test scores and selected conditions of their family environments. In the researchers' effort to interpret the computed relationships, they wrote:

> Family size is inversely correlated with student achievement, perhaps indicating less time and exposure to parental stimulation in large family households. In addition, there probably is less money for culturally and educationally stimulating materials and events in such households.
>
> Two-parent households are . . . significantly associated with [higher] Spanish [language] achievement. . . . Research shows that students who live in one-parent households are disadvantaged. [Footnote citation of other studies]. Some have argued that the negative effects are explained by the low income of one-parent families, whereas others have claimed that children from such situations are harmed by psychological stress and incomplete socialization. [Footnote citation of other studies] (Palafox, Prawda, & Velez, 1994, p. 176)

The authors' tentative estimates of cause may then become issues to investigate in future research—hypotheses to be tested by methods other than simply computing correlations. For the Mexico example, those methods might include extensive observations of family life (large versus small families, one-parent versus two-parent families) and interviews with parents and children.

A somewhat different approach to estimating causes of correlations was illustrated in the earlier-mentioned study of pupils' reading skills in 32 nations. The researchers posed the question: "What brings about these differences in achievement levels between nations?" In reply, they asserted that

Correlation studies cannot reveal causes. However, comparison between high- and low-scoring countries can identify factors which deserve closer study. . . . [Such closer study revealed that] factors which consistently differentiated high-scoring from low-scoring countries were large school libraries, large classroom libraries, regular book borrowing, frequent silent reading in class, frequent story reading aloud by teachers, and more scheduled hours spent teaching the language. (Elley, 1992, pp. xii, 33)

Hence, the study team avoided the direct claim that those factors contributed to reading skill. Nevertheless, offering the comparisons in such a manner could well encourage readers of the report to regard such factors as causes (not just incidental correlates) of the superior performance of students in high-scoring countries.

Challenges to Conventional Wisdom

Sometimes investigators conduct research intended to test popular beliefs that have derived from an accumulation of previous studies. Frequently the reason such investigators bother to initiate further studies is that they suspect the earlier research failed to evaluate all potentially influential causal conditions. An example of such a revisionist attempt is Campbell and Ramey's (1995) longitudinal experiment designed to measure long-term educational effects of intensive child training methods initiated in early infancy and continued into the elementary school years.

The conventional wisdom that the investigators sought to challenge was the conviction that efforts to prepare young children from economically and educationally disadvantaged families to succeed well in school were in the long run of no avail. This belief was supported by a host of assessments of such preschool training as the U.S. government's Head Start programs, assessments showing that any advantage that children from poor families displayed over their nonpreschool agemates upon entering primary school was washed out within a year or two. "A meta-analysis of Head Start's benefits indicated that, despite some exceptions, by the end of the second year in public school, educationally meaningful differences between Head Start participants and control children were no longer apparent" (Campbell & Ramey, 1995, p. 744).

Campbell and Ramey suggested that whereas preschool training of limited length and intensity might not equip children from disadvantaged environments for progressing well in school, long-term "continual, consistent enrichment of the early environment might alter the negative trend toward developmental retardation and also reduce academic failure in such children" (Campbell & Ramey, 1995, p. 746). To test their proposal, they designed an experiment involving four groups of children who were selected around four months after birth, all of them from low income families (98% African American) and all judged to be poor risks for growing up with normal mental ability and school achievement. The infants were first randomly assigned to two treatments: (a) a special, intensive preschool program (57 infants in a child-care center) and (b) a regular preschool program (54 infants). Five years later, as the children entered primary school, half of each group were given special training in addition to the regular school program, whereas the other half followed only the regular program.

Standardized tests administered at periodic intervals over the years enabled the researchers to assess children's progress between infancy and mid-adolescence (age 15) in their general development, in intellectual aptitude, and—during the school years—in mathematics and reading achievement. Test results at age 15 and the records of the participants' status in school led to the researchers to conclude that:

> (1) Through mid-adolescence, there were different patterns of intellectual development in individuals treated in the [special] preschool program compared to preschool controls; (2) a significant [superiority] in academic test performance was maintained through 10 years in school for both reading and mathematics; (3) there were significantly fewer assignments to special education and to retention in grade for those who had [special] preschool treatment; and (4) the more optimal timing for educational intervention was during the preschool years [rather than during the primary school years]. . . . It is quite plausible that, compared to the school-age program, enhancing the educational stimulus value of the infant and preschool environment through a full-day, year-round child care program represented a more powerful contrast to the early childhood environments of the preschool control children. (Campbell & Ramey, 1995, pp. 764-765)

Evaluations of the Testing Process

The meaning of test results is sometimes interpreted in relation to the testing methods used. For example, Marlaire and Maynard (1990) analyzed the procedure of administering individual intelligence tests in order to examine their hypothesis that such assessment is not objective measurement but, instead, is an interactive process by which tester and testee influence each other's behavior, with their interaction affecting the test results. By observing psychologists testing individual children, the researchers identified ways testers and their clients help determine each other's actions. At the outset of the testing session, the psychologist orients the client to the task ahead and seeks to learn if the client understands what is expected. The client's response then affects what the tester will next say and do. And throughout the testing session, such give and take continues. The authors interpreted their observations as signifying that:

> Clinicians change their responses, both formally and substantively, according to children's performance; engage reparative routines according to interpretations of children's incorrect answers; and, because of such interpretations, are

in the position of choosing to initiate repair in an almost arbitrary manner. Thus, clinicians, on an item-by-item basis, are more implicated or less implicated in the children's performance. Test scores, in all these ways, are collaborate productions. (Marlaire & Maynard, 1990, p. 99)

The authors then expanded their interpretation beyond the data they had collected in order to speculate:

It is plausible that such things as [social] class, race, gender, and so on may exert their effects through differences in co-orientation, expanded or reduced prompts, uses of and responses to "tentativeness," neutral and positive acknowledgments, repair sequences, gaze patterns, intonation, and other interactive practices. (Marlaire & Maynard, 1990, p. 99)

Research Projects' Limitations

Frequently the interpretation section of a research report not only proposes what the data mean but also identifies limitations on the conclusions that can properly be drawn. In way of illustration, consider an investigation of the impact of oral-reading instruction on children's silent-reading development (Reutzel, Hollingsworth, & Eldredge, 1994). The researchers compared two oral-reading instructional approaches (the Oral Recitation Lesson and the Shared Book Experience) that were used with second-grade pupils over a four-month period to determine how each method contributed to children's word-analysis, vocabulary, and comprehension skills as measured by the Iowa Tests of Basic Skills and a researcher-constructed Oral Reading/Retelling Test. The researchers' interpretation of the test results first led them to conclude that both of the instructional methods were effective for teaching young children to read narrative or literary text, with the Shared Book Experience the better approach for instruction in analyzing words within their contexts.

The authors then mentioned three limitations of their study. First, they stated that their conclusions applied to only two instructional approaches, so that future research could profitably compare other approaches as well. Second, their investigation focused solely on second-grade pupils. Children at other grade levels might progress differently under the two teaching methods. Third, the final Oral Reading/Retelling Test required that a child read and retell only one story—an Aesop fable, *The Fox and the Grapes*—so that "We cannot state with any authority how oral reading instruction might influence the development of reading abilities associated with expository or information texts" (Reutzel, Hollingsworth, & Eldredge, 1994). In effect, a wider range of testing methods could properly be used in future research.

When authors thus mention limitations of their work, they perform two useful services for people who read their report. First, by suggesting cautions to observe in interpreting the study, the authors likely increase readers' faith that the researchers have not generalized beyond their data; the authors, in effect, have refrained from making unreasonable claims for their findings. Second, the cited limitations serve to identify issues that can become the focus of research that readers themselves may choose to conduct.

The Resolution of Unexpected Outcomes

Inferred constructs often take the form of theories or models that are intended to explain how and why things operate as they do. For instance, the field of education includes numerous theories about the effect that different methods of teaching have on learning; and researchers frequently conduct studies designed to evaluate and refine such models, with tests usually playing a significant role in the evaluations. When the test results confirm what the researchers predicted on the basis of the theory, such outcomes can be interpreted as helping validate the theory. However, when the test results are contrary to expectations, investigators are obliged either to propose revisions in the theory itself or to locate the cause of the discrepancies in their research methods. The following example illustrates (a) how one researcher sought to interpret an unexpected test outcome and (b) how the test used in the experiment may not have accurately measured the study's target variable.

During the time that teachers are lecturing or leading a class discussion, they often pose oral questions for students to answer. On such occasions, the teacher waits momentarily after finishing a question before calling on a student for an answer. A research problem derived from this situation is: How does the length of a teacher's wait time (the post-question pause) affect students' learning? This was the query Duell (1994) attempted to answer in an experiment she conducted with university students who were studying test construction. She developed a scripted lecture on the subject of test reliability, with 21 questions interspersed throughout the lesson. Students were divided into three sets of classes which received identical lectures and questions, but the wait time following a question differed between one set of classes and another. In the first version of the lesson the wait time was 1 second, in the second version 3 seconds, and in the third version 6 seconds.

The theory of learning underlying Duell's study was an information-processing model which proposed that furnishing students time to formulate their answers to teachers' questions before the students speak improves the quality of students' answers, particularly if the answers require more than just recalling an item of information from memory.

> According to this model, to answer a recall question the learner must locate the relevant information in long-term memory, retrieve it into working memory, check to see if the retrieved information does answer the question, and then answer the question. On the other hand, when answering a question requiring the application of information (concepts or principles) to a new situation, besides

retrieving relevant information from long-term memory, the student applies the retrieved information to the new situation, decides if that application is correct, and if so is ready to answer the question. (Duell, 1994, p. 398)

In each of the classes, students first participated in the lecture session, then took a fill-in-the-blank short-answer test of 11 low-level knowledge items and 19 high-level application and synthesis items.

On the basis of her information-processing theory and of similar studies reported in the professional literature, Duell expected that a short wait time would be sufficient for students to process low-level knowledge adequately, so that students in a 1-second wait-time group would answer simple recall questions as accurately as students in 3-second and 6-second groups. But in the case of complex, high-level questions, she predicted that the longer the wait time, the more accurately students would process the material and thus provide better answers.

Upon analyzing the scores the students earned on the test, Duell found no significant differences among the three groups in their performance on low-level knowledge items. She interpreted this as support for her prediction that a 1-second pause enabled learners to process easy questions as effectively as did a 3-second or 6-second pause. However, her prediction about the superior effectiveness of a 6-second pause for complex questions was not supported, since students in the 6-second wait-time group scored significantly lower than those in the 3-second group.

Duell now faced the challenge of explaining why her data on the relationship between wait time and complex questions differed from the results of earlier studies and from her version of information-processing theory. In six pages of interpretation, she presented a wide range of potential explanations, including such possibilities as:

—The earlier studies used elementary and middle-school pupils who (a) would likely be less adept learners than her university subjects, (b) represented a wider range of aptitudes than did the university students, (c) were not taught identically scripted lessons, (d) were in groups taught by different teachers, and (e) were not asked an identical number and level of questions.
—Wait time may not be sufficiently important by itself to show an effect on the knowledge students acquire; instead, wait time may interact with a complex of other variables to influence learning.
—Before the university students participated in the lesson, some may already have known at least part of the information needed to answer the test questions, so the test may not have revealed what they learned during the lesson. Duell noted that her research design would have been better if it had included a pretest prior to the lesson so that she could have computed change scores (subtract students' pretest scores from their posttest scores) rather than just compare posttest scores.

A further possibility that Duell did not mention was that the test she created was perhaps not an accurate measure of the answers students had generated in their minds within the wait times following the teachers' questions during the class session. That is, each question during the class session was answered by only one student, so the researcher did not know what the other class members were thinking at the time. So the final written test measured most directly the answers that students generated while they took the test, that is, during an undetermined length of time between when they read a question and when they wrote their answer. Despite this problem of how accurately the paper-pencil test reflected what students thought in the wait times during the class session, Duell asserted in her final summary that

No matter how logical or satisfying it might be to believe that giving students more thinking time before they begin their answers to questions, [this study] found no evidence to support the hypothesis that just extending wait time for university students will enhance higher level achievement. (Duell, 1994, p. 412)

QUESTIONNAIRES

The term *questionnaire* refers to a paper-pencil instrument on which respondents write answers to questions that permit the researcher to locate respondents in classification categories. Or sometimes a questionnaire is filled out by a researcher who orally poses the instrument's queries to a respondent and then enters the answers on the instrument.

The following methods of interpreting questionnaire results analyze respondents' answers in terms of (a) correlations, without the researcher offering an estimate of the causes of such relationships, (b) evaluations of how closely the status of some educational phenomenon matches a standard of desirability, (c) personality traits, (d) the validity of personality inventories, (e) respondents' perceptual proclivities, (f) individuals' value preferences, (g) estimated effects of cultural contexts, and (h) theory testing followed by policy recommendations.

Correlations Without Causal Attributions

The "meaning" of questionnaire results often takes the form of correlations reported between respondents' answers and some aspect of the environment, without the researcher proposing that the environmental factors caused the events reflected in the answers. In way of illustration, after 6,758 middle-school and secondary-school youths in England answered a 25-item, multiple-choice questionnaire about bullying in their schools, Whitney and Smith (1993) calculated correlations between the incidence of bullying and five other variables. No significant correlation was found between the frequency of bullying and school size, class size, or the ethnic diversity of a school. However, somewhat more bullying occurred in schools located in socioeconomically disadvantaged neighborhoods. In addition, bullying was more frequent in schools where more pupils reported being alone at playtime rather than being with classmates.

Benchmark Comparisons

A commonly practiced mode of interpretation involves adopting a benchmark or baseline standard against which educational phenomena are compared. Interpretation consists of demonstrating how closely the phenomena approach the standard.

An illustrative case is a study of primary schools in 14 of the world's least-developed nations—Bangladesh, Benin, Bhutan, Burkina Faso, Cape Verde, Equatorial Guinea, Ethiopia, Madagascar, Maldives, Nepal, Tanzania, Togo, Uganda, and Zambia. The study, sponsored jointly by UNESCO and UNICEF, was carried out in 1995-1996 by a research team from Germany's University of Hamburg.

The purpose of the study was to assess the condition of primary education in representative least-developed societies five years after the *World Conference on Education for All* had been held in Jontien, Thailand, in 1990. The study team adopted two standards against which the results of their investigation might be judged. The first benchmark was the condition of the 14 nations' primary schools at the time of the Jontien conference. The second was the ideal of having all children of primary-school age instructed by well-prepared teachers in well-equipped schools. The researchers sought to determine how far the nations had advanced (a) beyond their 1990 position toward (b) the ideal standard.

By means of questionnaires completed by the heads of primary schools in the 14 countries, the study team collected information about 21 characteristics of schools, such as enrollment, class size, buildings, classroom equipment, pupils' books and supplies, and the numbers of teachers and their education. The survey results were interpreted in two ways—as general conclusions about the 14 nations together and as specific conclusions about each nation's status in relation to the 21 variables.

The general conclusions provided what the researchers called "fairly dismal reading" because in most instances primary schools in the 14 countries had deteriorated rather than improved since the Jontien conference, so the gap between the primary schools and the ideal of education-for-all had widened. Many school buildings were in need of major repairs, class sizes commonly ranged between 40 and 70 pupils, few students had their own textbooks, many children lacked a proper place to sit or a surface on which to write, and there were no classroom libraries. In some countries, large numbers of teachers had still received no form of teacher training (Schleicher, Siniscalco, & Postlethwaite, 1995).

Interpretation also focused on differences among nations. For instance, only in the Maldives did every child have a place to sit, but even then 42% of those pupils did not have a place to write. The availability of sitting and writing places was far better in Burkina Faso, Cape Verde, and Togo than in Benin, Equatorial Guinea, Ethiopia, Nepal, Tanzania, and Uganda, all of which suffered very serious shortages (Schleicher, Siniscalco, & Postlethwaite, 1995).

Personality Traits

In experiments, attitude inventories are often used to determine what changes may have occurred in people's personalities as the result of an experimental treatment they received. Typical of such investigations is a study in which 50 high school students in health-education classes were divided into two groups. Relaxation practice was included in the learning activities for one group but not for the other group. The researchers' purpose was to learn how physiological-relaxation training might affect the students' *self-esteem* and *locus of control.* (Self-esteem as a construct represents an individual's sense of competence in coping with problems. Locus of control as a construct reflects the degree to which people believe that they themselves, rather than other people and events, control their destiny.) The journal article reporting the research opened in this fashion:

> For many, adolescence is a difficult period of adjustment, fraught with problematic behaviors. Low self-esteem and an external locus of control have been shown to be associated with negative behavior and can contribute to feelings of depression [Goldney, 1982] and anxiety [Fimian & Cross, 1986]. They have also been associated with poor academic performance [Downs & Rose, 1991], delinquent behaviors [Downs & Rose, 1991], and increased drug and alcohol use [Uribe & Ostrov, 1989]. (Benson, et al., 1994, p. 226)

The experimental design was of the pretest-treatment-posttest variety. In both the pretest and posttest phases, the students' self-esteem and locus of control were assessed by means of questionnaire-type inventories—the Piers-Harris *Children's Self-Concept Scale* and the Nowicki-Strickland *Locus of Control Scale.* At the close of the experiment, the research team reported that

> Despite the relatively small numbers [of students], statistically significant changes in self esteem were observed following exposure to the relaxation-response based curriculum. . . . No such trend was evidenced following exposure to the control [non-relaxation training] curriculum. . . . With respect to locus of control, the group exposed to the relaxation response curriculum during the spring semester exhibited a statistically significant change toward internality [or a sense of self control, rather than control by outside forces].

The components of the research team's interpretation are worth noting. As implied in the research report, their line of reasoning included five beliefs.

1. That the pair of constructs labeled *self-esteem* and *locus of control* are not merely products of some theorist's imagination but, instead, are cohesive, measurable personality traits that significantly influence people's behavior.
2. That low self-esteem and a weak sense of internal control are "associated with" (implying that they "help cause") depression, anxiety, poor academic performance, delinquency, and drug and alcohol use.
3. That the two paper-pencil inventories used in the study's pretesting and posttesting phases provide accurate assessments of self-esteem and locus of control as those constructs operate in people's daily lives.
4. That the students' improved scores on the two inventories after practicing the relaxation exercises are convincing evidence that such exercises can improve adolescents' self-esteem and sense of control over their lives.
5. That relaxation activities may thus be expected to reduce the incidence of depression, anxiety, poor academic performance, delinquency, and drug and alcohol use among adolescents.

The confidence that readers attach to the study's conclusions depends on the degree of faith readers place in each element of such a process of interpretation.

The Validity of Personality Inventories

Research sometimes is directed by the twofold purpose of revealing the structure of personality constructs and of judging the validity of instruments designed to measure those constructs. A case in point is Marsh and Holmes' (1990) comparison of three inventories for assessing children's self-concepts.

For years, an issue debated in the professional literature is the question of whether *self-concept* is a unified rather than a multifaceted personality characteristic. Does a person have a single, overall conception of self that influences his or her behavior in all aspects of life, or is a person's sense of self divided into multiple subconcepts which are no more than loosely connected? Related to this issue is the question of what method of investigating people's self-concepts is the most accurate? These two questions provided the focus of a study in which 290 fifth-grade students in Sydney, Australia, filled out three paper-pencil inventories that have served in recent years as popular instruments for assessing individuals' self-concepts. The inventories were Harter's *Perceived Competence Scale*, the Piers-Harris *Children's Self-Concept Scales*, and Marsh's *Self-Description Questionnaire I*.

By applying factor analysis to the students' responses, the researchers endeavored to learn if the responses revealed a single, unified sense of self for each child or, instead, revealed different perceptions of self in different facets of life. Their interpretation of the factor analysis led the authors to conclude that:

—Self-concept is multidimensional, consisting of separate senses of self
relating to one's physical appearance, physical ability, social status,
academic competence (with a different self-perception for mathematical
ability than for verbal skills), and more.

—Of the three inventories, the *Self-Description Questionnaire I* was the
most effective for distinguishing among the sub-self-concepts, Harter's
Perceived Competence Scale was somewhat less effective, and the Piers-
Harris scale was the least effective.

As is frequently the case, the authors' interpretation concluded with words of
advice derived from their findings.

> Researchers and practitioners seeking to understand self-concept are cautioned
> not to rely primarily on global, undifferentiated notions of self-concept. . . .
> Children . . . apparently feel relatively better about themselves in some areas
> and poorer about themselves in other areas. . . . Understanding of self-concept
> in educational settings will improve if researchers focus on specific dimensions
> of self-concept that are appropriate for their particular purposes and that are
> assessed with psychometrically sound instruments. (Marsh & Holmes, 1990,
> pp. 113-114)

Perceptual Propensities

It is commonly believed by psychologists that the knowledge people have
acquired from their past experiences determines how they perceive new events in
their lives. In other words, one's knowledge serves as a lens or filter that
attributes meaning to new events. Questionnaires and interviews are sometimes
used by researchers to estimate the nature of people's perceptual tendencies.

An example of research that included the assessment of perceptual attitudes is a
study in which Mickelson (1990) compared the levels of academic performance
among 1,193 high school seniors with the opinions of those same students
about the worth of formal education. By means of a questionnaire, Mickelson
collected the youths' answers to questions about their abstract and concrete views
of education, their peers, their family backgrounds, and their leisure and work
activities. She compared these data with the grades the students had earned in
academic work during their high school career. Mickelson defined *abstract
attitudes* as perceptions based on the conventional view in society about the
value of education. In contrast, *concrete attitudes* were defined as perceptions
based on students' direct observations of everyday events. Her results revealed
that many black students expressed a high regard for education (abstract attitudes)
at the same time that they achieved very poorly in academic studies.

Mickelson's interpretation of the results of her research consisted of a five-
step line of logic. First, she applied the term *paradox* to the discrepancy between
students' positive view of education and their poor academic performance, an

outcome in conflict with the expectation that people who highly value education will perform well in school. Second, she asserted that

> The poor quality of schooling that many blacks, particularly those in inner-city schools, continue to receive certainly contributes to their academic performance. . . . Yet an often-neglected but critical factor in the level of achievement may well be the student's perception of what her or his efforts and accomplishments in school ultimately will bring from the larger society. . . . Adolescents see their parents' experiences in the labor market, in which class, race, and gender also influence returns on educational credentials. Young blacks are not bewitched by the rhetoric of equal opportunity through education; they hear another side of the story at the dinner table. (Mickelson, 1990, p. 59)

Mickelson provided no data from her own study to support this assumption about experiences "at the dinner table" but, instead, based her opinion on other people's writings and on a quoted comment from one of her former students.

Third, she proposed that (a) students' answers to her questionnaire items could be divided between the abstract and the concrete, and that (b) the positive attitudes were of the abstract variety, not based on direct personal experiences. Her paradox, then, was between abstract attitudes and academic achievement.

Fourth, she contended that students' achievement was based on their concrete experiences which suggested that studying hard in school would not yield the desired rewards (favorable job opportunities), so they felt that working diligently on school assignments was not worth the effort.

> In a reasonable and rational process, material realities are the foundation of concrete attitudes toward education. This is the logic and the structure of the often-reported lower performance of black and working-class youths. (Mickelson, 1990, p. 60)

As her final step, Mickelson concluded that the underachievement of minority and working-class students is likely to continue unless basic changes occur in the vocational and social opportunities they face, regardless of any improvements in the efficiency of the education system.

Value Preferences and Extended Interpretations

In the present context, the term *values* refers to people's beliefs about the desirability or propriety or goodness of something. The "something" may be a person, an object, a place, an event, a procedure, a goal, or the like. A *value* is thus a mental construct that is assumed to influence a person's behavior. The term *value preference* means a person's favoring one value over another.

Questionnaires are often used in educational research to reveal people's values. To illustrate, a research team mailed Ennis and Hooper's (1988) *Values Orientation Inventory* (VOI) to physical education instructors in the Washington,

DC, area in order to learn how instructors' value orientations affected their daily decisions.

> The values of teachers in a predominantly black metropolitan school district were studied to determine the extent to which they made consistent curricular and instructional decisions that reflected five educational value orientations. Using a paper and pencil inventory (the VOI), teachers compared examples of educational situations (goals, strategies, activities, and evaluation procedures) representative of each value perspective and then ranked their preferences based on their educational beliefs. (Ennis, Chen, & Ross, 1992, p. 157)

The five value positions tapped by the VOI were defined as:

1. Disciplinary mastery—promote students' knowledge of the traditional body of subject matter.
2. Self-actualization—nurture each student's growth in self-esteem, autonomy, and responsibility.
3. Learning process—teach students how to learn.
4. Social reconstruction—increase students' awareness of inequities in society and equip them with strategies for effecting change.
5. Ecological integration—achieve a balance among the learner's interests, the importance of knowledge, and the influence of society.

Of the 172 teachers who received the inventory, 68% returned usable answers. Eighty percent of the respondents were white; 78% of the students in their classes were black.

The research team's interpretation of the inventory answers included two phases. The first phase involved summarizing the central findings.

> The majority of teachers in this sample consistently selected items from the social reconstruction orientation. . . . Although the traditional goals of disciplinary mastery, learning process, and self-actualization were present, they received a relatively low priority when compared to items reflecting social justice and reform. (Ennis, Chen, & Ross, 1992, p. 162)

In the second phase of the interpretation, the authors did not confine their conclusions to the sample of 117 physical education instructors in the Washington area. Instead, they broadened their interpretation (a) by extending their conclusions to teachers in general and (b) by proposing that teaching students to reconstruct the society is a suitable method of meeting students' needs, although the nature of those needs was not explained.

> At a time when schools are facing increasing pressures to create responsive environments, findings from this research suggest that teachers are sensitive to these issues and are able to consistently select content and instructional strategies to meet students' evolving needs. (Ennis, Chen, & Ross, 1992, p. 163)

Critical readers might question the wisdom of founding such a broad generalization on the sort of data the authors had collected. Readers might also ask whether the teachers' responses on the mailed paper-pencil inventory accurately represented their daily practice in the classroom and on the playfield. In-class observations of a sample of the respondents might have answered this question.

Estimated Effects of Cultural Contexts

Researchers sometimes account for the outcomes of an investigation by citing the study's cultural milieu as a significant determinant of the results. The term *cultural milieu* or *cultural context*, as intended here, refers to the set of ideals and values shared in common by members of a community. Cultural contexts can vary in their degree of cohesiveness. A more cohesive milieu is represented by a high level of agreement within the community about the ideals and values that should guide people's lives. A less cohesive milieu is represented by a high level of diversity in the ideals and values to which community members subscribe.

An appeal to the nature of cultural contexts is found in the interpretation offered by Saad and Hendrix (1993) for the results of their study in Israel of teachers' views of proper pupil-teacher relations. A questionnaire focusing on teachers' pupil-control ideologies was administered to teachers in four school settings: (1) urban Jewish schools, (2) rural kibbutzim Jewish schools, (3) urban Arab schools, and (4) rural Arab schools. The questionnaire (*Pupil Control Ideology Scale* by Willower, Eidell, and Hoy, 1967) was designed to distinguish between two orientations toward controlling elementary school pupils—the custodial and the humanistic. The custodial emphasized the maintenance of order, a rigid hierarchy of pupil-teacher status, and the expectation that pupils would accept teachers' decisions without question. The humanistic conceived the school to be a democratic community within which pupils learned by means of cooperation, pupil self-discipline, and two-way communication between pupil and teacher.

The questionnaire results showed that Arab teachers in rural schools were more custodial in their philosophies than Arab teachers in urban schools, a finding in keeping with earlier studies reported in the educational literature. But among Jewish teachers, the outcome was quite the opposite. Rural Jewish teachers displayed a more humanistic orientation than those in urban Jewish schools. The authors explained this seemingly exceptional finding as a consequence of the cultural settings of two sorts of Jewish schools.

> Kibbutzim are small, homogeneous, egalitarian, and relatively affluent communities that are based on a cooperative, socialist, and highly participatory model of organization. People join a kibbutzim by choice, and membership is dependent on sharing these values. Since the whole community strives to embody nonauthoritarian, cooperative, and democratic values, it is logical that

the schools would exhibit such humanistic characteristics. It is not surprising that teachers' [questionnaire] scores in Jewish city schools are less humanistic than those of the teachers in the kibbutz schools. City schools exist in larger, more diverse communities where people do not all share the same cultural background and values. In addition, the schools themselves are larger. This, according to some researchers, leads to higher levels of bureaucracy and student alienation, which in turn results in teachers with more custodial [questionnaire scores]. (Saad & Hendrix, 1993, pp. 28-29)

Theory Testing and Policy Recommendations

Questionnaire results are sometimes used for two stages of interpretation—(a) estimating which of several theories best explains the results and (b) suggesting educational policies based on the theory that proved most convincing. Such was the procedure in a survey of sexual harassment within a nationally representative sample of 1,203 eighth- to eleventh-grade students enrolled in 79 U.S. secondary schools (Lee, Croniger, Linn, & Chen, 1996).

The research team's threefold aim was to learn the type and extent of sexual harassment among secondary-school students, to judge which of 10 theories best accounted for such harassment, and to suggest policies educators might adopt to reduce the incidence of harassment. As the source of their data, the team used the results of a questionnaire survey sponsored earlier by the American Association of University Women and published in the book *Hostile Hallways* (1993).

Sexual harassment was defined as a student receiving any unwanted verbal or physical sexual attention. A total of 74% of the students reported receiving such attention at least once, chiefly from peers rather than from school staff members. In seeking to explain the widespread prevalence of harassment, the investigators examined the questionnaire results (describing the nature and consequences of the incidents) from the perspectives of 10 theories of sexual harassment found in the professional literature. The theory labels and their foundational precepts can be summarized as follows:

> *Biological theory*—The hormonal and body size differences between males and females make males the aggressive perpetrators of harassment and females the victims.
>
> *Development theory*—Young people have trouble expressing sexual feelings in socially acceptable ways, but they achieve better control as they mature.
>
> *Pathology theory*—Being victimized by trauma in their lives damages people's ability to empathize so that they do hurtful things to others.
>
> *Abuse of power I: Exclusionary intimidation*—Males seek to "keep women in their place" by harassing them sexually.
>
> *Abuse of power II: Abuse of organizational power*—People in positions of power take sexual advantage of people under their authority.
>
> *Abuse of power III: Abuse of societal power*—Traditional superior power and status of males in society cause them to sexually exploit females.

Cultural theories—The culture of a particular context (the school, the work site) permits or encourages harassment.

Cultural theory I: Psychoanalytic approach—The culture fails to repress people's potentially destructive sexual and aggressive instincts.

Cultural theory II: Structural approach—The culture's (school's) rules, tolerance of rituals, selected heroes, and methods of handling discipline tolerate or encourage harassment.

Cultural theory III: Critical theory—Sexual harassment in schools reflects violence and sexual aggression in the larger society, as in advertising and capitalist consumption.

Cultural theory IV: Ethical perspective—Existing societal organizations (family, school, church, government) fail to instill ethical integrity in their members.

After examining the questionnaire data from the viewpoints of the 10 theories, the authors concluded that a combination of three models provided the most reasonable interpretation of the results—(a) abuse of organizational power, (b) the structure of the school culture, and (c) the ethical characteristics of that culture. This interpretation served as the foundation for three proposed changes in school policies: (1) Expand the schools' agenda to include the discussion of sexuality (both wanted and unwanted) in both the elementary and secondary schools' formal and informal curricula. (2) Hold students accountable for their harassing behavior, and help them understand "their own ambivalence about sexual harassment (indeed, about sexuality generally)." (3) Examine the behavior of school personnel to ensure that they serve as constructive models for students to emulate (Lee, Croniger, Linn, & Chen, 1996, p. 410).

INTERVIEWS

As noted earlier, interviewing involves a researcher posing oral questions for respondents to answer orally. The following four modes of interpreting interviews involve: (a) extracting themes from the pattern of respondents' answers, (b) introducing a novel perspective, (c) evaluating a pedagogical innovation, and (d) eliciting people's meanings.

Central Themes

A commonly applied method of interpreting interview answers consists of identifying themes that dominate respondents' replies. For instance, in South Africa researchers interviewed 25 principals of high schools that formerly had restricted their clientele to white, Indian, or colored students but that now were obliged to accept applicants of various racial origins. The interviewers' purpose was to learn the attitudes of principals toward new racial-integration policies.

The task of interpreting interviews consisted of extracting attitudes that typified the viewpoints of the principals as a group.

> The most powerful theme to emerge from these interviews is the generally held belief that to open schools to children of "other races" is a "good thing" and that it is both morally right and economically expedient to do so. . . . A second major theme . . . was apprehension and uncertainty . . . [concerning] [1] the cultural background of African students . . . [2] whether [academic and social] standards would be maintained, . . . and [3] the extent of local control over schools by school management councils. (Penny, et al., 1993, pp. 415-416)

Introduction of a Novel Perspective

The aim of some research is to introduce and elucidate a novel way of viewing educational practice. This general goal is typically composed of several subgoals —those of defining the concepts at the core of the new perspective, identifying how the perspective differs from traditional viewpoints, illustrating the perspective with empirical examples, interpreting the examples from the new vantage point, and suggesting ways educational practice would benefit if the new perspective was adopted.

An illustration of this sort of research is McKay and Wong's (1996) two-year case study of four Chinese immigrant students enrolled in ESL (English as a second language) classes in a California junior high school. The researchers' purpose was to introduce a non-traditional way of conceptualizing the second-language-learning situation. In their report of the investigation, the authors first contrasted their *contextual perspective* to a pair of traditional ways of conceiving second language learning:

(a) Second language learning as *code-based*, emphasizing "the learner's need to master and adjust him/herself to the rules of appropriateness in the target language" (McKay & Wong, 1996, p. 579).
(b) Second language learning as a *process* of acquiring learning strategies that can differ from one individual and social context to another.

The authors then introduced the key features of their contextual perspective, a viewpoint picturing the second-language learner as a person seeking to achieve a secure and satisfying *identity* by performing effectively (that is, by displaying *agency*) in a social context that offers communication encounters (*discourses*) heavily loaded with the participants' cultural histories, expectations, unstated understandings, values, and attitudes. Key people involved in the second-language learner's discourses include teachers, fellow students, counselors, and administrators. These people's impressions of the immigrant student's abilities, habits, appearance, motivations, and attitudes influence the power relationships reflected in their social interactions and affect how adequately the immigrant student invests time and energy in mastering English.

The bulk of the authors' account details the way each of the four Chinese adolescents coped with the discourses in which they engaged. The data for the case studies were collected primarily by extensive interviews with the four students, their teachers, teacher aides, administrators, classmates, and parents, as well as by 155 hours of observation in and outside of classes.

The following are among the interpretations McKay and Wong drew from their data analysis.

—[Learners] exist in extremely complex social environments that consist of overwhelmingly asymmetrical power relations and that subject the learners to multiple discourses.

—The learners' . . . needs, desires, and negotiations are not simply distractions from the proper task of language learning. . . . Rather, they must be regarded as constituting the very fabric of students' lives and as determining their investment in learning the target language.

—Contrary to common belief, the four [language] skills [listening, speaking, reading, writing] do not develop sequentially, nor is proficiency in one necessarily an indicator of proficiency in another. The four skills also have different values for the learner in terms of how his/her identities are defined and how well they help meet his/her social and academic demands. (McKay, & Wong, 1996, pp. 603-604)

In respect to how their contextual perspective might influence educational practice, the researchers refrained from offering specific "recipes for pedagogical change" since they believed that discourses and relations of power (teacher/ student, native/immigrant, adult/child) are not "amenable to quick intervention." Instead, the authors implied that educators' greater awareness of such matters might cause them to alter their practices in ways more beneficial to students in second-language programs.

Appraisal of a Pedagogical Innovation

The introduction of a novel teaching or administrative procedure often becomes the stimulus for a research project. The intent of the research is to evaluate the effectiveness of the innovation and to estimate what the adoption of such a procedure suggests for changes in the conduct of education.

One example is the evaluation of a program designed to teach 19 African-American adolescent mothers constructive ways to promote their young children's literacy and cognitive development. The mothers had dropped out of school as a consequence of childbearing, poor academic achievement, substance abuse, and/or poverty; and they were now enrolled in a yearlong literacy program, with accompanying child care furnished for their young children.

The learning sessions assumed the form of small-group discussions (four or five mothers) centering on questions designed to elicit adolescent parents' beliefs about learning, and early literacy in particular. The sessions, in essence, functioned as group interviews that started with rather general queries and progressed to questions of more pointed focus. A guide sheet for the discussion leader suggested such a sequence of opening questions as:

—What is a mother? Is a mother different from a father?
—In what ways are you like your own mother? How would you like to be like your own mother? In what ways would you not want to be like your mother? Why?
—What makes a mother a good mother? Why? (Ask for specific words.)
—What makes a mother a bad mother? Why? (Ask for specific words.) (Neuman, Hagedorn, Celano, & Daly, 1995, pp. 822-823)

The interview technique was intended to engage the mothers and discussion leaders in a mutual exchange of opinions and information. During the sessions, several members of the research team watched and took notes from an observation booth, and the discussions were videotaped for later review. The data analysis was interpreted as confirming the success of the group-interview approach for

> establishing a *posture of reciprocity* between parents and professionals [that] may require a delicate shift in the balance of power between schools and communities. This power shift must be founded on a basic respect for families, their knowledge and beliefs, and their cultural community as a primary context for children's early development and learning. (Neuman, Hagedorn, Celano, & Daly, 1995, p. 822)

People's Expressed Meanings

In the studies reviewed so far in this chapter, the questions posed for respondents have been designed (a) to elicit answers that could be classified in ways that allow researchers (b) to propose what such answers mean in terms of personality traits, the influence of environments, the validity of theories, and more. However, sometimes the answers are not intended to serve as the grist for researchers' interpretive mills. Instead, the sought-for meanings are contained in the answers themselves, since the interviewee is being asked, essentially, "What do you mean by . . . ?" Because the role of the interviewer in this situation is limited to that of collecting and conveying information and not interpreting it (other than perhaps summarizing central themes of the expressed meanings), some people would label the activity *journalism* rather than *research*, thereby reserving the term *research* for studies which require that investigators play an active part in data interpretation.

An example of such an expressed-meanings study is a published interview with Harvard University philosopher Cornel West about his conception of relationships among homophobia (antipathy toward homosexuals and homosexuality), patriarchy (paternal, male supremacy), and racism (contention that one race is superior to another). The interview questions posed to West were intended to reveal his values, personal experiences related to those values, beliefs about social justice, and recommendations for action to rectify injustice. Here are three such questions:

Interviewer—We've often heard you speak about the connections among homophobia, patriarchy, and racism. Why do you talk about these issues, and how do you see them linked? And would you also talk about some of the personal challenges you face as a heterosexual Black man, in taking such a vocal stance against heterosexism?

Interviewer—With highly charged political and moral issues such as sexuality, how do democratic educators balance a respect for diverse community values with respect for their own democratic ideals, particularly where community values may run counter to them?

Interviewer—The question about identity is linked to a question about destructive divisions between liberation struggles for people of color and liberation struggles for gays and lesbians. The hierarchy of oppressions—"my oppression is worse than your oppression"—gets in the way of coalition building. What can be done to foster coalition? (Eisen & Kenyatta, 1996, pp. 357-362)

RESEARCH PROJECT CHECKLIST

1. In my research project, do I intend to gather data by means of tests? If so, which forms of interpretation do I intend to employ?

___1.1 Comparisons of individuals and groups. (Specify which tests will be used and which kinds of individuals and groups will be compared.)

___1.2 Evaluations of how closely participants' responses approach a standard of desirability. (Explain what factor or variable is to be tested, and tell how and why the particular standard was selected.)

___1.3 The patterning of achievements or aptitudes within individuals' or groups' test performances. (Identify which types of tests will be used.)

___1.4 Estimates of the likely causes of correlations between test scores and other measures of variability. (Tell which tests and other assessment methods will be used and why.)

___1.5 Assessments of the validity of conventional wisdom or traditional practices. (Identify which conventions or practices are to be appraised.)

___1.6 Evaluations of tests' validity or of the testing process. (Tell which tests or testing processes are to be evaluated.)

___1.7 Other (explain)_____

(Note: The last two functions of test-result interpretation illustrated early in this chapter [*research-project limitations* and *the resolution of unexpected outcomes*] cannot adequately be foreseen during a project's planning stage, because both are discoveries made during the implementation phase of the research. Therefore, neither of them is included in this check list.)

2. In my research project, do I intend to gather data by means of questionnaires? If so, which forms of interpretation do I intend to employ?

___2.1 Identification of correlations, without offering an estimate of their causes. (Specify the variables whose degree of relationship will be computed or estimated.)

___2.2 Evaluation of how closely the status of some educational phenomenon matches a bench mark or standard. (Identify the educational phenomenon or variable, and explain how and why the particular standard was selected.)

___2.3 Investigation of personality traits. (Define the traits to be studied and describe the instruments to be used in appraising them.)

___2.4 The validation of personality inventories. (Identify the inventories to be assessed, and describe the method to be used in determining their validity.)

___2.5 Identification of respondents' perceptual proclivities. (Explain what sorts of perceptual tendencies will be studied and why.)

___2.6 Identification of individuals' value preferences.

___2.7 Estimated effects of cultural contexts. (Specify which cultural contexts will be inspected, and tell what instruments will be used for estimating what kinds of effects.)

___2.8 Theory testing. (Explain what theory or theories are to be tested by the use of what instruments.)

___2.9 Policy and practice recommendations. (Identify the kinds of educational policies or practices that might warrant revision on the basis of the questionnaire results obtained in the intended project.)

___2.10 Other (explain)_____

3. In my research project, do I intend to gather data by means of interviews? If so, which forms of interpretation do I intend to employ?

___3.1 Central themes. (Specify the questions to be asked of the kinds of respondents to be interviewed in order to extract key themes from respondents' answers.)

___3.2 Introduction of a novel perspective. (Label and define the perspective that will be introduced, and identify the competing perspectives with which it will be compared.)

___3.3 Evaluation of a pedagogical innovation. (Tell what educational innovation will be evaluated, identify who will be interviewed, and describe the questions that interviewees will be asked.)

___3.4 People's meanings. (Describe the interview questions to be asked for eliciting the respondent's beliefs and intentions.)

___3.5 Other (explain)_____

Stage V:

Reporting the Outcomes

In the two chapters that comprise Stage V, the word *publishing* refers to issuing a research report in some form available to people other than the report's author. Thus, publishing outlets include such diverse media as theses, dissertations, books, booklets, articles in academic journals or popular magazines, newspaper accounts, encyclopedia entries, videos, radio and television programs, lectures, debates, panel discussions, presentations at professional conferences, microfilm, microfiche, computer renditions on the internet and worldwide web, and the like. Chapter 14, entitled "Where to Publish," identifies characteristics of such media that authors can profitably consider as they plan to disseminate the outcomes of their research.

Chapter 15, "How to Publish," guides researchers through typical steps in the process of selecting an appropriate publishing medium, casting the report in a suitable form, negotiating with editors, and carrying the project through to completion.

14

Where to Publish

The characteristics of different types of publishing outlets render certain outlets more appropriate than others for disseminating a given research report. Consequently, researchers can profit from recognizing the available variety of publishing sources and their distinguishing features. The purpose of this chapter is to describe principal sources in terms of features that can influence an author's choice of which type will be most suitable for reporting the results of a particular research effort.

PUBLISHING SOURCES AND THEIR CHARACTERISTICS

The types of outlets reviewed in this chapter include theses and dissertations, conference presentations, academic journals, popular periodicals, books, chapters in books, microfiche reproductions, taped and broadcast presentations, Internet publishing, and researcher-created print publications. Each type is described in relation to nine variables—the length of the research report, the intended audience, the likely breadth of dissemination, the probability that the report will be accepted for publication, the time lapse before publication, the author's contribution, the publisher's contribution, the extent of author control over the publication's final form, and the extent of control wielded by the publisher.

Theses and Dissertations

One important advantage of graduate students' theses and dissertations is that rarely are restrictions placed on their length. This means that a research report can include quantities of detail and supporting evidence not possible in a journal article or conference presentation.

The most immediate audience for a thesis or dissertation is the faculty committee that supervises the research. A wider audience consists of other students and faculty members in the author's college or university. These are people who obtain the document from the institution's library. In the case of dissertations, a brief synopsis of the work may be available to readers outside the institution through the periodical *Dissertation Abstracts*, which is a series available in libraries of major colleges and universities. Most theses and dissertations apparently reach a very small number of readers, probably fewer than a dozen. For this reason, students often wish to appeal to a broader audience by issuing their work in some additional form as well—a journal article, a presentation at a professional conference, or a chapter in someone's book.

Ultimate control over the content and quality of a thesis rests in the hands of the faculty committee that guides and monitors the research. Whereas the student bears responsibility for conducting the investigation and writing the results, the committee is responsible for giving advice and ensuring that the ultimate product exemplifies sound scholarship.

There is hardly any time lapse between when the finished report is accepted by the supervising committee and the document becomes available to readers. The only delay results from the time it takes to have the work bound and accessioned by the library staff.

Conference Presentations

In many institutions graduate students have opportunities to describe their research in seminars or colloquia attended by their peers and faculty members. However, they can reach a far larger audience when they present their findings at conferences of such academic and professional organizations as the American Educational Research Association, the Comparative and International Education Society, the American Psychological Association, and the like.

The presentation format at such events can be of various kinds—lectures, panels organized around themes, debates, question-answer sessions, open discussions, and poster displays. The poster presentation is a relatively recent innovation that consists of researchers being assigned positions in a room or hallway where each one displays key elements of her or his work and discusses the work with whatever interested individuals choose to stop by. The size of the audience reached by a presentation depends on several factors—the number of people attending the conference, the reputation of the presenter, the popularity of the topic being discussed, the time of day, and the number of parallel sessions going on at the same time so that the total audience is divided among multiple sessions. Because of such conditions, the number of people reached by a presentation can vary from more than a thousand to only two or three.

The length of time allotted to a speaker at a conference can vary from five minutes to an hour or so, depending on the eminence of the position the researcher enjoys in the field of interest and on the number of presentations the conference organizers have chosen to include. A speaker with a distinguished reputation or a breakthrough discovery will be assigned more time than will a graduate student or assistant professor who is reporting on a sound but hardly startling research effort. Fifteen minutes is a rather typical length of time allowed each presenter, thereby providing the opportunity to describe no more than the highlights of the research method and results.

The chance of having a research paper accepted for delivery at a conference is usually far greater than having it accepted for publication in a journal or as a chapter in a book. Conference planning committees, compared to journal and book editors, are typically more lenient in the standards they apply in judging submissions, and competition for having a paper accepted for a conference is usually less than for a journal. Frequently the opportunity to present a paper is limited to members of the organization that sponsors the conference.

There is usually little or no time lag between a researcher completing a research report and presenting it at a conference.

Academic Journals

The world's academic journals number in the thousands. Journals can be issued monthly, bimonthly, quarterly, semiannually, or annually. The most common publication schedule is perhaps quarterly. Each journal accepts articles in a defined realm of interest that may be quite narrow (*Journal of Industrial Teacher Education, Rural Special Education Quarterly*) or quite broad (*Education, Educational Studies, Journal of Thought*). The journal's subject-matter focus can be:

An academic discipline—*Journal of Research in Music Education, Business Education Forum, Oral History Review, Economics of Education Review*
A region—*Journal of Asian and African Studies, The Middle East Journal, Australian Journal of Language and Literacy, Georgia Historical Society*
A sociogeographic entity—*Research in Rural Education, Education and Urban Society*
A professional specialization—*Journal of Correctional Education, Journal of the Association for the Severely Handicapped, The American Music Teacher*
An ethnic group—*Black Issues in Higher Education*
A gender category—*Women's Studies Quarterly, Women's Rights Law Reporter*
A religious denomination—*Muslim Education Quarterly, U.S. Catholic, Lutheran Theological Journal, Journal of Jewish Communal Services*

The size and type of a journal's reading audience are influenced by several factors—the publication's subject-matter focus, its reputation, its cost, how widely it is advertised, and whether it is issued by a professional society or association. Whenever a journal is a key publication of a professional group or scholarly society, everyone belonging to the society usually receives the journal as a right of membership. Thus, the larger the membership in the society, the larger the guaranteed reading audience. In way of illustration, the *Educational*

Researcher, published by the American Educational Research Association, is sent monthly to all 21,000 of the association's members. However, many other journals—not published by a society or not automatically distributed to a society's members—must depend solely on paid subscriptions for their distribution. Because subscription prices are frequently high, individuals often avoid buying such publications themselves and depend, instead, on using copies in a college or university library. However, in recent years, as library funds have diminished, many libraries have eliminated subscriptions to journals that are seldom read or are especially expensive, so the reading audience for such publications has dwindled.

Journals can differ dramatically in the proportion of submitted articles that they ultimately publish. The most prestigious and popular journals may accept as few as 15% or 20% of the papers they receive. In contrast, journals of particularly lower status or a small potential audience may publish 80% or more of the submitted items. Journal editors usually maintain strong control over the form, topics, and scholarly quality of the articles they accept so that authors are obliged to abide strictly by journal editors' standards and preferences. Consequently, authors enjoy far less freedom and control over articles in journals than they do over conference presentations, researcher-produced publications, microfiche content, and—in many cases—book manuscripts.

The acceptable length of articles can vary considerably from one journal to another. Some publications limit entries to ten printed pages or less. Others accept reports as long as 40 or 50 pages. Occasionally a lengthy work will be considered of such import that the editors will dedicate an entire issue of the journal to the report. Frequently the periodical's policy regarding length is described on the journal's inside cover (front or rear) in a notice to potential contributors. For example, a notice in *Child Development* (the key publication of the Society for the Study of Child Development) informs readers that:

> Most single experiment studies can be presented in less than 15 double-spaced [typewritten] pages, including tables and references. It is recognized that more space may be necessary in papers involving complex methodology, multiple studies, and reviews. If a paper of over 25 pages is submitted, a cover letter justifying its length should be included. A paper of over 60 [typewritten] pages is unlikely to be accepted but it may be referred to the [Society's] *Monographs*. (Notice to Contributors, 1994)

The time lag between an author's submitting a paper to a journal and the paper's actually appearing in print can differ significantly from one journal to another. This time lapse can be affected by a number of conditions—the number of steps in the publishing process, the efficiency of the journal's personnel, the number of submissions the journal receives, the backlog of accepted papers, the frequency with which the journal is issued, and the number of pages in each issue of the publication.

The publishing process for some journals is quite simple. A single editor takes responsibility for deciding which papers to publish, the editor makes few if any changes in the accepted manuscripts, the author submits a revised copy (if changes have been required), the author's typescript is photocopied instead of being newly set in type, the editor places the current issue's articles in a desired sequence, and that issue is printed.

However, for many journals, the publishing process is far more complex. If many articles are submitted during the same period of time, they may rest idly on some busy editor's desk until he or she gets to them. This is likely to occur when editors bear their editorial duties as a sideline, with their principal occupation being that of a college professor, therapist, business executive, government employee, or the like. After one or more editors in the journal office briefly review a submitted paper, it is mailed to three or four evaluators— known as *referees*, *reviewers*, or *readers*—who are considered to be experts in the paper's subject-matter. The referees are asked to evaluate the paper for the significance of its contribution to knowledge, the quality of its research, and its form of presentation. This reviewing procedure may take from one month to four or five months or more, depending on the efficiency and diligence of the referees. When the reviewers' judgments have all been received in the editorial office, the editors may find that the referees have disagreed about the quality of the paper. In this event, the paper may be sent to further reviewers for their opinions. Finally, when all reviews have been received, an editor—or group of editors—may decide to reject the submission, so they inform the author that the item has been judged unsuitable for the journal, and they may include the reviewers' comments about the piece (with the reviewers' names omitted from the page of comments). Frequently a paper will be accepted on the condition that specified improvements be made in its content or style. The author is informed of what needs to be done, so there is an additional time lapse while the author makes the changes and submits the revised document, which is once again inspected by one or more editors. If they decide the piece is now satisfactory, they schedule it for publication. But if more changes are required, the paper is returned to the author for additional work. After being deemed acceptable, the article is placed in line for publication. For a journal that is published quarterly, that publication date could be as early as six months from the time the final version has been approved or as late as three years after the final approval. Some journals inform potential contributors of the time lag to be expected. For example, an announcement appearing in each issue of *Child Development* states that:

> The initial review process seldom requires more than 3 months. . . . The time between initial submission and appearance in print of accepted manuscripts seldom exceeds 1 year. (Notice to Contributors, 1994)

Some journals do not accept unsolicited manuscripts but use only material from authors who have been invited to prepare articles on special themes.

Journals are not all alike in their policies regarding the costs that authors are expected to bear and the payments authors may receive. Most journals neither charge authors anything for publishing their articles nor do they pay authors for their work. However, some require that authors contribute to the expense of publication (usually a given amount per printed page), whereas others pay writers a nominal sum for articles. Authors usually receive two or three free copies of the issue of the journal in which their paper appears, and they may also be sent 25 or more offprints of their article.

Popular Periodicals

The term *popular periodicals* in the present context refers to magazines, newspapers, and newsletters read by the general public. Contributions to periodicals may be submitted on an author's own initiative, at the suggestion of an author's literary agent, or at the invitation of the periodical's editors.

Compared with journal articles, versions of research studies published in the public press are usually briefer, contain few if any technical terms, limit statistics to percentages and averages, include illustrative examples familiar to a lay audience, and may suggest applications of the research results to everyday life. Authors of such works are often paid for their contributions, except in the case of letters to the editor of a magazine or newspaper.

Magazine editors usually maintain greater control over the focus and style of articles than do newspaper editors. The editing of material for a newspaper may be limited to simplifying complex sentences and shortening the piece to fit the available space.

A significant advantage of popular periodicals over the typical journal is that they reach far more readers. Whereas a journal may have only 1,000 or 1,500 subscribers, the Sunday edition of a major newspaper ends up in hundreds of thousands of homes.

Books

For the purpose of the following discussion, books can be divided into two types—trade and academic. Trade books are intended for the general reading public and are available in regular bookstores and public libraries. Academic books are intended for such specialized audiences as students and faculty members in colleges and universities, teachers and administrators in elementary and secondary schools, early-childhood educators, physicians, social workers, therapists, engineers, industrialists, architects, lawyers, and the like. Academic books are found in the libraries of higher-education institutions, in college and university bookstores, and in academic publishers' catalogues.

Although most educational research is best suited for publication in academic books, a small proportion may appeal to the general public and thus qualify for the trade market. Some books can be successfully distributed through both general and specialized channels.

The procedure for offering manuscripts to publishers can be different for trade than for academic books. Particularly in the case of popular trade fiction, such as detective stories and romantic novels, publishers are not likely to accept submissions directly from authors. It thus becomes necessary for an author to hire a literary agent to provide the initial screening of a manuscript. The agent first reviews the author's manuscript, estimates its potential, and advises the author about changes needed. Only then will the agent seek out a publisher who is willing to consider the manuscript. But in the case of academic publishing, an agent is unnecessary. Publishers of scholarly works are usually willing to receive submissions directly from authors. However, an author's manuscript may receive more serious and prompt attention if someone of respected stature in academia recommends the work to the editors.

Publishers can differ markedly in the amount of control they seek to wield over the content, structure, and format of the books they issue. For example, at the *least-control* end of the responsibility scale are publishers who conduct what are essentially *printing services*. In other words, they leave decisions about the subject-matter content, structure, and writing style entirely in the hands of the authors. The responsibility of such publishing houses is thus limited to ensuring that the final printed book is free from typographical errors, bound attractively, and advertised to the potential readers. In contrast, publishers at the *most-control* end of the scale conceive their responsibility to include verifying and—if judged necessary—changing the technical content of the work, revising the structure (altering the sequence of chapters, moving paragraphs, eliminating portions), altering the writing style (changing phrasing and vocabulary), determining the book's type font and format, binding the work, and marketing the finished product. Some publishers adjust their degree of control to the characteristics of the author and the submitted manuscript. The work of a prestigious, highly influential researcher is less likely to be altered than is that of an unknown neophyte. A brilliantly crafted manuscript can pass through the editorial process unscathed, whereas a carelessly written document can be subjected to major editorial changes.

The monetary agreement between publisher and author can differ from one publishing house to another. The most common arrangement is for the publisher to pay nearly all production costs and to pay the author a royalty on each copy of the book that is sold. The amount of the royalty can be influenced by the size of the book's probable market, the reputation of the author, and the bargaining skill of the author or the author's agent. Here are examples of typical clauses regarding royalties as they appeared in the contracts offered to an author by two publishers of academic books.

First Publisher In the case of a regular clothbound edition of the book sold in the United States and its territories and dependencies, on the net price of the work (actual cash received), the author will receive a total royalty of 8% of the net price for all copies sold to 1,000 copies sold; 10% of the net price for all copies sold from 1,001 to 2,000 copies sold; and 12% of the net price for all copies sold in excess of 2,000 copies sold. One-half of the foregoing royalties will be paid on all sales made outside the United States and its dependencies and territories.

Second Publisher The publisher shall pay to the author in respect of its sales of the work a royalty calculated as follows: 10% of all income received on sales worldwide.

If a work appears to have the potential for greater sales, the publisher's royalty offer may be twelve-and-one-half percent on the first 1,000 or 1,500 copies sold and 15% on sales beyond 1,000. But royalties higher than 15% are extremely rare for academic publications these days (though more common in the distant past), unless the author or agent can argue an unusually strong case.

For authors, publishing educational research is seldom a reasonable money-making venture. Only when a work is adopted widely as a textbook will it sell in the thousands. Most academic publications are not adopted as texts, but are purchased chiefly by university libraries rather than by individual readers, so their sales total no more than a few hundred over the life of the work. Hence, the most rational motives authors have for publishing research projects in book form are to gain prestige, to enjoy a sense of accomplishment, and to make a contribution to knowledge—but not to become rich.

The time lag between the initial submission of the manuscript and the eventual publication of the book can vary between eight or ten months and three or four years, with the average perhaps about 12 to 16 months. Among the conditions that affect this length of time are the number of manuscripts being reviewed by the publisher, the efficiency of editorial personnel at the publishing house, the quantity of revisions the author is required to make, how soon the author submits the revisions, delays in receiving permission to quote copyrighted passages from other books, and the backlog of edited manuscripts waiting to be printed.

Chapters in Books

Research reports are often published in an edited book, with each report forming a separate chapter. The various contributors to such collections receive the opportunity to have their chapter included in the collection by one of three means.

First, a person who is editing a volume on a particular topic selects the authors who will be asked to submit chapters for the volume. Such was the case with *Cultural Literacy and the Idea of General Education*—13 chapters (Westbury

& Purves, 1988), *Curriculum Development in East Asia*—12 chapters (Marsh & Morris, 1991), and *Quality in Education*—38 chapters (Watson, Modgil, & Modgil, 1997).

Second, an editor selects a variety of already-published journal articles or excerpts from books to be reissued as chapters of a book. The result can be such volumes as *The Human Encounter: Readings in Education* (Stoff & Schwartzberg, 1969) and *Improving Instruction with Microcomputers* (Tashner, 1984).

Third, papers presented at a conference comprise a book's contents. Examples of volumes published from selected papers at three conferences of the Comparative and International Education Society's western region are *Human Rights and Education*—13 chapters (Tarrow, 1987), *Education's Role in National Development Plans*—12 chapters (Thomas, 1992), and *Education in the Urban Context*—12 chapters (Stromquist, 1994).

Editors of collections can vary considerably in the amount of control they seek to exert over the content and quality of contributors' chapters. Some editors publish the offerings without change, except for correcting spelling and grammar errors. Other editors return offerings to the authors with directions for substantial changes, or else an editor may choose to thoroughly rewrite submissions. Because the quality of chapters submitted for an edited volume frequently vary markedly from one author to another, an editor may accept certain manuscripts in their initial form while revising others in minor or major ways.

Authors usually receive a free copy of the volume in which their chapter appears but they are seldom paid for their work.

The ERIC Microfiche Collection

The acronym *ERIC* stands for *Educational Resources Information Centers,* a collection of agencies that compose a network of 16 clearinghouses for educational publications under the sponsorship of the U.S. Department of Education. Each clearinghouse specializes in a particular aspect of education, such as higher education, reading and communication skills, educational management, elementary and early childhood education, handicapped and gifted children, and the like. (See the Appendix at the end of this book for the 16 agencies' titles and addresses.)

The ERIC network is designed to collect educational documents and make them available to researchers, administrators, teachers, students, and other interested persons. The network publishes a monthly journal of abstracts, *Resources in Education,* announcing all documents that are acquired and that meet ERIC selection criteria.

A manuscript published by ERIC is not issued as an article in a journal but, rather, as one or more separate microfiche sheets containing miniaturized photographic reproductions of the author's original submission. Each microfiche is a

4-by-6-inch transparent plastic sheet on which tiny reproductions of a manuscript's pages are arranged in succession. A single 4-by-6-inch microfiche can
contain nearly 100 letter-size pages. Obviously, such material cannot be read by
the naked eye, so that reading a microfiche requires a machine that magnifies the
pages to their original size or larger. Not only are ERIC documents available in
microfiche form, but most can also be obtained as reproduced paper copies at
nominal cost.

As a publishing outlet, the ERIC network has a variety of advantages. There
are no limitations on the length of submissions. Documents can be as short or
as long as an author desires. Furthermore, there are no limits on the number of
manuscripts that can be accepted. Everything that meets ERIC's quality
standards can be published. In addition, it is not necessary for users of ERIC
documents to purchase microfiche copies themselves, because additions to the
collection are regularly distributed to over 700 subscribers (mostly libraries) in
North America and abroad. Documents newly issued by ERIC are announced
monthly to more than 4,000 organizations that receive *Resources in Education.*
Authors pay no fees to have their work included in the collection, nor do they
receive royalties for their submissions.

A great variety of educational writings can qualify for inclusion in the ERIC
files—research reports, program descriptions, speeches, evaluation studies,
instructional materials, syllabi, handbooks, conference papers, taxonomies,
annotated bibliographies, and dissertations.

At each ERIC center, when a document is received, experts judge the
suitability of the work in terms of its intended audience, likely contribution to
knowledge, newness, significance for current educational priorities, effectiveness
of presentation, thoroughness of reporting, and the authoritative status of the
document's sources.

Taped and Broadcast Presentations

At an increasing pace, reports of research projects recorded on audiotapes and
videotapes are being broadcast over radio and television or presented directly to
such on-site audiences as students in classrooms and participants attending
professional conferences. In addition, the computer Internet and World Wide
Web are being adopted as media for disseminating research results.

Taped presentations can be produced by researchers themselves or by others,
such as radio or television news reporters, talk show personnel, and the like.

Researchers maintain the greatest control over the content and quality of tape-
recorded reports when they create tapes themselves. Audiotapes are the simpler
kind to produce, since they require a minimum of equipment, and program
participants' comments can be recorded in nearly any quiet location. In contrast,
videotapes require more elaborate equipment and proper visual settings in which
to record program content. However, the extra bother that videotapes entail is
compensated for by their ability to visually portray the episodes and people who

are the objects of the research. Videotapes also permit the inclusion of information in cartoon, graph, map, or tabular form. Researcher-created tapes are more often used for classroom instruction and for conference presentations than for radio and television broadcasts, thereby enabling their creators to maintain greater control over the timing of their presentation. Unless the production of such tapes is financed by a research grant or an institution, the cost of the work must be borne by the investigators themselves.

Taped and live radio and television broadcasts produced by people other than researchers themselves are in the form of news spots, talk show appearances, and special programs. A news spot is a brief segment within a half-hour or one-hour general program of current events, with the segment featuring a report of the principal conclusions of a project bearing on a topic of interest to the general public. A talk show appearance consists of the researcher being interviewed during a half-hour program by the show's host. The program may include questions and comments by members of a studio audience or by listeners who phone in their opinions. Special programs are usually taped productions treating a research topic of public interest, with the program dedicated either to the work of a single scholar or to the findings of a variety of investigators who have studied that topic.

Internet Publishing

Recent years have witnessed the creation of a worldwide computer network consisting of millions of *hosts* (*information servers* that connect to the network) and over 25 million *users* (consumers who attach their computers to the network) at more than 500,000 sites—with more hosts and users added each year. The Internet was initially created in the United States during the 1960s to facilitate rapid communication among military researchers and scientists situated in different locations. The system enabled a computer at one site to exchange quantities of information with computers at distant sites by means of telephone lines or communication satellites. Rapid expansion of the network began in the 1980s when the National Science Foundation took over Internet supervision and insisted that access to the system be extended to as many educational institutions as possible. Soon commercial organizations and corporations linked their own networks into the Internet, and many thousands of library catalogues, files, and other information resources were added. By the latter 1990s the Internet still played a vital role in higher education and scientific research but had also expanded to include millions of individuals and organizations in other walks of life. In the mid-1990s there were sites in over 140 nations from which Internet users could obtain information, simply by accessing the sources via a personal computer at home or in the office (Franks, 1995; Harris, 1996).

The rapid growth of the Internet and the subsequent World Wide Web has provided a new outlet for research reports, an outlet bound to expand at a fast pace in the near future as the amount of research continues to accelerate at the same time that traditional outlets (journals, printed books) have become so expensive to maintain that scholars face diminishing opportunities for getting their work into print and widely disseminated. At present there are two principal ways that researchers can distribute their reports via the Internet and World Wide Web.

The simplest way is by e-mail (electronic mail), which operates in much the same fashion as postal mail, except that messages are delivered over the computer network rather than by a mail carrier. An author, seated at a computer, transmits the research report either (a) to particular readers at their network addresses (with the names and e-mail addresses of people interested in the researcher's topic obtained from mailing lists available on the Internet) or (b) to one or more of the thousands of special interest groups found on the Internet, with appropriate interest groups identified and reached by means of the USENET (short for *users' network*) service that the Internet furnishes (Pike & Pike, 1994). Information intended for a particular type of audience is assigned by the author to an electronic "bulletin board."

> A single message posted on a popular bulletin board or sent to a mailing list might reach and engage millions of people. . . . Each bulletin board or news-group has a name, and anyone interested can "hang out" there. . . . Almost any topic you can name has a group communicating about it on the network. (Gates, 1995, pp. 123-125)

A second publishing option is to transmit the manuscript via the Internet to the editor of a journal or magazine that issues its products solely on the Internet. With the costs of print publishing rising and the number of subscribers to many scholarly journals declining, traditional journals increasingly experience financial difficulties. Thus, a growing number are turning to electronic publishing as a solution to their money problems. University libraries are usually equipped to furnish an author the names of electronic periodicals suitable for publishing the particular research report that the author wants to distribute.

Electronic publishing via e-mail has a number of advantages over print media. First, e-mail delivers the finished product to readers far more quickly than does print publishing. With books and journals, a year or two can elapse between the time a completed manuscript is submitted to editors and the time the work is finally in print. With electronic publishing, there is little or no wait between when the author puts the report on the network and it becomes available to readers. Furthermore, electronic publishing eliminates problems of distance. The World Wide Web now reaches virtually all parts of the world in which computers are available, so readers anywhere can receive the researcher's report as soon as it appears. Whereas traditional journals and books cannot be conveniently altered once they are in print, materials on the web can be revised at any time—corrected, lengthened, updated. Publishing on the network also enables an author to receive rapid feedback from readers who send their comments to the author by e-mail. Documents placed on the Internet (with the World Wide Web as the *server* or intermediary) can include full color illustrations to accompany the text, which is a feature that is expensive in print media but is included at little cost on the Internet. Finally, in e-mail publishing, the author maintains complete control over the form of the report, since no editors are involved, except in the case of formal Internet journals and books that must pass through the editorial process before being issued on the Internet. However, a disadvantage of shortcutting the editorial process is that the author then lacks the professional aid with the writing style and the elimination of errors that editors usually provide.

Researcher-Created Print Publications

The advent of the personal computer in the 1980s equipped researchers—at home or in the office—to produce high-quality printed reports of their studies. This movement is popularly referred to as *desk-top publishing*. With no more than an up-to-date word processing program, an author can create book or journal pages that appear to be professionally typeset. This means that the author, rather than the editors in a publishing house, maintains complete control over the format and quality of the final product. Furthermore, if a photocopy machine is available, the researcher can print quantities of the report.

However, there are several important disadvantages to self-published books and articles. For instance, when a professional publishing facility is involved, editors, copyreaders, and proofreaders assume responsibility for ensuring that a manuscript's structure, grammar, syntax, and spelling are accurate. But in the case of researcher-produced publications, authors themselves must perform the laborious editing tasks and accept the blame for errors in the final product. And though authors can easily do the typesetting, few have the equipment and skill needed to bind a book or periodical proficiently. Thus, the task of binding must be contracted out to professionals, with the author paying the cost that would be borne by the publisher if the book or article were issued by a publishing house.

Then there is the problem of how to disseminate the finished work to a suitable audience. This is one of the most important functions of publishing firms. They typically conduct a sophisticated marketing system, complete with specialists in writing advertising copy, providing lists of libraries and members of professional societies who are potential buyers, shipping books to book-sellers, displaying booths at conferences, and delivering books and journals to customers. In the case of self-produced reports, authors are obliged either to market the reports themselves or else contract out the distribution tasks to an organization that provides such service.

Whether books, audiotapes, videotapes, and other materials are issued by a publisher or by researchers themselves, authors can seek to enhance the dissemination of their works in several ways—presentations at conferences, announcements in newsletters and journals of professional societies, articles in newspapers and popular magazines, and appearances on radio and television talk shows. For authors who do not wish to spend the time and bother that such advertising efforts require, issuing their work through a professional publisher is likely a better method than desktop publishing for ensuring that their reports reach a wide audience.

RESEARCH PROJECT CHECKLIST

Which one or more modes of disseminating my research report do I intend to use?

___1. Master's degree thesis

___2. Doctoral dissertation

___3. Conference presentation
      (Name one or more conferences that would be suitable occasions
      for presenting the report.)

___4. Academic journal article
      (Name journals that would seem to be suitable outlets for the
      the report.)

___5. Article in a popular periodical
      (Name magazines, newspapers, or newsletters that would seem
      to be suitable outlets for the report.)

___6. Book

   ___6.1 Academic publication

   ___6.2 Trade publication
      (Name firms that would seem to be suitable publishers for such
      a book.)

___7. Chapter in someone else's book
      (Suggest how the opportunity to publish the report as a chapter
      might be sought.)

___8. An entry in the ERIC collection.
      (Identify the ERIC center to which the report might best be sent.
      For each center's specialization, see the Appendix on page 351.)

___9. Taped or broadcast presentation

   ___9.1 Audiotape—researcher produced

   ___9.2 Videotape—researcher produced

   ___9.3 Radio broadcast

      ___9.3.1 News spot

      ___9.3.2 Talk show interview

      ___9.3.3 Special program

   ___9.4 Television broadcast

      ___9.4.1 News spot

      ___9.4.2 Talk show interview

      ___9.4.3 Special program

___10. Computer-network entry—the Internet
___11. Researcher-created publication
   ___11.1 Pamphlet
   ___11.2 Book
   ___11.3 Other (specify)_____

15

How to Publish

The task of publishing a research report can be seen as consisting of eleven steps, with the decisions at each step influenced by a variety of conditions. Chapter 15 inspects each of the steps in relation to the conditions that can profitably be weighed in resolving the issues that each step entails.

STEPS IN THE PUBLISHING PROCESS

The eleven steps are labeled: (1) choosing the publishing form, (2) locating a publishing outlet, (3) organizing the manuscript, (4) submitting a proposal, (5) negotiating the publishing conditions, (6) obtaining copyright permission, (7) furnishing a completed manuscript, (8) responding to copyediting, (9) preparing an index, (10) proofreading, and (11) distributing the final product.

Choosing the Publishing Form

When selecting a publishing outlet, researchers can be guided by the considerations reviewed in Chapter 14, such as the intended audience, length of the report, expense to the author, probability of acceptance by a publisher, amount of control maintained by the author, and more.

At the outset it is useful to recognize that authors may choose more than one form in which to issue their findings. For instance, doctoral students may first offer their results in a detailed dissertation, then subsequently report the main findings in a short journal article, or they may write a brief summary of the results in a style suitable for a popular magazine or newspaper.

The following five cases illustrate typical patterns that the choosing process can assume under different circumstances.

Case 1: To gain research experience before attempting her thesis investigation, a master's degree candidate in the field of international education carried out an individual study project under the guidance of her academic advisor. The topic she studied was educational policy for ethnic minorities in Nicaragua under successive governments. Her academic advisor considered the completed project of high quality, worthy of dissemination to a professional audience, so he suggested it be submitted to an ERIC center. The paper was subsequently accepted by ERIC editors for inclusion in their microfiche collection (Rippberger, 1988).

Case 2: To gather data for his doctoral dissertation, a graduate student received permission from a school district to attend high school classes in the role of a student. His purpose was to study teachers' classroom management techniques and, by associating with high school students on a regular basis, to understand the students' perspectives toward teachers' management styles, to observe the students' strategies in interacting with teachers, and to learn the goals that such strategies were intended to achieve. The completed dissertation was 359 pages long.   Two years after finishing the research, the author prepared a much shortened form of the study that was accepted for eventual publication in the *American Educational Research Journal* (Allen, 1986). The journal version was limited to 23 pages; thus, it could describe only a segment of the original research.

Case 3: A doctoral student in the field of educational psychology accepted a teaching position in an inner-city high school in order to conduct dissertation research focusing on a method of helping students from deprived families succeed in school. Upon finishing her investigation and earning the doctorate, she continued for three more years as a teacher at the school in order to study her students' lives in detail and to help them surmount the difficulties they faced in their violent, socially disordered community. At the end of the three years, she was appointed to the teacher-education faculty of a state university. Now, as a university professor, she used her dissertation and her subsequent experiences at the high school as the source of a book-length ethnographic account of the plight of students in a poverty-ridden ghetto, an account entitled *Lives in the Balance* (Diver-Stamnes, 1995). She chose to report her investigation in book form in order to include the detail necessary for tracing the complex patterns of students' lives against a background of theory and societal conditions that she extracted from the professional literature. If she had attempted to report her findings as a journal article, she would have been forced to sacrifice most of the study's enlightening detail.

Case 4: A widely published comparative-education expert at a major U.S. university received an invitation from a British professor to submit a proposal for a chapter suitable for inclusion in a book to be titled *Power and Responsibility in Education.* The invitation identified the general nature of appropriate topics, the desired chapter length, and the dates that the proposal and completed chapter were due. Because the book was in the American professor's field of expertise, he welcomed the opportunity and sent a proposal describing a study of school decentralization that he could conduct to provide the contents of the chapter. His proposal was accepted, and the final product was published in the book under the title "Not Decentralization but Integration" (McGinn, 1997). In this case, the researcher was not only freed from the problem of locating a suitable publishing source, but the invitation to contribute to the book served as the stimulus for carrying out the study that provided the substance of the chapter. Such opportunities as this are enjoyed chiefly by scholars who have already compiled a respected record of publication.

Case 5: Coincident with the appearance of the sixth edition of a college textbook entitled *The Whole Child: Developmental Education for the Early Years* (Hendrick, 1996), a philanthropic foundation sponsored the preparation of a series of 13 half-hour television programs based on the contents of the book. The volume's eighteen chapters presented the author's summary of research on child development and the practical application of the research results to child rearing. The series was designed for the U.S. Public Broadcasting System's adult learning service and was made available to educational institutions on video cassettes. The decision by the book's publisher and the philanthropic foundation to issue the author's work as a televised course was based on the popularity of the first five editions of the book as a college text and as a resource for the lay public.

Locating a Publishing Outlet

The way to find the names and addresses of potential publishing outlets differs somewhat from one medium to another. The nature of those differences can be illustrated with the examples of dissertations, journal articles, books, and microfiche reproductions.

Locating a publishing source is obviously not a problem for the authors of theses and dissertations, since copies of their works are automatically placed in the library of the college or university they attend and are usually made available to other institutions through the interlibrary loan service. Furthermore, in most universities that offer doctoral studies, authors of dissertations have brief summaries of their work published in *Dissertation Abstracts*, which is a reference series available in the libraries of most higher-learning institutions in the United States.

Identifying journals in which to place an article can involve:

—Asking the advice of someone who has published on topics similar to the topic of one's own report.
—Inspecting the bibliographies in books bearing on topics similar to that of one's own project in order to find the names of suitable journals cited in those volumes' lists of references.

—Searching through past issues of a library's journals that are related to the field of one's own work so as to judge which journals include articles of the same type as one's own.

The process of finding an appropriate book publisher can include:

—Asking the advice of someone who has already published academic books or has read widely in the literature related to the topic of one's research.
—Using key words from one's own research project for searching universities' computerized library catalogues in order to locate books on similar topics and thus find the names of the publishers of those books.
—In a college or university library: entering key words into the computerized catalogue of holdings to identify books related to one's research; noting the call numbers of such books, and using the call numbers to find the sections of the library stacks in which the books are stored; then browsing through those sections to find books on topics similar to that of one's own research, and noting the names of the publishers of those volumes.
—Finding the addresses of the editorial offices of publishers by searching in the latest edition of *Books in Print,* a publication found in the reference section of nearly every library.

As explained in Chapter 14, the ERIC microfiche collection emanates from a network of 16 research-documentation centers, each specializing in a particular aspect of education. To decide which center will be the appropriate editorial site to which a research report should be sent, authors can be guided by the list of sites and their fields of emphasis found in the Appendix at the end of this book. If an author is uncertain about which clearinghouse is the appropriate outlet for a particular manuscript, the manuscript can be sent to the following address from where it will be forwarded to the most suitable center.

> ERIC Processing and Reference Facility
> 1301 Piccard Drive, Suite 300
> Rockville, MD 20850-4305

Organizing the Manuscript

Once the potential publishing outlet has been chosen, the author is ready to cast the research report in an appropriate form. Matters of form include the writing style, the sections into which the report is divided (chapters, subheadings within chapters), the order in which the sections are presented, the method of citing references within the body of the work, the bibliographic form, and the footnote style.

Theses and Dissertations

In the case of theses and dissertations, the proper format is dictated by regulations governing such matters in the student's particular college or university. Such regulations are often available in printed form at the institution's library or bookstore, or in the department of the student's academic major. The patterning of theses and dissertations is also influenced by the preferences of the student's research advisor and by the opinions of other members of the committee charged with supervising the work.

Journals

Academic journals often differ from each other in their format policies. Virtually all journals require a particular style of citing references and listing bibliographies. For example, some locate each reference in a footnote at the bottom of the page on which the reference appears. Others place the referenced authors' names and the date of publication in parentheses within the body of the text, then list the complete reference to that item at the end of the volume (as is the practice in this book you are now reading). Although there are variations among journals in their style requirements, most of those published in North America follow one of two general forms. The form used most often in the natural and social sciences and frequently in the field of education is found in the *Publication Manual of the American Psychological Association* (1994). The alternative form commonly appears in journals focusing on the humanities and, in some instances, on education. Both forms are described in detail in *The Chicago Manual of Style* (1993).

By inspecting copies of a journal, researchers are able to identify the range of manuscript forms considered acceptable. Furthermore, information about a journal's style requirements is frequently printed on the inside of the front or back cover of each issue of the publication.

When authors prepare their reports for a journal, they are also obliged to abide by that journal's policy regarding the length of an article.

Not only do journals vary in their requirements for such technical details as the form of footnotes and references, but they differ as well in their policies about the sequence in which the contents of an article are presented. Some periodicals, such as the *Comparative Education Review* and the *International Review of Education* accept virtually any pattern of presentation that is logical and readily grasped by readers. In contrast, other journals require that research reports follow a set pattern. One rather common pattern consists of five sections arranged in this order: (1) summary (a précis of the study's methods and results), (2) the research problem (the research question as set against a background of theory and previous studies bearing on the same or similar topics), (3) methodology (the steps and instruments used in collecting data, and the way sites and participants for the study were chosen), (4) results (the outcomes of data-gathering described in narrative and/or statistical form), (5) discussion (an interpretation of what the outcomes mean in relation to the research problem, theories, previous studies, and practical applications to real-life situations).

Authors who have little or no experience with journal publication sometimes assume that they need not cast their manuscript in a particular style—that the editors will consider the content of the piece of such worth that the editors themselves will take responsibility for adjusting the submitted work to the journal's format. This is rarely the case. Submitting a manuscript that fails to conform to the journal's style usually results in its rejection or at least in the work being returned to the author for revision.

Books

When preparing a manuscript for its initial presentation to a publisher, an author needs to decide the form in which to cast the material. Designing a research report for publication as a book usually allows the writer far more freedom in terms of organization and style than does designing the report as a journal entry. Book editors generally accept authors' judgments about the sequence in which to present ideas, the number of chapters to include, the subdivisions within chapters, and such matters, so long as the book's ideas are in a logical, readily comprehended order. In regard to the work's bibliography, footnotes, and method of citing references, some editors will accept any of several styles commonly found in academic publications. Other editors will require that the book's final form be in a particular style to which their publishing house is dedicated. However, these issues of format need not be important considerations for the initial submission of the work, since such matters can be attended to later during the copyediting phase of the publishing process.

Chapters in Books

As noted in Chapter 14, a researcher's report becomes a chapter in someone else's book under one of three circumstances—(1) the editor of a book focusing on a particular field of interest invites each of several researchers who work in that field to write a chapter for the book, (2) the report is first presented at a conference and then, along with papers from other conference participants, is included as a chapter in an edited volume, or (3) the researcher's report has already appeared in print—in journal or book form—and is now reprinted as a chapter for a book of readings on a particular topic.

When a book chapter was initially a conference paper, the book's compiler may either accept the paper in its original form or may specify the way the author should revise the piece—perhaps shorten it or expand it with additional data, embellish it with educational applications, and the like.

If the chapter is to be newly written at the invitation of the book's editor (who typically will be an academic in the same field as the author), the editor will usually offer guidelines delineating the book's purpose, the intended role to be played by chapters, the desired length of chapters (how many double-spaced typed pages or how many words), and such format features as the method of citing references, the placement of explanatory notes, the bibliographic style, and the form of subheadings to use. Sometimes an editor will write the introductory chapter of the book, therein explaining the purpose and organization of the work, and send the chapter to authors to aid them with their assignment.

Chapters that are reprints of journal articles or book excerpts usually require no additional work by the author, for they are either published in their original form or else recast by the editor into a style that is consistent from one chapter to another.

Popular Periodicals

The simplest way to discover the appropriate writing style and length of articles for a particular magazine, newsletter, and newspaper is to inspect a variety of articles in the publication to which the research report will be sent. The most common form in which to submit an article is as typed, double-spaced material, with wide margins, on letter-size sheets. If the author produces the manuscript by means of a word-processing program on a computer, the editor may also appreciate receiving a floppy disk containing the article, a procedure that may hasten the editing of the article if it is indeed accepted for publication.

Microfiche and Microfilm

Authors maintain control over the structure, writing style, and format of works to be published on microfiche or microfilm. In regard to manuscript form, the only requirements are that the contents be logically organized and free from typographical errors. Documents are most convenient to reproduce photographically if they are typed either single- or double-spaced on letter-size white paper, with the type size no smaller than 12-point so that the miniaturized pages can easily be read when enlarged on a microfiche or microfilm machine.

Researcher-Created Print Publications

It should be apparent that authors achieve the greatest control over the timing and quality of a publication when they perform all of the publishing tasks themselves. This means that authors also bear the blame for any shortcomings of the final product.

The control provided by desktop publishing enables an author to skip over certain intermediate steps in the publishing process by writing the document in the exact form in which it will finally be issued. Typically, a manuscript submitted to a journal or book publisher is originally typed double-spaced on letter-size sheets. Later, after the material has been copyedited, it is set in type in the form that it will ultimately assume in print. However, a researcher who composes the document on a computer can skip the double-spaced stage and work directly on the printed-version stage. That is, the author can decide at the outset on the page size, the typeface styles and type sizes for the body of the work and for headings, and the bibliographic form of the final product. These features can be incorporated into the document as it is composed, so that by the time the author arrives at the last page the material is in publishable form.

Submitting a Proposal

The phrase *submitting a proposal* refers to an author's initially tendering a research report to a potential publisher to learn whether the publisher is willing to issue the report and, if so, under what conditions. People with little or no experience with academic publishing often seek answers to four questions: At what point in a report's development should I approach a publisher? What should I include in my initial submission? Is it wise to send my proposal to more than one publisher at the same time? How should I react to a publisher's rejecting my work? As illustrated in the following paragraphs, the answers to these questions can differ somewhat from one publishing medium to another.

Theses and Dissertations

The manner in which a graduate student selects a thesis or dissertation topic and casts it in the form of a proposal is typically negotiated between the student and the student's main academic adviser. This procedure is often regulated by the particular university's graduate-study policies.

Journals

Although some journal editors occasionally invite selected scholars to submit articles on a particular theme, most entries in journals are ones submitted at the initiative of the authors themselves. A few journals charge authors a fee to cover the cost of having their manuscripts reviewed for possible publication, but most charge nothing for evaluating submissions.

Journals usually follow one of two reviewing procedures. The first consists of editors deciding for themselves whether a manuscript should be published. The second consists of the editors sending a copy of the manuscript to each of several outside referees (who are usually academics well versed in the topic of the article at hand) for their assessments of the document's suitability for that journal. Referees are asked to identify the work's strengths and weaknesses and to recommend whether the article be (a) published in its present state, (b) revised in a described fashion and then published, or (c) rejected. The editors subsequently compare the referees' judgments (which are sometimes at odds with each other) and add their own assessments in order to arrive at a decision about publishing the article.

When editors reject a manuscript, they usually inform the author in one of two ways. Some simply thank the writer for the submission and say that the paper does not fit into the journal's current publishing program. Others send the author copies of the referees' remarks (with the referees' names deleted) to explain why the manuscript was deemed unacceptable. Frequently a submission is neither accepted nor rejected outright. Instead, revisions are suggested, and the author is invited to resubmit the article after making the revisions. The author then needs to decide (a) whether the requested changes seem desirable or reasonable and (b) whether it is possible or feasible to attempt such changes. On the basis of this decision, the researcher either resubmits the manuscript in a new form or else decides to send it elsewhere.

Anyone who has an article turned down is bound to be disappointed. However, rejection is usually most discouraging to writers who are still new to publishing, because the refusal may be interpreted as indisputable evidence from impeccable authority that the author's work is entirely unacceptable. But writers need to realize that editors and referees display the same virtues and faults as do ordinary mortals. The rejected manuscript has been judged unacceptable by only one or two individuals whose appraisal could have been affected by a variety of factors—their limited knowledge of the author's topic, their propensity to favor submissions from their friends or from prestigious scholars, their preferences for particular theories or research methods, their mood at the time they read the manuscript, the number of other articles already accepted for publication, and more. Therefore, instead of setting the article aside in despair, the author can more profitably respond to the rejection in two ways. The first is to seriously examine any reasons that the editors or referees offer for turning down the manuscript. Frequently the reviewers' criticisms are well founded and can serve as useful guides to improving the work. In effect, the journal's review process can provide writers with free expert guidance toward enhancing a report's style of presentation, definition of terms, background information, theoretical context, or interpretation. The writer may thus choose to revise the document in keeping with the referees' complaints and suggestions. Or, if the complaints seem unjustified or they cannot feasibly be accommodated in a reconstructed version of the article, the criticisms can simply be ignored. The author's second response, then, is to send the manuscript—in either its original or revised condition—to another journal. The longer that the work lies idle on the researcher's desk, the older the data and the author grow. Useful advice is: Keep completed manuscripts on editors' desks, not on your own.

Authors sometimes wonder if it is appropriate to submit the same article simultaneously to more than one journal, so that if one journal turns down the material there is a chance that the other journal will accept it; as a result, no time has been lost in getting the work published. In deciding whether such simultaneous submission is a wise practice, an author can usefully estimate what is likely to happen if two or more journals accept the article for publication. The writer is then obliged to withdraw the paper from all but one journal, and the editors of the rejected journals are bound to remember this incident if that author ever offers another paper in the future. The damage to the author's reputation is even worse if the article is actually published in two or more journals. Angry editors will then not only blacklist the writer but also warn editors of other journals that the author is not to be trusted. In short, sending an article to more than one periodical at the same time is a risky venture.

Books

As noted in Chapter 14, it is rarely necessary for authors to hire a literary agent in order to have their manuscripts considered by publishers of research reports. Only when a work is designed for publication as a trade book aimed at the general reading public is it advantageous to employ an agent.

There are several common procedures for submitting a proposal to book publishers. The following are four of the more popular approaches. Which approach will be most suitable in a given case depends on such factors as the author's reputation and publishing record, the popularity of the author's topic, and the volume of manuscripts that editors must handle.

Phone Call. To learn whether to bother even sending material to a publisher by mail or by computer (fax or e-mail), the author may first choose to telephone the publishing house and ask to speak with an editor who handles manuscripts in the author's field of interest. The author can then explain to the editor the nature of the intended book and thereby learn (a) whether the editor considers it worthwhile to submit a proposal and, if so, (b) what sort of material the editor would like to receive—a brief outline, some sample chapters, or a completed manuscript.

Brief Outline. Frequently editors initially wish to see a brief description of the purpose of the book and its contents, including either a paragraph specifying the contents of each chapter or a list of the subtopics treated within each chapter. The outline may enable the editors—or the academics they consult—to decide whether the proposed work fits into the publisher's fields of emphasis, is innovative, is marketable, and is academically respectable. On the basis of this sample of the author's plan, the editors may inform the author that the proposal "is not suited to our publishing program at this time." Or, instead, they may encourage to author to "send us a few chapters when you have them ready so we can see how your plan is worked out in detail."

In a few cases, editors will offer the writer a contract on the basis of the brief outline. This most often occurs in the cases of researchers who already have an established record of well respected publishing in the field of interest.

Sample Chapters. Editors recognize that researchers who can produce a convincing outline for a book may be ill equipped to write chapters that are readily understood, well documented, and interesting. Thus, before offering an author a contract, editors usually wish to examine not only a general outline of the book, but also one or more representative chapters. Writers may therefore profit from including a few sample chapters when they first submit their proposal. If the outline and chapters initially show promise, the editors will probably send the material to be evaluated by consultants well versed in the themes of the chapters. Then, on the basis of the consultants' and editors' appraisals, (a) the author's proposal may be turned down, (b) the author may be offered a contract to publish the work, or (c) or the author may be encouraged to "send us the entire manuscript to review when you have it available."

Completed Manuscript. Sometimes editors prefer to see a finished manuscript before offering the author a contract, particularly in the case of writers who have no prior record of book publishing. Reviewing a finished product enables editors and their consultants to judge how well the entire work hangs together. It also convinces them that the author will actually complete the writing task rather than being distracted by other interests or succumbing to the malady labeled *writer's block.*

Although sending the same manuscript to several journals at the same time is unwise, it is more acceptable to send a book manuscript simultaneously to more than one publisher. Editors are not pleased with such a practice, since they would prefer not to spend time evaluating a work when it may end up being issued by another publishing house. However, most of them will put up with the practice. Some authors, when submitting their work, explain that it is being reviewed by more than one publisher.

Popular Periodicals, Radio, and Television

Authors without a distinguished record of publication will usually find that their proposed articles for magazines, newsletters, and newspapers are best submitted as completed manuscripts. It is often desirable to phone the magazine or newspaper ahead of time to learn the name of the editor to whom the material should be sent. This helps ensure that the manuscript reaches the person responsible for deciding whether the piece will be published.

Researchers who wish to air their projects over radio or television may initially wish to offer the broadcasters a brief summary of the intended program's content and mode of presentation, a summary sent by phone or letter. If the station's production editors express interest, it is time to furnish them a more detailed prospectus of what the researcher has in mind.

Microfiche and Microfilm

A research report intended for the ERIC microfiche collection should be in the form of a completed manuscript. At least one copy should be mailed to the ERIC center responsible for manuscripts in the particular educational specialty on which the author's paper focuses.

Negotiating the Publishing Conditions

The word *negotiating* refers to the way in which authors seek concessions or "the best deal" in the process of settling the terms under which their work will be published.

In the case of theses and dissertations, such negotiating is carried out between the student and the committee of faculty members (usually a principal adviser plus two or three subsidiary research advisers) working within the requirements set for such studies in their particular college or university.

Authors rarely are able to negotiate with journal editors for special treatment. Leading journals have so many acceptable articles submitted that they need not yield to individual authors' pressures for concessions. However, magazine and newspaper editors are sometimes more flexible in their demands; so if a submitted article is of particular high quality and high interest level, they may be willing to pay a higher price for it or to display it more prominently in their publication. Such is also true of research reports intended for radio or television broadcasts.

Whether the publishing conditions for invited book chapters can be negotiated depends mainly on the compiler who is editing the book. Some compilers set strict guidelines that permit no exceptions. Others are amenable to authors' appeals. Some editors will yield to suggestions that appear to improve the quality of the book. They also may yield to the demands of authors who are so prominent that the stature of the book would suffer if those contributors were left out.

The greatest possibility of negotiating terms is in book publishing. Publishers typically signify their desire to issue a manuscript by sending the author a *standard contract*. Such a contract is a printed document stipulating an extensive list of conditions under which the material will be published. The portion of the contract specifying the royalties to be paid will often not be printed but, rather, will be typewritten, thereby indicating that different royalty arrangements are possible for different authors and their books. So the amount of royalty payments is one matter that may be negotiable. In addition, some of the printed portions may be negotiable as well. For example, here is a clause commonly found in contracts:

> The Author gives the Publisher the exclusive option to publish his or her next substantial work. The Publisher shall be entitled to a period of sixty (60) days after the submission of the completed manuscript in which to notify the Author in writing whether it desires to publish such manuscript.

I see no good reason for authors to accept such a limitation. All of the advantage is on the publisher's side. Therefore, when faced with a contract that includes such a stipulation, I cross out the paragraph and place my initials beside the deleted segment to indicate that, in signing the document, I do not agree to that condition.

Obtaining Copyright Permission

Copyright laws are designed to protect printed materials (as well as other forms of communication) from being extracted and published without the consent of the owner of the copyright, who typically is either the author or the publisher of the work. Anyone who wishes to quote a substantial portion of copyrighted material to use in a journal article or book is legally obligated to obtain the copyright owner's written permission to use the quoted passages. The copyright owner can either charge a fee for this privilege or can grant the request without requiring payment. However, the law governing copyrights in the United States also includes a *fair-use* provision that allows an author to quote a limited portion of a copyrighted publication without obtaining the permission of the copyright holder. But one difficulty authors face in taking advantage of this provision is that the law fails to specify how much material—in terms of a given number of words—constitutes fair use. As a result, different publishers have created their own specifications of fair use that represent what they conceive to reflect the spirit of the law. They begin "by establishing a cut-off point that varies from [publishing] house to [publishing] house but ranges typically between 100 and 500 words of prose and between zero and 10 lines of poetry. . . . The limits at most houses have dropped in recent years" (Rinzler, 1985, p. 204).

Defining fair use in terms of a number of words is influenced by the nature of the publication in which the quoted material will appear. Reports of research, in whatever form they are published, are intended as contributions to the world's knowledge and are not simply designed to entertain the public and make authors rich. Copyright law recognizes the socially-constructive, educational nature of research products by permitting greater leeway in defining fair use for academic works than for trade books aimed at a broad reading public. (Not all publications are copyrighted. Some, such as government publications, are in the public domain so that no permission is required to quote from such sources. However, the source should be identified in a reference citation.)

In my own writing, I have considered quoted material totaling 150 words or less from a book or from an extended journal article to fall within the intent of the fair-use provision, thereby not requiring the copyright holder's permission.

Not only do publishers (journal, book, magazine) differ in their interpretations of fair use, but they differ as well in their efficiency and generosity in responding to permission requests. This fact was dramatically demonstrated to me in 1996 as I sought permission from several publishers to quote passages exceeding 150 words from books whose copyrights they controlled. I asked Harvard University Press for permission to quote segments totaling 422 words from Vicinus and

Nergaard's *Ever Yours, Florence Nightingale* and was immediately granted use of the material free of charge. I asked Houghton Mifflin Company for permission to excerpt a total of 672 words from Manheim's translation of Adolf Hitler's *Mein Kampf,* and my request was promptly granted, also free of charge. Because Houghton Mifflin held the copyright for only the United States, I was obliged to ask permission as well from the British firm, Random Century Group, that held rights to Manheim's translation for the rest of the world. Again, I was granted permission at no charge. I had this same good fortune with three other publishers.

But trouble arose with my request to reproduce a small figure from a 1938 book published by the New York division of Oxford University Press. The material was a simple diagram that included 34 words. (Permission must be requested to use graphic material of any size.) When, after two months, I had received no response to my request, I wrote again to New York. In reply, I was asked to send a photocopy of the page of their book, for they could not find the book. I complied with this request, filled out a required form, and sent a check for the $50 they charged to use the figure. When I received no reply after more than a month, the editor who was handling my book phoned the Oxford Press to inquire about the permission. She was told that they had never received either the required form or my check. They sent me another form to complete and they requested $50, so I sent another check. Two more months passed without news of the permission, so my editor phoned the Press again and was again told that no $50 check had been received. But a short time later I found among the monthly set of my canceled checks from my bank that the Press had cashed both $50 checks. That same week I received a notice from the head of the Oxford permissions department informing me that I could use the figure from the 1938 book if I filled out an enclosed request form and sent $40 as the permissions fee. Since I had now lost all patience, I compiled the seven months of correspondence and sent copies (including photocopies of the cashed checks) to both the head of the permissions department and the head of the academic-books division. Three days later I received a phone call from the permissions head to inform me that the whole affair had been very unfortunate but nothing could be done to rectify any errors. In the end, permission was granted and the Press kept the $100, even though the final charge had been set at $40. This comedic series of events had delayed the publication of my book by nearly six months, since my publisher was unable to put the work into production until all of the permissions were in order.

What, then, are publishers' policies on charging fees? In answer, Rinzler has observed that:

Fees charged by publishers are negotiable, but they range generally from $15 to $100 per page of prose, from $5 to $25 per line of poetry. . . . One calculation [that] permissions departments typically engage in is a sort of what-the-traffic-will-bear test. . . . Some publishers have raised minimum fees or are contemplating setting them; some are starting to charge for uses they admit clearly fall under the fair use exception. At these latter houses, you may say, fair use stops when you ask [permission]. (Rinzler, 1985, pp. 204-205)

Implied in the foregoing discussion are three decisions faced by writers who contemplate quoting passages from published sources: What standard should I adopt for determining that a quotation qualifies as fair use? What should I do if a fee appears exorbitant? How can I avoid the need to seek permission?

Usually the most practical standard is the one used by the journal or book publisher who will be issuing the author's work. If there are quotations in the writer's original manuscript that exceed the publisher's standard, permission must be requested for those passages; or the writer can reduce the length of quotations so they fit within the adopted fair-use limit.

If a fee for using quoted material appears unreasonably high, the author can either try to negotiate a lower payment or simply eliminate the quoted material from the manuscript.

Authors who wish to quote material found on the Internet may ask whether they need permission for Internet quotations that extend beyond fair use. The answer is that copyright laws apply equally to print and electronic publishing. Extensive quotations and graphics from the Internet require the same permission as similar material extracted from print media.

One way for an author to avoid the need to request permission is to keep the length of quotations below whatever fair-use limit has been chosen. Another way is to eschew quoting other sources entirely and simply summarize in one's own words the themes or concepts conveyed in those sources.

Furnishing a Completed Manuscript

The three most common forms in which completed manuscripts are submitted are (a) as a double-spaced typescript (from a typewriter or computer) on letter-size paper, (b) as camera-ready copy, or (c) as a computer disk.

A double-spaced typescript is the traditional, and still most popular, form. It's the style in which theses and dissertations are usually cast. In the case of journal articles and books, a double-spaced typescript permits a copy editor to mark the material for typesetting by identifying the desired type size and style for the body of the work as well as for headings. The copy editor also rephrases awkward or misleading passages, corrects spelling and grammar errors, and—in some cases— reorganizes the placement of portions of the work. The marked manuscript is then ready to be set in type and printed.

Camera-ready copy is material presented in the exact form in which it will finally appear in print. Today's computer word-processing programs equip researchers to cast their reports in formats that precisely simulate professionally typeset documents. This mode of submission often appeals to publishers, for it saves time and typesetting expense, so long as the final version of the material calls for few, if any, changes. But if an editor suspects that the author's work will require considerable correction or revision, the editor will ask the author first to submit a double-spaced typescript for copyediting and then, on the basis of changes and corrections made on the typescript, to resubmit the corrected version in camera-ready form.

Authors have two main choices in the way they prepare camera-ready copy. As one alternative, they can initially compose the document on their computer as a double-spaced typescript. Subsequently, after receiving from the publisher a style sheet describing the form that camera-ready material should assume, they can recast the document in camera-ready style—with page dimensions, type sizes, headings, and bibliography conforming to the publisher's requirements.

As a second choice, authors who are already acquainted with the publisher's camera-ready style have the option of formatting the document at the time they originally compose it. Such is the method I used in writing this book. I decided at the outset what the final style should be, and then wrote the chapters in that style from the beginning.

The third way of submitting an article, chapter, or book is to present it on a computer floppy disk.   This is a recent practice, as yet in relatively little use but growing in popularity.   Because typesetting today is usually done on computers rather than on linotype machines as in the past, it is convenient for editors to have in hand a manuscript's disk version that can be displayed on a computer screen for whatever revision and formatting is required. Increasingly, authors of book chapters and journal articles are being asked to submit both a paper copy and a disk version of their work.

Responding to Copyediting

A *copy editor* or *copy reader* is a person, other than the author, who tries to ensure that a document is readable and free from spelling, punctuation, and grammar errors. Sometimes copy editors also try to determine whether the facts in the document are accurate.

The responsibility for copyediting theses and dissertations is typically assumed by the faculty member who supervises the student's research, by a friend of the student, or by someone the student hires for the task. In a journal- or book-publishing house, copy editing is performed by professionals who specialize in such work.

How much a copy editor will change an author's manuscript is determined by several considerations, including the publisher's copyediting policies, the quality of the author's writing, and the particular copy editor's own preferences in vocabulary use and writing style. Authors are typically grateful when copy editors locate spelling and grammar errors or recast an obviously awkward phrase to render it clear and felicitous. But frequently a measure of tension develops between the author and the copy editor, with the author resenting "unnecessary and unwanted" changes made in a manuscript "simply to suit the copy editor's personal taste." On these occasions, the author can either accept such revisions without complaint or seek to negotiate with the production editor to have the most egregious changes reversed.

Preparing an Index

The task of creating an index is a concern only for book authors and the compilers of books consisting of chapters by different authors. Indexing can be performed either by the author or by someone the author or publisher hires for the job. Authors who create indexes themselves have the advantage of deciding which topics readers might wish to locate in the book. In addition, self-produced indexes save the substantial expense an author incurs when the publisher pays someone to do the work. However, some authors feel that avoiding the time and trouble that indexing requires is well worth the expense of farming the job out.

There are two principal ways an index can be constructed. The most familiar way involves a person poring over the book's final page proofs to list in alphabetical order all words that readers would likely wish to look up. The traditional way of performing this operation has consisted of placing each word on a separate card on which the author accumulates the numbers of all proof pages on which the word appears. Finally, the cards are arranged in alphabetical order and their contents typed as either a typescript or camera-ready copy. In a recent version to this approach, the index compiler enters words and page numbers into a computer rather than on cards as he or she progresses through the page proofs. Consequently, upon reaching the final page, the computer holds a finished version of the index ready to print.

An alternative to the traditional approach is provided by computer word-processing programs that enable authors, as they originally create a document, to flag each word they wish to include in the index. The program simultaneously collects and organizes the flagged words and page numbers; so by the time the author has written the book's last page, the index is complete.

Proofreading

Proofreading involves examining the final edited version of a document to ensure that it is free of errors. In the publishing field, proofreading traditionally has consisted of two stages—galley proofs and page proofs. At the galley-proof stage, the document is printed on long sheets not yet divided into pages. At the page-proof stage the material is in the exact form in which it will appear as a book or article. In the past, authors were usually first sent galley proofs, then at a later time sent page proofs to be inspected and corrected. However, in recent years it has become more common to skip the galley-proof stage and send authors page proofs only.

Publishers can differ in their proof-reading practices. Some maintain a staff that scrutinizes both galley and page proofs in detail before and after the proofs have been checked by the author. Others expect the author to do the principal careful proofing, with the publisher's production editors limiting their proofreading to spot checking portions of the final version before it goes to press.

Distributing the Final Product

Methods of informing potential consumers of research and of getting copies of reports into their hands can vary from one medium to another.

Lists of theses and dissertations are found in the library catalogue of the institution in which the authors earned their degrees. As already mentioned, many—but not all—doctoral dissertations are cited in *Dissertation Abstracts*.

Articles in journals and popular magazines come to the attention of the institutions and individuals who subscribe to those periodicals.

Book publishers advertise their products in several ways. They issue catalogues and send announcements of individual books to libraries and to individual members of organizations whose interests are in the area of the books' topics. They also send a copy of the book to each editor whose journal includes reviews of books that focus on the journal's academic emphasis, and they sometimes arrange for the author to appear on radio and television programs, at autograph sessions in bookstores, or at the meetings of academic societies. Book and journal publishers commonly display their wares at professional conferences.

As noted in Chapter 14, additions to the ERIC microfiche collection are regularly distributed to over 700 institutions. Documents newly issued by ERIC are announced monthly to more than 4,000 subscribers that receive the periodical *Resources in Education*.

When authors publish their own works, they can disseminate the products by themselves or can contract with a professional distributor to market their publications. Researchers who accept the entire responsibility for marketing their own works are obliged to find (usually purchase) lists of the names and addresses of potential buyers, prepare an advertising campaign, process orders for the products, ship the products to the customers, and assume the entire expense of this dissemination process.

If the task of selling researcher-created publications is delegated to a firm that specializes in distributing such materials, all the steps of dissemination are performed by the firm, which takes its expenses and profits out of the book's or journal's sales receipts. However, authors should recognize that distributors "cannot sell your books without your help. You must be prepared to back up their sales efforts with your own advertising and publicity campaign" (Kremer,

1990, p. 247). Names and addresses of distributors are found in such publications as the *Book Publishing Resource Guide* (Kremer, 1987). When selecting a distributor, authors can profit from:

—Learning the discount or fee charged to authors. Most ask for 15% to 30% of the net sales receipts, which in turn may be discounted 30% to 50% from the advertised retail price of the book (Kremer, 1990, p. 247).
—Seeing a sample contract to learn its duration, how it can be terminated, and the distributor's responsibilities as compared to those of the author.
—Asking for the names and addresses of other people whose books the firm handles, then contacting those people to learn how satisfactory their relationship with the distributor has been.

For aid in publishing and distributing their own works, authors can consult such volumes as *The Self-Publishing Manual* (Poynter, 1996) and *The Complete Guide to Self-Publishing* (Ross & Ross, 1985).

RESEARCH PROJECT CHECKLIST

1. Which methods do I plan to use to locate a suitable publishing outlet?
   ___Ask for advice (Identify persons whose adive will be sought.)
   ___Search through bibliographies in books to locate suitable journals or book publishers
   ___Inspect journals related to my research topic (Tell which journals.)
   ___Other (explain)_____
2. How do I intend to organize my research report in terms of a sections into which it will be divided, the form in which references will be cited, and the arrangement of the bibliography?
3. How do I plan to submit my research proposal to a potential publishing outlet?
   ___As a brief description of the work's purpose and results (sent by phone or by letter)
   ___In the case of a book, as an outline of the contents, plus one or two sample chapters
   ___As a completed product
4. In my report, do I plan to quote passages from published materials? If so,
   ___What standard will I adopt for defining *fair use*? (explain)
   ___If I plan to seek permission to quote material, from whom will I seek permission and when will I do it?

5. In what form do I expect to submit the final version of the report for publication?

    ___As a double-spaced typescript

    ___In camera-ready format

    ___As a computer disk

    ___As both a typescript and computer disk

6. Will an index be needed for my report? If so, who will prepare the index?

    ___I, myself

    ___Someone I hire

    ___The publisher

7. How do I expect to have my report advertised and disseminated?

    ___By the publisher

        ___At professional conferences

        ___Through book catalogues

        ___Through mailed brochures sent to potential customers

        ___Other (explain)_____

    ___By my own efforts

        ___At professional conferences, meetings, or presentations

        ___Through mailed brochures sent to potential customers

        ___Other (explain)_____

16

Opportunities Ahead

The purpose of this final chapter is to speculate briefly about several appealing prospects that educational researchers face in the near future. The prospects concern improving the speed and accuracy of studies, rendering complexity understandable, and extending researchers' reach. Because technological innovations play such a vital role in facilitating such opportunities, the discussion begins with a vision of technological advances that may be expected in the coming years.

TECHNOLOGY'S TRENDS AND RESEARCH IMPLICATIONS

Previous chapters have cited a variety of technological innovations useful in educational research. The purpose of the following overview is to summarize key characteristics of those innovations and to hazard predictions about advances to be expected in their development in the coming decades. The discussion identifies eleven trends in the evolution of research technologies—trends toward greater digitalization, speed, accuracy, capacity, sensitivity, miniaturization, versatility, popularity, and ease of control. An additional trend involves the dollar expense of devices—a mixture of both increased and decreased costs.

Digitalization

The word *digital*, when applied to electronic devices, refers to the manner in which information is processed in a device (computer, camera, audio recorder) and communicated to other devices. The implications of digital systems is perhaps best exemplified in electronic computers.

Computers are of three classes—analog, digital, and hybrid. Analog computers operate on the basis of continuous variables, just as a thermostat functions along an unbroken array of temperatures, ranging from very cold to very hot. In along an unbroken array of temperatures, ranging from very cold to very hot. In contrast, digital computers operate on the basis of discrete variables, just as the typical electric-light switch can assume only two positions—completely on and completely off. Hybrid computers combine certain features of both analog and digital devices. But because analog computers are rarely used in the field of education or in the social sciences, our concern in educational research is limited to digital varieties (even though digital machines may include some analog elements).

In computer parlance, each binary on/off switch in a digital circuit is called a *bit*. Because a bit has only two possible positions (the digit *1* for on, the digit *0* for off), it cannot hold or convey much information. However, when eight bits are clustered to form a unit called a *byte*, the large quantity of on/off permutations that this 8-bit cluster assumes can represent a great variety of symbols. For example, a single meaningful character—such as a letter of the alphabet, a number, or a punctuation mark—can be assigned a set code of eight on/off (1/0) combinations. The byte pattern representing letter A is 01000001, the pattern for letter B is 01000010, and so on. Furthermore, in order to provide more flexibility in defining symbols manipulated by computers, byte size has been extended from 8 to 16 bits in recently designed systems.

Because great quantities of bytes are needed for the complex operations of the computer, bytes are usually not referred to as single units but, rather, as *kilobytes*, a term often abbreviated as K or KB. The prefix *kilo* normally means 1000. However, a digital computer's counting system is binary, based on the number 2 rather than on the number 10 in the decimal system, so one kilobyte contains 1024 individual bytes (since 2 multiplied by itself nine times equals 1024). The operating capacity of computers is often referred to in terms of kilobytes or in such larger units as *megabyte* (one million bytes), *gigabyte*, (one billion bytes), and *terabyte* (one trillion bytes).

In summary, one trend in digitalization has been that of increasing the number of bits that comprise a byte and of increasing the number of bytes that a given computer has available for manipulating and storing data. A researcher who in the early 1980s operated a desktop computer that had a maximum of 128 kilobytes of working memory was, at the end of the 1990s, operating a note-book-size computer that provideed a few dozen megabytes of working memory (random-access memory) and several gigabytes of long-term storage on a hard disk.

A further trend has been the digitalization of an increasing variety of research devices that formerly operated on principals other than the digital computer's 0/1 binary principle. The recording of visual images, which traditionally has depended on film, is increasingly recorded in digital form in both still cameras and motion-picture cameras (television *camcorders*). A digital camera that is operated as easily as an instamatic camera enables a person to photograph scenes that are captured into the camera's random-access memory or on a special diskette and then transferred into a personal computer. The computer displays the picture on its screen, where the researcher is able to edit the scene—adding, altering, or eliminating elements—and then print out the result as a full-color photograph.

The recording of sound (speech, music, sounds in nature) that traditionally took the form of vibrations in grooves on a plastic disk (phonograph records) or magnetic impulses on a wire or tape (tape recorder) increasingly depends on digital devices. For example, the grooves on a compact disc contain pits that a laser beam reads as either of two depths, one signifying *1* and the other signifying *0*. The quality of these digital visual and sound representations is superior to that of their nondigital predecessors.

Speed

One of the more dramatic impacts of modern technologies on research activities is that of increasing the speed of operations.

Transistors began replacing vacuum tubes in computers in the early 1960s, making it then possible for computers to execute up to 100,000 instructions per second. Since then, the speed of computation has increased many fold. Desktop computers within seconds perform calculations that would require months of time with a hand calculator. In no more than a second, mainframe computers carry out billions of calculations, with the speed of such devices continuing to increase by the year. As a result, determining the degree of correlation among several thousand students' test scores in a variety of subject-matter areas is a task requiring no more than a moment.

The velocity of transporting information from one site to another also continues to accelerate. Whereas postal service can require days or weeks to carry messages, facsimile copies of documents are sent instantaneously via telephone lines and satellites to nearly any city in the world. Electronic mail provides researchers a similar quick way to exchange ideas.

Although traditional methods of producing photographs and motion pictures have required a delay of hours or days for the film to be processed, researchers now can immediately see the results of their photographic efforts. A snapshot of a school building (taken with a Polaroid or digital camera) or a motion picture of a student dance performance (taken with a television camera—a camcorder) can be viewed the moment after it's recorded.

Accuracy

Although bank tellers, supermarket clerks, and insurance adjusters are apt to blame mistakes of computation or billing on "computer error," it is rarely the case that something wrong with the computer's hardware is at fault. Computers are generally highly accurate and reliable. In the great majority of instances, when errors do occur, the fault lies either with the person who wrote the software program which carries out the computations or else with the people who are operating the computer. There is always the danger that a computer programmer—out of ineptitude or malice—will insert malevolent instructions into a program which subsequently act as a virus, harmfully infecting the operation of other computers with which that machine communicates. Virus-protection programs have thus been developed to cope with this danger of viruses. But again, the blame for viruses must be borne by people, not the computers themselves.

In sum, computers are far more accurate than are people in performing computations, storing quantities of information, and verifying the storage operations; and new methods for ensuring accuracy continue to appear.

Capacity

In 1974, the Intel Corporation's 8080 computer chip that represents the heart of the system contained 4,800 transistors. In 1993, Intel introduced its Pentium chip that provided 3,200,000 transistors, with future chips promising to expand such capacity at an accelerating rate (Muroga, 1994, p. 641). On the average, each newly developed computer chip doubles computer operating capacity every 18 months (Gates, 1995, p. 31). Consequently, educational researchers are able to manipulate and store ever-growing quantities of complicated variables. For example, carrying out computations involving multiple scores for thousands of students who inhabit complex and diverse environments has become increasingly feasible.

Sensitivity

Recorders for capturing sounds and sights provide a good example of the increasing sensitivity of electronic devices. The passing years witness advances in the ability of audiotape devices and video cameras to record events from greater distances and in difficult environments.

In the past, the task of editing a research report for publication required that an editor first peruse a handwritten or typewritten document in order to mark corrections and make format changes, then have the material set in type for printing. However, today a document can be digitized into a computer by means of an image scanner equipped with an optical character recognition function (OCR software). Each page of the author's document is thereby transformed into an image on the computer screen so that an editor can read and alter the material as if it had originally been typed into the computer. The more sophisticated present-day OCR programs are highly sensitive, able to distinguish the shapes, sizes, and pitch of symbols—including handwriting—and to learn from experience. The edited, newly-formatted version of the material can be printed as typeset copy, ready to be photographed for printing in a final published form.

Although a universal OCR machine is not yet available to read all versions of even a single alphabet, the likelihood that such software will be perfected seems bright.

The ability of computers to achieve reasonable translations of documents from one language into another can be expected as well, a great boon to researchers whose own foreign language skills are limited.

Miniaturization

To house a computer in the 1950s, a large room was needed to accommodate the forest of vacuum tubes that performed the machine's data manipulation and storage. By the 1990s the size of computers had so dramatically decreased that an electronic gadget smaller than a deck of playing cards could carry out far more operations and far more quickly than had its 1950 ancestors. Two inventions made such miniaturization possible. First was the creation of transistors to replace vacuum tubes. Second was the development of integrated-circuit chips into which multiple transistors could be encased. By the 1990s, millions of transistors could be imbedded in a single silicon chip no larger than an infant's finger nail.

Audio and video recording equipment has likewise become more compact each year. The widespread adoption of wire and tape recorders in the mid-20th century eliminated the need for a bulky collection of machinery to record and playback speech and music. Since that time, audio recorders have become increasingly small and sensitive. By the end of the century, tape recorders no larger than a small child's hand and weighing no more than a few ounces were commonly used by researchers to record interviews and group discussions. Such devices were voice activated, starting to record only when someone spoke, then stopping until another voice was heard, thereby permitting a researcher to record inter-mittent conversations without being immediately present to personally start and stop the instrument.

Miniature video cameras, placed in inconspicuous locations and operated by remote-control devices from a distance, enabled investigators to record sights and sounds of a classroom, office, or discussion group without intimidating the par-ticipants with the presence of onlookers or highly visible equipment.

As the miniaturization trend continues at a rapid pace into the 21st century, further advantages for educational research can be expected.

Versatility

Tasks that were performed by individual instruments in the past are increas-ingly being performed by a single device. Prior to the advent of "talking pictures" in the late 1920s, motion-picture cameras recorded sights but not sounds, whereas phonograph recording devices captured sounds but not sights. Since those early years, the ability of a single, combining instrument to carry out multiple functions has markedly improved. Therefore, by the end of the 20th century, a relatively inexpensive videocamera (camcorder) could simultaneously record the sights and sounds of an event, either up close or at a distance (via telephoto lenses and remote microphones), with the results immediately available for display on a computer screen and ready to be edited—portions eliminated, sequences altered, details enlarged, and the pace of events slowed or quickened.

Popularity

The pace at which attractive technological innovations are disseminated can be illustrated with the worldwide distribution of computers over the decade 1985-1995. In 1985, an estimated 38.1 million computers were in use throughout the world. The total grew by 260% to 129.4 million in 1991 and by 575% to 257.2 million in 1995. The expected total by year 2000 was projected at 535.6 million, 14 times greater than the number sold 15 years earlier. However, the distribution by nations has been very uneven, with the United States in 1995 having 345 computers per 1,000 people, a number expected to reach 580 by year 2000. Following the United States, the nations with the highest per capita incidence of computers by year 2000 are expected to be Australia (526 per 1,000 population), Norway (515), Canada (512), Denmark (510), Finland (505), Sweden (109), New Zealand (500), and Great Britain (441). Less favored are such countries as Mexico (66 per 1,000), Russia (62), Brazil (48), and China (11). The worldwide rate has been predicted at 90 per 1,000 people by the opening of the 21st century (Johnson, 1997, pp. 566-567).

Ease of Control

The electronics industry made rapid progress over the last half of the 20th century in rendering their projects more "user friendly," with further progress due in the years ahead.

During the 1940s, producing a monaural phonograph recording required a special studio, complicated equipment, and the services of a skilled technician. By the close of the century, a child with minimal training could produce a stereo sound tape recording of far greater fidelity than the skilled technician's phonograph disk of the forties.

During the early 1960s, producing a black-and-white television sequence required a complicated, weighty camera and a trained operator. If the sequence was to be saved for transmission at a later time, it had to be recorded on motion-picture film as a *kinescope*. But by the 1990s, nearly anyone with a few minutes' instruction could successfully produce a full-color television sequence by means of a lightweight camcorder that conveniently fit into the palm of the hand and simultaneously converted the pictured scenes into digitized codes on magnetic tape that could be saved for later viewing.

In the 1970s, an investigator who wished to use a computer to calculate the frequency of a large quantity of respondents' answers to questionnaire items and to compute correlations among types of items was obliged to enter the data and calculation instructions into a mainframe computer by means of a rather complicated programming language, such as Fortran. By the 1990s, that same task could be accomplished on a laptop personal computer equipped with an easily understood statistical program that provided the user with far more kinds of information than would a mainframe computer 25 years earlier. Furthermore, the personal computer allowed the investigator to insert the outcome of the computations into the research report—which the author was currently writing on the machine—and include full-color graphic displays of the summarized data.

Cost

With the passing of time, the purchase price of a technological innovation typically assumes a familiar pattern—very high cost at the outset, with the cost then progressively diminishing as the device is mass produced, improvements are effected in its design, and competition heats up among manufacturers.

A mainframe computer that filled a large room and cost $1 million in the 1960s could be replaced in the 1990s by a desktop personal computer that was 1,000 times cheaper but had comparable computational power. In the mid-1990s a $2,000 laptop computer was more powerful than a $10 million IBM mainframe computer 20 years earlier (Gates, 1995, p. 34). In the mid-1970s a handheld electronic calculator that could only add, subtract, multiply, and divide cost $250 at an office supply store. In the 1990s, an even smaller calculator that performed far more operations than the 1970 model cost $2 at the corner supermarket.

In summary, the 21st century should witness the improvement of such technology at an accelerating pace, equipping researchers with an expanding range of devices that improve the speed and accuracy of collecting and storing data, classifying information, and publishing the results.

RENDERING COMPLEXITY UNDERSTANDABLE

Most thoughtful people likely recognize that (a) every educational event is the result of a host of causal factors, (b) each event can contribute to a diversity of after-effects, and (c) any event can be viewed from a variety of vantage points, each of which yields a different understanding. In short, educational activities are extremely complicated phenomena.

Not only does every event involve multiple variables and many facets, but no event is static—frozen in time. Each is in continual transition, shifting from one status to another as its constituent variables interact. Consequently, a student's achievement-test scores are valid only for that one testing occasion and can be expected to change as the student gains experience and views matters in a different light. Likewise, the pattern of decision making in a nation's ministry of education is bound to alter, at least in subtle ways, as the days pass. And the amount of effort a group of pupils devote to their learning tasks can differ with the advancing moments.

When educational studies are cast against such a backdrop of reality—the reality of a highly complicated and ephemeral world—it becomes apparent that all research projects represent only bits and pieces of a constantly shifting picture puzzle. Hence, scholars are confronted with two daunting tasks—how to encompass all of this complexity and how to render such complexity understandable to their audience. The ability to perform such tasks is constrained by the limitations of the human mind and the fallibility of human communication. People's capacity to simultaneously interrelate a host of variables is restricted, because their minds are engineered to consider one thing at a time. Although ideas may follow in rapid succession, they still generally march in single file. Furthermore, human memories—as the raw materials of most thought—are elusive and often imprecise. Consequently, a researcher trying to accomplish the goal of completely elucidating educational events in all their tangled complications is rather like the man, in Stephen Crane's verse, who chased the horizon. Yet, however impossible the goal may be, the need for people to understand and manage educational affairs requires that the goal be pursued, even though, for the sake of practicality, it must be reduced to a more modest and achievable aim. Such a modest aim can be that of designing studies which accommodate as many influential variables and viewpoints as feasible and of admitting the limitations of the conclusions.

Thus, the position adopted here is that investigators cannot legitimately dismiss complexity simply with such clichés as "Other things being equal . . ." or "Setting other factors aside . . . ." The trouble is that "other things" are never equal—"other things" affect outcomes in either large or small ways. Nor can "other factors" be set aside without risking inaccurate interpretations of results. Consequently, researchers can at least attempt to place their projects within a broader domain of related events and to estimate not only what their work means within that domain but also to propose which features of the domain are not addressed by their work.

This modest aim of expanding the purview of a research project beyond the data collected in the project itself involves placing the project in a broader context by such methods as (a) literature surveys, (b) meta-analysis, (c) classification systems (typologies and taxonomies), and (d) explanatory theories. As methods, all four of these have been used in the past; so, as general approaches, none of them is novel. Thus, the opportunities they open in the future must depend on improvements in their implementation. Consider, then, the likely nature of those improvements.

Literature Surveys

As mentioned in Chapter 4, one reason a researcher surveys books, journals, conference proceedings, and dissertations is to suggest where, in the realm of education, the researcher's present research effort is situated. The general question guiding this inquiry is: How does my work relate to that of other investigators? Specific questions subsumed under this general inquiry include: How do key concepts or terms that I use fit into a broader range of related terms? How are the topics or questions that I study linked to different fields of interest? How do the results of my research compare with the results of others' research?

The most dramatic future change in literature reviews will appear in the expanded scope of studies that a researcher can survey by means of computer networks. Not only are the titles of an increasing quantity of library holdings around the world already available to investigators, but the complete contents of journal articles are increasingly being included in computer data banks. Soon entire theses, dissertations, and books can be expected to appear in those banks. As a result, people sitting at home before their personal computers can read and print out passages of a worldwide range of studies bearing on a topic of interest.

Not only will literature surveys become more complete, but the time needed to compile studies will be drastically reduced. This means that researchers can finish their projects in a fraction of the time required in the past. They can efficiently complete one project and move immediately to the next, thereby contributing to a rapid proliferation of studies.

Meta-analysis

Meta-analysis is a special way of reviewing literature created in recent decades by critics who observed that:

> The traditional process of integrating [the conclusions from] a body of research literature is essentially intuitive and the style of reporting narrative. Because the reviewer's methods are often unspecified, it is usually difficult to discern how the original research findings have contributed to the integration. A careful analysis can sometimes reveal that different reviewers use the same research reports in support of contrary conclusions. . . . The most serious problem for reviewers to cope with is the volume of relevant research literature to be integrated. Most reviewers appear to deal with this by choosing only a subset of the studies. Some take the studies they know most intimately. Others take those they value most highly, usually on the basis of methodological quality.

Few, however, give any indication of the means by which they selected studies for review. (McGaw, 1985, p. 3322)

The term meta-analysis can be applied to any quantitative integration of empirical research results. The two most popular approaches to defining the domain of pertinent studies and calculating the commonalties and differences among studies are those described by Glass, McGaw, and Smith (1981) and by Hunter, Schmidt, and Jackson (1982).

Proponents of meta-analysis note that the technique has equipped researchers to reveal consistencies in several bodies of studies in which narrative reviewers were only able to discern marked variation, suggesting that wider use of the technique may "help reestablish public faith in the efficacy of empirical research in education by making clearer what has already been achieved" by schools (McGaw, 1985, p. 3330).

Larger quantities of increasingly precise meta-analyses can be expected as computer networks provide investigators access to so many more studies and as more refined statistical programs are produced. The ability of computers to calculate complex relationships among a host of variables within the space of a few seconds will equip researchers with the capacity to conduct meta-analyses that would have been impossible a few years ago.

Classification Systems—Taxonomies and Typologies

Taxonomies and typologies were identified in Chapter 8 as formal systems for classifying phenomena. The intention of such schemes is to provide a complete mapping of a realm, with the realm usually identified by such a label as "types of affective educational objectives" (Krathwohl, Bloom, & Masia, 1964), "forms of differential education of the gifted" (Jellen & Verduin, 1986), or "taxonomies of misdeeds, sanctions, and aims of sanctions" (Thomas, 1995).

Although computer networks expand the variety of studies available to researchers, that expansion does not render the realm of a researcher's topic more readily understood. Indeed, an expansion of collected studies can easily do the opposite—increase the difficulty of comprehending the additional variables that an augmented search typically produces. This means that, in the future, investigators need to devise new classification schemes that lucidly portray the extended variety of variables comprising a domain of interest.

There are two principal approaches to creating a classification scheme—by logical deduction and by a method of statistical comparison known as *numerical taxonomy* (Sokal & Sneath, 1963). Logical deduction consists of a person inspecting a collection of data (in the present case it's a collection of studies in some domain of education) and proposing enough categories to accommodate all of the data (all of the studies). The categories generally form a hierarchy, with more specific classes subsumed under more general ones. In contrast, the numerical-taxonomy approach consists of a person (a) identifying a series of defining characteristics of the collected data, then (b) statistically comparing the individual items (studies) to determine how much one is like another in terms of those characteristics. The greater the correlation among items (studies), the more they belong together within the same category or within closely related categories. In way of illustration, the characteristics to be compared among studies that comprise the domain *school finance* might include (a) size of a school system's enrollment, (b) size of the school budget, (c) budget categories, (c) sources of income, (d) accounting procedures, and such. Producing a numerical taxonomy of school finance would consist of calculating the degree of similarities among research studies in terms of the array of characteristics.

The logical deduction approach has been by far the more popular method. However, with the capacity of computers to calculate complicated relationships, numerical approaches to constructing taxonomies may be more widely adopted in the years ahead.

One important way researchers use a classification system is to show where within a domain of knowledge their particular study is located. In other words, taxonomies help investigators portray how their research project fits into the pattern of other studies conducted in a particular area of education.

Explanatory Theories

Whereas taxonomies and typologies are designed to show relationships among phenomena without accounting for the causes of such connections, *theories*—as the term is used here—serve as formal explanations of why educational events occur as they do. More precisely, the relationships depicted in theories are assumed to be cause-and-effect linkages among phenomena. For instance, a theorist may assert that the nation's lack of progress in furnishing adequate educational facilities for all learners has been caused by a combination of economic recession, skirmishes between political parties, and a reactionary educational bureaucracy. Another theorist may account for an adolescent's sudden spurt of progress in school by changes in the boy's environment— encouragement from an admired teacher, the youth's election as a class officer, and his parents' promise to buy him a car upon graduation if he earns a place on the academic honor role.

To create an explanatory model, a theorist abstracts from a type of educational phenomenon the assumed key components of that phenomenon and then proposes how such components interact to produce the phenomenon's outcomes. Thus, a theory of educational administration proposes the sorts of units (people, departments, agencies) that make up the administrative structure and the manner in which those units influence each other. Statements of influence take the form of speculation about who is responsible for what actions, who has authority over whom, how information flows among the units, what sanctions one unit can impose on others, and more. In like manner, a theory of student discipline identifies the units that participate in any instance of student misbehavior and postulates the kinds of interactions among those units that produce the results of the event.

What, then, does the theorist's expanding ability to compile studies and theories portend for the future? That ability can:

(a) Increase the sophistication of theories (increasing the components that theories include and the interactions envisioned among components) by obliging theorists to consider a greater diversity of variables found in a wider range of studies conducted with different people in different contexts.
(b) Enhance the ability of theorists to compare their models with others' versions, thereby assisting them in recognizing shortcomings of their own proposals that invite correction, revision, and explanation.
(c) Challenge researchers to explain increasingly complex relationships in ways that other people can readily understand, particularly by utilizing the capacity of computers to display animated graphic versions of complicated models.

One way to compare theories is in terms of the range of phenomena they intend to explain. From such a perspective, theories can be arrayed along a scale extending from the most encompassing macrotheories at one end to the most restricted minitheories at the other end. To illustrate, in the field of biology, Darwin's (1975) theory of how all living species evolved over eons of time embraces more phenomena than does Wenner's (Wenner & Wells, 1990) theory of how honey bees communicate to their hive-mates the location of a bed of nectar-rich blossoms. Darwin's proposal, in effect, belongs toward the macro-end of the scale while Wenner's belongs toward the mini-end. In the realm of education, Carroll's model of school learning (Carroll, 1963; Clark, 1985) is a macrotheory that focuses on teaching toward any sort of objective, whereas Downing's (1979) model of teaching beginning reading is a minitheory focusing on structural (phonics) and semantic features of written language.

The chief advantage of macrotheories is that they are designed to explain a wide range of events on the basis of a relatively few components and principles. However, in proposing to explain so much in such a simple way, they can fail to account for exactly how a specific event in a particular context has occurred. For this reason, some critics in the fields of human development and education contend that minitheories are apt to have greater explanatory and predictive power because they are obligated to explain a narrower range of variables than are the all-embracing macrotheories (Elsom-Cook, 1994). Thus, one challenge theorists face in the future is to bridge the gap between mini- and macrotheories by depicting how more precise subcomponents and subprinciples fit within more general components and principles. Theorists' improved ability to survey the professional literature, combined with the capacity of computers to manipulate variables, should contribute to greater integration of the macro and the mini.

EXTENDING THE RESEARCHER'S REACH

The expression *extending the researcher's reach* concerns ways that recent and expected technological innovations equip investigators to gather data from sources not readily available in the past. For convenience of discussion, the sources can be divided into three types—veiled, distant, and simulated.

Veiled Sources

Veiled sources of information are ones hidden from direct sight, sound, or touch. In way of illustration, three techniques invented in recent decades for diagnosing conditions of the brain and nervous system should prove useful for educational research in the future (Clayman, 1989).

The first technique is *computerized tomography* (CT) or *computerized axial tomography* (CAT) scanning, which involves passing X-rays through the brain at different angles to reveal cross-sectional images (slices) of the tissues being examined. Information from the X-ray scanner is processed by a computer and displayed as images on a TV screen. CT scanning has the advantages of being quick and accurate, and it involves only modest exposure to radiation. One important use of the method has been to show brain structure characteristics, such as tumors, that may account for a patient's learning or behavior disorders.

The second technique is *magnetic resonance imaging* (MRI), which does not use X-rays but, rather, depends on the behavior of protons (nuclei) of hydrogen atoms that are exposed to a powerful magnetic field and radio waves. When so exposed, the protons emit radio signals that are detected and then transformed by a computer into images on a screen. MRI scanning involves no radiation risk and produces sharper distinctions between white and gray brain matter than does CT scanning.

The third approach is *positron emission tomography* (PET) scanning, which uses a radioactive substance introduced into the body to produce an image that reflects the level of activity of the tissues being studied. The image created by the computer on a TV screen is similar to a CT scan. The method is often used for investigating brain tumors, identifying the source of epileptic activity, and studying the brain functions related to various sorts of mental illness.

As improvements in these scanners' physical features render the machines less cumbersome, scanning techniques should enable researchers to more easily inspect the operation of the brain while people are engaged in learning activities, retrieving memories, undergoing psychotherapy, or involved in emotional encounters. The resulting information can enrich educators' understanding of the connections among people's observed learning behavior, their statements about their thought processes, and the accompanying operation of their brains.

Distant Sources

In the mid-20th century, the postal service, telephone, and airplane were the most influential media for extending researchers' capacity to collect data from a distance. At the close of the century, fax machines and such computer networks as the Internet and World Wide Web eclipsed those earlier devices' ability to reduce the distance barrier in researchers' data-gathering activities.

Furthermore, improvements achieved in the more traditional media permitted researchers to conduct a greater range of distant business from their own office or home. For example, the invention of telephones that furnished a television image of the speaker at the other end of the line enabled interviewers not only to conduct inquiries from any distance, but also to see the individuals with whom they were speaking. In addition, the devices already in widespread use to record phone conversations on tape could soon be replaced with ones that recorded both the telephone-transmitted sounds and sights in a computer for storage and display.

Simulated Sources

A simulated source is a substitute for an actual data source that cannot be studied directly. The researcher's aim in creating a simulation is to make the significant characteristics of the substitute source resemble as closely as possible the significant features of the original source. Prominent among forms of simulations bearing on education are studies of artificial intelligence.

Artificial intelligence (AI) has been described as "the science of making machines do things that would require intelligence if done by men" (Minsky in Crevier, 1993, p. 8). The machines in this instance are electronic computers. Developers of artificial-intelligence schemes assume that if they can devise computer programs that arrive at the same answers to problems that humans would provide, the steps of logic in those computer programs are likely similar to—if not identical to—the steps of human thought. In the field of artificial intelligence, the term *expert systems* refers to the patterns of information and decision-making rules applied by human experts to arrive at their solutions. A system necessary for solving one sort of problem can be different from the system for solving another. For instance, the information and rules employed by a chess master are not identical to those employed by an adroit reader of French literature, an adept auto mechanic, or a skilled teacher of children who suffer from dyslexia.

Noteworthy success in creating computer programs that solve complex problems has been achieved in the playing of such table games as checkers, tic-tac-toe, and chess. For example, consider the development of chess-player simulations. After three decades of efforts, computer scientists by the early 1990s had created a chess program named Deep Thought that could defeat 99.9%

of human players. Designers then began working on a new version that would deploy integrated-circuit chips one thousand times faster than those available in the mid-1990s, chips that would inspect about one billion chess positions per second (Crevier, 1993, p. 233; Belford, 1994, p. 635). But the scientists' joy in creating a machine that could defeat all but the most adept grand masters was dampened by their realizing that the machine's success derived from its exceptional speed of computation and not from its use of human-like logic. Hence, while success with computer chess failed to meet the researchers' "hope of learning about the human mind . . . it nevertheless led them to discover thinking processes different from our own—[a discovery illustrating] the serendipity of science" (Crevier, 1993, p. 236).

Undaunted, computer scientists and psychologists continue to pursue the challenges of artificial intelligence, including challenges relating to human learning issues important to educators. However, up to now

> Every prediction about major advances in artificial intelligence has proved to be overly optimistic. Today even simple learning tasks still go well beyond the world's most capable computer. When computers appear to be intelligent it is because they have been specially programmed to handle some task in a straightforward fashion—like trying out billions of chess moves in order to play master-level chess. . . . The computer has the potential to be a tool to leverage human intelligence for the foreseeable future. (Gates, 1995, pp. 255-256)

One advantage of computers in this pursuit is their demand for clear thinking.

> Formulating a hypothesis so precisely that it will run on a computer forces crystal clarity on it. Computers tolerate neither hand waving nor fuzzy thinking and keep you honest. Unrealized, implicit, or unspoken assumptions are mercilessly weeded out. Weaknesses of construction appear as if under a magnifying glass. (Crevier, 1993, p. 247)

A second advantage is the computer's ability to isolate aspects of mind in the form of simulated mental functions, enabling researchers to evaluate theories about how people learn and how they store and recall memories. In doing so, computers can organize and compare far larger masses of data—scores, measurements, symptoms, behaviors—in a far shorter time and more accurately than can humans, thereby providing investigators better tests of their theories than would otherwise be possible.

Educational applications of artificial intelligence have already appeared in the field of instructional design, particular in the analysis of the structure of subject-matter areas and of students' thought patterns as they solve problems (Elsom-Cook, 1994).

In sum, the field of artificial intelligence offers educational researchers a seemingly unlimited range of opportunities.

CONCLUSION

As the contents of this chapter suggest, educational research faces a bright future as a result of technological advances that enhance the scope, speed, accuracy, and complexity of collecting and manipulating information and that foster greater worldwide communication among researchers.

Appendix:

Locations of ERIC Specializations

The following are addresses and professional specializations of Educational Research Information Centers that publish research reports in microfiche and printed-document form.

ERIC Clearinghouse on *Adult, Career, and Vocational Education*
  Ohio State University
  Center on Education and Training for Employment
  1900 Kenny Road
  Columbus, OH 43210-1090

ERIC Clearinghouse on *Assessment and Evaluation*
  Catholic University of America
  210 O'Boyle Hall
  Washington, DC 20064-4035

ERIC Clearinghouse on *Community Colleges*
  University of California (UCLA)
  3051 Moore Hall
  405 Hilgard Avenue
  Los Angeles, CA 90024-1521

ERIC Clearinghouse on *Counseling and Student Services*
  University of North Carolina at Greensboro
  School of Education, 101 Park Building
  Greensboro, NC 27412-5001

ERIC Clearinghouse on *Disabilities and Gifted Children*
  Council for Exceptional Children (CEC)
  1920 Association Drive
  Reston, VA 22091-1589

ERIC Clearinghouse on *Educational Management*
  University of Oregon
  1787 Agate Street
  Eugene, OR 97403-5207

ERIC Clearinghouse on *Elementary and Early Childhood Education*
  University of Illinois
  805 West Pennsylvania Ave.
  Urbana, IL 61801-4897

ERIC Clearinghouse on *Higher Education*
  George Washington University
  One Dupont Circle, NW., Suite 630
  Washington, DC 20036-1183

ERIC Clearinghouse on *Information and Technology*
  Syracuse University
  Center for Science and Technology
  4th Floor, Room 194
  Syracuse, NY 13244-4100

ERIC Clearinghouse on *Languages and Linguistics*
  Center for Applied Linguistics
  1118 22nd Street, NW
  Washington, DC 20037-0037

ERIC Clearinghouse on *Reading, English, and Communication*
  Indiana University
  Smith Research Center, Suite 150
  2805 E. 10th Street
  Bloomington, IN 47408-2698

ERIC Clearinghouse on *Rural Education and Small Schools*
  Appalachia Educational Laboratory
  1031 Quarrier Street
  P. O. Box 1348
  Charleston, WV 25325-1348

ERIC Clearinghouse on *Science, Mathematics, and Environmental Education*
  Ohio State University
  1929 Kenny Road
  Columbus, OH 43210-1080

ERIC Clearinghouse on *Social Studies/ Social Science Education*
  Indiana University
  Social Studies Development Center
  2805 East 10th Street, Suite 120
  Bloomington, IN 47408-2698

ERIC Clearinghouse on *Teaching and Teacher Education*
American Association of Colleges of Teacher Education
One Dupont Circle, N. S., Suite 610
Washington, DC 20036-1186

ERIC Clearinghouse on *Urban Education*
Teachers College, Columbia University
Institute for Urban and Minority Education
Main Hall, Room 3030, Box 40
525 West 120th Street
New York, NY 10027-9998

If an author does not know which specialization is most appropriate for a particular research report, the item can be sent to the following address, from which it will be forwarded to the most suitable ERIC location.

ERIC Processing and Reference Facility
1301 Piccard Drive, Suite 300
Rockville, MD 20850-4305

References

AAUW. (1993). *Hostile hallways.* Washington, DC: American Association of University Women's Educational Foundation.

Abraham, M. F. (1980). *Perspectives on modernization: Toward a general theory of third world development.* Washington, DC: University Press of America.

Achter, J. A., Lubinski, D., & Benbow, C. P. (1996). Multipotentiality among the intellectually gifted: "It was never there and already it's vanishing." *Journal of Counseling Psychology, 43* (1), pp. 65-76.

Adjangba, A. M. (1993). Problems of African nationalism. In K. Schleicher, *Nationalism in education* (pp. 193-212). Frankfurt am Main: Peter Lang.

AERA, APA, & NCME. (1985). *Standards for educational and psychological testing.* Washington, DC: American Educational Research Association, American Psychological Association, & National Council on Measurement in Education.

Aiken, L. R. (1996). *Rating scales and check lists: Evaluating behavior, personality, and attitudes.* New York: Wiley

Allen, J. D. (1982). *Classroom management: A field study of students' perspectives, goals, and strategies.* Unpublished doctoral dissertation, University of California, Santa Barbara.

Allen, J. D. (1986). Classroom management: Students' perspectives, goals, and strategies. *American Educational Research Journal, 23* (3), pp. 437-459.

Alschuler, L. R. (1978). *Predicting development, dependency, and conflict in Latin America.* Ottawa: University of Ottawa Press.

Altbach, P. G., & Kelly, G. P. (Eds.). (1991). *Education and the colonial experience* (2nd ed.). New York: Advent Books.

Ambert, A. M. (1995). Toward a theory of peer abuse. *Sociological Studies of Children, 7,* pp. 177-205.

Anderson, L. W., & Sosniak, L. A. (Eds.). (1994). *Bloom's taxonomy: A forty-year retrospective.* Chicago: National Society for the Study of Education.

Anderson, N. H. (1991a).   Preface. In N. H. Anderson (Ed.), *Contributions to information integration theory: Volume II: Developmental* (p. 1). Hillsdale, NJ: Erlbaum.

Anderson, N. H. (1991b).   Moral-social development. In N. H. Anderson (Ed.), *Contributions to information integration theory: Volume II: Developmental* (pp. 137-187). Hillsdale, NJ: Erlbaum.

Anwkah, T. G. (1983).   *Undergirding educational action in Nigeria with responsive curriculum theory.* Lagos: Comparative Education Study and Adaptation Centre.

APA. (1974).   *Standards for educational and psychological tests.* Washington, DC: American Psychological Association.

Apple, M. (1982).   *Education and power.* Boston: Routledge & Kegan Paul.

Arnove, R. F. (1986).   *Education and revolution in Nicaragua.* New York: Praeger.

Ashley, M. (1992).   The validity of sociometric status. *Educational Research, 34* (2), pp. 149-154.

Axinn, G. H., & Sudhaker, T. (1972).   *Modernizing world agriculture.* New York: Praeger.

Babad, E. (1993).   Pygmalion—25 years after interpersonal expectations in the classroom.   In P. D. Blanck (Ed.), *Interpersonal expectations* (pp. 125-153). Cambridge, England: Cambridge University Press.

Babbie, E. R. (1990).   *Survey research methods* (2nd ed.). Belmont, CA: Wadsworth.

Bacharach, M., & Hurley, S. (Eds.). (1991).   *Foundations of decision theory: Issues and advances.* Cambridge, MA: Blackwell.

Bailey, S. K. (1978).   Thomas Jefferson and the purposes of education.   In E. K. Mosher & J. L. Wagoner, Jr. (Eds.), *The changing politics of education* (pp. 5-41). Berkeley, CA: McCutchen.

Ball, S. (1985). Reactive effects in research and evaluation.   In T. Husén & T. N. Postlethwaite (Eds.), *International Encyclopedia of Education: Research and Studies* (1st ed., vol. 7, p. 4200). Oxford: Pergamon.

Bandura, A. (1986).   *Social foundations of thought and action: A social cognitive theory.* Englewood Cliffs, NJ: Prentice-Hall.

Barker, R. G. (Ed.). (1978).   *Habitats, environments, and human behavior.* San Francisco: Jossey-Bass.

Barker, R. G., & Gump, P. V. (1964).   *Big school, small school.* Stanford, CA: Stanford University Press.

Barker, R. G., & Wright, H. F. (1951). *One boy's day.* New York: Harper.

Barnett, V. (1991).   *Sample survey principles and methods.* New York: Oxford University Press.

Baroody, A. J. (1989).   *A guide to teaching mathematics in the primary grades.* Boston: Allyn & Bacon.

Bartusch, D. J., & Matsueda, R. L. (1996). Gender, reflected appraisals, and labeling: A cross-group test of an interactionist theory of delinquency. *Social Forces, 75* (1), pp. 145-166.

Baum, R. N. (1996). "What I have learned to feel": The pedagogical emotion of Holocaust education. *College Literature, 23* (3), pp. 44-57.

Bauman, R. (1972). An ethnographic framework for the investigation of com-municative behavior. In R. D. Abraham & R. Troike (Eds.), *Language and cultural diversity in American education.* Englewood Cliffs, NJ: Prentice-Hall.

Beaglehole, E., & Beaglehole, P. (1941). *Pangai: A village in Tonga.* Wellington, New Zealand: The Polynesian Society.

Becker, G. S. (1993). *Human capital: A theoretical and empirical analysis with special reference to education* (3rd ed.). Chicago: University of Chicago Press.

Beeby, C. E. (1966). *The quality of education in developing countries.* Cambridge, MA: Harvard University Press.

Belford, G. G. (1994). Computer science. *Encyclopaedia Britannica* (vol. 16, pp. 629-638). Chicago: Encyclopaedia Britannica.

Benavot, A. (1992). Curricular content, educational expansion, and economic growth. *Comparative Education Review, 36* (2), pp. 150-174.

Bennett, G. K., Seashore, H. G., & Wesman, A. G. (1952). *Differential aptitude tests: Manual* (2nd ed.). New York: Psychological Corporation.

Bennett, R. E., Gottesman, R. L., Rock, D. A., & Cerullo, F. (1993). Influence of behavior perceptions and gender on teachers' judgments of students' academic skill. *Journal of educational psychology, 85* (2), pp. 347-356.

Benson, H., Kornhaber, A., Kornhaber, C., LeChanu, M. N., Zuttermeister, P. C., Myers, P., & Friedman, R. (1994). Increases in positive psychological characteristics with a new relaxation-response curriculum in high school students. *Journal of Research and Development in Education, 27* (4), pp. 226-231.

Bess, J. L. (1988). *Collegiality and bureaucracy in the modern university.* New York: Teachers College Press.

Billigmeier, R. H. (1985). Social discrimination and human development. In T. Husén & T. N. Postlethwaite (Eds.), *International encyclopedia of education: Research and studies* (1st ed., vol. 8, pp. 4630-4633). Oxford: Pergamon.

Blalock, H. M., Jr. (1989). *Power and conflict: Toward a general theory.* Newbury Park, CA: Sage.

Bloom, B. S. (Ed.). (1956). *Taxonomy of educational objectives: Handbook I: Cognitive domain.* New York: Longmans, Green.

Boorstin, D. J. (1948). *The lost world of Thomas Jefferson.* New York: Henry Holt.

Booth, A., & Edwards, J. N. (1992). Starting over. *Journal of Family Issues, 13* (2), pp. 179-194.

Bottani, N. (1995). Comparing educational output. *OECD Observer* (193), pp. 6-7.

Bozarth-Campbell, A. (1979). *The word's body.* University, AL: University of Alabama Press.

Bracey, G. W. (1993). More looks at SIMS. *Phi Delta Kappan, 75* (2), p. 187.

Bray, M. (1992). Colonialism, scale, and politics: Divergence and convergence of educational development in Hong Kong and Macau. *Comparative Education Review, 36* (3), pp. 322-342.

Bray, M., & Thomas, R. M. (1995). Levels of comparison in educational studies: Different insights from different literatures and the value of multilevel analyses. *Harvard Educational Review, 65* (3), pp. 472-490.

Bronfenbrenner, U. (1972). *Two worlds of childhood: U.S. and U.S.S.R.* New York: Simon & Schuster.

Bronfenbrenner, U. (1979). *The ecology of human development.* Cambridge, MA: Harvard University Press.

Bronfenbrenner, U. (1993). The ecology of cognitive development. In R. H. Wozniak & K. W. Fischer (Eds.), *Development in context: Acting and thinking in specific environments.* Hillsdale, NJ: Erlbaum.

Bryant, S. E., & Fox, S. K. (1995). Behavior modeling training and generalization: Interaction of learning type and number of modeling scenarios. *Psychological Reports, 45* (3), pp. 495-503.

Burton, J. (Ed.). (1990). *Conflict: Human needs theory.* New York: St. Martin's.

Cahn, S. M. (Ed). (1977). *New studies in the philosophy of John Dewey.* Hanover, NH: University Press of New England.

Campbell, D. P., & Hansen, J-I. C. (1985). *Manual for the SVIB-SCII—Strong-Campbell Interest Inventory* (4th ed.). Stanford, CA: Stanford University Press.

Campbell, D. T., & Stanley, J. C. (1966). *Experimental and quasi-experimental designs for research.* Chicago: Rand McNally.

Campbell, F. A., & Ramey, C. T. (1995). Cognitive and school outcomes for high-risk African-American students at middle adolescence: Positive effects of early intervention. *American Educational Research Journal, 32* (4), pp. 743-772.

Carey, K. B. (1993). Situational determinants of heavy drinking among college students. *Journal of Counseling Psychology, 40* (2), pp. 217-220.

Carney, T. F. (1972). *Content analysis: A technique for systematic inference from communications.* Winnipeg: University of Manitoba Press.

Carnoy, M. (1974). *Education and cultural imperialism.* New York: McKay.

Carroll, J. B. (1963). A model of school learning. *Teachers College Record, 64*, pp. 723-733.

Carroll-Rowan, L. A., & Miltenberger, R. G. (1994). A comparison of procedures for teaching abduction prevention to preschoolers. *Education and Treatment of Children, 17* (1), pp. 113-128.

Case, R. (1992). *The mind's staircase.* Hillsdale, NJ: Erlbaum.

Castro, C. de M. (1993). Models of vocational education and training. *The Forum for Advancing Basic Education and Literacy, 3* (1), 12-13.

Chase-Dunn, C., & Grimes, P. (1995). World-systems analysis. *Annual Review of Sociology, 21*, pp. 387-417.

Chaudhuri, A., & Vos, J. W. E. (1988). *Unified theory and strategies of survey sampling.* New York: Elsevier.

Chicago manual of style (14th ed.). (1993). Chicago: University of Chicago Press.

Chung, R.C.Y., & Walkey, R. H. (1989). Educational and achievement aspirations of New Zealand Chinese and European secondary school students. *Youth & Society, 21* (2), pp. 139-152.

Clark, C. M. (1985). Carroll model of school learning. In T. Husén & T. N. Postlethwaite (Eds.), *International encyclopedia of education: Research and studies* (1st ed., vol. 2, pp. 641-645). Oxford: Pergamon.

Clayman, C. B. (Ed.). (1989). *The American Medical Association encyclopedia of medicine.* New York: Random House.

Coker, D. R., & White, J. (1993). Selecting and applying learning theory to classroom teaching strategies. *Education, 114* (1), pp. 77-80.

Colangelo, N., & Kerr, B. A. (1990). Extreme academic talent: Profiles of perfect scores. *Journal of Educational Psychology, 82* (3), pp. 404-409.

Collins, R. (1993). What does conflict theory predict about America's future? *Sociological Perspectives, 36* (4), pp. 289-313.

Colomb, G. G. (1989). Cultural literacy and the theory of meaning. *New Literary History, 20* (2), pp. 411-450.

Conoley, J. C., & Impara, J. C. (Eds.). (1994). *Supplement to the eleventh mental measurements yearbook.* Lincoln, NE: University of Nebraska Press.

Conoley, J. C., & Impara, J. C. (Eds.). (1995). *Twelfth mental measurements yearbook.* Lincoln, NE: University of Nebraska Press.

Conoley, J. C., & Kramer, J. J. (Eds.). (1989). *Tenth mental measurements yearbook.* Lincoln, NE: University of Nebraska Press.

Conoley, J. C., & Kramer, J. J. (Eds.). (1992). *Eleventh mental measurements yearbook.* Lincoln, NE: University of Nebraska Press.

Coombs, P. H. (1985). *The world crisis in education.* New York: Oxford University Press.

Cremin, L. A. (1970). *American education: The colonial experience 1607-1783.* New York: Harper & Row.

Cremin, L. A. (1980). *American education: The national experience 1783-1876.* New York: Harper & Row.

Cremin, L. A. (1988). *American education: The metropolitan experience 1876-1980.* New York: Harper & Row.

Crevier, D. (1993). *AI: The tumultuous history of the search for artificial intelligence.* New York: Basic Books.

Crozier, B. (1975). *A theory of conflict.* New York: Scribner.

Cruikshank, D. E., & Sheffield, L. J. (1992). *Teaching and learning elementary and middle school mathematics* (2nd ed.). New York: Merrill.

Culture. (1994). *The new Encyclopaedia Britannica* (vol. 3). Chicago: Encyclopaedia Britannica.

Cunningham, A. E., & Stanovich, K. E. (1990). Early spelling acquisition: Writing beats the computer. *Journal of Educational Psychology, 82* (1), pp. 159-162.

Darwin, C. (1975). *The origin of species.* New York: Norton.

Davey, G., & Cullen, C. (1988). *Human operant conditioning and behavior modification.* New York: Wiley.

Davison, J., & Kanyuka, M. (1992). Girls' participation in basic education in Southern Malawi. *Comparative Education Review, 36,* (4), pp. 446-466.

Dawes, R. M. (1972). *Fundamentals of attitude measurement.* New York: Wiley.

Demoulin, D. F. (1987). *Juvenile delinquents, the martial arts, and behavior modification: An experimental study of social intervention.* Washington, DC: U.S. Office of Research and Improvement.

Denzin, N. K. (1997). *Interpretive ethnography.* Thousand Oaks, CA: Sage.

Deolikar, A. B. (1993). Gender differences in the returns to schooling and in school enrollment rates in Indonesia. *Journal of Human Resources, 28* (4), pp. 899-932.

Diver-Stamnes, A. C. (1995). *Lives in the balance—Youth, poverty, and education in Watts.* Albany: State University of New York Press.

Diver-Stamnes, A. C., & Thomas, R. M. (1995). *Prevent, repent, reform, revenge: A study in adolescent moral development.* Westport, CT: Greenwood.

Do you know which patients can't read? (1996). *Patient Care, 30* (6), p. 13.

Donohue, J. W. (1996). Brandishing the rod. *America, 174* (1), pp. 4-6.

Downing, J. A. (1979). *Reading and reasoning.* New York: Springer-Verlag.

Duell, O. K. (1994). Extended wait time and university student achievement. *American Educational Research Journal, 31* (2), pp. 397-414.

Dufresne-Tasse, C., & Lefebvre, A. (1994). The museum of adult education: A psychological study of visitor reactions. *International Review of Education, 40* (6), pp. 469-484.

Duncan, J., Emslie, H., & Williams, P. (1996). Intelligence and the frontal lobe. *Cognitive Psychology, 30* (3), pp. 257-303.

Eccles, J. S. (1994). Understanding women's educational choices. *Psychology of Women Quarterly, 18* (4), pp. 585-609.

Educational Testing Service. (1990). *The ETS test collection catalog: Volume 4: Cognitive aptitude and intelligence tests.* Phoenix, AZ: Oryx Press.

Eisen, V., & Kenyatta, M. (1996). Cornel West on heterosexism and transformation: An interview. *Harvard Educational Review, 66* (2), pp. 357-367.

Eisner, E. W., & Peshkin, A. (Eds.). (1990). *Qualitative inquiry in education.* New York: Teachers College, Columbia University.

Elkind, D. (1976). *Child development and education.* New York: Oxford.

Elley, W. B. (1992). *How in the world do students read?* The Hague: International Association for the Evaluation of Educational Achievement.

Elsom-Cook, M. T. (1994). Artificial intelligence as a contributing field to instructional design. In T. Husén & T. N. Postlethwaite (Eds.), *International encyclopedia of education: Research and studies* (2nd ed., vol. 1, pp. 343-348). Oxford: Pergamon.

Emmanouel, C., Zervas, Y., & Vagenas, G. (1992). Effects of four physical education teaching methods on development of motor skill, self-concept, and social attitudes of fifth-grade children. *Perceptual and Motor Skills, 74* (3), pp. 1151-1167.

Ennis, C. D., Chen, A., & Ross, J. (1992). Educational value orientations as a theoretical framework for experienced urban teachers' curricular decision making. *Journal of Research and Development in Education, 25* (3), pp. 156-164.

Ennis, C. D., & Hooper, L. M. (1988). Development of an instrument for assessing educational value orientations. *Journal of Curriculum Studies, 20,* pp. 277-280.

Ermarth, M. (1978). *Wilhelm Dilthey: The critique of historical reason.* Chicago: University of Chicago Press.

Ethnography. (1994). *The new Encyclopaedia Britannica* (vol. 4). Chicago: Encyclopaedia Britannica.

Fagerlind, I., & Saha, L. J. (1989). *Education and national development* (2nd ed.). Oxford: Pergamon.

Farkas, A. J. (1991). Cognitive algebra of interpersonal unfairness. In N. H. Anderson (Ed.), *Contributions to information integration theory: Volume II: Developmental* (pp. 43-99). Hillsdale, NJ: Erlbaum.

Farnworth, M., & Leiber, M. J. (1989). Strain theory revisited: Economic goals, educational means, and delinquency. *American Sociological Review, 54* (2), pp. 263-274.

Fernandez, R. (1995). *Education finance reform and investment in human capital: Lessons from California.* Cambridge, MA: National Bureau of Economic Research.

Fischer, K. W. (1980). A theory of cognitive development: The control and construction of hierarchies of skills. *Psychological Review, 87* (6), pp. 477-531.

Fishbein, H. D., Eckart, T., Lauver, E., Van Leeuwen, R., & Langmeyer, D. (1990). Learners' questions and comprehension in a tutoring setting. *Journal of Educational Psychology, 82* (1), pp. 163-170.

Fishbein, M. (1967). *Readings in attitude theory and measurement.* New York: Wiley.

Fisher, C. W., & Berliner, D. C. (1984). *Perspectives on instructional time.* New York: Longman.

Flexner, S. B. (1987). *The Random House dictionary of the English language.* New York: Random House.

Foley, D. E. (1991). Rethinking school ethnographies of colonial settings: A performance perspective of reproduction and resistance. *Comparative Education Review, 35* (3), pp. 532-551.

Follman, J. (1984). Cornucopia of correlations. *American Psychologist, 39*, pp. 701-702.

Ford, D. H., & Lerner, R. M. (1992). *Developmental systems theory.* Thousand Oaks, CA: Sage.

Foster, G. P. (1991). Cultural relativism and the theory of value: The educational implications. *American Journal of Economics and Sociology, 50* (3), pp. 257-267.

Foucault, M. (1984). Nietzsche, geneology, history. In P. Rabinow (Ed.), *The Foucault reader* (pp. 76-100). New York: Pantheon.

Franklin, B. (1866/1941). *The autobiography of Benjamin Franklin.* New York: Walter J. Black. (The autobiography was originally in four parts written at different times. Not until 1866 did John Bigelow recover the original manuscripts and published them as a unit. All subsequent editions, including the 1941 printing, have followed Bigelow's text.)

Franks, M. (1995). *The Internet publishing handbook.* Reading, MA: Addison-Wesley.

Freire, P. (1970). *Pedagogy of the oppressed.* New York: Herder & Herder.

Freire, P. (1985). *The politics of education.* Westport, CT: Bergin & Garvey.

Friedman, E. E. (1987). *Who wrote the Bible?* New York: Summit Books.

Furth, H. G., & Wachs, W. (1975). *Thinking goes to school.* New York: Oxford.

Gadamar, H. G. (1975). *Truth and method.* London: Harvester Press.

Gamoran, A. (1992). The variable effects of high school tracking. *American Sociological Review, 57*, pp. 812-828.

Gardner, H. (1983). *Frames of mind.* New York: Basic Books.

Garfinkel, A. (1981). *Forms of explanation.* New Haven: Yale University Press.

Gates, B. (1995). *The road ahead.* New York: Viking.

Gerbert, E. (1993). Lessons from the Kokugo (national language) readers. *Comparative Education Review, 37* (2), 152-180.

Gilligan, C. (1982). *In a different voice: Psychological theory and women's development.* Cambridge, MA: Harvard University Press.

Giroux, H. (1983). *Theory and resistance in education: A pedagogy of the opposition.* London: Heinemann.

Glass, G. V. (1988). Quasi-experiments: The case of interrupted time series. In R. M. Jaeger (Ed.), *Complementary methods for research in education* (pp. 445-463). Washington, DC: American Educational Research Association.

Glass, G. V., & Hopkins, K. D. (1984). *Statistical methods in education and psychology* (2nd ed.). Englewood Cliffs, NJ: Prentice-Hall.

Glass, G. V., McGaw, B., & Smith, M. L. (1981). *Meta-analysis in social research.* Thousand Oaks, CA: Sage.

Goldthorpe, J. H. (1996). Class analysis and the reorientation of class theory. *British Journal of Sociology, 66* (2), pp. 413-414.

Goodenough, W. H. (1976). Multiculturalism as the normal human experience. *Anthropology and Education Quarterly, 7* (4), pp. 4-7.

Greenlees, J. (1993). New texts on brutal past. *Times Educational Supplement* (July 2) p. 14.

Guilford, J. P. (1967). *The nature of human intelligence.* New York: McGraw-Hill.

Guthrie, G. P. (1992). Bilingual education in a Chinese community: An ethnography in progress. In M. Saravia-Shore & S. F. Arivizu (Eds.), *Cross-cultural literacy* (pp. 173-210). New York: Garland.

Guttman, L. (1950). The basis for scalogram analysis. In S. A. Stouffer (Ed.), *Measurement and prediction.* Princeton, NJ: Princeton University Press.

Habermas, J. (1972). *Communication and the evolution of society.* London: Heinemann.

Haddad, S. (Ed.). (1996). Special section: Adult education—the legislative and policy environment. *International Review of Education, 42* (1-3), pp. 9-186.

Hall, G. S. (1965). *Health, growth, and heredity.* New York: Teachers College Press.

Hambleton, R. K., & Zaal, J. N. (Eds.). (1991). *Advances in educational and psychological testing.* Boston: Kluwer.

Harnischfeger, A. (1985). Active learning time. In T. Husén & T. N. Postlethwaite (Eds.), *International encyclopedia of education: Research and studies* (1st ed., vol. 1, pp. 42-45). Oxford: Pergamon.

Harris, C. (1996). *An Internet education.* Belmont: Wadsworth.

Harris, J. R. (1995). Where is the child's environment? A group socialization theory of development. *Psychological Review, 102* (3), pp. 458-459.

Harris, M. L., & Harris, C. H. (1971). A factor analytic interpretation strategy. *Educational and Psychological Measurement, 31* (3), pp. 589-606.

Heaton, J. B. (1990). *Classroom testing.* New York: Longman.

Heermann, E. F., & Braskamp, L. A. (1970). *Readings in statistics for the behavioral sciences.* Englewood Cliffs, NJ: Prentice-Hall.

Held, D. (1980). *Introduction to critical theory: Horkheimer to Habermas.* London: Hutchinson.

Hendrick, J. (1996). *The whole child: Developmental education for the early years.* Columbus, OH: Merrill/Prentice-Hall.

Henry, G. T. (1990). *Practical sampling.* Newbury Park, CA: Sage.

Henry, G. T. (1996). Community accountability: A theory of information, accountability, and school improvement. *Phi Delta Kappan, 78* (1), pp. 85-90.

Hersh, R. H., Miller, J. P, & Fielding, G D. (1980). *Models of moral education.* New York: Longman.

Hewitt, J. P. (1994). *Self and society: A symbiotic interactionist social psychology* (6th ed.). Boston: Allyn & Bacon.

Hinde, R. A. (1983). Ethology and child development. In M. M. Haith & J. J. Campos (Eds.), *Handbook of child psychology. Vol. II: Infancy and developmental psychobiology* (pp. 27-93). New York: Wiley.

Hlebowitsh, P. S. (1993). *Radical curriculum theory reconsidered: A historical approach.* New York: Teachers College Press.

Hommers, W., & Anderson, N. H. (1991). Moral algebra of harm and recompense. In N. H. Anderson (Ed.), *Contributions to information integration theory: Volume II: Developmental* (pp. 101-141). Hillsdale, NJ: Erlbaum.

Hopkins, C. D., & Antes, R. L. (1989). *Classroom testing* (2nd ed.). Itasca, IL: Peacock.

Hopkins, T. K., & Wallerstein, I. (1982). *World-systems analysis: Theory and methodology.* Beverly Hills, CA: Sage.

Hoy, W. K., Tarter, C. J., & Witkoskie, L. (1992). Faculty trust in colleagues: Linking the school principal with school effectiveness. *Journal of Research and Development in Education, 26* (1), pp. 38-45.

Hunter, J. E., Schmidt, F. L., & Jackson, G. B. (1982). *Meta-analysis: Cumulating research findings across studies.* Beverly Hills, CA: Sage.

Husén, T., & Postlethwaite, T. N. (Eds.). (1985). *International encyclopedia of education: Research and studies* (1st ed.). Oxford: Pergamon.

Husén, T., & Postlethwaite, T. N. (Eds.). (1994). *International encyclopedia of education: Research and studies* (2nd ed.). Oxford: Pergamon.

Husén, T., & Tuijnman, A. (1994). Monitoring standards in education: Why and how it came about. In A. C. Tuijnman & T. N. Postlethwaite (Eds.), *Monitoring the standards of education* (pp. 1-21). Oxford: Pergamon.

Illich, I. D. (1970). *Deschooling society.* New York: Harper & Row.

Impoco, J. (1996). TV's frisky family values. *U.S. News & World Report, 120* (15), pp. 58-62.

Inglis, F. (1985). *The management of ignorance: A political theory of the curriculum.* New York: Blackwell.

Inhelder, B., & Piaget, J. (1964). *The growth of logical thinking in the child.* London: Routledge & Kegan Paul.

Ishumi, A.G.M. (1992). Colonial forces and ethnic resistance in African education. In K. Schleicher & T. Kozma (Eds.), *Ethnocentrism in education* (pp. 121-138). Frankfurt au Main: Peter Lang.

Iverson, P. (1981). *The Navajo nation.* Westport, CT: Greenwood.

Jallife, F. R. (1986). *Survey design and analysis.* New York: Halsted.

Jellen, H. G., & Verduin, J. G., Jr. (1986). *Handbook for differential education for the gifted.* Carbondale, IL: Southern Illinois University Press.

Jensen, A. R. (1972). *Genetics and education.* New York: Harper & Row.

Jensen, A. R. (1973). *Educability and group differences.* New York: Harper & Row.

Johnson, O. (Ed.). (1997). *Information please almanac.* Boston: Houghton Mifflin.

Johnston, D. K. (1988). Adolescents' solutions to dilemmas in fables: Two moral orientations—two problem solving strategies. In C. Gilligan, J. V. Ward, & J. M. Taylor (Eds.), *Mapping the moral domain: A contribution of women's thinking to psychological theory and education* (pp. 49-71). Cambridge, MA: Harvard University Press.

Kalekin-Fishman, D. (1991). Latent messages: The acoustical environments of kindergartens in Israel and West Germany. *Sociology of Education, 64*, pp. 209-222.

Kamil, C., & DeVries, R. (1980). *Group games in early education.* Washington, DC: National Association for the Education of Young Children.

Kapavalu, H. (1993). Dealing with the dark side in the ethnography of childhood: Child punishment in Tonga. *Oceania, 63* (4), pp. 313-329.

Karlsson, J. L. (1978). *Inheritance of creative intelligence.* Chicago: Nelson Hall.

Karweit, N. L., & Slavin, R. L. (1980). *Measuring time on task.* Baltimore, MD: Johns Hopkins University Press.

Keith, A. B. (1925). *The religion and philosophy of the Vedas and Upanishads.* Cambridge, MA: Harvard University Press.

Kelly, G. P. (1987). The transfer of an education operation system: French educational management organization in the colonies. In R. M. Thomas & V. N. Kobayashi (Eds.), *Educational technology* (pp. 233-252). Oxford: Pergamon.

Kennedy, E. & Park, H. S. (1994). Home language as a predictor of academic achievement: A comparative study of Mexican- and Asican-American youth. *Journal of Research and Development in Education, 27* (3), pp. 188-202.

Kerwin, C., Ponterotto, J. B., Jackson, B. L., & Harris, A. (1993). Racial identity in biracial children: A qualitative investigation. *Journal of Counseling Psychology, 40* (2), pp. 221-231.

Kish, L. (1965). *Survey sampling.* New York: Wiley.

Kohlberg, L. (1984). *The psychology of moral development.* San Francisco: Harper & Row.

Kramer, J. J., & Conoley, J. C. (Eds.). (1990). *Supplement to the tenth mental measurements yearbook.* Lincoln, NE: University of Nebraska Press.

Krathwohl, D. R., Bloom, B. S., & Masia, B. B. (1964). *Taxonomy of educational objectives: Handbook II: Affective domain.* New York: McKay.

Kravetz, N. (1983). The United States of America: The languages of education: New ethnicity and the drive to power. In R. M. Thomas (Ed.), *Politics and education* (pp. 104-121). Oxford: Pergamon.

Kremer, J. (1987). *Book publishing resource guide.* Fairfield, IA: Ad-Lib Publications.

Kremer, J. (1990). *1001 ways to market your book.* Fairfield, IA: Ad-Lib Publications.

Kyle, N. J. (1992). Can you do as you're told? The nineteenth century preparation of a female teacher in England and Australia. *Comparative Education Review, 36* (4), pp. 467-486.

Lebra, W. P. (1966). *Okinawan religion.* Honolulu: University of Hawaii Press.

LeCompte, M. D., & Preissle, J. (1993). *Ethnography and qualitative design in educational research* (2nd ed.). San Diego: Academic.

Lee, V. E., Croniger, R. G., Linn, E., & Chen, X. (1996). The culture of sexual harassment in secondary schools. *American Educational Research Journal, 33* (2), pp. 383-417.

Lesser, H. (1977). *Television and the preschool child: A psychological theory of instruction and curriculum development.* New York: Academic.

Likert, R. (1932). A technique for the measurement of attitudes. *Archives of psychology* (No. 140).

Limage, L. J. (1990). Language and education. In. R. M. Thomas (Ed.), *International comparative education* (pp. 227-250). Oxford: Pergamon.

Lin, H. Y. (1985). *Moral development and children's literature in Taiwan.* Unpublished doctoral dissertation, University of California, Santa Barbara.

Lin, H. Y., Davidman, P., Petersen, G., & Thomas, R. M. (1998). Teachers' views of moral-education topics—Taiwan and the USA. *International Review of Education, 44* (1), pp. 65-83.

Lundberg, I., & Linnakylä, P. (1993). *Teaching reading around the world.* The Hague: International Association or the Evaluation of Educational Achievement.

Lundgren, U. P. (1985). Frame factors and the teaching process. In T. Husén & T. N. Postlethwaite (Eds.), *International encyclopedia of education: Research and studies* (1st ed., vol. 4, pp. 1957-1962). Oxford: Pergamon.

Luria, A. R. (1976). *Cognitive development: Its cultural and social foundations.* Cambridge, MA: Harvard University Press.

Macsporran, I. (1982). Hermeneutics: An alternative set of philosophical assumptions for comparative education? In R. Cowen & P. Stokes (Eds.), *Methodological issues in comparative education* (pp. 47-51). London: London Association of Comparative Educationists.

Maddox, R. (1994). Culture, schooling, and the politics of class identity in an Andalusian town. *Comparative Education Review, 38* (1), pp. 88-114.

Malinowski, B. (1922). *Argonauts of the Western Pacific.* London: Routledge.

Mannien, J., & Tuomela, R. (Eds.). (1976). *Essays on explanation and understanding.* Dordrech, Netherlands: D. Reidel.

Marcus, B. A., & Vollmer, T. R. (1996). Combining noncontingent reinforcement and differential reinforcement schedules as treatment for aberrant behavior. *Journal of Applied Behavioral Analysis, 29* (1), pp. 43-51.

Marlaire, C. L., & Maynard, D. W. (1990). Standardized testing as an interactional phenomenon. *Sociology of Education, 63*, pp. 83-101.

Marsh, C., & Morris, P. (Eds.). (1991). *Curriculum development in East Asia.* London: Falmer.

Marsh, H. W., & Holmes, I.W.M. (1990). Multidimensional self-concepts: Construct validation of responses by children. *American Educational Research Journal, 27* (1), pp. 89-117.

Martin, J. D., Blair, G. E., & Bledsoe, J. R. (1990). Measures of concurrent validity and alternate-form reliability of the Test of Nonverbal Intelligence. *Psychological Reports, 66* (2), pp. 503-508.

Martin, R., Zimmerman, S. E., Long, B., & West, A. (1995). A content assessment and comparative analysis of prison-based AIDS education programs for inmates. *Prison Journal, 75* (1), pp. 5-47.

Marx, K. (1859). Excerpt from: A contribution to the critique of political economy. In K. Marx & F. Engels, *Karl Marx and Frederick Engels: Selected Works* (vol. 1, pp. 327-331). Moscow: Foreign Language Publishing House (1951).

Marx, K. (1898). Wages, price, and profit. In K. Marx & F. Engels, *Karl Marx and Frederick Engels: Selected Works* (vol. 1). Moscow: Foreign Language Publishing House (1951).

Marx, K., & Engels, F. (1848). The manifesto of the communist party. In K. Marx & F. Engels, *Karl Marx and Frederick Engels: Selected Works* (vol. 1, pp. 33-61). Moscow: Foreign Language Publishing House (1951).

Mazzeo, J. A. (1978). *Varieties of interpretation.* Notre Dame, IN: University of Notre Dame Press.

Mboya, N. M. (1995). Peer differences in teachers' behavior in relation to adolescents' self concepts. *Psychological Abstracts, 77* (3), pp. 831-839.

McCafferty, B. (1996). Credit where it is due. *Times Educational Supplement,* (4163), p. 2.

McGaw, B. (1985). Meta-analysis. In T. Husén & T. N. Postlethwaite (Eds.), *International encyclopedia of education: Research and studies* (1st ed., vol. 6, pp. 3322-3330). Oxford: Pergamon.

McGinn, N. F. (1987). The creation and development of an educational operating system: The bureaucratic organization of the French national system of state education. In R. M. Thomas & V. N. Kobayashi (Eds.), *Educational technology* (pp. 209-232). Oxford: Pergamon.

McGinn, N. F. (1997). Not decentralization but integration. In K. Watson, C. Modgil, & S. Modgil (Eds.), *Power and responsibility in education* (pp. 17-24). London: Cassell.

McGraha, J. E., & Leoni, E. L. (1995). Family violence, abuse, and related family issues of incarcerated delinquents with alcoholic parents compared to those with nonalcoholic parents. *Adolescence, 30* (118), pp. 473-482.

Mcguire, M. (1994). Cultural stances informing storytelling among bilingual children in Quebec. *Comparative Education Review, 38* (1), pp. 115-143.

McKay, S. L., & Wong, S.L.C. (1996). Multiple discourses, multiple identities: Investment and agency in second-language learning among Chinese adolescent immigrant students. *Harvard Educational Review, 66* (3), pp. 577-606.

Mevarech, Z., Shir, N., & Movshovitz-Hadar, N. (1992). Is more always better? The separate and combined effects of a computer and video programme on mathematics learning. *British Journal of Educational Psychology, 62,* pp. 106-116.

Mickelson, R. A. (1990). The attitude-achievement paradox among black adolescents. *Sociology of Education, 63,* pp. 44-61.

Miles, M. B., & Huberman, A. M. (1994). *Qualitative data analysis* (2nd ed.). Thousand Oaks, CA: Sage.

Miles, M. B., & Weitzman, E. A. (1994). Appendix: Choosing computer programs for qualitative data analysis. In M. B. Miles & A. M. Huberman, *Qualitative data analysis* (2nd ed.). Thousand Oaks, CA: Sage.

Mitchell, J. V., Jr. (Ed.). (1985). *Ninth mental measurements yearbook.* Lincoln, NE: University of Nebraska Press.

Moore, J. E. (1985). *Measuring and increasing time on task.* Washington, DC: National Institute of Education.

Mounoud, P. (1986). Similarities between developmental sequences at different age periods. In I. Levin (Ed.), *Stage and structure: Reopening the debate* (pp. 40-58). Norwood, NJ: Ablex.

Muroga, S. (1994). Computers. *Encyclopaedia Britannica* (vol. 16, pp. 639-652). Chicago: Encyclopaedia Britannica.

Murray, F. B. (Ed.). (1979). *The impact of Piagetian theory on education, philosophy, psychiatry, and psychology.* Baltimore: University Park Press.

Neuman, S. B., Hagedorn, T., Celano, D., & Daly, P. (1995). Toward a collaborative approach to parent involvement in early education: A study of teenage mothers in an African-American community. *American Educational Research Journal, 32* (4), pp. 801-827.

Newman, H. H., Freeman, F., & Holzinger, K. J. (1937). *Twins: A student of heredity and environment.* Chicago: University of Chicago Press.

Newman, R. S., & Goldin, L. (1990). Children's reluctance to seek help with schoolwork. *Journal of Educational Psychology, 82* (1), pp. 92-100.

Nightingale, F. (1963). *Notes on hospitals.* London: Longmans, Green.

Nikandrov, N. D. (1995). Russian education after perestroika: The search for new values. *International Review of Education, 41* (1-2), pp. 47-57.

Nisbet, R. A. (1969). *Social change and history: Aspects of the Western theory of development.* New York: Oxford University Press.

Notice to contributors. (1994). *Child Development, 65,* inside back cover.

Nyerere, J. K. (1968). Education for self-reliance. In J. K. Nyerere, *Freedom and socialism: A selection from writings and speeches 1965-1967* (pp. 267-290). Oxford: Oxford University Press.

Odman, P. J. (1985). Hermeneutics. In T. Husén & T. N. Postlethwaite (Eds.), *International encyclopedia of education: Research and studies* (1st ed.). Oxford: Pergamon.

Oosterhof, A. (1996). *Developing and using classroom assessments.* Englewood Cliffs, NJ: Prentice-Hall.

Oppenheim, A. N. (1966). *Questionnaire design and attitude measurement.* New York: Basic Books.

Ormiston, G. L., & Schrift, A. D. (Eds.). (1990). *The hermeneutic tradition.* Albany: State University of New York Press.

Osgood, C. E. (1952). The nature and measurement of meaning. *Psychological Bulletin, 49,* pp. 197-237.

Palafox, J. C., Prawda, J., & Velez, E. (1994). Primary school quality in Mexico. *Comparative Education Review, 38* (2), pp. 167-180.

Palmer, R. E. (1969). *Hermeneutics: Interpretation theory in Scheiermacher, Dilthey, Heidegger, and Gadamer.* Evanston, IL: Northwestern University Press.

Pelham, W. E., Jr., et al. (1993). Separate and combined effects of methylphenidate and behavior modification on boys with attention-deficit hyperactivity disorder in the classroom. *Journal of Consulting & Clinical Psychology, 61* (3), pp. 506-515.

Pendidikan moral pancasila. (1982-83). Jakarta: Departemen Pendidikan dan Kebudayaan, Vols. 1-6.

Penny, A., Appel, S., Gultig, J., Harley, K., & Muir, R. (1993). Just sort of fumbling in the dark: A case study of the advent of racial integration in South African schools. *Comparative Education Review, 37* (4), pp. 412-433

Piaget, J. (1930). *The child's conception of physical causality.* London: Routledge & Kegan Paul.

Piaget, J. (1969). *The child's conception of movement and speed.* New York: Basic Books.

Piaget, J. (1970). *The science of education and the psychology of the child.* New York: Orion.

Piaget, J. (1973a). *The child and reality.* New York: Viking.

Piaget, J. (1973b). *To understand is to invent: The future of education.* New York: Grossman.

Piaget, J., & Inhelder, B. (1969). *The psychology of the child.* New York: Basic Books.

Pike, M. A., & Pike, T. (1994). *The Internet quickstart.* Indianapolis, IN: Que.

Pinnell, G. S., Lyons, C. A., DeFord, D. E., Byrk, A. S., & Seltzer, M. (1994). Comparing instructional models for the literacy education of high-risk first graders. *Reading Research Quarterly, 39* (1), pp. 8-38.

Plante, P. R. (1987). *The art of decision making: Issues and cases in higher education.* New York: Macmillan.

Portes, P. G. (1991). Assessing children's cognitive environment through parent-child interactions. *Journal of Research and Development in Education, 24* (3), pp. 30-37.

Postlethwaite, T. N. (1994). Monitoring and evaluation in different education systems. In A. C. Tuijnman & T. N. Postlethwaite (Eds.), *Monitoring the standards of education,* (pp. 23-46). Oxford: Pergamon.

Postlethwaite, T. N., & Ross, K. N. (1992). *Effective schools in reading.* The Hague: International Association for the Evaluation of Educational Achievement.

Postlethwaite, T. N., & Wiley, D. E. (1992). *The IEA study of science II: Science achievement in twenty-three countries.* Oxford: Pergamon.

Poynter, D. (1996). *The self-publishing manual* (9th ed.). Santa Barbara, CA: Para.

Prewett, P. N. (1992). The relationship between the Kaufman Brief Intelligence Test and the WISC-R with incarcerated juvenile delinquents. *Educational and Psychological Measurement, 52* (4), pp. 977-982.

Prucha, F. P. (1979). *The churches and the Indian schools, 1888-1912.* Lincoln, NE: University of Nebraska Press.

Publication manual of the American Psychological Association (4th ed.). (1994). Washington, DC: American Psychological Association.

Purdie, N., Hattie, J., & Douglas, G. (1996). Student conceptions of learning and their use of self-regulated learning strategies: A cross-cultural comparison. *Journal of Educational Psychology, 88* (1), pp. 87-100.

Raggio, D. J. (1993). Correlations of the Kahn Intelligence Test and the WISC-R IQs among mentally retarded adults. *Perceptual and Motor Skills, 76* (1), pp. 252-254.

Razel, M. (1989). The intelligence test as a measure of knowledge and the nonconstancy of the intelligence score. *Perceptual and Motor Skills, 68* (2), pp. 655-574.

Rea, L. M., & Parker, R. A. (1992). *Designing and conducting survey research.* San Francisco: Jossey-Bass.

Reichard, G. A. (1963). *Navaho religion: A study of symbolism* (2nd ed.). New York: Random House.

Resnick, D. (1996). Jekyll and Hyde in the classroom: A comparative case study i n educational failure. *International Review of Education, 42* (1-3), pp. 227-241.

Reutzel, D. R., Hollingsworth, P. M., & Eldredge, J. L. (1994). Oral reading instruction: The impact on student reading development. *Reading Research Quarterly, 29* (2), pp. 40-62.

Ricoeur, P. (1976). *Interpretation theory.* Fort Worth, TX: Christian University Press.

Rinzler, C. E. (1985). What's fair about "fair use"? In B. H. Weil, & B. F. Polansky (Eds.), *Modern copyright fundamentals* (pp. 203-205). New York: Van Nostrand Reinhold.

Rippberger, S. J. (1988). *Nicaragua: Educational policy for ethnic minorities.* ERIC microfiches collection, ED 329446.

Rippberger, S. J. (1993). Ideological shifts in bilingual education: Mexico and the United States. *Comparative Education Review, 37* (1), pp. 50-61.

Roid, G. H., & Haladyna, T. H. (1982). *A technology for test-item writing.* New York: Academic.

Rosenthal, R., & Jacobson, L. (1968). *Pygmalion in the classroom.* New York: Holt, Rinehart, & Winston.

Ross, H. (1992). The tunnel at the end of the light: Research and teaching on gender and education. *Comparative Education Review, 36* (3), pp. 343-354.

Ross, K. N. (1985). Sampling. In T. Husén & T. N. Postlethwaite (Eds.), *International encyclopedia of education: Research and studies* (1st ed., vol. 8, p p. 4370-4381). Oxford: Pergamon.

Ross, K. N., & Postlethwaite, T. N. (1992). *Indicators of the quality of education: A summary of a national study of primary schools in Zimbabwe.* Paris: International Institute for Educational Planning.

Ross, T., & Ross, M. (1985). *The complete guide to self-publishing.* Cincinnati, OH: Writer's Digest Books.

Rousseau, J. J. (1773). *Emilius; or, A treatise on education.* Edinburgh: W. Coke.

Rüegg, W. (1993). Nationalism and internationalism: A need for balanced identities. In K. Schleicher (Ed.), *Nationalism in education* (pp. 41-53). Frankfurt am Main: Peter Lang.

Rumberger, R. W. (1985). *Correspondence theory.* In T. Husén & T. N. Postlethwaite (Eds.), *International encyclopedia of education: Research and studies* (1st ed., vol. 2, pp. 1030-1031). Oxford: Pergamon.

Saad, I. A., & Hendrix, V.I. (1993). Pupil control ideology in a multicultural society: Arab and Jewish teachers in Israeli elementary schools. *Comparative Education Review, 37* (1), pp. 21-30.

Sanderson, S. K. (1995). *Social transformation: A general theory of historical development.* Cambridge, MA: Blackwell.

Schleicher, A., Siniscalco, M. T., & Postlethwaite, T. N. (1995). *The conditions of primary schools: A pilot study in the least-developed countries.* Hamburg: UNESCO/UNICEF.

Schofield, J. W., Eurich-Fulcer, R., & Britt, C. L. (1994). Teachers, computer tutors, and teaching: The artificially intelligent tutor as an agent for classroom change. *American Educational Research Journal, 31* (3), pp. 579-607.

370 References

Schoppa, L. J. (1991). *Education reform in Japan: A case for immobilist politics.* London: Routledge.

Schwartz, R. M. (1997). Self-monitoring in beginning reading. *Reading Teacher, 51* (1), pp. 40-48.

Scott, C. V. (1995). *Gender and development: Rethinking modernization and dependency theory.* Boulder, CO: L. Rienner.

Seavey, O. (1988). *Becoming Benjamin Franklin.* University Park: Pennsylvania State University Press.

Shepardson, D. P., & Pizzini, E. L. (1992). Gender bias in female elementary teachers' perceptions of scientific ability in students. *Science Education, 76* (2), pp. 147-153.

Shields, J. J., Jr. (1992). Book review. *Comparative Education Review, 36* (4), 546-547.

Shimabukuro, K. (1950). Okinawa no minzoku to shinko [Religion and folk customs in Okinawa]. *Minzokugaku Kenkyu* [Ethnological Studies], *15,* pp. 136-148.

Sinclair, A. (1994). Prediction making as an instructional strategy. *Journal of Research and Development in Education, 27* (3), pp. 153-161.

Singer, M. (1968). The concept of culture. *International encyclopedia of the social sciences* (vol. 3). New York: Macmillan.

Skinner, B. F. (1969). *Contingencies of reinforcement: A theoretical analysis.* Englewood Cliffs, NJ: Prentice-Hall.

Skinner, B. F. (1974). *About behaviorism.* New York: Knopf.

Skinner, B. F. (1984). The shame of American education. *American Psychologist, 39* (9), pp. 947-954.

Slavin, R. E. (1984). *Research methods in education.* Englewood Cliffs, NJ: Prentice-Hall.

Smith, M., & Glass, G. (1977). Meta-analysis of psychotherapy outcomes. *American Psychologist, 32,* pp. 752-760.

Smith, T. L. (1995). The resource center: Finding solutions for illiteracy. *HR Focus, 72* (2), p. 7.

Socha, T. J., & Kelly, B. (1994). Children making "fun": Humorous communication, impression management, and moral development. *Child Study Journal, 24* (3), pp. 237-252.

Sokal, R. R., & Sneath, P.H.A. (1963). *Principals of numerical taxonomy.* San Francisco: Freeman.

Sorensen, C. W. (1994). Success and education in South Korea. *Comparative Education Review, 38* (1), pp. 10-35.

Spearritt, D. (1985). Factor analysis. In T. Husén & T. N. Postlethwaite (Eds.), *International encyclopedia of education: Research and studies* (1st ed., vol. 4, pp. 1813-1824). Oxford: Pergamon.

Spradley, J. P. (1979). *The ethnographic overview.* New York: Holt, Rinehart, & Winston.

Spradley, J. P. (1980). *Participant observation.* New York: Holt, Rinehart, & Winston.

Stevenson, D. L. (1991). Deviant students as a collective resource in classroom control. *Sociology of Education, 64,* pp. 127-133.

Stoff, S., & Schwartzberg, H. (Eds.). (1969). *The human encounter: Readings in education.* New York: Harper & Row.

Strachey, L. (1933). *Eminent Victorians.* New York: Random House.

Stromquist, N. (Ed.). (1994). *Education in the urban context.* Westport, CT: Praeger.

Sukmadinata, N. (1978). *Pengajaran singkat tentang diagnosa dan pemechaan kesulitan belajar* (A short course in diagnosing and treating learning difficulties). Jakarta: Indonesian Ministry of Education and Culture.

Swift, J. (1980). *The annotated Gulliver's travels.* New York: C. N. Potter.

Talbani, A. (1996). Pedagogy, power, and discourse: Transformation of Islamic education. *Comparative Education Review, 40* (1), pp. 66-82.

Tarrow, N. B. (Ed.). (1987). *Human rights and education.* Oxford: Pergamon.

Tashner, J. H. (Ed.). (1984). *Improving instruction with microcomputers.* Phoenix, AZ: Oryx.

Taylor, P. A. (1981). Education, ethnicity, and cultural assimilation in the United States. *Ethnicity, 8*, pp. 31-49.

Telljohann, S. K., Everett, S. A., Durgin, J, & Price, J. H. (1996). Effects of an inservice workshop on the health teaching self efficacy of elementary school teachers. *Journal of School Health, 66* (7), pp. 261-265.

Terman, L. M., & Merrill, M. A. (1960a, 1973). *Stanford-Binet intelligence scale.* Boston: Houghton Mifflin.

Terman, L. M., & Merrill, M. A. (1960b). *Stanford-Binet intelligence scale: Manual for the third revision form L-M.* Boston: Houghton Mifflin.

Thomas, R. M. (1967). *The study of unmet educational needs: A discrepancy-score approach.* Santa Barbara, CA: Tri-County Supplementary Service Center.

Thomas, R. M. (1974). A pattern for teaching indigenous culture. *Comparative Education, 10* (1), pp. 49-55.

Thomas, R. M. (1976) Changing patterns of Samoan Games. *South Pacific Bulletin, 26* (2), pp. 18-23.

Thomas, R. M. (1987). The advent of hermeneutics in educational parlance. *Perspectives in Education, 3* (1), pp. 5-14.

Thomas, R. M. (Ed.). (1988). *Oriental theories of human development.* New York: Peter Lang.

Thomas, R. M. (1990a). Education law as a mirror of maturity: The Indonesian case. *International Review of Education, 36* (1), pp. 7-19.

Thomas, R. M. (1990b). Into the future. In R. M. Thomas (Ed.), *International comparative education* (pp. 302-325). Oxford: Pergamon.

Thomas, R. M. (Ed.). (1992). *Education's role in national development plans.* Westport, CT: Praeger.

Thomas, R. M. (1995). *Classifying reactions to wrongdoing: Taxonomies of misdeeds, sanctions, and aims of sanctions.* Westport, CT: Greenwood.

Thomas, R. M. (1996). *Comparing theories of child development* (4th. ed.). Pacific Grove, CA: Brooks/Cole.

Thomas, R. M. (1997a). *An integrated theory of moral development.* Westport, CT: Greenwood.

Thomas, R. M. (1997b). *Moral development theories: Secular and religious.* Westport, CT: Greenwood.

Thomas, R. M., & Diver-Stamnes, A. C. (1993). *What wrongdoers deserve.* Westport, CT: Greenwood.

Thomas, R. M., & Postlethwaite, T. N. (Eds.). (1983). *Schooling in East Asia..* Oxford: Pergamon.

Thomas, R. M., & Postlethwaite, T. N. (1984). *Schooling in the Pacific islands.* Oxford: Pergamon.

Thomas, R. M., & Titialii, T. (1973a). *A study of unmet educational needs in American Samoa: Overview and design.* Pago Pago: Government of American Samoa.

Thomas, R. M., & Titialii, T. (1973b). *Measuring Samoan-language silent-reading skills.* Pago Pago: Government of American Samoa.

Thorndike, R. L. (Ed.). (1971). *Educational measurement* (2nd ed.). Washington, DC: American Council on Education.

Thurstone, L. L. (1938). *Primary mental abilities.* Chicago: University of Chicago Press.

Thurstone, L. L., & Chave, E. J. (1929). *The measurement of attitudes.* Chicago: University of Chicago Press.

Trueba, H. T., Guthrie, G. P., & Au, K. H. (Eds.). (1981). *Culture and the bilingual classroom: Studies in classroom ethnography.* Rowley, MA: Newbury House.

Tulloch, M. I. (1995). Evaluating aggression: School students' responses to television portrayals of institutionalized violence. *Journal of Youth and Adolescence, 24* (1), pp. 95-115.

Uhlfelder, H. F. (1997). Ten critical traits of group dynamics. *Quality Progress, 30* (4), pp. 69-72.

Underwood, E. A. (1994). Florence Nightingale. In *The new Encyclopaedia Britannica,* (vol. 8, pp. 705-706). Chicago: Encyclopaedia Britannica.

UNESCO. (1995). *Statistical yearbook.* Lanham, MD: Bernan.

van der Veer, R., & Valsiner, J. (Eds.). (1994). *The Vygotsky reader.* Cambridge, MA: Blackwell.

Van Doren, C. (1938). *Benjamin Franklin.* New York: Viking.

Vandenburg, D. (1990). *Education as a human right: A theory of curriculum and pedagogy.* New York: Teachers College Press.

Varma, V. P., & Williams, P. (Eds.). (1976). *Piaget, psychology, and education.* Itasca, IL: Peacock.

Vicinus, M., & Nergaard, B. (1990). *Ever yours, Florence Nightingale—Selected letters.* Cambridge, MA: Harvard University Press.

von Wright, G. H. (1971). *Explanation and understanding.* Ithaca, NY: Cornell University Press.

Vygotsky, S. L. (1978). *Mind in society.* (Edited by M. Cole, V. John-Steiner, S. Scribner, & E. Souberman.) Cambridge, MA: Harvard University Press.

Wadsworth, B. J. (1989). *Piaget's theory of cognitive and affective development.* New York: Longman.

Wagner, R. K., Torgesen, J. K., Rashotte, C. A., & Hecht, S. A. (1997). Changing relations between phonological processing abilities and world-level reading as children develop from beginning to skilled readers: A 5-year longitudinal study. *Developmental Psychology, 33* (3), pp. 468-479.

Walberg, H. J. (1989). District size and student learning. *Education and Urban Society, 21* (2), pp. 154-162.

Walberg, H. J., Zhang, G., & Daniel, V. C. (1994). Toward an empirical taxonomy of world education systems. In A. C. Tuijnman & T. N. Postlethwaite (Eds.), *Monitoring the standards of education* (pp. 79-99). Oxford: Pergamon.

Walford, G. (1993). Book review. *Comparative Education Review, 37* (1), pp. 83-85.

Watson, K., Modgil, C., & Modgil, S. (Eds.). *Quality in education.* London: Cassell.

Webster's encyclopedic dictionary of the English language. (1989). New York: Portland House.

Weiler, H. (1983). Educational policy as compensatory legitimation. In R. M. Thomas (Ed.), *Politics and education: Cases from eleven nations* (pp. 33-54). Oxford: Pergamon.

Weitzman, E. A., & Miles, M. B. (1994). *Computer programs for qualitative data analysis.* Thousand Oaks, CA: Sage.

Wenner, A., & Wells, P. H. (1990). *Anatomy of a controversy: The question of language among bees.* New York: Columbia University Press.

West, D. (1990). *Authenticity and empowerment: A theory of liberation.* New York: Harvester Wheatsheaf.

Westbury, I., & Purves, A. C. (Eds.). (1988). *Cultural literacy and the idea of general education.* Chicago: National Association for the Study of Education.

Whitney, I., & Smith, P. K. (1993). A survey of the nature and extent of bullying in junior/middle and secondary schools. *Educational Research, 35* (1), pp. 3-25.

Wiggins, G. P. (1993). *Assessing student performance.* San Francisco: Jossey-Bass.

Williams, M. V., et al. (1995). Inadequate functional health literacy among patients at two public hospitals. *JAMA, The Journal of the American Medical Association, 274* (21), pp. 1677-1682.

Willower, D. J., Eidell, T. L., & Hoy, W. K. (1967). *The school and pupil-control ideology.* University Park, PA: Pennsylvania State University.

Wolcott, H. F. (1988). Ethnographic research in education. In R. M. Jaeger (Ed.), *Complementary methods for research in education* (pp. 187-210). Washington, DC: American Educational Research Association.

Woodhall, M. (1985). Earnings and education. In T. Husén & T. N. Postlethwaite (Eds.), *International encyclopedia of education: Research and studies* (1st ed., vol. 3, pp. 1495-1505). Oxford: Pergamon.

Woodham-Smith, C. (1951). *Lonely crusader.* New York: McGraw-Hill.

Wozniak, R. H., & Fischer, K. W. (Eds.). (1993). *Development in context: Acting and thinking in specific environments.* Hillsdale, NJ: Erlbaum.

Wright, C. (1988). Home school research: Critique and suggestions for the future. *Education and Urban Society, 21* (2), pp. 96-113.

Yanagita, K. (1951). *Minzokugaku jiten* [A dictionary of folk culture]. Tokyo: n.p.

Yogev, S. (1985). Sexism in education. In T. Husén & T. N. Postlethwaite (Eds.), *International encyclopedia of education: Research and studies* (1st ed., vol. 8, pp. 4557-4559). Oxford: Pergamon.

Zeng, K. M. (1996). Prayer, luck, and spiritual strength: The desecularization of entrance examination systems in East Asia. *Comparative Education Review, 40* (3), pp. 264-279.

Zilversmit, A. (1993). *Changing schools: Progressive education theory and practice, 1930-1960.* Chicago: University of Chicago Press.

Zoller Booth, M. (1995). Children of migrant fathers: The effects of father absence on Swazi children's preparedness for school. *Comparative Education Review, 39* (2), pp. 195-210.

Index

About the Author

R. MURRAY THOMAS is Professor Emeritus, Graduate School of Education, University of California at Santa Barbara, where he taught educational psychology and headed the program in international education over three decades. His published works exceed 300 and include *An Integrated Theory of Moral Development* (Greenwood, 1997), *Moral Development Theories—Secular and Religious* (Greenwood, 1997), *Classifying Reactions to Wrongdoing* (Greenwood, 1995), *Prevent, Repent, Reform, Revenge* (Greenwood, 1995), *What Wrongdoers Deserve* (Greenwood, 1993), and *Education's Role in National Development Plans* (Praeger, 1992).

ISBN 0-89789-609-2

EAN

9 780897 896092

90000>

HARDCOVER BAR CODE